The Design of Federations

Albert Breton
University of Toronto
and
Anthony Scott
University of British Columbia

The Institute for Research on Public Policy
L'Institut de recherches politiques

Montreal

ISBN 0 920380 43 3

Legal Deposit Second Quarter
Bibliothèque nationale du Québec

The Institute for Research on Public Policy/L'Institut de recherches politiques
2149 Mackay Street
Montreal, Quebec
H3G 2J2

Founded in 1972, THE INSTITUTE FOR RESEARCH ON PUBLIC POLICY is a national organization whose independence and autonomy are ensured by the revenues of an endowment fund, which is supported by the federal and provincial governments and by the private sector. In addition, The Institute receives grants and contracts from governments, corporations, and foundations to carry out specific research projects.

The *raison d'être* of The Institute is threefold:

— To act as a catalyst within the national community by helping to facilitate informed public debate on issues of major public interest

— To stimulate participation by all segments of the national community in the process that leads to public policy making

— To find practical solutions to important public policy problems, thus aiding in the development of sound public policies

The Institute is governed by a Board of Directors, which is the decision-making body, and a Council of Trustees, which advises the board on matters related to the research direction of The Institute. Day to day administration of The Institute's policies, programmes, and staff is the responsibility of the president.

The Institute operates in a decentralized way, employing researchers located across Canada. This ensures that research undertaken will include contributions from all regions of the country.

Wherever possible, The Institute will try to promote public understanding of, and discussion on, issues of national importance, whether they be controversial or not. It will publish its research findings with clarity and impartiality. Conclusions or recommendations in The Institute's publications are solely those of the author, and should not be attributed to the Board of Directors, Council of Trustees, or contributors to The Institute.

The president bears final responsibility for the decision to publish a manuscript under The Institute's imprint. In reaching this decision, he is advised on the accuracy and objectivity of a manuscript by both Institute staff and outside reviewers. Publication of a manuscript signifies that it is deemed to be a competent treatment of a subject worthy of public consideration.

Publications of The Institute are published in the language of the author, along with an executive summary in both of Canada's official languages.

iv

Dr. Mark Eliesen
  Director, Federal NDP Caucus Research
    Bureau, Ottawa
W.A. Friley
  President, Skyland Oil, Calgary
Judge Nathan Green
  The Law Courts, Halifax
Donald S. Harvie
  Chairman, Devonian Foundation, Calgary
Dr. Leon Katz
  Department of Physics, University of
    Saskatchewan, Saskatoon
Tom Kierans
  Vice-Chairman, McLeod, Young, Weir,
    Toronto
Dr. Leo Kristjanson
  Vice-President, Planning
    University of Saskatchewan, Saskatoon
Andrée Lajoie
  Director, Centre for Research on Public
    Law, University of Montreal
Allen T. Lambert
  Chairman, Toronto-Dominion Bank,
    Toronto
Terry Mactaggart
  Executive Director, Niagara Institute,
    Niagara-on-the-Lake
Professor William A.W. Neilson
  Faculty of Law, University of Victoria
Marilyn L. Pilkington
  Tory, Tory, DesLauriers, Binnington,
    Toronto
Adélard Savoie, Q.C.
  Yeoman, Savoie, LeBlanc & DeWitt,
    Moncton
Philip Vineberg, Q.C.
  Phillips, Vineberg, Goodman, Phillips &
    Rothman, Montreal
Dr. Norman Wagner
  President, University of Calgary
Ida Wasacase
  Director, Saskatchewan Indian Federated
    College, University of Regina
Professor Paul Weiler
  Mackenzie King Professor,
    Harvard University
Dr. John Tuzo Wilson
  Director General, Ontario Science Centre,
    Toronto
Rev. Lois Wilson
  Rector, Chalmers United Church, Kingston
Ray Wolfe
  President, The Oshawa Group, Toronto

Ex Officio Members
Dr. Owen Carrigan
  Representing the Canada Council
Denis Cole
  President, Institute of Public
    Administration of Canada
A.J. Earp
  President, Association of Universities &
    Colleges of Canada
Dr. Claude Fortier
  President, Science Council of Canada
Larkin Kerwin
  President, Royal Society of Canada
Dr. William G. Schneider
  President, National Research Council
Dr. René Simard
  President, Medical Research Council
Dr. David Slater
  Acting Chairman, Economic Council of
    Canada
Professor André Vachet
  Representing the Social Science Federation
    of Canada

We dedicate this book to the
memory of our friend
Harry G. Johnson

Forword

Canada is currently engaged in a national debate on federalism and the constitution, the outcome of which will profoundly affect the future of all Canadians. Much attention has been focused on the distribution of powers among the various levels of government, and on methods for dealing with regional disparities both within and across those levels.

The future of parliamentary government is the subject of this report. The authors employ conventional methods of economic analysis to arrive at some salient conclusions. They construct a model for a new federation in which truly representative government operates within a bureaucratic framework that ensures effective and efficient policy making and implementation.

Canada is on the verge of momentous changes and our future prosperity will in part be determined by the widsom of our present decisions. Such decisions must be based on a knowledge of all possible alternatives. The Institute for Research on Public Policy is pleased to contribute to the national debate by presenting an alternative for consideration.

Gordon Robertson
President
June 1980

Avant-propos

Le Canada est actuellement engagé dans un débat national sur le fédéralisme et la constitution. Ce qui émergera de cette prise de conscience aura des répercussions profondes sur l'avenir de tous les Canadiens. Deux questions préoccupent tout particulièrement l'opinion: le partage des pouvoirs entre les divers ordres de gouvernement et les moyens de résoudre le problème des disparités régionales tant en deça des aires de compétence politique et administrative que par delà.

Le thème de cette étude est l'avenir du gouvernement parlementaire. Les conclusions saillantes des auteurs reposent sur des méthodes orthodoxes d'analyse économique. Ils ont établi un modèle de fédération dans lequel le gouvernement, réellement représentatif, est étayé dans ses fonctions par une bureaucratie qui assure la formulation efficace des principes directeurs et leur fructueuse application.

Des changements de très grande importance se préparent. Notre prospérité de demain dépendra en partie de la sagesse qui inspirera nos décisions d'aujourd'hui. Il faudra fonder ces décisions sur une conscience éclairée de toutes les options possibles. L'Institut de recherches politiques est heureux de contribuer au débat national en présentant au lecteur une de ces options.

Le président,
Gordon Robertson
Juin 1980

Preface

We have long been interested in federalism and the problem of federal states. Five years ago that interest led us to join forces to try to break out of the framework used by economists to analyse multi-level governmental structures because we felt that the framework was too narrow and that it had become unproductive.

The result of our collaboration was *The Economic Constitution of Federal States*, a book published by the University of Toronto Press in the spring of 1978. In that book, which is cast at a high level of abstraction, we sought to develop a theory of federalism that was general enough, without being empty, to provide the tools that would allow anyone to analyse systematically the numerous questions that arise in multi-level, multi-layered governmental structures.

When Michael Kirby of the Institute for Research on Public Policy asked us to apply the ideas and the theory of our book to one or more issues of interest in Canada, we thought we could do no better than to try to use our framework to inquire into the ways and means of improving the functioning of the Canadian federal system.

As is usually the case in such exercises, we discovered that our framework had to be extended and adjusted; that turned out to be a fairly smooth exercise, which we took as an indication that the basic framework was fundamentally sound and robust.

In a way, therefore, the pages that follow are an extension as well as an application of the results of our earlier collaboration, possibly a bit more of the former than of the latter. We offer this as a lame explanation of the fact, which the reader will soon discover, that this small book is not easy reading.

We wish to add, however, that beyond our literary clumsiness, the problems of government and of governmental structures are inherently difficult ones. Despite the impression that a reading of the morning paper may convey, they are not problems and issues that lead to slogans and facile solutions. It is partly to act as an antidote to morning newspapers that we have chosen to express ourselves in a rather formal and detached style. It is not that we do not feel strongly about the issues examined in the following pages, but we would like our style to convey to the reader our belief that even in matters of federalism there is place for reasoned argument in addition to passionate eloquence.

We thank Michael Kirby for providing us with the opportunity to work together again to test our ideas anew, after being away from them for almost two years. We are also grateful to Louise Dalhouse for typing numerous drafts of the manuscript.

Albert Breton
Anthony Scott
1979

The Authors

Albert Breton is a graduate of the University of Manitoba and received a Ph.D. in economics from Columbia University. He was later a Post-Doctoral Fellow at the University of Chicago.

Professor Breton has taught at the Université de Montréal, the Université Catholique de Louvain, the London School of Economics, and Harvard University. He is a Professor of Economics and an Associate of the Institute for Policy Analysis at the University of Toronto.

Professor Breton has written several books and articles. He is a Fellow of the Royal Society of Canada.

Anthony Scott is a graduate of the University of British Columbia and Harvard University, and received a doctorate from the London School of Economics. He is a Professor of Economics at the University of British Columbia.

Professor Scott's writings include several books and numerous articles. He has served on the editorial boards of several professional journals including *Land Economics* and *Western Economic Journal*.

Professor Scott is a Fellow of the Royal Society of Canada.

Table of Contents

Executive Summary

A larger and more representative 'constituent assembly' is needed to redesign the Canadian federation according to this report, *Design of Federations*, which uses the methods of economic analysis to arrive at this conclusion.

Unlike the closest body to a constituent assembly Canada now has—first ministers' conferences—the proposed assembly would be enlarged considerably to include government and opposition members from federal, provincial, and local levels of government, as well as a certain number of interested citizens from outside the political system. At its largest it could be just somewhat smaller than the delegations that elect leaders at federal and provincial political party conventions in Canada.

Members would stand for election to the constituent assembly. They would expect to serve on an ongoing basis, and to be re-elected. In other words, they would not be 'disinterested' citizens nobly trying to design an ideal constitution, but politicians acting on their normal bases of self-interest.

The reason for this is based on an economic theory that has been around since Adam Smith: a host of economic agents acting in their own self-interest unknowingly will make the best economic decisions for society. Therefore, rather than trying to reform the individuals to be elected to the constituent assembly, it should be designed to take advantage of this basic principle. An extension of this economic theory states that in any market the more buyers and sellers there are, the more likely an equilibrium price will be established at least cost to society. Similarly, the larger and more representative the constituent assembly is, the less will be the cost of the federation it designs. As in any commodity market, many participants make it less likely the flow of information concerning the real costs of any constitutional option could be restricted.

This is typical of the economic analysis used to support the ideas developed in this report. The authors suggest that the mode of analysis used in economics can be used in areas wider than those where problems are easily expressed in money terms. As long as choice and decision making by individuals are involved, economic analysis can be applied. Thus they are quick to point out that their arguments are not confined to "economic welfare," but pertain to all issues of concern to citizens.

For example, current federal-provincial negotiating sessions can be viewed as markets for 'powers'. The two levels of government trade with each other. Goods other than actual powers, such as money in the form of transfer payments or the expectation of future favours, can be exchanged. In Canada, the normal practice is for the federal government to be the buyer of powers (the responsibility for legislating in a certain domain) from the provinces in exchange for money transfers because it commands the strongest tax base. However, a more representative constituent assembly, induced to consider all the real 'costs' involved in a federal system, might decide to distribute taxing powers more efficiently between the federal and provincial levels of government. Because assignment of responsibilities between these two levels of government lies at the heart of Canada's current constitutional impasse, this is where the assembly's first efforts should be focused. But other questions, such as entrenching basic rights in a constitution, could be addressed in due course.

Whatever aspect of designing a federal structure an extended constituent assembly takes up, it will tend to a solution that makes organizational costs as small as possible. The notion of organizational costs as used here does not include the costs of providing day-to-day government services. It is assumed throughout this report that these latter costs are held constant. This is done only to emphasize the crucial role of organizational costs. These are the costs of signalling preferences, mobility between jurisdictions, co-ordination of intergovernmental actions, and administration. The assembly is influenced by them because each is affected differently by whatever the assembly decides about what the report calls the "constitutional dimensions."

It is less costly for citizens to signal their preferences to governments that are smaller and closer geographically because the smaller the territory the more homogeneous are the citizens' preferences. This cost therefore decreases with the degree of decentralization. But if a group of citizens in a given jurisdiction in a federal system disagree strongly enough with the public policies of the government in their jurisdiction they can simply leave it for another. As can be seen by comparing the options open to the citizens of a federation of many jurisdictions to those in a unitary state, who can only move to an outside country, the cost of mobility is also expected to decrease with the degree of decentralization.

On the other hand, the more decentralized a state is, the more the co-ordination or negotiation that will have to be carried on between the different jurisdictions. Therefore, the total cost of co-ordination increases as the degree of decentralization increases. The fourth organizational cost, administration, consists of all the day-to-day costs not included in the normal provision of government services already presumed to remain constant. Although these administration costs decline as the size of jurisdictions declines, an increasing number of jurisdictions would balance out this cost.

It can be imagined that the sum total of these organizational costs can be minimized by taking all the possible combinations for every degree of federalization, and throwing them into a computer that would churn out the best result. But it would be mechanical at best, and unrealistic because it assumes that politicans may be given only a neutral role to play. Because politicians naturally would prefer to assign to their own jurisdictions those powers that would best enable them to be re-elected, their organizational cost solution would not be as low as one produced by a computer. But as indicated before, an extended constituent assembly would produce through its more competitive nature a realistic least-cost arrangement.

This argument, of course, is based on the premise that a federal form of government should be adopted if it is less costly to citizens than other forms such as a unitary state. The resulting advocacy of federalism is supported by mentioning its other advantages. For example, individual liberty can be preserved to a greater extent by fragmenting political power among a number of jurisdictions at different levels than leaving that political power in the hands of a single government. In fact a distinction can be made between one-level federations, characterized in Canada by provincial governments and their 'creature' governments such as municipalities, where real control rests with the former, and two-level federations, typified by the relationship between the Canadian central government and provincial governments, where power is shared by the two levels. Two-level federations, because they provide a greater measure of choice, are preferred. That is not to say that there are no disadvantages to federalism. There are a number, such as forgone opportunities for economies of scale in providing government services. But a major claim is that making organizational costs as low as possible tends to strike the best balance between the advantages and disadvantages of the various degrees of federalization.

In sum, the report argues that federations can be designed based on organizational costs that are kept as low as possible. Because the more competition the better, an extended constituent assembly would reduce organizational costs more than the current one-level and two-level assemblies that are too insulated from competitive pressures. Economic theory suggests that attempting to reform the self-interested behaviour of politicians is decidedly inferior to channelling it in the most socially constructive direction.

Abrégé

Les méthodes d'analyse économique appliquées dans ce rapport ont permis de tirer la conclusion suivante: pour renouveler le pacte fédératif canadien, il est nécessaire de former une "assemblée constituante" composée d'un plus grand nombre de membres et donc plus représentative.

À la différence du corps constitué ressemblant le plus à une assemblée constituante dont dispose actuellement le Canada, à savoir les conférences des premiers ministres, l'assemblée proposée serait considérablement élargie pour accueillir des membres du gouvernement et de l'opposition aux niveaux fédéral, provincial et régional, ainsi qu'un certain nombre de citoyens intéressés n'appartenant pas au système politique. Sous sa forme la plus élaborée, cette assemblée serait à peine plus petite que les délégations qui élisent les chefs de parti au cours des assemblées politiques fédérales et provinciales au Canada.

Les membres poseraient leur candidature à l'assemblée constituante. Il serait prévu qu'ils restent en fonction en permanence et qu'ils soient réélus. En d'autres termes, il ne s'agirait pas de citoyens "désintéressés" essayant noblement de concevoir une constitution idéale, mais de politiciens agissant hors des limites traditionnelles de leur intérêt particulier.

Cette perspective est fondée sur une théorie économique connue depuis Adam Smith: une foule d'agents économiques, agissant dans leur intérêt particulier, prendront inconsciemment les meilleures décisions économiques pour l'intérêt général. Plutôt que d'essayer de réformer les personnes qui seront élues à l'assemblée constituante, il faudrait donc concevoir cette assemblée de manière à tirer parti de ce principe fondamental.

Cette théorie économique établit par ailleurs que, plus il y a d'acheteurs et de vendeurs dans un marché, plus il y a de chances de stabiliser les prix au moindre coût pour la société. De même, plus l'assemblée constituante sera grande et représentative, moins il en coûtera à la confédération qu'elle conçoit. Comme sur le marché de n'importe quelle marchandise, plus les participants sont nombreux, plus il est difficile de restreindre l'accès à l'information relative au coût réel de l'option constitutionnelle.

Cela est caractéristique de la méthode d'analyse économique appliquée pour illustrer les idées exposées dans ce rapport. Les auteurs suggèrent que le mode d'analyse utilisé en sciences économiques peut être appliqué au-delà des secteurs où les problèmes peuvent facilement être formulés en termes monétaires. L'analyse économique s'appliquerait à tout ce qui touche à des choix et à des décisions individuelles. Cependant, les auteurs s'empressent de souligner que leurs arguments ne se limitent pas au "bien-être économique" et qu'ils ont trait à toutes les questions concernant les citoyens.

Par exemple, les sessions de négociations fédérales-provinciales en cours peuvent être considérées comme un marché de "pouvoirs". Les deux niveaux de gouvernement "traitent" entre eux. Ils peuvent échanger des marchandises autres que le pouvoir effectif, telles que l'argent, sous la forme de transfert de paiements, ou l'attente de faveurs ultérieures. Au Canada, la pratique normale veut que le gouvernement fédéral soit acheteur des pouvoirs (responsabilité de légiférer dans un certain domaine) des provinces en échange de transferts monétaires parce qu'il commande la masse d'imposition la plus importante. Cependant, une assemblée constituante plus représentative, consciente du "coût" réel du système fédéral, pourrait décider de répartir les pouvoirs d'imposition plus équitablement entre les gouvernements fédéral et provinciaux. L'attribution des responsabilités entre ces deux niveaux de gouvernement est au coeur de l'impasse constitutionnelle au Canada; c'est donc sur cette question que devraient porter les premiers efforts de l'assemblée. D'autres questions, telles que l'inscription des droits fondamentaux dans une constitution, pourraient être étudiées en temps voulu.

Quel que soit l'aspect de la conceptualisation d'une structure fédérale sur laquelle se pencherait une assemblée constituante élargie, elle recherchera une solution qui minimise autant que possible les dépenses d'organisation. La notion de dépenses d'organisation, telle qu'utilisée ici, n'inclut pas le coût de distribution journalière des services gouvernementaux. Nous supposons, dans ce rapport, que le coût de ces services demeure constant. Nous faisons cette supposition uniquement pour mettre en lumière le rôle capital des coûts d'organisation. Il s'agit du coût d'indication des préférences, du coût de la mobilité entre les régions administratives, du coût de la coordination des activités intergouvernementales et du coût de l'administration. Ces coûts retiendront l'attention de l'assemblée, car ils seront soumis, chacun de façon différente, aux décisions qu'elle prendra concernant les "aspects constitutionnels" dont parle le rapport.

Il en coûte moins aux citoyens d'indiquer leurs préférences aux gouvernements qui sont plus petits et plus proches géographiquement parce que, plus le territoire est petit, plus les préférences des citoyens sont homogènes. Ce coût diminue donc avec le degré de décentralisation. Mais si, dans un système fédéral, un groupe de citoyens d'une région administrative donnée est en désaccord profond avec les politiques publiques d'un gouvernement dans sa région, il peut simplement la quitter pour s'installer dans une autre région. Comme on le constate en comparant les options ouvertes au citoyen d'une fédération de multiples collectivités avec celles qu'il aurait dans un État unitaire où il ne pourrait que passer à l'étranger, on s'attend aussi que le coût de la mobilité diminue selon le degré de décentralisation des pouvoirs.

D'un autre côté, plus un État est décentralisé, plus il faudra de coordination ou de négociations entre les différents composants administratifs. Le coût total de coordination augmente donc avec le degré de décentralisation. Le quatrième élément du coût, soit celui de l'administration, se compose de tous les coûts journaliers non inclus dans la fourniture normale des services gouvernementaux que nous avons supposé rester constants. Les coûts administratifs diminuent avec la taille des entités, et l'augmentation du nombre de ces entités administratives neutraliserait cet avantage.

On peut imaginer que la somme totale de ces coûts d'organisation pourrait être minimisée en envisageant toutes les combinaisons possibles à chaque degré de "fédéralisation" et en les entrant dans un ordinateur qui fournirait la meilleure solution. Il s'agirait d'une solution mécanique au mieux et non réaliste, car elle suppose que les hommes politiques ne joueraient qu'un rôle neutre. Les politiciens préféreraient conférer à leurs circonscriptions respectives des pouvoirs leur assurant une réélection facile; leur solution, du point de vue du coût d'organisation, ne serait donc pas aussi économique que celle qui serait fournie par l'ordinateur. Mais, comme nous l'avons expliqué plus haut, une assemblée constituante élargie produirait, du fait même de sa nature plus concurrentielle, une solution réaliste, au coût le moins élevé possible.

Cet argument repose naturellement sur le principe qu'une forme fédérale de gouvernement devrait être adoptée si elle coûte moins cher aux citoyens que d'autres structures politiques, telles que l'État unitaire. On renforce aussi la cause du fédéralisme en mentionnant les autres avantages du système. Par exemple, la liberté individuelle est mieux préservée en fragmentant le pouvoir politique en un nombre d'entités de niveaux différents qu'en laissant ce pouvoir politique entre les mains d'un gouvernement central. En fait, on peut établir une distinction entre la fédération à un niveau, caractérisée au Canada par des gouvernements provinciaux et leurs gouvernements "créatures", tels que les municipalités, où le vrai contrôle reste entre les mains du gouvernement provincial, et la fédération à deux niveaux, illustrée par la relation existant entre le gouvernement central canadien et les gouvernements provinciaux, où le pouvoir est partagé entre ces deux niveaux de gouvernement. Les fédérations à deux niveaux ont la préférence, car elles permettent un plus grand choix. Il ne faudrait pas en conclure que le fédéralisme ne présente pas d'inconvénients. Il en amène quelques-uns telles l'impossibilité de réaliser des économies sur une grande échelle en ce qui concerne la fourniture des services gouvernementaux. Mais l'un des principaux arguments, c'est que, en maintenant les coûts d'organisation à leur plus bas niveau possible, on tend à réaliser le meilleur équilibre entre les avantages et les inconvénients de chaque degré de "fédéralisation".

En conclusion, ce rapport démontre que les fédérations peuvent être conçues en fonction de coûts d'organisation aussi bas que possible. Plus il y a de concurrence, mieux cela vaut, et une assemblée constituante élargie réduirait les coûts d'organisation bien plus que ne le font les assemblées actuelles à un et deux niveaux, qui sont trop protégées des pressions concurrentielles. La théorie économique suggère qu'il est moins utile de réformer le comportement intéressé des hommes politiques que de le réorienter au service du bien commun.

Chapter One

Building Blocks

•

INTRODUCTION

There is a widespread consensus among the public about what constitutes the domain of economic questions and about what economists can be expected to say on these questions. This consensus and the accompanying expectation are generally correct but sometimes, especially with regard to areas of active research, they are too narrow. This, we suspect, is the case for a topic such as federalism. If members of the public were asked about what occupied those economists who are students of the problems that pertain to federal states, most would mention interjurisdictional grants and payments, harmonization of expenditure and tax structures, interjurisdictional income redistribution, and other problems of that kind. Economics students of federalism do devote much of their time to these kinds of issues, but they also use the tools of economics to analyse broader and more fundamental problems that pertain to federal states. It is with these that we are mainly concerned in the following pages.

Before defining these problems, we set out in Section 1 our view of what constitutes the economic approach to federalism and to other issues of that kind. In Section 2, we define the particular aspects of federalism which occupy us in these pages. Throughout we use words which are in day-to-day use, but sometimes in a slightly different sense than in that usage, and we seek to restrict the number of meanings to one. Section 3 is devoted to a definition of some of these words; among them is the word "federalism" itself, as well as "constitution" and "constitutional," "jurisdictional level," "division of powers," and others.

Having outlined the domain of our investigation and the principal terms we use, our last task in this introductory chapter will be to set down some of the more important assumptions that underlie our analysis; those assumptions are in Section 4.

1. THE ECONOMIC APPROACH

Economics is at once a set of substantive propositions or theorems and a method of analysis; furthermore, these two components of the discipline are separable from each other in the sense that the methods, although necessary

1

to derive the substantive propositions, can be used independently to analyse various situations. It is because of this that the method of economic analysis has been applied in recent years to such questions as fertility, crime, racial discrimination, nationalism, education, federalism, and many others, all of which had not been considered historically within the field of economics and which some still consider to be non-economic questions.

At the heart of the distinction between theorems and method is the view that it is not the subject matter, but the mode of analysis, which distinguishes the economic from the other approaches to issues—such as the sociological and the anthropological. For example, an economist using the methods of economics can analyse the functioning of the labour markets and the effects on adjustments in these markets of policies such as unemployment insurance and minimum wage legislation. A sociologist using the methods of sociology can also proceed to an analysis of labour markets and of the effect of these policies on those markets. Both will have studied the same subject matter and both will come out with substantive propositions which should be consistent with each other. The substantive propositions of the economist and the sociologist would be different, however, and in our eyes both would be useful. In the following pages we apply the methods of economics to one decision that must be made about each potential federation, namely its design.

We remind our reader that the methods of economics should not be restricted to domains in which the magnitudes can be measured in terms of money and in which goods are exchanged for money. It is true that much of economics deals with the production, exchange, and consumption of goods and services whose values are easily expressed in money terms, but it is no less true that much of the apparatus of production, exchange, and consumption theory is an apparatus of choice and decision making by individuals. As such, it can be modified to apply to such problems as that of the decision to have or not to have children, of committing or not committing a crime, of supporting or withholding support from a political party, of discriminating or not against women. In none of the decisions is the monetary dimension the dominant one, but being choice problems, they are amenable to economic analysis. Typically, the methods of economics consist in breaking a problem in two parts. A first one consists, as we have just intimated, in the study of individual choices; a second, in the analysis of institutional adjustment to exogenous changes. In the first, economists focus on the factors that govern individual decisions and the derived sets of propositions carry such names as the theory of consumer behaviour and the theory of the firm. In the second, markets are examined, as are coalitions and, as will be seen below, constituent assemblies, and how each responds to outside changes. The two parts are very closely related and each has an impact on the other.

The typical approach to individual choices is based on a calculus of the advantages and disadvantages of the outcomes of decisions. The assumption is made that the course of action with the most attractive outcome is the one chosen by individuals. Such an assumption prompts the following questions. Most attractive in terms of what? Most attractive to whom? At the level of the individual, the answer to these questions characterizes the economic approach to economic, social, and political issues.

Economists assume that the attractiveness of outcomes is appreciated by each person subjectively, and give the name of utility or satisfaction to the value which each places on the outcomes of alternative courses of action. The advantages and disadvantages which are balanced against each other in the decision maker's calculus are therefore advantages and disadvantages measured in terms of utility. Sometimes that utility converts easily into monetary units, but that conversion is not essential to the calculus nor to the methodology of economics, although it sometimes simplifies the task of measuring.

It is already implicit in what we have said that the attractiveness of outcomes must be to the decision maker. This is sometimes labelled the hypothesis of self-interest. We must note immediately that the pursuit of self-interest by a decision maker is not inconsistent with a concern for others, or with a concern for the environment and other things of that kind. There are difficulties here which centre on the definition of self-interest, but the notion can be made broad enough to encompass behaviours which have traditionally been considered inconsistent with self-interest.

There is a final point. The notion that individuals pursue their own interest is, in the economic approach, associated with the assumption of individual rationality or, to put it differently, with the assumption that individuals maximize their utility. Many find this idea difficult to accept. For this reason, we want to stress that it is not as restrictive as it is sometimes made to be. First, rationality applies to means, not to ends. It says, in other words, that given any goal or objective, the decision maker will seek to attain that goal by use of the most efficient means available to him, that is, by means that use up the smallest amount of the scarce resources at his disposal. The concept of rationality, secondly, is one that applies in a world in which knowledge is unevenly shared and is costly—so that decision makers are not assumed to know all relevant facts—and in which the outcome of decisions may be less than certain. Thirdly, it is a concept that recognizes that the range of choice open to decison makers is always—sometimes severely—narrowed by the existence of technological, social, political, legal, environmental, and economic constraints of one kind or another. As it applies to individual decisions—distinguished from institutions such as markets, governments, or constituent assemblies—the economic approach therefore consists in listing the goals or objectives of a particular class of actors, defining the advantages and disadvantages attached to each means of achieving these goals, specifying the constraints operating on the actors, and assuming that they will select the means toward their various goals which "maximize their own utility."

In the exercises of the next chapters, the actors with whom we are most concerned are politicians and citizens. Politicians will be seen to be pursuing one or more objectives depending on circumstances and on their own tastes or preferences. These objectives, which are all associated with the implementation of public policies, may include the pursuit of some private notion of the public good—what may be called an ideology; the resolution of a problem of national or local concern; an exalted place in history; the accumulation of private wealth for themselves or others such as relatives or friends; the guarantee of a good pension; the possibility of coming out of obscurity without much effort; and others. We assume that these varied objectives, from which politicians derive utility, are attainable only by being in office and consequently, in seeking maximum utility, politicians will be constrained by the need of re-election.

The analysis of institutional adjustments and of responses to exogenous change is in essence an analysis of the reconciliation of individual decisions that, in general, will be at variance with each other. In slightly more abstract terms, it is an analysis of the determination of the "equilibrium" values of many of the factors which govern individual choices.

Our purpose in the following pages is to outline an analysis of the design of federations for a world in which that design is elaborated by politicians— usually more than one of them—whose decisions have to be reconciled in institutions which we call constituent assemblies. Since politicians have to be re-elected if they are to achieve maximum utility, the views of the citizens who elect them will play a role in shaping the outcome of the deliberations of these constituent assemblies.

2. THE PROBLEM

What do we mean by the expression "the design of federations"? What attributes of a federation are encompassed by these words? To develop our answer we need to distinguish between two separate, but not completely independent, classes of governmental activities. Following other students of governments, we will call them the constitutional and the policy activities. The first, as the word indicates, refers to the constitutional dimensions of the governmental system, the second, to the day-to-day decisions of governments with regard to new policies and the implementation of older ones. Our focus is on the first of these.

How are these constitutional dimensions defined? First, we should indicate that we give to the word constitution a wider meaning than is customary in day-to-day speech. For us, the constitutional dimensions of the governmental system include such characteristics as the number of jurisdictional levels in the system: at the outset, whether the system should be unitary or federal,[1] and if the latter, how many levels—such as provincial, regional, and municipal—it should have; the number of governmental units at each level—sometimes called the boundary problem; the specification of the broad functions and precise powers to be assigned to each level; and the rules of representation, including not only the rules for the selection of representatives, but also the constitutional rules governing decisions about day-to-day policies and the constitutional rules regulating the amendment of these same constitutional rules. That short list is not exhaustive, but it is sufficient to give an indication of what we mean by the constitutional dimensions of the public sector.

It should be easy to visualize that all of these constitutional dimensions will have an effect on the particular configuration of public policies that the public sector as a whole will produce. In other words, a change in the number of jurisdictional levels, a change in the number of governmental units, a reassignment of powers, or a change in the rules of representation will affect the quantity, or quality, or configuration of public policies produced by governments at various levels. This interdependence of constitutional dimensions and policy decisions should not, however, obscure the fact that it is not only possible but essential to distinguish the two orders of decision making. The tendency to confuse decisions about constitutional dimensions governing policy making with the day-to-day choice of policies has led to repeated unsuccessful attempts to resolve problems related to constitutional dimensions as if they were simply policy problems.

In the pages that follow, we restrict ourselves to constitutional dimensions. Our efforts do, of course, have implications for the level and configuration of public policies. But we do not take these into account, since to do so would immensely complicate our tasks without adding much to the results. But we restrict ourselves even more. Indeed, the economic approach to decison making as applied to consitituional dimensions is in a very uneven state of development. Consequently, in the next chapters, we tend to emphasize some dimensions to the neglect and even to the exclusion of others. Since our earlier book on federalism focused most of its attention on the question of the assignment of powers to different jurisdictions, we tend to illustrate what we have to say about decision making that relates to constitutional dimensions by reference to the assignment-of-powers issue. This restriction is not as dramatic as it may appear. Indeed, many of the factors which affect the choice of a particular assignment also affect the outcome with respect to other constitutional dimensions so that the approach we put forward has wider application than a reading of the following pages may suggest.

To summarize, then, this book is concerned with the constitutional dimensions of governmental systems. It seeks to define the forces and mechanisms that operate in decisions related to these and therefore to the design of federations. Our focus in illustrating these problems is often the assignment-of-powers issue, but other issues would serve as well. Again, although the forces and mechanisms we describe are related and overlap those that govern decision making with respect to day-to-day policies of governments, we stress that the two domains are distinct, and that the theories that pertain to each are also distinct.

Before proceeding, we must pause to note the meaning we give to the term public policies which we have been using throughout this section. Briefly, these words are used to account for everything that is supplied by governments to the population of their jurisdictions on a day-to-day basis. Included are such things as national defence, roads, bridges, police protection, law and order, the administration of the courts, as well as such things as tariffs, quotas, taxes, pollution controls, censorship, anti-abortion laws, minimum wage legislation, and the host of other regulations affecting the activities of persons and institutions. The concept is even broader: it includes those actions of governments as fall under headings such as nationalism, anti-Semitism, and discrimination. The term public policy encompasses all the non-constitutional actions of governments; on a day-to-day basis, all the supply or provision activities of governments are public policies.

3. SOME DEFINITIONS

We have provided a distinction between constitutional dimensions and policies and offered definitions. We have also used such words as federation and federal structure, jurisdictional level and jurisdiction; these need to be defined more precisely. We must also say what we mean by concepts such as constituent assembly, organizational activities, administration, co-ordination, mobility, and signalling, which play an important role in our approach. Finally, we must say a few words on constitutional powers.

The words federation and federal structure have a fairly precise meaning in ordinary conversation. They refer to that characteristic of governmental systems whereby the responsibility for public policies (the powers) is divided between two jurisdictional levels *and* is entrenched either in a constitutional document, in tradition or custom, or in both. Under that definition, Australia, Austria, Canada, Germany, India, and the United States are federations, while Belgium, France, and the United Kingdom are not. We do *not* use the word federation in that sense.

Throughout this book without exception, words such as federation, federal structure, and federal state refer to governmental systems in which responsibility for public policies is divided between two, but usually between a larger number of jurisdictional levels as in the day-to-day definition; we do not, however, make it a part of our definition that the division of powers is entrenched in any document or custom. Consequently, regional, municipal, local, and any special-purpose jurisdictional levels are considered bona fide levels. It follows that under our definition Belgium, France, and the United Kingdom are federations in the sense that our approach to the problem of ''who can do what?'' will apply.

Is that to say that there are no differences in our approach between those structures that all call federal and those which only we and other economists call federal? Not only is there a difference in the real world between these two kinds of structures, but there is also an important difference in our approach. As the following discussion, but in particular that of Chapter 3, emphasizes, in a federation in which the division of powers is entrenched in a document or custom, it is much more difficult—that is, much more costly—to operate changes in assignment than it is in a structure in which that division is not so entrenched. As the reader will discover, these costs play a very important role in our approach.

Our use of the word federation to cover countries that are not usually considered to be federal countries does not, therefore, prejudge the reality; it only provides us with a word that is convenient for our purpose.

Words such as jurisdiction and jurisdictional level are not used consistently in ordinary conversation. We use them in the following way: a jurisdictional level is made up of a set of one or more governmental units at the same level in the federal hierarchy. Consequently, the central government itself constitutes a jurisdictional level often called the national level. Another level is made up of provincial, state, canton, or *land* governments, sometimes in large and sometimes in small numbers; that level is called the provincial, state, or cantonal level. The provincial level may be directly under the national level, but there could also exist a number of intermediate levels in which subsets of provincial governments decided to plan and act together as subsets. One could, in the same way, define regional, metropolitan, municipal, and local levels of government.

When analysing the assignment of powers, it is well to keep in mind that powers are assigned to jurisdictional levels or, more exactly, to all governments located at a particular jurisdictional level. The word jurisdiction has two meanings: as a substantive, it is a synonym of government; that is the meaning we usually give it. When used in such terms as ''to have jurisdiction,'' it is a synonym of ''to have responsibility over'' or ''to have been assigned power over.'' Because of this dual meaning we abstain from using the word jurisdiction except when the context makes it very clear.

We call the body to whom we give the responsibility for making decisions about the constitutional dimensions of governmental systems a constituent assembly. That assembly is not always easy to identify with a real world counterpart because few of the bodies that meet to make choices about constitutional dimensions are called, or even call themselves, constituent assemblies. We return to this question in the next chapters; for the present, it is sufficient to note that whenever a body with the appropriate authority meets to take decisions about any one of the constitutional dimensions of the governmental system of a society, it is acting as a constituent assembly.

We should, however, note immediately a distinction that plays an important role in our discussion. We distinguish between what we call one-level and two-level constituent assemblies. In the first type, decisions with respect to constitutional dimensions are taken unilaterally by assembly-men who are usually also politicians in governments at one of the jurisdictional levels; in the second type, decisions are made by assemblymen from governments at two jurisdictional levels. Decisions pertaining to constitutional dimensions in Britain, France, Quebec, and California are decisions of one-level assemblies, while those made by the first ministers in Canada are decisions of two-level constituent assemblies.

The distinction between types of constituent assemblies which we make for analytical reasons, as the discussion in forthcoming chapters shows, does, however, reduce the difference between our definition of federations and the commonly accepted one. Indeed, all federations which common usage calls federations are ruled by two-level assemblies, while the others are ruled by one-level assemblies.

As the next chapter makes clear, the approach we are suggesting to choices that pertain to constitutional dimensions rests heavily on the cost of four organizational activities in which citizens and politicians engage. These are the signalling of preferences and the mobility between jurisdictions for citizens and for governments, administration, consisting of the whole package of activities surrounding the setting-up and the running of governments, as well as co-ordination of intergovernmental actions.

These organizational activities which give rise to organizational costs are defined in such a way as to be all-inclusive. In other words, there are no activities of governments which relate to administration and co-ordination or to the signalling of preferences and the political mobility of citizens which are not encompassed by that concept. Consequently, when we use the concept of organizational costs, we are using a concept which *by definition* is all-inclusive. We need not dwell on the definition of these terms further here, since they are defined as they are introduced in the next chapter; we must, however, indicate some of the assumptions we make about these organizational activities and costs.

4. SOME ASSUMPTIONS

There is a distinction which is implicit in the last few paragraphs which we must now bring into the open. The notion of an all-encompassing concept of organizational costs implies a distinction or separation between these costs and those directly involved in the provision of public policies proper. It will be easier to elucidate this notion if we proceed with the use of examples. Suppose that the citizens of a town decide that they would like to have a sewage disposal system to replace the *ad hoc* and privately owned individual system now in use. They may decide that the first step that they have to take is to elect a small committee to analyse the situation, to investigate the various modes of sewage disposal, to receive estimates, and to report to the whole assembly of citizens. It may be necessary to rent a hall, to buy forms for balloting, and to engage in other activities of that kind, but it will be necessary to pay whoever makes studies and draws up estimates.

The sum of all these costs—rental of a hall, purchase of forms, paper, pencils, salaries for studies and estimates, and so on—are the "organizational costs" of coming to a decision on a sewage disposal system. So is the cost of supervising those who will build it. These costs have to be distinguished from the cost of the sewage system itself. The reason for the distinction is that the two types of costs—organizational and output costs—do not respond to and vary with the same factors.

Consequently, we will assume that organizational costs are independent of the provision or output costs of public policies. Indeed, to simplify, we will assume throughout that the level or size of public policy output is constant, and that the cost of the output is also constant. That simplification will help us to focus on organizational activities and costs without having to pay attention to what is happening to decisions about public policies. In some way, our distinction between constitutional dimensions and policies is mirrored in the distinction between organizational and output costs. We associate constitutional dimensions and the level of organizational costs with each other and policies and their output costs together.

Another assumption, which follows arithmetically from the one that the output of the public sector is fixed, is that the relative size of the public and private sectors is fixed, except for variations in organizational costs. Another way of saying this is to recognize that the size of the public relative to that of the private sector will change only with changes in organizational costs. The public sector will grow if these are growing; if they are falling, it will be shrinking.

This last assumption is of some importance because it brings out the fact that all organizational costs are "public expenses" which have to be paid by citizens somehow, whether directly in the form of taxes to meet administrative costs, or indirectly in the form of individual expenditures to meet signalling and mobility costs. This fact must be borne in mind if certain of the conclusions of the forthcoming chapters are to be well understood.

Note to Chapter 1

[1] This question is discussed in some detail in the next chapter.

Chapter Two

Design by Machine

INTRODUCTION

The organization of this chapter is based on the recognition that in designing institutions for the public sector, one should distinguish between two orders or levels of decisions which, although not completely independent of each other, are sufficiently different to warrant and justify the distinction. The first pertains to whether a society should adopt a federal or a unitary form of government; the second, if the first choice is for a federal form, relates to the degree of federalization or, in less abstract terms, to the centralization or decentralization the governmental system should display.

To approach the question of the choice between unitary and federal forms of government we must possess a more precise definition than the ones given in the last chapter. We begin with the first. We say that the governmental system of a society is unitary when, in that society, only one jurisdictional level exists and when there is only one governmental unit at that level. As formulated, this definition will do for all cases of unitary states but, in contrasting unitary with federal structures, it is helpful to recognize that, for any given spatial unit, the adoption of a unitary form of government can signify either of two things: a unique government for the whole of the spatial unit, or a multitude of governments, unitary in each of the sub-units into which the same space is divided. We should, consequently, distinguish between simple-unitary and "balkanized" unitary states.

The usefulness of the distinction can be appreciated by considering the meaning of an index of the degree of centralizaiton of any federal structure. Suppose that the extent of centralization is measured by a number that varies between zero and one, with the degree of centralization increasing as the number approaches one. Another way of interpreting such an index is to say that when it is at one, all constitutional powers have been assigned to one government at a jurisdictional level; observing the index at one, therefore, tells us of the existence of a unitary state. But when the index is at zero, all powers have been assigned to a very large number of minuscule governmental units—this is what we mean by balkanization. Therefore, when the index is at zero as well as when it is at one, it indicates a unitary form of government.

A federation, we shall see, is different from simple unitary states; but it is also different from a balkanized system of states. In discussing the merits of federal versus unitary structures, we must at all times keep the above distinction clearly in mind, otherwise we will very easily impute to federalism benefits which are also reaped by balkanized unitary forms of government, a mistake that is often made.

An illustration may help. It is sometimes claimed that a federal structure is superior to a unitary one in that it permits small groups to be catered to by proportionately small governmental units, instead of by a larger unit in which, as a minority, their preferences would be neglected or overridden. In this form, this is not an argument for federalism because a balkanized structure of unitary states would also permit small governmental units.

Let us now turn from unitary states to the definition of federalism. A state which is federal has more than one jurisdictional level and at least one of these levels possesses more than one governmental unit. It can, for example, have a "central" level and a "municipal" level, as is the case for countries such as Britain and France and such political units as British Columbia and Ontario; it can, however, have a "central" level, a "provincial" level, and a "local" level, as is the case for Canada, Germany, India, Italy, Switzerland, the Union of Soviet Socialist Republics, the United States, and Yugoslavia.

As indicated in Chapter 1, that definition of federalism is useful for our work; it does not correspond to the everyday usage of the word, but also it does not depart very much from current usage. In summary, in defining constituent assemblies we distinguished between one- and two-level assemblies. We noted that all the countries and political units which we call federations, but which common usage does *not* so label, are one-level-constituent-assembly federations, while those which we and common usage call federations are all two-level-constituent-assembly federations. To some extent the difference between current usage and our own is reflected in a difference between types of constituent assemblies.

These definitional matters cleared up, we can return to the distinction between the orders or level of decisions in the design of governmental institutions. To give substance to that distinction we devote the next section to a comparison of federal and unitary forms of government. We conclude that federal forms are to be preferred to unitary forms and, anticipating the conclusion of the next chapter, that two-level are preferable to one-level-constituent-assembly forms.

But however superior federal forms may be to unitary forms of government, one must recognize that their multi-level, multi-unit structures create well-known "problems." We devote Section 2 to investigating the nature of these "problems" which, in the language of economics, are all externalities and forgone economies-of-scale problems. In Section 3, we examine what has now become the conventional solution to these "problems," namely to centralize to the extent that the mounting benefits so obtained are not swamped by the increasing ''problems'' of decentralization. This solution was to the best of our knowledge invented by economists, and has now been widely adopted by political scientists and public administration specialists. We argue that it is unacceptable.

We then devote Section 4 to an alternative solution to the ''problems'' posed by the existence of a federal form of government. This alternative solution, unlike the conventional one, is logically correct. It also has other virtues. It is possible, if one is so inclined, to use it as a bench-mark to evaluate other solutions. Secondly, with slight modification, it can be made to serve as a building-block in devising other solutions. These two uses are important because, even if logically correct, this new solution possesses certain features which make it impossible to apply in the real world. Briefly, the new solution—a mechanical solution, hence the title of the present chapter—has computational requirements which could only be satisfied at very high costs. We develop this point in Section 5.

As indicated, the materials of this chapter play a crucial role in the development of Chapters 3 and 4. This is why they are so important.

1. UNITARY VERSUS FEDERAL STRUCTURES

The strongest argument for federalism can be couched in the language of the authors of *The Federalist Papers*[1] who were seeking a political basis for the maintenance and blossoming of individual civil liberties in the face of governmental power. On the recognition that a unitary government has unlimited political power to coerce, they reasoned that a fragmentation of political power among a number of governmental units at different jurisdictional levels must place a limit on the restriction of individual liberty because those units will compete with each other. In brief, since political power curtails the exercise and enjoyment of individual liberty, a fragmentation of political power among competing units will, other things remaining the same, curtail liberty to a lesser extent.

This compelling argument requires clarification and emphasis at several points. First, all terms in the argument are important: the fragmentation of political power[2] between a number of units, the resulting competition between them, and the consequent greater individual liberty. The argument in fact claims that because power is fragmented between competing units, there is less of it and hence there is more liberty. The argument does not say that federalism creates and guarantees the exercise of liberty: it recognizes that in some federations all governments may be dictatorial or authoritarian and that in some unitary states (and in some one-level-constituent-assembly federations) individual liberty may flourish—that is why a ''other things remaining the same'' qualification is incorporated in the argument. But it does say that individual liberty will be greater in a federation in which all governments are authoritarian than it would be in a system in which all these governmental units had been collapsed into a single unit that was also dictatorial. Similarly, it says that in those unitary systems in which it exists, liberty would blossom even more if the unitary was replaced by a federal governmental system.

The argument that by denying a concentration of political power federalism improves the conditions for the manifestation of liberty applies with special force to two-level-constituent-assembly federations. Indeed, as we will endeavour to show in the next chapter, the natural workings of one-level constituent assemblies is such that the concentration of political power is always greater in such federations than in the two-level-assembly variety. The argument does extend, however, albeit with less force, to one-level-assembly federations.

A second point to note about the argument is that it rests on the existence of competition between political units. The manifestations of competition among units in a governmental structure are manifold. In one sense, competition refers to government-versus-government conflicts, involving controversies, disputes, apparent bickering and quarrelling, as well as haggling and chaffering in negotiations and transactions. These conflicts can be desirable in the same sense that the checks and balances and hence the conflicts that arise from the division of governments in three branches—the judiciary, the legislative, and the executive—are desirable: they provide restrictions to the use of power by a governmental unit.

In another sense, the existence of competition is attractive because it suggests that choices are possible and that preferences can be satisfied in more than one way. For example, as between units at the same level in a federal structure, competition enables the citizen to compare and to choose between jurisdictions—to migrate to the bundle of policies they like best. Also, as between higher and lower levels of government, competition frees the citizen from complete dependence on a particular government; alternative public goods and services, or superior recourse or appeal may be available when there are more than one level. In general, competition implies the existence of alternatives. This is widely recognized, and often criticized, as involving duplication and overlap; but those who fault federalism for competitiveness and duplication fault it for its main virtue!

A third and final point about the above argument is that it does not extend to balkanized states. In such states, the disputation and rivalry that may be going on between units do not improve the conditions for the exercise of liberty, because there is no fragmentation of political power. Each unit is a unitary state.

The foregoing argument is essentially political in nature. A more economic argument, which is roughly parallel to it, can also be made. It is based on the recognition that a federal structure, of necessity, possesses many governmental units, each providing goods and service—what in the last chapter we called policies—to its citizens. The resulting possible diversity in quantity, quality, and composition of some policies coupled with the simultaneous uniformity in quantity, quality, and composition of others is the key to an appreciation of the economic superiority of federalism over unitary systems of government. We stress that it is not the diversity of supply—which can be achieved by balkanization—nor the uniformity of provision—easily obtained in unitary systems—but the simultaneous satisfaction of preferences for different policies on some issues and for similar policies on other issues which define the superiority of a federal structure. In developing this argument we concentrate first on the benefits of diversity, then turn to those of uniformity. The reader should keep in mind, however, that it is the simultaneity of both that is the essence of the case.

To visualize the benefits that follow from the diversity of output, assume that the regions (provinces or states) of a country contain people that differ in preferences and opportunities. If one looks at the country taken as a whole, there will be for each policy a majority which will favour one outcome and a minority which will oppose it. By allowing diversity of quantity and quality that results from fragmenting the system in a larger number of governmental sub-units, the majorities in each sub-unit will decide the pattern of output. It can easily be shown that the sum of people who make up these regional majorities is never less than the majority for the country taken as a whole.

The point is important enough that we should provide an example. Suppose, therefore, that in a country there live 100 citizens. Between the two policies A and B, a majority of 60 favour A and a minority of 40 oppose it. Policy A will therefore be the one selected by the majority under a unitary form of government. If the same country was divided in two "provinces," each of 50 citizens, we could have the following outcome: if, in province X, 40 citizens favour A and 10 favour B, A will be implemented; if in province Y, 20 favour A and 30 favour B, then B will be the policy outcome selected by the majority. In the "federal" structure, 70 (out of 100) citizens would have had their preferences satisfied, while in a unitary system only 60 (out of 100) would have had them satisfied.

More generally, we can say that because it features a number of governmental units at each jurisdictional level—except at the highest—a federal system reduces the chance that citizens will be in a minority in some jurisdiction. Put another way, an increase in the number of governmental units increases the probability that any person living in any jurisdiction will be a member of a majority able to secure for him or herself the quantity and quality of public policies that he or she (and others of his or her group) prefer.

Given a slightly different twist, this reasoning can be made into a second economic argument for federalism. Suppose that geographical and spatial conditions differ between the regions of a country (or of an area within a country), but that the preferences of citizens are the same across regions. Public policies supplied by regional or local governments could still meet the preferences of the population better than could policies supplied by a central government because of the improvement in efficiency that a knowledge and an adjustment to local conditions permit.

Similarly, it will be easier—that is, less costly—for citizens to signal their preferences to their governments if these governments are local, municipal, or regional governments—that is, smaller governments—than if they are national and hence larger governments. Although this argument in support of federal over unitary systems has been developed many times in the literature, it is often wrongly stated, and is not as simple as it is often made to sound. Consequently, we devote some space to an elucidation of its significance. We argue in fact that the correct way of stating this type of advantage of federalism is to say that its costs are lower.

One often hears or reads that junior governments are more "responsive"; that is, they react more promptly and more adequately to the preferences of citizens than do more senior ones. Hence, the argument goes, local governments are more responsive to the preferences of citizens than regional governments, these more than provincial, and these, in turn, more than central ones. No empirical evidence has been submitted in support of this view which must, therefore, be taken as an assertion; it is, consequently, a weak base for developing a case in favour of federalism.

We would argue that a much more convincing case can be made that the cost of signalling preferences and of eliciting a response from junior governments is smaller than it is from more senior ones. Why? If the total population is distributed among different regions, and if preferences differ from region to region, the fragmentation of the governmental system into a larger number of units will almost of necessity imply that within each unit preferences will be more homogeneous than over the whole of the territory. This homogeneity in turn will mean that the cost of signalling for each citizen will be smaller because, once the preferences have been ascertained by the government, each will have at most to acquiesce in the diagnosis. The homogeneity of preferences also means that it is easier—less costly—for the government of a small unit to react to the preferences of its citizens, since everyone, or a large fraction of the population in its jurisdiction, wants the same policies, or almost the same policies. This way of formulating the argument would lead us to conclude, if evidence that senior governments are less responsive than junior ones was brought forth, that that evidence supports our view on the cost of signalling and of reacting, not on some inherent capacity to respond.

Another way of making this point would be to say that because of the more heterogeneous preferences they face, the job of senior governments is more difficult to fulfil than that of junior ones. Either way, the benefits of federalism may be said to reside in lowering the overall cost of operating the governmental system by reducing the overall heterogeneity of preference facing each governmental unit.

A last argument, based on the diversity which a federal structure permits, recognizes the possibility that citizens who are dissatisfied with one or more of the public policies supplied by the government of the jurisdiction in which they live can choose to move to another jurisdiction within the same country, or the same province, or the same region. This so-called "voting with one's feet" or political mobility is sometimes given a much exaggerated place in the literature on federalism, but the recent fairly large out-migration from the Province of Quebec to other areas of Canada in response to language laws is a good indication that it is not an empty case in favour of federalism. For members of some minorities, it may indeed provide the best alternative open to extricate themselves from a degree of coercion which is judged to be excessive.

Again, we must stress, it is not on the possibility of voting with one's feet that the case for federalism rests, but on the lower cost of political mobility which a federation permits as compared to a balkanized system. People can usually move from country to country, but the cost measured in terms of the acquisition of permits, visas, citizenship, and so on, is larger than an equivalent move within a country.

So far we have taken diversity of preferences and opportunities— diversity of individuals—as a datum, a feature of the world we live in, and argued that federalism is the form of government which can best accommodate and not conflict with that diversity. Our discussion was implicitly based on the assumption that although diversity is a source of "difficulties," it must be respected. Individuals should be able to provide themselves with public policies that meet their preferences and, to the extent that these differ between groups, with policies that differ.

But for many, diversity is not a source of "difficulties," but is itself a desirable feature. From this point of view, societies are "better," in some senses, when there is diversity in them so that, to the extent feasible, differences should be encouraged and fostered. There can be little doubt that, to the extent that political systems can nurture the growth of diversity, a federal form must be vastly superior to a unitary form, which tends to ignore or suppress diversity.

But we must avoid traps in this line of reasoning. It is common, in Canada, to hear the view that the country is very regionalized, that is, diversified, and that consequently decentralization of powers from the centre to the provinces is a necessity for the stability of society. By some, this argument is used to promote an ever-increasing degree of decentralization. As stated the argument is either incomplete or wrong. What is missing is a statement that the observed diversity is autonomous and independent of the degree of decentralization. Indeed, if diversity is, to a degree, a consequence of federalism, the argument cannot be used to promote decentralization and still less, ever-increasing decentralization. In other words, if the exercise of political power in the separate units of the federation is to some extent the source of diversity among the regions, it is circular to use diversity as a basis of an argument for decentralization. It would be using diversity to argue for decentralization to protect diversity!

All of the above discussion, based on the existence or on the promotion of diversity, would be fatally incomplete if we did not recognize that federalism also permits simultaneous uniformity in the provision of some public policies. In other words, while a federal structure allows the satisfaction of diverse preferences, it also permits the provision of policies which are unquestionably "national" or "provincial" in character, have a dimension or span over people or space broader than local or provincial, or are of value to some citizens only if they are also received by others. This is especially the case for policies that display lower unit costs when produced on a larger scale—what economists call economies of scale—or whose benefits cannot be withheld from a large number of individuals—policies characterized by external effects. These are policies such as national defence, broadcasting, transportation, postal service, and others like them which constitute some part of the overhead equipment—or productive infrastructure—of a society.

The whole notion of reconciling diversity and uniformity has been given the following schematic form. Assume that it is possible to realistically classify public policies according to the spatial span of the benefits and amenities they yield. To the extent that such a classification contains policies with a broad span, policies which we could call "national"; other policies with a smaller span, which could be called "provincial"; others which would be "regional"; then "metropolitan" and local ones; a federal structure then allows an assignment of policies according to such spans which, it can be shown, is more efficient from an economic point of view. A federal structure, then, can accommodate uniformity in the supply of public policies without sacrificing diversity.

Federalism's superiority to unitary states can be argued from an altogether different vantage point. This argument is more dynamic in that it focuses on the greater capacity to minimize the risk of errors in the implementation of policies in a world of changing technologies, preferences, incomes, and opportunities, in a world, in other words, of uncertainty.

Briefly stated, the point is that smaller governmental units can try out new solutions, provide new responses, and engage in experiments that, of necessity, involve smaller populations. These smaller units introduce new policies to deal with local problems and opportunities, but by doing so they, at the same time, serve as "pilot projects" for the rest of the country. If the experiment is unsuccessful, only a small part of the country has had to endure its consequences. Consequently, at the same time that risks of large errors, implicit in large or national projects, are avoided or, more exactly, minimized, experimentation on a small scale provides an efficient way of learning.

An example may be the best way to illustrate this argument. All over Canada, the environment is threatened by infestations of insects in farms and forests, and of weeds and algae in lakes and rivers. These are of concern to those with direct economic interests in the environment, such as farmers, logging firms, navigational and hydroelectric companies, but they are also of concern to those who live on or near these farms, forests, lakes, and rivers. All are concerned because they may suffer either from the infestations or from the solutions, which usually involve control of the intrusions by the use of chemicals. In Canada the responsibility for dealing with this class of problems is widely distributed among levels of government and among the agencies of all governmental units. The dynamic case for federalism is that this division of responsibility leading to a multiplicity of suggestions for solutions, to a multitude and even to a duplication of research efforts, and to a large number of governmental responses to the problems and to the complaints of citizens is a productive way of ''learning by doing'' and of avoiding the risks of large mistakes.

The argument so far is incomplete. A federal form of government will be more efficient in permitting learning by doing and the minimization of risks through small-scale experimentation only if it also makes it easier for the various sub-units to co-operate with one another. This may be the result of actions of the central government seeking to facilitate and to co-ordinate—possibly even to assist financially—the experimental and knowledge-seeking activities of the sub-units. In any case, this argument for federalism requires the possibility of putting the experiments more easily to use in a federal structure, otherwise it applies with equal force to balkanized unitary states.

2. ''PROBLEMS'' OF FEDERALISM

If a society opts for a federal form of government, it will, at the same time, have to face the fact that that decision, based on the value placed on liberty, diversity, and adaptability to risk, cannot be implemented without giving rise to certain problems. We must therefore first examine these problems and then devote some space to an analysis of solutions that have been proposed to deal with them. We analyse the problems in this section and look at alternative solutions, which we find unacceptable, in the remaining sections of this chapter. Acceptable solutions begin to emerge in the next two chapters.

We can classify the problems of federalism in five broad classes. In the language of economics, they are
 i. Forgone benefits of economies of large-scale production
 ii. Interjurisdictional consumption spill-overs
iii. Interjurisdictional production spill-overs
iv. Empathy or interdependence between persons across jurisdictional boundaries
 v. Interjurisdictional trade and financial leakages
We will look at each of these in turn, although the formal similarity between consumption and production spill-overs will allow us to treat these two sources of problems as one.

Before we engage in this exercise, we must, however, be clear on the exact meaning which is to be given to the word 'problem' in all these five cases. Let us illustrate this with the forgone economies of mass production. Suppose a policy dealing with national defence, the administration of justice, or international diplomacy is produced under technical conditions such that the cost per unit of output is smaller if produced centrally than if it is produced in a fragmented structure. Then if the production of that policy is assigned to a junior level, the output of each unit will be smaller and the total cost of production—that is, the cost of all units added up together—will be larger than if the production had been assigned to a senior central government. The higher cost or the forgone benefits from mass production, which the fragmentation implies, is one of the problems of federalism to which a solution must be found. In other words, the fact that a federal form implies multiplicity of production units means that in the production of some public policies the benefits of economies of scale—which are in the nature of lower-unit production costs—have to be given up, unless a solution can be found to the problem.

It will require no demonstration that the greater the fragmentation—that is, the greater the degree of decentralization in the assignment of powers to junior jurisdictional levels—the more likely it will be that larger benefits from economies of scale will be forgone. We cannot be absolutely sure that that will be the case, since decentralization and fragmentation apply to powers, while forgone economies of scale apply to the implementation of policies; and even if powers are decentralized, one cannot be certain that they will be used to implement policies under them. To the extent that powers are used, however, more decentralization will be accompanied by larger forgone benefits from economies of mass production.

The problems posed by consumption[3] spill-overs are not identical to those resulting from decreasing unit costs, but they have a family resemblance. Public policies that yield benefits that spill over (hence the jargon ''spill-over'') the boundaries of the governmental unit in which they are produced will be under-supplied in a federal as compared to a unitary state. The technicalities of this subject can be confusing, but the essential is easy. Imagine that the benefits from a public policy produced in one unit of a fragmented political structure are enjoyed (that is, consumed) in neighbouring jurisdictions. Assume also that the flow of consumer benefits across boundaries is unavoidable, being the result of technical features of the public policy produced; finally, assume that in the producing jurisdiction no one is affected by that interjurisdictional flow or spill-over. The problems of a federal system arise from the likelihood that the quantity produced of the public policy that spills over will be too small or its quality too low, because the government of the producing unit will have no incentive to increase quantity, quality, or both to the level that would satisfy the demands of citizens in the neighbouring jurisdictions. Why? Because these citizens neither vote nor pay taxes for the benefits they receive.

In a unitary structure, the central government would be motivated to respond to the demand of all citizens and if it levied taxes from all according to the benefits received—something it could, in principle do, since it has authority over all who partake in the benefits—the public policy would not be under-supplied.[4]

Spill-overs are in all likelihood greater between municipal than between provincial governments because, as with economies of large scale, spill-overs probably increase with the degree of decentralization. The more fragmented the governmental system, the greater will be the probability of under-supply of public policies yielding benefits and the greater the problems posed by a federal structure.

In the list of problems above, we have used the word ''empathy.'' Much of what one would like to say under this heading is formally similar to what goes under the heading of ''spill-overs.'' We can consequently be brief. The formal similarity of empathy and spill-overs should not, however, blind us to the great substantive difference between the two realities they describe. Empathy relates to feelings of interdependence between people which can be based on kinship, propinquity, friendship, or on some more abstract reality. The existence of empathy may lead people to want a redistribution of income or of goods from themselves to those *vis-à-vis* whom it exists. The demand for such redistributions will then stimulate the formulation of public policies to give it form.

In a federal structure, because of the fragmentation of the instrumentality of government, it may be difficult to implement such policies so that a part of the demand for redistribution may remain unsatisfied, whereas in a unitary structure the government can reach everyone and therefore can carry out the desired policies. The problem is compounded by the fact that the amount of redistribution an individual may want can be affected by the amount desired by others.

In all probability the problems posed by empathy will be greater, the more decentralized the governmental system. It is for the reasons given earlier that all we can make is a probabilistic statement. The difference between powers and policies, on which it is based, is central to our view of federalism and will be referred to again later.

The last class of problems of federal structures originate with the existence of leakages. The best way to understand what these are is to consider all purchases, whether public or private, by members of one governmental unit from another, as imports. Expenditures by individuals in a jurisdiction can then be divided into expenditures on goods and services in the jurisdiction and expenditures on imports. The fraction of expenditures on imports measures the size of the leakage ''abroad,'' and the larger such leakages the less efficient will be aggregate macro-economic stabilization policies originating within a jurisdiction of a fragmented system. Since the size of the leakages will in all likelihood increase as the degree of decentralization increases, so will the relative inefficiency of macro-economic policies. The reader should keep in mind that the average size of leakages increases with decentralization only if decentralization is associated with the assignment of stabilization powers to smaller-size governmental units. To put this point differently, balkanized states—even though each unitary—would suffer large leakages. As we will see later on, what federalism does is to facilitate the solution of this problem.

3. THE CONVENTIONAL SOLUTION

How can the above problems be resolved? In this section, we would like to outline one solution that is due, we believe, to economists, and which is now in a way part of the folklore.

At its most simple, this conventional solution consists in trying to solve the problems by seeking to capture all the possible economies of scale, by eliminating the spill-overs, by making internal to jurisdictions as much as possible of the amounts associated with empathies and leakages. How is this to be achieved? Simply by reassigning each power to higher and higher jurisdictional levels until all interjurisdictional spill-overs, the economies of scale, and as many of the leakages as possible, have disappeared.

It is on these grounds that it has been recommended that all powers related to macro-economic stabilization and all those related to redistribution be assigned to the highest level of government, namely the central government. Furthermore, the recognition that in a society in which a large fraction of the population is very mobile—there exists almost automatically a large amount of spill-overs of various sorts—has also led to the view that powers should be more centralized in order to eliminate their spill-overs.

Consequently, this conventional solution, which aims at a more efficient allocation of resources in production and in consumption, as well as at more efficient policies for redistribution and stabilization, is one which operates almost exclusively in a centralizing direction. We say ''almost exclusively,'' because that tendency was recognized by some students of federalism who have sought to develop a more complex calculus of assignments that would prevent the steady ''upward'' drift of powers in federal structures. These efforts, in which we participated during the 1960s, were, on the whole, unsuccessful. They were based on a recognition that as powers become more centralized the benefits of federalism—those related to the exercise of liberty, to meeting the requirements of diversity, and to the possibility of learning by doing at lower risks—were reduced. A calculus based on weighing the loss in these benefits against the gains in efficiency emerged; a calculus which superficially gave the impression that an optimal division of powers could be derived.

The efforts failed for a number of reasons. One was that the benefits and the costs were not of the same dimensions and hence could not legitimately be compared. A second one was that even if the calculus was apparently associated with powers, it was, at least with respect to spill-overs, economies of scale, empathy, and leakages, really associated with the level of policy implementation. On that ground too the calculus was therefore thwarted. A third reason for the failure was that the calculus could not really be generalized to more than one power at a time. This third reason is not really independent of the first two, but the recognition that only one power could be reassigned, while all others were held at some pre-specified level, was sufficient to call forth efforts in another direction.

4. MINIMUM COST SOLUTION

We call this new solution, a minimum cost one, but we could just as appropriately have called it an "organizational cost" solution, since it originated in our recognition that *all the gains in efficiency* from capturing economies of scale, from eliminating spill-overs, and from adjusting to empathy and leakages could be reaped, not only by transferring powers from one jurisdictional level to another, but as well through co-ordination of policies between the governments involved. To illustrate, suppose that a spill-over creates a problem because citizens in the recipient jurisdiction cannot be taxed by the producing jurisdiction and hence the amount produced is too small. The governments of the two jurisdictions can get together and negotiate about the amount of output that produces the spill-over *and* about the amount of payment to be surrendered by the recipient jurisdiction to the producing one. Powers need not be reassigned, but the efficient outcome can be obtained through negotiation and hence through co-ordination of activities.

Such co-ordination is costly, it must be recognized, using up resources such as time, real goods, and energy. Furthermore, if we assume for expository purposes only that the cost of each unit of co-ordination is the same or non-decreasing, the total cost of co-ordination will increase as more and more co-ordination is engaged in. One of the factors which affects the amount of co-ordination is the degree of decentralization or extent of federalization. We will simply take it to be a good approximation of reality that the total cost of co-ordination increases as the degree of decentralization increases. Further consideration quickly brings the realization that co-ordination is not the only costly activity that is dependent on the structure of government and assignment of powers. In addition to it, we can distinguish three main categories of activities which vary with the structure of government, with the assignment of powers, and with representation rules. We call these four activities the "organizational" activities of the public sector and label them as follows.

Under any structure of government, citizens engage in two distinguishable activities: *signalling*, or conveying, to governments and to other citizens their demands and preferences (by voting and by engaging in other individual or collective political activities); and *mobility*, or moving, from jurisdiction to jurisdiction to improve the combination of policies bearing on them.

We postulate that the total costs of signalling decrease as the size of the typical jurisdiction decreases. This means that a change in the structure of government in the federal direction, bringing more levels and smaller jurisdictions into existence, will tend to reduce the costs of signalling to citizens. The reader will observe that this postulate about signalling is consistent with and is one explanation of the claim cited earlier that one of the advantages of a federal form of government is that diverse citizens can communicate and obtain responses to their particular preferences. Less evidence is available on political mobility, but we postulate that the cost of mobility also declines as the structure of government is altered in the federal direction.

Governments also engage in two organizational activities, which are also influenced by the degree of decentralization of the public sector. We have already mentioned *co-ordination*. The other is *administration*. It consists in the set of all activities that include setting up and operating governments on a day-to-day basis from the purchase of the services of bureaucrats and of paper as well as of the operations of parliaments and of other councils of state.

We have already indicated how total co-ordination costs behave as the degree of decentralization is changed. Administration costs will also vary with the extent of fragmentation of the structure of the government system. Because administration is an aggregation of a long list of specific activities, it is not obvious how its total will behave as we move in the direction of a more federal structure of government. We postulate that administration activities in each jurisdiction decline as the size of jurisdictions declines, but that the consequent decline in administration costs is matched by a simultaneous increase in the number of governments undertaking administration activities. On balance, therefore, we believe that total administration costs remain roughly constant as the structure of government is varied.[5]

Two points must be re-emphasized. First, administration and co-ordination costs are not the cost of public policies. They are analogous to the compliance, information, and other transactions and contracting costs incurred by consumers and business in the private sector, which are the subject of analysis in the literature of industrial organization. Second, signalling, political mobility, administration, and co-ordination costs are, by definition, all the organizational costs of the public sector; there are no others.[6] We can now imagine that the sum total of all these organizational costs is minimized. We can, in other words, conceive of a constituent assembly—a body, it will be remembered, which we introduced in the last chapter and to which we gave the task of making all decisions with respect to the constitutional dimensions of the public sector—that adds up the four organizational costs for each possible degree of federalization or of fragmentation of the governmental system and then chooses, as the one to be implemented, the degree for which total costs are the smallest.

That operation is strictly mechanical; because of this we call the government structure which it yields one that is designed by machine. It is mechanical in the specific sense that "members" of the constituent assembly have no views and preferences that count in the design. Data on the cost of signalling, of political mobility, of co-ordination, and of administration for every possible degree of federalization are fed as in a computer and the minimum cost solution is found.

Finding the governmental structure at which organizational costs are minimized means finding the number of jurisdictional levels, the boundaries of governmental units, the assignment of powers, the rules of representation, and the other constitutional dimensions for which these costs are a minimum. It is also the same thing as finding the structure for which the benefits from forgone economies of scale are the smallest, the shortfalls of output from the optimum caused by spill-overs are the least, the distortion in redistribution of goods and income from disregarded empathy a minimum, and the distortion in stabilization of overall economic activity due to leakages the smallest.

One could call such a solution an "ideal" solution and the governmental structure to which it gives rise an "ideal" structure, but we stay away from such a view for the present, because the minimum organizational cost structure cannot be attained by machines. Let us examine why.

5. THE HIGH COST OF THE MINIMUM COST SOLUTION

The minimum cost solution, unlike the solution of Section 3, is logically correct. It cannot, however, be used in the form presented for two reasons. The first, sufficient in itself to reject it, is its cost; the second, important in practice but not a sufficient reason in itself for rejection, is the role given to the members of the constituent assembly in the search for that solution.

The first reason is that the costs of finding and of collecting the data, as well as the cost of computing the solution, are too high. To appreciate this, it must be remembered that the solution requires that organizational costs must be computed by first combining every possible assignment of powers with every possible pattern of jurisdictional levels and every possible pattern of governmental units for all rules of decision and representation. Secondly, organizational costs for all levels of policies, as the number of levels, the boundaries of units, and the assignment of powers change, must be calculated. Thirdly, data on all of these dimensions must be collected for every possible shock to which the system may be subjected.

The reader may wonder whether such thoroughness is necessary in practice. Would not calculations in the neighbourhood of equilibrium or for small changes from any existing point be sufficient? Possibly, but since little is known, in practice, about the relationships between organizational costs and the various constitutional dimensions of the public sector, it is difficult to be sure. It is not known, for example, whether these relationships are regular and well-behaved or whether, instead, they display numerous peaks and valleys which make it difficult to know whether a "local" minimum is a true general or global minimum.

But computational costs and data requirements are not the only shortcoming of the minimum cost solution. Notice that the member of this assembly are assumed to be willing to act like robots, either having no preferences of their own, or being unwilling to act on them, concerning the constitutional dimensions of their country's governmental system. Such individuals no doubt exist, but they would be unlikely to find their way to a constituent assembly. Real-life assemblymen (politicians, statesmen, community leaders, and interest-group spokesmen) could be kept from interfering in the recommendations only if decision rules for the constituent assembly could be devised to bar them from pressing their own interests, or principles. But here the very notion of a constituent assembly becomes a nebulous and even a flawed construct. Indeed, can one imagine a group of constituent assemblymen making rules for themselves that would force them to rubber-stamp the recommendations of a computer, and prevent them from exercising the very function for which they would have been selected?

Notes to Chapter 2

[1] A. Hamilton, J. Jay and J. Madison, The *Federalist* (New York, 1937). See especially Madison's Federalist No. 10.

[2] The argument extends to other types of power, such as bureaucratic power, and corporate power, but for obvious reasons we restrict our discussion here to political power.

[3] We restrict ourselves to consumption spill-overs, because the argument that applies to them is intuitively easier to grasp than it is for production spill-overs, but technically there is no difference between the two.

[4] If the public policy affects neighbouring jurisdictions adversely, it would be over-supplied. The argument can easily be formulated for damages, as well as for benefits.

[5] The interested reader is referred to Chapter 5 of our *The Economic Constitution of Federal States* (Toronto: University of Toronto Press, 1978) for a discussion and justification of these postulates and assumptions.

[6] See Chapter 1, Section 4 above.

Chapter Three

Design by Politicians

INTRODUCTION

It is now time to abandon some of the simplifications of the last chapter, simplifications which allowed us to represent the constituent assembly as a machine capable of finding the best or optimal constitutional dimensions of any government system—dimensions such as the number of jurisdictional levels, the size of units, the assignment of powers, and the rules of representation—simply by making the total cost of organizing the public sector as small as possible. To achieve the move from that simplified approach to a more realistic one, we need assumptions that meet the two following requirements: (i) they must be simple enough that it will be relatively easy to work with them, and (ii) they must be descriptive enough to represent adequately the essential features of the Canadian federation.

These two requirements, as a minute of reflection will show, are in conflict with each other: the simpler the assumptions the less they will be descriptive of Canadian realities and, conversely, the more descriptive or realistic the assumptions the less easy it will be to manipulate them and the fewer the results it will be possible to derive from them. We hope that the reader will find our solution to this trade-off problem a felicitous one.

In Section 1, therefore, we set down our assumptions and explain their meaning. Then in Sections 2 and 3, we examine some of the results which follow from these assumptions when they are combined with the building-blocks of Chapters 1 and 2, minus the mechanical nature of the constituent assembly assumed in the second of those chapters.

1. THE ASSUMPTION

We begin by replacing the machine which makes the decisions about the constitutional dimensions of the public sector with human beings. Throughout this chapter the only difference between the men and women who make up the constituent assembly and the rest of us is that they are politicians, while the rest of us are not engaged in politics. These persons are, in other words, politicians elected to the governmental units of the federation. Otherwise they are like other citizens. In particular, when they make decisions about boundaries, assignments, and the other constitutional matters that come up before them, these politicians will be guided by the givens and by the constraints of the situation (which we shall examine in more detail in the two following sections) but, of most importance, they will also be governed by their own self-interest as politicians. As we have noted in the first chapter, the notion that individual choices are governed by self-interest is a hallmark of the economic approach. Although a simplification of reality, this notion is a productive one to which can be attached many of the important results of modern economic science.

It is not easy in a small space to define the interest of politicians. It will be sufficient for the development of our argument if we define them as the amenities—monetary, but most important, non-monetary—derived from tenure of office; these do, as we need not insist, vary greatly between governing and opposition politicians. These amenities are also difficult to define. They may comprise the pursuit of some notion of the public good, an exalted place in history, personal wealth, and the kudos that sometimes attaches to the solution of difficult problems. Since these amenities and others more or less like them are derived from tenure in office we conclude that politicians will not voluntarily make decisions that harm their chances of re-election.

The decisions of self-interested politicians, as members of a constituent assembly, are therefore going to be partly governed by a search for these amenities and indirectly by a desire to improve the probability of their re-election. Specifically this means that in making decisions with respect to the constitutional dimensions of the public sector, politicians, in their roles as members of a constituent assembly, will be governed in part by the bundle of amenities that best provides them with individual satisfaction. They will not be governed by an urge to provide the least-cost constitution described in the last chapter unless, by accident, the design of such a constitution coincided with the realization of their personal goals.

It would be unduly repetitive to examine in turn how the interests of politicians are related to each of the constitutional dimensions of governmental systems but, to illustrate the nature of our argument, we will examine this dependence for the assignment of powers. At the most elementary level, we can say that governing politicians will want a power or a function assigned to the jurisdictional level at which they are located if the policies that they could implement under that power would lead to an increase in the probability of their re-election; similarly they would want a power assigned to another level if all the policies implementable under that power would only reduce their chances of re-election. We need not insist that the relationship between the probability of re-election and implementable policies under any power is not an immutable property of nature, but something that differs between collectivities and between historical periods. The desired assignment of powers will consequently vary between societies and time periods.

To illustrate, suppose that a number of the policies that can be introduced and implemented under the power which gives responsibility for social welfare are policies which elicit the support of a large fraction of the electorate—certainly that of those who are net recipients of welfare payments, but also of those who favour a more equal distribution of income—then self-interested politicians would prefer that that power be assigned to the level at which they themselves are located. In the case of the power that confers responsibility with respect to abortion, if all implementable policies are divisive and unlikely to be approved by a majority of the electorate, the preference of politicians would be that that power be assigned to another jurisdictional level than the one at which they are located.

We have so far been discussing the preferences of politicians, as members of constituent assemblies, without giving any indication of the characteristics of these assemblies. In that, we have been prolonging the practice of the last chapter; we cannot continue in that way. In Chapter 2, it was not necessary to say anything about the structure of constituent assemblies because the outcome was not affected by whether there was one or one hundred machines in the assembly, or by whether these were elected, chosen by lot, or delivered by a computing machine company since, in all cases, they were instructed to search for the least-cost outcome.

Once the constituent assembly is made up of elected politicians, however, the characteristics of the assembly become very important, since they determine in good part how members of the assembly interact with each other and make constitutional decisions. There are many kinds of constituent assemblies in the world. In this chapter, we restrict ourselves to two types, because in the Canadian context what we can most readily identify as constituent assemblies are of two types. In the next chapter, however, we suggest the possibility of at least one other type.

It is not always easy, as we noted earlier, to distinguish in the real world between constituent assemblies, legislative assemblies, consultative assemblies, and other kinds of assemblies. Many times, for example, the parliament of a province shifts in a matter of minutes from being a legislative assembly making policy decisions into the role of a constituent assembly making constitutional decisions. We return to this identification problem at the end of this section, but the reader should keep in mind that in the real world decisions such as those we are concerned with in this book are seldom made by assemblies which confine themselves to constitutional decisions. It is the nature of the subject-matter and of the decision which helps us to identify a constituent assembly.

Without simplifying much, it is possible to say that in Canada there exist two broad types of constituent assemblies. The first we have already called one-level assemblies and the second two-level assemblies. The one-level assemblies are exemplified by provincial legislatures making unilateral decisions about the size of municipalities and school boards; about new jurisdictional levels such as metropolitan and regional governments; about the assignment of powers between regional governments, municipal governments, municipal boards, school districts and, of course, themselves as legislative assemblies and executive bodies; and about the rule of representation for these governmental units, deciding that some will be bureaucracies, that others will be democratic and, in that case, deciding on the extent and nature of the franchise as it affects age groups, property versus non-property owners, et cetera.

The two-level assemblies, on the other hand, are made up of politicians from two jurisdictional levels: in Canada, the federal and the provincial levels. In these assemblies decisions are not taken unilaterally by one level, but involve parties from both levels in an essential way. The *modus operandi* of these two-level assemblies will occupy us in Section 3. In recent years, in Canada, these two-level assemblies have often been meetings of first ministers, which have not always been announced as constituent assemblies, but in which decisions about one or more of the constitutional dimensions of the Canadian governmental system have been made.

The identification of one- and two-level constituent assemblies in the Canadian context is therefore made first by a consideration of whether one or two jurisdictional levels take joint decisions and secondly, by a consideration of the subjects on which decisions are made, whether they pertain to the number of jurisdictional levels, the boundaries of units, the assignment of powers, or the rules of representation, or whether they pertain to day-to-day policies.

2. ONE-LEVEL ASSEMBLIES[1]

A good part of the reality of one-level constituent assemblies can be captured by looking at the relationships between provincial and municipal governments in Canada and by taking note of the fact that the latter are, in popular parlance, "creatures" of the former, while in the case of two-level assemblies neither is a "creature" of the other. A little more of this reality can be captured by making reference to the language—but more tangentially to the substance—of economic theory, which would identify one-level assemblies with monopolies and two-level assemblies with bilateral monopolies.[2]

It is useful to push the analogy with monopolies—for the case of one-level assemblies—a little further. A monopolist wants to make as large a profit as possible, but the levels of sales on which that profit depends are a function of the demand for the product that he is alone to sell. A monopolist's sales and hence his profits are, therefore, governed not only by his own efforts, but also by the resistance, as it were, which he encounters in the market. Similarly, a one-level constituent assembly will have preferences for the number of jurisdictional levels, the size of governmental units, the assignment of powers, and the rules of representation that pertain to the jurisdictions that are its "creatures," but the final outcome with respect to these constitutional dimensions and others will depend on the resistance it will encounter and not only on its own preferences.

The nature of the problem can be illustrated by reference to the division of powers. To visualize how the outcome is reached, let us imagine that the one-level constituent assembly has a ranking or preference ordering of all the powers or functions that have to be assigned between itself and the level of government which is its junior. This ranking will depend on two dominant factors. First and foremost, it will depend on the characteristics of the policies that can be implemented under each power and in particular on the weights given to each characteristic in terms of votes gained and votes lost whenever a policy is implemented. If a power allows the implementation of policies which possess, or can be imputed, characteristics which on the average raise the probability of re-election substantially and hence permit obtaining many desirable amenities, that power will occupy a high position in the preference ordering of governing politicians; otherwise it will occupy a lower rank.

Because the calculus just mentioned will not usually give the same value to all powers, that exercise alone should produce a ranking for one-level constituent assemblies. But there is a second factor at work. The amenities derived from office do not all have the same value. Indeed, it seems reasonable to assume that the increase in the total satisfaction derived from amenities associated with policies is less for each increment in amenities. Let us say, for example, that the first unit of the amenities produced yields fifty units of satisfaction, then our assumption is simply that the second unit will produce something less than the fifty units yielded by the first.[3] This second factor, together with the first, should guarantee that a preference ranking of powers will exist. The existence of the ranking does not of itself tell us anything about whether a one-level constituent assembly will want all powers for itself as a legislative body, apart from telling us that the implementation of powers which permit the implementation of nothing else but policies which have a negative value for politicians will be spurned by them.

To simplify, let us suppose that all powers have a positive value for the constituent assembly. Will it then proceed to take all these for itself? Will it, in other words, if it is a provincial assembly, seek to take all powers away from municipalities and thus centralize all powers? To answer that question, we must return to the discussion of organizational costs in Section 4 of the last chapter. There we saw that as powers moved from one jurisdictional level to another, the amount of resources used up by citizens for interjurisdictional or political mobility and for signalling their preferences to governments as well as the amount used up by governments for administration and interjurisdictional co-ordination varied. To know how far members of one-level constituent assemblies will go in transferring powers to the level of government at which they, as politicians, are located, it is necessary to look at the behaviour of all these organizational costs taken together as powers are transferred in larger and larger numbers from the municipal (or ''creature'') to the provincial level.

If we accept, as the bulk of the literature on that subject suggests we should, that when powers become more centralized the cost to citizens of signalling their preferences increases, and if we take note of the fact that interjurisdictional mobility is necessarily impeded or worth less as centralization increases, we must conclude that centralization increases the organizational costs borne directly by citizens. As far as the organizational costs that are initially[4] borne by governments are concerned, decentralization—that is, devolution of powers—will usually lead to an increase in co-ordination expenditures. Whether it leads to an increase in administration costs, however, is an open question. If one believes that larger organizations need more control devices to monitor the bureaucracy, then centralization would lead to higher expenditures on administration. If changes in co-ordination and in administration expenditures more or less cancel each other out, however, the overall pattern of total organizational costs will be governed by the behaviour of signalling and political mobility costs, and therefore will rise as centralization increases.

The same result can be obtained by an alternative route. If one concedes that the division of powers that minimizes total organizational costs—that is the total of signalling, mobility, administration, and co-ordination costs—is one that assigns some powers to all jurisdictional levels (not only to one level), it follows that beyond a certain point organizational costs will rise as centralization is increased.

We must immediately emphasize, however, that the constituent assembly we are examining is not directly concerned with organizational costs; indeed, if the increase in these costs had no effect on their personal position and status, the members of the constituent assembly would disregard them and proceed to transfer to the jurisdictional level at which they are located all the powers which have a positive value.

But as we have noted above, all organizational costs are ultimately borne by citizens. As both the direct and indirect burden of these costs increases, it seems reasonable to assume that citizens will give less and less of their support to the governing party so that the probability of its re-election will fall. We conclude that as the members of one-level constituent assemblies transfer more and more powers to the jurisdictional level at which they operate in their role as politicians, the declining extra value of amenities that these powers make possible will become equal to the increasing additional burden of popular resistance to higher organizational costs and, therefore, the process of transfer will come to an end. An equilibrium division of powers will have been determined.

Will that equilibrium division of powers be one that is more centralized than the minimum cost one determined in the last chapter? Or, to put it differently, will a one-level constituent assembly assign more powers to itself than one that focused exclusively on organizational costs and sought to minimize them? The answer must be in the affirmative. First, in the cost-minimizing or machine assembly, the members have no direct preferences or direct demand for powers while in the one-level assembly they have, and that demand can be satisfied by unilateral action up to the point at which the increasing burden of higher organizational costs affects the probability of re-election in a way that is adverse enough to counter the positive effects of policies implementable under the acquired powers. Second, when organizational costs begin to increase, the effect is not direct, but manifests itself through the average probabiltiy of re-election. Since the higher centralization that results from one-level assemblies is particularly dependent on this second factor, we must stress its significance. A cost-minimizing mechanical assembly adds *all* organizational costs and, proceeding with its calculus, decides on the best assignment of powers. Members of a one-level assembly, on the other hand, are affected by organizational cost only in so far as its burden lowers their probability of re-election as governing politicians; since that probability can be raised by many other events and actions, the governing party, acting as a constituent assembly, can unilaterally transfer powers to itself by "compensating" those citizens who react strongly to the increasing burden of organizational costs by implementing other policies chosen to retain their loyalty.

That compensating, or "balancing," act cannot be pursued indefinitely, but it can be engaged in sufficiently to generate a fairly centralized structure for a part of the public sector. For those reasons, the degree of centralization will be higher in federations designed by one-level constituent assemblies than in those designed by machine or cost-minimizing ones.

We have developed the argument pertaining to one-level assemblies by focusing on one constitutional dimension of the public sector: the assignment of powers. We would like to be in a position to tell the reader that the conclusions arrived at for that dimension hold for all or a good many of the other dimensions, so that the best we can do is to indicate our belief that similar processes are at work on jurisdictional levels and on boundaries. We cannot be certain at this stage, however, of the outcome of further research.

We therefore end this section by noting that in every province in Canada the division of powers between the provincial governments and their junior or "creature" governments is one that is too highly centralized, in the sense that it is one in which the burden of organizational costs is higher than it need be. This is an important conclusion; it is especially important if one recalls that many—not all—provincial governments have been voicing the view that devolution of powers is a good thing, a proposition they apply to their relationship with the national government. But if decentralization is a good thing, it must also be good with respect to junior governments.

3. TWO-LEVEL ASSEMBLIES

We noted earlier that two-level constituent assemblies are those in which the constitutional dimensions of the public sector are determined by two levels of government participating in the decision-making process in an essential way. In Canada, the prototype two-level constituent assembly is represented by meetings of federal and provincial representatives—often, but not always, first ministers—meeting to decide on one or more of the constitutional dimension of one part of the Canadian governmental system.

There are two different kinds of two-level constituent assemblies which have to be distinguished if we are to understand how constitutional decisions are made. First, there are two-level assemblies in which the members at each level have come to a common view, or more precisely, have developed a common collective preference ordering. In the Canadian context of federal-provincial assemblies, this first kind exists when the provinces have come to one view about what they desire for a particular constitutional dimension. This common view may have been reached in meetings of provincial representatives preceding the convocation of a federal-provincial assembly, by correspondence or in some other way.

The common view or common preference ordering is always the result of exchange or trade between the members of one jurisdictional level, what economists, following political scientists, have come to call "log-rolling." At its simplest a log-rolling process is one in which groups or parties involved exchange not goods for money, but the support of one group or party on a particular issue against the support of another on a different issue; log-rolling is in effect vote trading and when votes are not explicitly cast, it is "support trading." When both jurisdictional levels have arrived at a common preference ordering, constitutional decision making may be said to involve two parties as is the case in a bilateral monopoly situation. In the Canadian context, log-rolling cannot take place at the federal level, since there is only one government at that level, but it can and often does take place at the provincial level with the ten provincial governments. If these can come to a common preference ordering through log-rolling they can then "face" the federal government as one, engaging together in some sort of bilateral monopoly process in making decisions about some of the constitutional dimensions of Canada's governmental system.

The second kind of two-level constituent assembly is one in which the parties on each side—in the Canadian federal-provincial case, on the provincial side only since there is only one party on the federal side—are not able, through log-rolling, to come to a commonly agreed view or to arrive at a common preference ordering. What we have to say about this second kind of two-level assembly applies not only to the case where no log-rolling whatsoever is possible, but also to that where log-rolling leads to the appearance of small coalitions of groups of provinces. For example, the Atlantic Provinces may come to a common view, the Western Provinces to another, while Ontario and Quebec each have their own views. In that case, on the provincial side of the constituent assembly, there would be four "coalitions," or views, facing the federal government.

What is the nature of the mechanism that leads to decision on constitutional dimensions in two-level assemblies? How is this mechanism affected by the complete or partial success of log-rolling between the parties at the provincial level who have to make constitutional decisions? We will look at each of these two questions in turn; in answering them, however, we will, as in the last section, focus our attention on the division of powers, because we know more about this constitutional dimension than about the others. The reader should, however, verify for himself that what we have to say about the assignment of powers appears to be extendible to some of the other constitutional dimensions of the governmental system.

We suggest that at its simplest the operations of a two-level constituent assembly seeking a solution with respect to the assignment of one or more powers should be conceived as the operations of a "market for powers." In other words, we are suggesting that the outcome of decisions with respect to the division of powers in the two-level assembly case is the outcome of trade or exchange between the parties involved. That trade may be one of "bartering" powers for powers, or it may be one of "selling" or "lending" (buying or renting) powers for money, or it may consist in exchanging powers for political support or other types of non-monetary amenities.

We suggest that when discussions and negotiations are going on between federal and provincial representatives—assuming for the moment a unique coalition on the provincial side—these negotiations are in effect negotiations over the "price" of a given power or of a set of powers or, what is the same thing, are negotiations over the value of powers to each party.

Appearances are deceiving and language is just as often used to becloud reality and issues as to shed light on them. We would therefore enjoin the reader not to think that a characterization of activities of two-level constituent assemblies as a type of market is cynical. It is not. The theory of markets is one that, even if in need of improvement and extension, does contain a number of tested, powerful propositions. If these propositions can be applied to constituent assemblies—that is, if assemblies can be conceived as markets for powers—they will help us to understand better what is going on. In any case the test is the result.

When the market for powers is in equilibrium, neither side wants to trade. This implies that, given what they would have to sacrifice, all parties are satisfied with the continuing division of powers. One might still hear speeches to the effect that the existing assignment is too centralized or too decentralized, or one might still observe some parties seeking to occupy some vacant powers but, if the equilibrium is at all real, there should be very little activity going on in the market for that constitutional dimension.

When the environment changes, powers are revalued by the trading partners, since at the prevailing exchange rates they are now dissatisfied with their holdings of certain, or possibly of all, powers. The market for powers is in disequilibrium; consequently, opportunities exist for trading to commence and to continue until a new equilibrium is reached. In other words, the two-level constituent assembly will meet and negotiations will be undertaken.

The theory of markets suggests what we should be looking for. Some parties will now want powers they do not have: they will be demanders of powers. Others will offer powers they have: they will be suppliers. Demanders will make bids and offer to pay a price as a quid pro quo. The price may take the form of other powers which are now less valuable to the demander, of money, or of other kinds of valuables such as political support. The powers demanded and the price offered can have a wide variety of time patterns. For example, demanders may seek only to borrow or to rent a power, instead of effecting a permanent reassignment. Or, they may seek a power for future delivery, but be willing to commence payment now. Still another type of trade could involve both the transfer of a power and payment to begin at some future date. Renting or borrowing a power can then be seen as an offer to buy a power now, and to reverse the transaction at a later date. The demander must have a quid pro quo to offer, and the supplier must be willing to accept it or suggest another of different amount or form. Both parties may be willing to transfer a power, but be unable to agree on a quid pro quo: if trading were restricted to the exchange of powers, it would often prove impossible to deal, for there are comparatively few powers, few of them are divisible, and fewer still are of roughly equal value. The opportunity to use money as a quid pro quo here, as in all markets, therefore greatly expands the number of mutually advantageous improvements in each party's holdings of powers that can be achieved by trading.

For example, suppose that a new deal is struck and that the coalition of all provinces agrees to transfer a given power to the federal level in exchange for a price. The transfer may be a sale or only a rental. Before proceeding the reader may appreciate a translation of this proposition in non-economic language. Such a translation could take the following form. The outcome of negotiations between the two levels of government—or in the language of Richard Simeon, of ''federal-provincial diplomacy''[5]—is that the federal government will henceforth (a sale), or for the next five years (a rental), have responsibility for legislation in such and such a domain. The federal government will also undertake to pay the provinces a sum of money as an unconditional grant. As our ''translation'' seeks to indicate, the process of trade is usually not recognized, the word trade is not used—but in addition, the connection or link between the power ceded and the grant (price) received is not even acknowledged. But that does not affect the reality of the situation, nor of the benefits of analysing it with the tools of economic theory. In this example, the federal government is the demander, the provinces are the suppliers, and the grant is the price paid for the power to legislate under the power being traded and transferred.

We must answer the following questions:

i. Why is the federal government the demander?
ii. Why are the provinces acting as suppliers?
iii. Is the price—the size of the grant—a determinate or predictable magnitude?
iv. Will the price always take the form of a cash grant?
v. Are there limits to the size of the transactions, that is, to the number of powers reassigned?

In our example the federal government is the demander for two reasons. First, the value (in the language of economic theory, the utility measured in terms of some bench-mark) it places on the power is greater than that placed by the provinces; and second, it possesses the resources necessary to act on the desire derived from its valuation of the power. The first reason need not detain us, since it pertains to the preference orderings attributed to the parties; we must, however, inquire further into the second reason. Indeed, if, for purpose of exposition, we neglect the first reason, it can be seen that a necessary condition for the federal government to be the demander is that it be able to command sufficient resources to pay for the power it wishes to acquire. We suggest that, in general, it will be the level of government that can bring together sufficient resources that will be active as demander and that this will often, but not always (see below), be the level of government with the most productive tax basis.[6]

Why would the provinces act as suppliers? Simply because rental agreements can be such that the provinces—more exactly, the provincial politicians—will benefit from ''fall-outs'' from the federal payment (grant or price). This argument provides a rationale for the observed fact that when the federal government has less revenues, for whatever reasons, the fall-outs will be less and the provinces will want to renegotiate a new agreement in which the power or powers are returned to them.

Thirdly, will the negotiated price be one that we could in principle predict? The answer to this question must be in the negative. In other words, the price paid by the federal government could easily be much higher than the highest price that the provinces would have accepted or it could be just a little higher. There are no forces, in a context in which only two or only a few parties trade with each other, to ensure that the amount paid by demanders approaches closely the amount desired by suppliers. This difference between the ask and the bid prices, or more exactly the suspicion that such a difference exists, explains why federal-provincial relations, in a country such as

Canada, are always complicated and slow moving, involving complex strategies on both sides: one seeking to find out what is the lowest price in order to pay it, and the other trying to extract a high one. Such contexts are always conducive to posturing, as is also easily observed and verified in labour relations and business take-overs.

Our fourth question has already been touched upon. It has to do with whether the price paid by the demander will always take the form of cash grants. As we have already said, that will not be the case. Sometimes the price paid will be in the form of other powers, an agreement in which the ''fall-outs'' take alternative present or future forms, and sometimes it will take the form of present or future political support. It may be objected that the payment for powers has to be paid to all suppliers and that consequently it cannot easily take the form of explicit political support: it is unlikely, in other words, that the same political party will be in office at the same time in all jurisdictions. This argument has some force, but it must be recalled that there are powers which are relevant to only a number of governmental units at a given jurisdictional level. Such is the case with fisheries, with wheat, and with offshore oil in Canada. In cases such as these, the coalition of suppliers are limited to two, three, or four governmental units, and the price paid need be advantageous only to their governing politicians.

More generally, the expression ''political support'' should not be restricted to explicit public support of a political party or of a government. Political support extends to the creation of a political climate that is favourable to certain politicians or to certain parties whether in office or in opposition. To find a way to aid some politicians in all provinces is not easy, but is certainly not inconceivable. For example, certain policies under federal power can be implemented in ways that relieve political pressure on provincial governments, either by lightening the burdens of local taxes by changing the federal tax laws or by accepting the ''blame'' for unpopular policies under concurrent powers, or in other ways. In additon, political support includes the ability and willingness to mobilize a population or an important fraction of that population; that capacity is then a resource that a government can use to pay for the acquisition of powers as well as of other goods.

Our fifth and last question pertains to the limits or constraints on the overall number of powers that can be transferred from one level to another, in our example, from the provincial to the federal level. To give substance to the issues raised by this question, let us suppose that the amount of resources which the tax base makes available to the federal authorities is very large, so that these authorities can enter the market for powers to buy a large number of them. What will be the effect of their successive purchases on adjustments in the market? Will the cost of powers to the federal level remain unchanged, as they buy or rent more and more powers? No, the cost will rise. Why? For two reasons about which we can be brief, since we have already discussed them in the previous section. The first is that the value of powers remaining with the provinces will rise as purchases by the federal government proceed, because of the principle of diminishing marginal value, and consequently the provinces will ask for higher and higher prices. The second reason is that as more powers are transferred upwards the total of organizational costs will rise as the degree of centralization rises, and therefore the monetary equivalent is nothing but the direct and indirect burden placed on citizens by a political system that is more and more over-centralized. The increase in the cost of powers to the federal purchasers will act as a check on the number of powers bought even if the productivity of tax bases is such as to make resources available in relatively large amounts.

What will be the consequence of having multiple subcoalitions at the provincial level instead of one grand coalition? The process we have described will, of course, be the same, but the price paid by the demander will be different. Indeed, that price will in general be lower. Why? Simply that as the number of market participants increases the degree of competition will also increase, and the outcome will reflect more accurately the relative values placed by all parties on the various powers.

Does all this mean that the division of powers between the two jurisdictional levels in the market for powers will be one that is optimal in some sense or that approximates the assignment that makes the sum total of all organizational costs a minimum? The answer must be in the negative. Why? We have just seen that the strength of the demand for, relative to the supply of, powers that manifests itself in the market for powers—that is, in the constituent assembly—reflects three things: first, the preferences of demanders; second, the distribution of command over resources, defined to include money, but other things as well; and third, the incrementally increasing cost of powers to demanders as determined, in part, by the preferences of suppliers and, in part, by the relationship of aggregate organizational costs, and hence of the average probability of re-election for all governing politicians to the degree of centralization.

It is time to recognize that, as in all markets, trade is governed by rules. These rules, which include those governing amendments to the rules themselves, dictate which trades can be carried out, as well as the conditions of trading. The division of powers is, therefore, determined by the preferences of demanders and suppliers, by the distribution of command over resources, by the reaction of citizens to the burden of increasing organizational costs and, last but not necessarily least, by the rules governing trade.

But rules are the product of constituent assemblies. In one-level assemblies the rules are set unilaterally by the senior ''partner,'' while in two-level assemblies they are set bilaterally if log-rolling produces a grand coalition on the provincial side, and multilaterally if log-rolling is not successful. It must therefore be the case that, as between one- and two-level assemblies, the degree of centralization will be smaller in the latter than in the former. Let us be more explicit about this. Suppose that in equilibrium one-level and two-level assemblies have produced a governmental system that is over-centralized. This means that the provinces have taken too many powers from the levels that are junior to themselves and that the central government has acquired too many powers from the provinces. But what must be emphasized, as the discussion of the last section and of this one shows, is that the excess centralization at the provincial level is *greater* than the excess centralization at the federal level.

For the same reasons as those which led us to argue that a one-level assembly would not, except by accident, generate a minimum cost assignment of powers, a two-level assembly will not either produce the least-cost outcome. But, in all likelihood, it will approach that outcome more closely than a one-level assembly would. In the next chapter, we develop the logic of this argument further as a proposal to improve the design of federations.

4. SUNDRY NOTES AND CONCLUSIONS

The analysis of the market for powers and of the market for all constitutional dimensions is in its infancy. It is full of promise but so far it has helped us primarily to focus on certain issues, rather than provide us with many definite conclusions. It has helped us to focus on the structure of the preference orderings for the various items under each constitutional dimension and therefore it has helped us articulate the concepts of the demand for and of supply of these dimensions—more concretely, of the demand and supply for powers, for boundaries, for jurisdictional levels, and so on.

The usefulness of this approach lies in identifying price and resources as the proximate forces determining the demand for and the supply of powers or of other constitutional dimensions. It is because of the existence of demand and of supply that we can identify the distinction between structures of constituent assemblies—whether one- or two-level—as one factor determining price paid and received and hence amount demanded and supplied, alongside the distribution of command over resources as a second factor in the constitutional market-place.

Behaviour in all market-places is also affected significantly by the legal system and hence by the structure of property rights in force in these market-places. We noted that something similar exists in markets for constitutional dimensions in that these markets are also governed by rules which affect the price at which trade takes place between the parties involved.

In this connection, it is interesting to note that in some markets for constitutional dimensions the right of veto sometimes exists, whereby any one party can prevent a trade from taking place. In virtually all proposals that have been made in Canada for rules to amend the constitution, some parties would have been given veto power. How can such power be explained? Is it one that is socially desirable? Within our framework, we can think of two reasons why some market participants may want to have veto power. One is simply that this power confers on whoever has it the capacity of raising the price of objects sold. Veto power provides a way of extracting what economists call rents from buyers. The second reason is that veto can be used to prevent pairwise trades between two other partners which would be at the expense of, or a diseconomy to, the first party. As such it may be socially beneficial.

We should also note by way of conclusion that constituent assemblies, either of the one- or two-level varieties, will be subjected to the pressures of lobbies and of interest groups. It is difficult to be precise on the effect of these groups, but we can illustrate how they will operate. Suppose that two powers which are complements[7] have, in the past, been assigned to two different levels of government. If the lobby members do a large part of their public business with one level—let us say 80 or 90 per cent of their business—they will be able to increase their effectiveness or reduce their costs of operation by having both powers at the same level. Then all their pressure-group activities will have a joint or common fixed cost, and can be based on a common investment in communication or goodwill leading to sympathetic understanding by governing parties and bureaucrats. They will therefore lobby for the reassignment of the second power at the level at which they do the bulk of their business. Does this phenomenon explain why, as the budgets and hence the capacity for patronage of provincial governments in Canada have grown, the pressure emanating from some business quarters seems to have been in favour of decentralization towards the provinces? We cannot yet answer such questions, but they are tantalizing enough to warrant further study.

Notes to Chapter 3

[1] The analysis of this and of the following sections would be enriched by the inclusion of self-interested bureaucrats and some results would be altered, but at the cost of much complication. Since the argument of this chapter is made in view of that in the next, and that argument is not altered by neglecting bureaucrats, we feel that the simplification is justified.

[2] On the analogy with bilateral monopoly, see, however, Section 4 of this chapter.

[3] This is the well-known principle of diminishing marginal utility or increasing marginal rate of substitution which we apply here to the amenities derived from policies implementable under different powers. The principle could alternatively be applied to the vote-begetting capacity of policies implementable under different powers. Whatever approach one chooses, certain conditions, which we do not discuss here, have to be satisfied. We assume that they are.

[4] All organizational costs are ultimately borne directly by citizens or indirectly in their role of taxpayers. We use the word "initially" to note that some of these costs are first paid by governments before being charged to citizens as taxes.

[5] In Richard Simeon, *Federal-Provincial Diplomacy: The Making of Recent Policy in Canada* (Toronto: University of Toronto Press, 1972).

[6] A productive tax base is one with a high revenue elasticity, so that a 1 per cent increase in the size of the base leads to an increase in revenue in excess of 1 per cent.

[7] We have not yet acknowledged the fact that powers can be either substitutes, complements, or independent. That follows from the existence of a demand for them. Complementarity means that the value of a power to someone is closely associated to the value of another.

Chapter Four

Towards a Better Constitutional Design

INTRODUCTION

In the previous chapter we showed that the structure of the federation at the national-provincial level is determined and altered by a trading process, in which the transactions are between elected, governing politicians. This process differs from that employed at the provincial-local level, in which the division of provincial and municipal powers is done by the governing party at the provincial level only.

In Section 2 of that chapter, we also drew an analogy between these two processes and two systems well known in the economics of industrial organization: bilateral monopoly and simple monopoly. Our intention here is to explore further the application of the economics of the effectiveness and performance of markets to the effectiveness and performance of constituent assemblies; this does not mean more concentration on commercial and money matters than those which, we have recognized, already exist.

This extension of economic reasoning to constituent assemblies culminates in the conclusion that large numbers and a more competitive atmosphere lead to better decisions and performance than obtained from unilateral and bilateral systems. The argument leading to this conclusion starts from the recognition that in any real-world assembly all decisions related to constitutional dimensions will usually be taken by politicians (from various levels and parties). Their self-interested behaviour induces them to act in a way which those who consider the design of constituent assemblies should seek to exploit, rather than to deplore. How can these energies be harnessed to work in the social interest?

Examination of existing constituent assemblies reveals that the small number of members that make them up represent only a fraction of the views of those who could potentially be interested in the design of the constitution. This limited membership naturally restricts trading to only those proposals for constitutional change that are of mutual interest to those present and to omit other proposals, those unlikely to attract profitable offers. Thus we observe that two-level assemblies confine themselves to dealing in only a few of the constitutional dimensions of a society, omitting some that, from a social point of view, may be of equal importance. This restricted scope is aggravated by the limited perspective of participants. The accident of being

43

in office at the time when a constituent assembly is active may give undue opportunity to one small coalition of participants to bias the outcome in particular (perhaps eccentric or even random) directions.

These observations therefore suggest that the design of constitutions would be better performed if the extent of the designing institution was broadened. The same conclusion also emerges from the application of orthodox economic doctrine concerning small numbers in markets. This doctrine teaches us that an increase in numbers reduces the dominance and the "bargaining power" of particular actors and increases the opportunity for a jointly determined trading outcome to approach a "competitive" equilibrium. In this latter condition, traders have no incentive to seek gains by holding back what they have to offer, by colluding with a grouping of other traders, or by withholding information about, or misrepresenting, their own ultimate willingness to buy or sell. Instead, competitive pressure forces each of them to declare their offers in a forthright manner, and to explore every avenue by which their self-interest can be satisfied. In this condition, on the one hand constrained by consumer demand and resources, and on the other by competitive pressure from other traders, participants jointly converge on transactions that benefit those whom they serve or would like to serve. Applied to the constituent assembly, this approach suggests that as the number of political participants is increased, the role of each shrinks from that of major actor to that of intermediary, seeking to make the best of the demands of his own electorate in the face of the demands of other jurisdictions for adjustments in the assignment of powers and in the other constitutional dimensions.

This argument is developed in the following sections. In Section 1 we enlarge on the defects of constitutional designs such as those outlined in the previous chapter. In Section 2 we marshal the arguments for a larger and more diverse constituent assembly. In Section 3 we discuss some practical questions about the scope and organization of the larger constituent assembly, and in Section 4 we contrast our enlarged assembly with more theoretical constructs, such as those involving a social contract. These are followed by a prediction that the extended assembly would design a federal structure with lower organizational costs than would emerge from existing assemblies.

1. DEFICIENCIES OF CONTEMPORARY CONSTITUENT ASSEMBLIES

In this section we present a critique of one- and two-level constituent assemblies.

Concentrating our attention on the assignment of powers between levels of government, we concluded in Chapter 3 that both forms of assembly tend to produce a federal structure that is over-centralized, that is, more centralized than a structure which minimized organizational costs. We reached that conclusion on the basis of certain similarities between constituent assemblies and market structures. We noted two things. First, that desire for re-election of political participants in both types of assembly can be likened to the profit-maximizing motive of those who participate in decision making in monopolistic and bilateral-monopoly markets. And in both types of assembly, the constraint on the political participants from voters' mounting resistance to increases in organizational costs can be likened to the limits imposed on monopolistic sellers by mounting resistance of buyer to price increases.

The second thing is that one- and two-level assemblies would not, in the same circumstances, make the same decisions. Not surprisingly, the divergence from a least-cost federal structure is likely to be greater when the participants are less inhibited by the counterbalancing forces of other participants. Hence, in the one-level assembly, where one governing party is, at any given time, restrained in its plans to reassign power only by its legislative opposition, inhibitions on reassignments arising from citizen reaction to changes in organizational costs may be weak and sporadic. Two-level assemblies, however, are not free to stray so far from the least-cost structure, because with two or more participants the reassignment of powers involves trading, and trading imposes taxes or other costs on the citizens of the jurisdiction buying or renting powers. Thus, in the two-level assembly there will be more scope than in the one-level one for organizational costs to have an influence on the structure of the federation.

This comparison of the two types of assembly suggests our main criticism. Starting from the position that the aim is to create a federal structure with minimum organizational costs, we note that while the level of these costs is not recognized as a determinant of the structure in either type of assembly, its influence is stronger in the assembly with the larger number of participants. This leads us to suspect that the number of participants is important in several ways, and to hypothesize that the chief fault of contemporary constituent assemblies is that they are too similar to small-number institutions in economic life. In these, strategic struggles among a few rivals lead to equilibria that differ from the cost-minimizing equilibria expected from the battle for gain and for suvival when large numbers compete.

Of course, it must be recognized that simply adding to the number of participants in constituent assemblies will not be sufficient to induce an assembly to choose a minimum cost assignment of powers. Some larger assemblies might be just as indifferent as smaller ones to organizational costs. Furthermore, larger assemblies might run into difficult decision-making problems, and for such reasons might fail to give weight to the organizational costs their decisions were imposing on society. These are possibilities. But we shall argue that larger assemblies are more likely to make decisions that reduce organizational costs. Our basic argument is that an increase in size makes it more difficult for the assembly to ignore or bypass any constitutional dimensions.

In developing this argument, we should first step back from the minutiae of logic to remind ourselves of the broad social scope of constitution making and constitution amending.[1] Any assembly must be concerned with creating or preserving basic individual liberties and social obligations, rules for individual relations with other persons, and with governments. Its concern with governmental structure is only a part of this broad concern, and its concern with a dimension like the assignment of powers in a federation focuses still more narrowly on one of the aspects of governmental structure.

Seen in this broad context, the relegation of the assignment of powers to the decisions of one- and two-level assemblies (such as those in Canada) might therefore be seen by some as an indication of the minor importance of this task. We agree that this would be a reasonable deduction but, minor or not, we would argue that this task should not and cannot be separated from that of constitution making in all its concerns with liberties and obligations, and with the role, scope, and structure of government. This is because the liberties and obligations of the citizen, the rights of the individual with respect to government, and the structure of government are not independent of each other. While in many respects they are properly treated as absolute ends in themselves, they have aspects in which they are complements, so that individual rights, for example, have more meaning in one structure of government than in another.[2] Furthermore, since in some other aspects they are substitutes, especially with respect to governmental structure, an assignment of powers, for example, has a clear meaning only when some or all of the other dimensions are specified. To illustrate, the assignment of a power to municipalities might have quite different consequences for citizens in a two-level than in a three-level governmental structure.

This sounds like an obvious conclusion. Most people realize that a constitution must be internally consistent and that its provisions must not conflict with one another. For that reason, written constitutions do eventually present a harmonious set of principles, rules, and structures. The harmony has been written into the document or documents by the original draftsmen, and added to it by subsequent amendments, judicial interpretations, and informal extensions and reinterpretations. Thus a constitution which guarantees certain rights to individuals, but also gives the power to one or more levels of government to infringe such rights, is bound to be tested eventually, and to have such inconsistencies resolved.

It is not so clear, however, that constituent assemblies will select the structure with the lowest organizational costs from the set of all possible types of federal structures. It must be admitted that when a conflict between citizens' rights and the powers of one or more governments is foreseen, the constituent assembly will design a constitution where such conflict either will not arise, or will be reduced by efficient co-ordination procedures (including recourse to judicial settlement). When assemblies act in this way, they are in our terms attempting to reduce the organizational costs of conflict resolution. But once open internal contradiction or inconsistency has been removed from a constitution, concern about the remaining organizational costs is much less immediate. There is little to take the place of overt conflict to induce assemblymen to take account of the weight of organizational activities and of their costs.

Furthermore, there is little to induce them even to distinguish adequately between decision making with respect to constitutional dimensions and with respect to day-to-day policies. In deciding on the first they should be induced to be foresighted enough to permit citizens, politicians, and bureaucrats to act with certainty in dealing with each other, with their economic opportunities, and with their governments. But one- and two-level assemblies are not set up in such a way as to give force to the distinction between constitutional dimensions and policies. In the first, the governing or majority party will take decisions about constitutional dimensions no differently than it will take decisions about any other piece of legislation which will affect the members' political future. In the second, the same criticism applies although with less force. This is because in a two-level assembly most business is part of the strategic diplomacy and trading in respect of spill-overs, economies of scale, and other matters of common concern. Even though much may hang on the decisions, these procedures are not necessarily part of constitution making, but are simply co-ordination activities, such as are called for whenever a governmental structure is not strictly unitary.

In brief, in both types of assembly, short-run strategic behaviour, unexceptionable and necessary in day-to-day government policy making, and intergovernmental policy co-ordination are inextricably mixed up with long-run decision making with respect to the constitutional dimensions, and are therefore necessarily decided on much the same criteria.

How can this be avoided? It is obvious that there is more than one way of distinguishing between constitutional and policy matters. For example, a one-level body could meet in a different place, or at a different time, to deal with constitutional business. Similarly, two-level meetings could be announced as convened for "constitutional," as opposed to, say, tax-policy, decisions. But these devices change nothing. The decisions of a provincial legislature, whenever it meets, will be shaped by its governing and opposition parties and their respective electoral strategies. And the decisions of an intergovernmental meeting, wherever and whenever it meets, will be determined by the same appliances, differences, and opportunities for obstruction or trading. In brief, however the meetings are set up, the same people with the same motives and *influenced by the same constraints* will be present. Changing the venue will not change the forces operating on decision makers.

Thus our criticism of one- and two-level assemblies comes down to a criticism of their structure and in particular to the narrowness of their membership. We shall argue below that neglect of organizational costs is due to their preoccupation with day-to-day concerns. Without an extension of their membership, organizational costs will never be more than one among many constraints, sometimes heeded, but often not influential enough to become a *criterion* for assembly decisions.

Before concluding this section, we should point out that we are by no means the first to argue that legislatures and federal-provincial conferences are too narrow in membership to serve as truly efficient constituent assemblies and that they need a broader composition. For example, plebiscites and referenda, common methods of changing, or of approving changes in, constitutions elsewhere, are already sometimes used in Canada at the provincial-local level, and have been suggested by some for the federal-provincial level. Furthermore, federal constitutions of the nineteenth and twentieth centuries have been for the most part the work of special constitutional conventions; in many of these, some pluralistic representation scheme, sometimes involving proportional representation, and sometimes other devices for obtaining more than one cross-section of national membership, was employed. Thus our criticism of the one- and two-level assemblies as having too narrow memberships is not unique, except in its emphasis on the need to get a system in which the minimization of organizational costs will have an influential role.

Up to this point, the whole thrust of our discussion comes down to this: the governing party in one-level assemblies and the assemblymen in two-level assemblies are attempting by trade to strengthen their electoral positions. They are not induced to become interested in any changes which would not promote this end. Thus, because they are not interested in discussing the constitution with politicians, persons, and parties who have no powers or positions to trade, many opinions, preferences, and voices, which we may broadly describe as those of a collection of minorities, are altogether ignored. Still less is their assembly composition one to be entrusted with the reduction of organizational costs.

2. AN EXPANDED CONSTITUENT ASSEMBLY

In this section we propose, and defend, a better way of designing constitutions. The substance of our proposal was anticipated in our criticisms of existing procedures.

First, today's one-level constituent assemblies should be replaced by two-level assemblies. This means that, in Canada, the provincial legislature's role as a body that takes decisions about the constitutional dimensions that apply to municipalities and school boards would be relinquished. This work would become the assignment of a two-level provincial-local constituent assembly. The coverage of this body would include all the constitutional dimensions mentioned in this and earlier chapters. The membership of this assembly would include members of the provincial governing party, and also other (opposition) politicians working at that level; representatives of incumbent and opposition politicians working at the municipal and school level; and perhaps others representative of strata of the population who because of geographical dispersion or for other reasons are not heard under existing rules of representation.

Second, today's two-level assemblies should be similarly reformed, both with respect to coverage and membership. Opposition politicians and perhaps potential representatives of other strata of society from two levels of government would become members.

Thus one-level assemblies would disappear, and central-provincial and provincial-local assemblies, both two-level, would have many characteristics in common. All such assemblies would certainly be larger than the present two-level assemblies in Canada. But how much larger? If they were too small, they could be ineffective in overcoming the reluctance of governing parties to debate or revise the existing constitutional structure. If they were too large, the consequent complete loss of party power or personal leadership might cause their deliberations to become formless and unwieldy. But at their largest, we would guess that such assemblies would be smaller than today's national or provincial party leadership conventions. (We note that in 1948 the complex West German ''basic law'' was worked out by sixty-five delegates from eleven Länder, representing about fifty million people. There were no central government delegates.)

Third, today's two sets of constituent assemblies, those dealing with central-provincial dimensions, and those dealing with provincial-local dimensions, would be fused into one super assembly. Thus the membership would include assemblymen from all three levels, so that local school-board representatives and national politicians would jointly participate in dealing with the expanded coverage of the assembly: all constitutional dimensions, at all jurisdictional levels.

The reader will perceive that the guesses above about the size of the respective assemblies could only be tentative. The size of any decision-making body is influenced not only by its rules of representation but also by its decision rules. In general, rules of representation that provided delegates to represent each minute interest, point of view, or political jurisdiction, thus leading to a very large potential membership, would tend to ''represent'' each citizen more than once; that is, each citizen would be ''spoken for'' or represented not only by assemblymen chosen by familiar electoral methods from each of the three levels of government, but by others as well. But the extent of such multi-representation would differ among citizens: those who were ''extremists'' in their constitutional views (or interests) being represented less frequently than those whose options and goals lay near the median.

It can be seen that, in such circumstances, the assembly's choice of its own decision rules must have an important effect on its design of a constitution. Assume, for example, that every delegate has one vote. Then a simple-majority rule would give "extremists" a better chance for their proposals for the dimensions of the constitution to win acceptance than would, say, a two-thirds majority rule, (or a rule that constitutional amendments must be confirmed by popular referendum.) The example illustrates that there is a trade-off between representation rules that give "extremists" many seats in a constitutional assembly, and decision rules that reduce the size of the majority (or the number of delegates they must win over) needed to gain acceptances.

The justification of these three proposals, implicit both in the critique concluding the last chapter, and in Section 1 of this chapter, stems almost entirely from broadening the membership to include persons outside the present governing parties. This would encourage three improvements in the work of constituent assemblies.

In the first place, by bringing in opposition, potential, and inactive politicians, it would broaden the scope of constituent assemblies to include all the constitutional dimensions of the public sector. Furthermore, it would reduce the dominance of the cabinet, or of the small number of active traders in present assemblies, and of the relatively small proportion of the electorate that is sufficient to keep them in power, and would create, or increase, influence from other persons now ineffective in constitutional matters. This point, closely related to the improvement described in the paragraph above, depends on the decision rules of the extended assembly. In our opinion, the broadened participation would tend to improve the efficiency of trading as an instrument of change along any of the dimensions of governmental structure. Trading, as barter, as log-rolling, for a cash quid pro quo between governments will come to resemble competitive trading more than bilateral or oligopolistic trading. This question will be dealt with in a later section. In addition, the broadened political membership, in touch with citizens in a mosaic of governmental levels, cultural, church, professional, and industrial groups, and regional and sectoral interests, might well be more sensitive to one or more of the organizational costs corresponding to the different combinations of the dimensions of government structure, especially those borne by citizens. We return to this possibility in Section 4.

3. SOME PRACTICAL DETAILS

The previous section is not concrete, and readers may well be dissatisfied with its obvious lack of plan of action for immediate reform. But our role is not to supplant the constitutional, legal, and administrative specialists, who will know better than we what rules and procedures are practicable. What follows, therefore, consists merely of brief notes, mentioning aspects of assembly organization that seem to us important if the aim of an improved federal structure is to be achieved.

In the first place, its rules of representation will have to be handed down to it in advance. Our remarks about narrowness of membership will have conveyed our firm belief that the assemblymen should be selected on a wider basis than as representatives of existing governments. But this criterion leaves much scope for further choice, including such systems as direct election of all assemblymen on a proportional basis, direct appointment of some from provincial and national parliaments, and various combinations and extensions of these two methods. Precedents do exist abroad: many countries have convoked constituent assemblies, and some of these have been federal countries. Consequently, models do exist to inspire a suitable variant. The first sentence of this paragraph only conveys our belief that the assembly cannot be asked to determine its own membership, but that it will have to make the best of whatever representativeness it is given.

In the second place, the assembly will have to determine its own rules of order and procedure, taking its membership into account. For example, it seems probable that its members would find it difficult to proceed on any except the familiar one-man, one-vote system, and that the simple majority system is as good as any. But alternative systems do exist, and some have recently been proposed for a reformed Senate of Canada. (Under one system, for instance, members would sit and vote as provincially instructed blocs. This system would work out much as today's federal-provincial conferences, with the addition of formally weighted voting. In practice, it would be little improvement over the small-group, power-trading assemblies of the present two-level assemblies, as discussed in Chapter 3.)

In the third place, we would expect the assembly to reconvene periodically, and we would expect assemblymen to act politically in attempting to gain seats in the assembly.

In the fourth place, we would expect that its agenda would evolve through time with experience and with need. At the present time, the pressing federal need in Canada is for a constitutional assembly to win wide consensus on the dimension of the assignment of powers among jurisdictions and levels. Another issue, less federal in nature, is the entrenchment of civil rights in a constitutional document. Later on, the other dimensions of federalism, especially the number of units and levels, must be dealt with. But once a procedure exists, and is freed of the need for ''agreement by trading'' between a small number of governments, these other dimensions can gradually be examined and reformed. We would expect the assembly to debate and determine its own agenda and timetable.

Other important procedural details will occur to the reader as needing careful consideration. What should be the role of referenda and of plebiscites? Should a certain number of provinces, a certain specified part of the population, or a certain region have a veto on changes in certain dimensions? Should the assembly be able to subdivide, dealing with problems of certain dimensions within certain regions without drawing in all assemblymen from other regions? We cannot see any insuperable objections to adaptations of all these well-known devices.

Nothing that we wish to urge in this chapter depends crucially on how these detailed questions are answered. We have attempted to draw attention to the defects of coverage and membership in the present assemblies, and to show how they might be dealt with. In the next section we turn to the probable performance of such a body with respect to recommendations about centralization; that is, with respect to attempting to take account of the organizational costs of alternative governmental structures.

4. SOME DISTINCTIONS AND PREDICTIONS

To Canadian readers, accustomed to decades of argument about patriation and amendment of their Constitution, our proposal may seem both insubstantial, in that many practical details are not discussed, and Utopian, in that it seems more concerned with principles than with means. We accept such criticisms, for we did not set out to design a constitution, but only to talk about alternative criteria by which one might be designed.

There is, however, one misunderstanding against which we must protect our analysis. Some readers may believe that, as is now fashionable, we are attempting to set up an assembly to draw up a social contract, in the manner suggested by writers such as Hobbes, Locke, or Rousseau. There is more danger of some misunderstanding of that kind today, when many economist-philosophers are using similar modes of analysis to distil the elements of a good, or just, economy. Whatever the merits of these works (of which that by John Rawls[3] is the most noteworthy), they are not the models for our proposed assembly.

The important distinguishing feature is as follows. Rawls and kindred writers imagine a representative assembly of ordinary men, possessing certain knowledge about the world, but none about themselves or their careers, meeting to make rules behind what is then labelled "a veil of ignorance." The purpose of imposing this veil on them is to force them to act unselfishly (since they cannot know what rules would be in their own interest). Such an assembly obviously cannot exist in the real world: it is a hypothetical pedagogical device.

The assembly we propose is one that could exist in the real world. All or most of its assemblymen would be actual politicians, interested in winning office, and therefore in having a federal constitution that could work in their favour. Of course, nothing would prevent them, or some of them, from acting in a disinterested or unselfish way. But we have not proposed an institution that relies on their being "statesmanlike" or unselfish. We hope, as we have said earlier, that such an assembly, because large and representative, will harness the energies of politicians in such a way as to evolve a better federation. Right or wrong, it would be totally unlike the deliberations of a Rawlsian assembly of non-political, "behind-a-veil-of-ignorance" men and women.

How would we predict that our assembly would work? First, we may point out that broadening the coverage of a constituent assembly, and including more classes of politicians among those participating may have more benefits than the obvious one of exposing the assembly to a wider range of ideas about constitutional dimensions. To put the point strongly, it could be argued that there would be advantages even if the expanded membership consisted entirely of persons whose opinions about the dimensions of governmental structure simply replicated the cross-section of views represented in a small two-level constituent assembly.

Why should this be so? We do not wish to produce a proof, so we shall rely on an analogy with economic models of commodity markets. In such markets transactions take place between traders at rates, in volumes, and in qualities that are the results of each trader's efforts to maximize his profits. If the number of traders is not restricted, buyers and sellers will continuously explore every possible type of transaction. Whenever profitable opportunities for trade are discovered, the new market will be invaded by other traders, until profits are reduced to the "normal" amount necessary to maintain activity. In the absence of changes or disturbances in costs or tastes, the market will eventually settle down to a condition where every variety of the commodity is being traded at a price that just covers the extra costs of production, including the transactions costs of the traders.

A restriction in the number of traders makes it possible for the smaller number to combine. By supplying smaller amounts and a narrower range of products they are able to raise prices, so that final consumers cannot obtain all they would be willing to take at the cost of producing the marginal unit. Then those traders make a higher than normal profit, and products are not available in the amounts or at the times that consumers would prefer. Note that this result does not depend on the particular characteristics of the traders who participate in, and those who are excluded from, the market. The tendency to form coalitions or combines, and to restrict quality and quantity, remains even if all actual potential market participants are identical. Trading in search of profit exists both when there are many participants, and when there are few.

Our argument is that increasing the number of participants in the constituent assembly has an effect similar to that of increasing the number of traders in a commodity market. The motives of the assemblymen are all similar: they are politicians seeking election or re-election in their respective governments. In the assembly they seek to bargain with one another, as outlined in Chapter 3. When their numbers are small, their powers to restrict the amounts offered allow them to restrict offers leading to changes in the constitutional dimensions of the governmental system. As we have seen, this restriction may lead to a situation where, in some dimensions, there are no transactions or changes. When trading does take place, the implicit gain to both buyer and seller may be high enough to bring each a substantial ''profit'' in terms of improved strength in the struggle for re-election. As suggested, this profit may arise because of restrictions in the amounts offered, and in the dimensions of the constitution explored for possible gains. Organizational costs to governments and citizens will be considered only if they affect a participant's electoral chances.

What is the effect of increasing the size of the assembly, and of permitting the participation of both governing and opposition politicians from all levels of government? As we have seen, the outcome will depend on the decision—and representation—rules under which the expanded assembly operates. We may, however, hazard the following general answer, which we offer on four simplifying assumptions. First, we assume that all have a single vote on each question before the assembly. Second, we assume that, regardless of the final ''package'' in which the changed constitution is announced, the assembly deals with the various dimensions of the constitution one by one, in a procedure similar to that followed when policy legislation is being hammered out at the committee stage. Third, we assume that the main decisions of the assembly are made in plenary sessions, visible to the public. Coalition formation and vote trading, of course, may go on anywhere. The reader may visualize the proceedings as being similar to those in which a multinational treaty, with many provisions and sections, is being negotiated. We have in mind such conclaves as were required to draft the great peace treaties; the United Nations charter; the successive GATT agreements; and the Law of the Sea convention. Fourth, we assume that while the assemblymen differ from one another in the objectives which they pursue with respect to the various constitutional dimensions, these differences are determined by their estimation of the best way to proceed to gain election or re-election, not by profound ideological principles to which they would adhere even if such adherence prevented them from ever becoming part of a policy-making government.

These assumptions, of course, are important. But, with the exception of the last, they are intended merely to simplify our development of the analogy with a market situation. The last assumption may, however, in some circumstances be crucial. If a large proportion of the participants are not politically minded, as we have defined that state of mind in Chapter 1, then the outcome of the assembly's work may be a set of constitutional dimensions which are not advantageous to the political careers of a majority of the participants, but satisfy them for some other, personal, reasons: private wealth, nationalism, or some more universalistic ethic or ideology. Such persons may be stubborn or adamant, and unwilling to make the best of the situation by any form of political action.

On these assumptions, we would expect the enlarged assembly to be more sensitive than the smaller one to the coverage of the dimensions of the constitution and, ultimately, to the organizational costs associated with various packages of decisions about these dimensions. We can suggest this by imagining the proceedings. The representatives of the governing parties will attempt, as before, to achieve the transfer of certain powers between their respective levels. Since such transfers will benefit traders at both levels, they will correspondingly threaten to weaken the electoral position of those assemblymen who are drawn from opposition parties or minority groups. These will, therefore, oppose the transfers, attempting to form groupings or coalitions with others, governments or opposition members, who would prevent the transfer in questions; their resistance, however, will not be inevitable or immovable. For example, it is possible that some of them, if ultimately their parties become the governments of their respective jurisdictions, will also benefit from the proposed transfer of powers. Others, for whom that is not the case, may benefit from some other transfer of powers, or from a change in some other dimension of the structure of government. Thus opportunities will be created for all politicians to trade votes, or trade support, among themselves with respect to different changes in the various constitutional dimensions. Shifting coalitions, negotiations, log-rolling—all these will be visible.

Partly because the deliberations will take place in public, organizational costs will have a better chance to emerge as a determining influence. The various participants will differ in the appeals they are making to the electorates in their respective jurisdictions, but all of them must be exposed to the ideas that the costs of administration, co-ordination, mobility, and signalling will be different under different assignments of powers and responsibilities.

Politicians in government, anxious to make trades or receive grants, would be confronted by evidence that such reassignments would not be costless. The different levels of administration and of co-ordination activity would be mentioned, and their costs would become public.

Arguments and claims that the burden of government (or the size of the bureaucracy) would be affected by the recommendations of the assembly would become part of the discussion. The great difference between these discussions and (previous) investigations and royal commissions abroad and in Canada dealing with the sharing and assignment of power is that these issues would be part of a political, not a semi-academic, exercise. Knowledge of administrative and co-ordination costs would not be mere background material, to be stressed or ignored at the whim of a small group of politicians; they would be part of the evidence, as it were, on which a large and diverse assembly would be asked to make lasting decisions that might affect many generations of citizens and many cohorts of local, provincial, and national ministries and cabinets. We must not press this point too hard: at any given time, sectoral, group and party interest would also be evident, pushing for particular solutions to the assignment question, and governmental organization costs would be unlikely to become the sole determining consideration. But neither do we see how they would be ignored.

The same would be true, to a certain extent, of the expected burden of citizen organizational activities. The costs of political participation, for example, do not get much mention nowadays (except when voting constituency boundaries are being redrawn). And they are rarely mentioned in connection with the assignment of powers. But the inclusion in the assembly of politicians with interests in local politics, and of some who have observed the difficulty of disgruntled or minority citizens in getting the ear of successful higher-level politicians and bureaucrats, should go part way at least to making the assembly aware of citizen signalling costs, and even of the costs of moving, when policies become intolerably inferior to those in other jurisdictions.

The costs of signalling are an unfamiliar topic for discussion or analysis. But an allied topic, the "responsiveness" of large and small jurisdictions, and of senior and junior governments, is sometimes debated. Hence, while we have some doubts that the constituent assembly we propose could, in its initial years at least, base much of its discussion on explicit evidence of citizen signalling costs, it is more likely that it could hear much about the merits of the various levels of government in hearing, and heeding, citizen demands and complaints. Such would, indirectly, cast light on the burden of signalling costs at various levels of centralization.

This brings us, finally, to the question posed in Sections 2 and 3 of the previous chapter. Would we expect that the distribution of powers in the expanded constituent assembly would be one that approximates an assignment that makes the sum total of organizational costs as small as possible? In Chapter 3 our answer, for one- and two-level assemblies, was in the negative. Here, it is not so emphatic, but it is that it would tend to that result.

This answer is based on two arguments. The first has to do with knowledge of organizational costs, and with the existence of an incentive to keep their impact on the public as low as possible. In the immediately preceding pages, we have shown why we would expect that in an expanded political constituent assembly, there would be opinions and influences present to raise "organizational costs" to the status of an issue to be quoted and cited in debate. Both the level of government and citizen organizational costs would be mentioned and used as arguments when proposals to reassign powers were advanced. This is all we need claim: it will be difficult or impossible for those who would reassign powers to ignore the effect of the change on organizational costs.

Our second argument has to do with financial resources. To the extent that trading of powers continues and is significant, we argued in Chapter 3 that under given conditions " . . . the distribution of command of resources is the prime determinant of the division of powers.'' A few paragraphs earlier, we had pointed to the fact that the federal government usually commanded the more productive tax bases. Our argument here is that, whereas in the trading in the two-level assembly, the trading process tended to gather powers into the central government *because* that government would hold on to its tax bases and use them to buy or rent other powers, the procedure of the expanded constituent assembly would not necessarily work this way. In particular, the expanded assembly would not necessarily regard as given the assignment of superior taxing powers (or, more generally, of financial resources) to the central government. (Even if it were decided to allocate access to the most productive tax base to the central government, that access need not be exclusive. The tax field could be shared, according to a wide variety of formulae, with the provincial and other levels of government.)

Once this is recognized, the force of our second argument becomes evident. On the evidence available, the expanded constituent assembly is just as likely to assign a productive tax base to a lower level of government, as it is to assign a power or responsibility to a higher level. We do not know which of these courses it will follow. But we do know that it will need some general criterion to guide its decision in such cases, if it is to avoid servile complaisance to the demands of the richest levels of government.

The obvious course to follow, when taxes and powers are being reassigned, is to pay attention to such matters as collection and compliance costs in considering the transfer of the tax base, and to compare them with administration, co-ordinating, signalling, and mobility costs in the case of the power that could be reassigned. In other words, it would tend to minimize organizational costs.

Notes to Chapter 4

[1] We remind the reader that we always use the word constitution in its broadest possible sense.

[2] See our discussion in Chapter 2.

[3] J. Rawls, *A Theory of Justice* (Cambridge: Belknap Press of Harvard University Press, 1971).

Chapter Five

Conclusion

The central conclusion of this book concerning the merits of an extended constituent assembly is based on several premises. A first one is that federations are institutions made up of a number of constitutional dimensions, all of which are susceptible to rational improvement. Consequently, federations can be designed. In adopting this premise we reject the views that federations are nothing more than historical accidents or political compromises between sectional interests. This, in itself, is a substantial break from tradition, since the acknowledged facts that many federations have been historical compromises and that a few have been accidents have often been interpreted to mean that there was no logic to federalism and, consequently, that the institution was not susceptible to rational improvement and design.

A second premise is that the design of federations should be based on organizational costs. In adopting this premise, we reject the views that the design of federations should rest on externalities or spill-overs, on economies of scale, on fiscal (tax and expenditure) harmonization, or on such meritorious criteria as autonomy, efficiency, responsibility, financial independence, or vertical balance. This completes much of our break from tradition.

A third premise, which is more in the nature of a basic assumption, is that the best design is the one which makes organizational costs as small as possible. This is a proper normative assumption, because our definition of organizational costs incorporates the welfare of citizens as well as the efficiency of governments (recall our definition of signalling and mobility). This criterion is then equivalent to one formulated in terms of maximum welfare or utility. This brings us in the mainstream of economic tradition!

Using the result from standard economic theory that increasing the degree of competition is generally beneficial, these premises lead us to conclude that an extended constituent assembly tends towards the minimization of organizational costs; in other words, to the best design for a federation. We wish to emphasize that although our argument is couched in economic language, our conclusion about a "best design" is not confined to "economic welfare," but is fully general, in that it encompasses all the objectives of citizens and groups of citizens which are within the purview of modern states. For example, the objectives of those who pursue the implementation of policies related to the degradation of the environment, to language rights, and to anti-abortion laws are taken into account in arriving at a "best design," in so far as these are revealed through signalling and mobility activities.

When an extended constituent assembly is contrasted with narrower bodies such as one- and two-level assemblies—the standard fare in Canada—its virtues are more easily appraised. One- and two-level assemblies are so organized that assemblymen are inevitably *insulated* from the competitive pressures that would lead them (unknowingly) to a federal structure in which organizational costs are the smallest. In contrast, in an extended assembly, the participation of assemblymen who must reflect the interests of all relevant citizens and groups of citizens would, in attempting to arrive at an acceptable design which all would agree on, be forced (in general unknowingly) to take the cost of alternative designs into account.

This result probably could not have been reached without the adoption of an economic approach. Indeed, the notion that socially desirable outcomes can emerge from collective behaviour without the necessity of the actors knowingly seeking these outcomes is central to modern economics, since its very first formulation by Bernard Mandeville and Adam Smith.

In seeking to improve the design of federations, the economic approach tells us that we should not seek to reform institutions by attempting to improve the behaviour or motivations of individuals. Rather we should seek to alter the institutional framework—in the present context, constituent assemblies—so that the self-interest of all will be channelled in the direction of what is the most socially desirable—in this case, a minimum cost federal structure. Hence, a race of supermen is not required, nor are idealists with any special view of the "national interest," although these are not ruled out and surely can play a role.

This brief conclusion summarizes some of the central elements of the framework which has governed our research. Not all of them may turn out to be essential, but most of them, we feel, are important. At least, they have served us well!

The Institute for Research on Public Policy
PUBLICATIONS AVAILABLE*
May, 1980

BOOKS

Leroy O. Stone &
Claude Marceau

Canadian Population Trends and Public Policy Through the 1980s. 1977 $4.00

Raymond Breton

The Canadian Condition: A Guide to Research in Public Policy. 1977 (No Charge)

Raymond Breton

Une orientation de la recherche politique dans le contexte canadien. 1978 (No Charge)

J.W. Rowley &
W.T. Stanbury, eds.

Competition Policy in Canada: Stage II, Bill C-13. 1978 $12.95

C.F. Smart &
W.T. Stanbury, eds.

Studies on Crisis Management. 1978 $9.95

W.T. Stanbury, ed.

Studies on Regulation in Canada. 1978 $9.95

Michael Hudson

Canada in the New Monetary Order—Borrow? Devalue? Restructure! 1978 $6.95

W.A.W. Neilson &
J.C. MacPherson, eds.

The Legislative Process in Canada: The Need for Reform. 1978 $12.95

David K. Foot, ed.

Public Employment and Compensation in Canada: Myths and Realities. 1978 $10.95

W.E. Cundiff &
Mado Reid, eds.

Issues in Canadian/U.S. Transborder Computer Data Flows. 1979 $6.50

G.B. Reschenthaler &
B. Roberts, eds.

Perspectives on Canadian Airline Regulation. 1979 $13.50

P.K. Gorecki &
W.T. Stanbury, eds.

Perspectives on the Royal Commission on Corporate Concentration. 1979 $15.95

David K. Foot

Public Employment in Canada: Statistical Series. 1979 $15.00

---

* Order Address: The Institute for Research on Public Policy
P.O. Box 9300, Station ''A''
TORONTO, Ontario
M5W 2C7

Meyer W. Bucovetsky, ed.

Studies on Public Employment and Compensation in Canada. 1979 $14.95

Richard French &
André Béliveau

The RCMP and the Management of National Security. 1979 $6.95

Richard French &
André Béliveau

La GRC et la gestion de la sécurité nationale. 1979
$6.95

Leroy O. Stone &
Michael J. MacLean

Future Income Prospects for Canada's Senior Citizens. 1979 $7.95

Douglas G. Hartle

Public Policy Decision Making and Regulation.
1979 $12.95

Richard Bird (in collaboration
with Bucovetsky & Foot)

The Growth of Public Employment in Canada. 1979
$12.95

G. Bruce Doern &
Allan M. Maslove, eds.

The Public Evaluation of Government Spending.
1979 $10.95

Richard Price, ed.

The Spirit of the Alberta Indian Treaties. 1979
$8.95

Peter N. Nemetz, ed.

Energy Policy: The Global Challenge. 1979
$16.95

Richard J. Schultz

Federalism and the Regulatory Process. 1979
$1.50

Richard J. Schultz

Le fédéralisme et le processus de réglementation.
1979 $1.50

Lionel D. Feldman &
Katherine A. Graham

Bargaining for Cities, Municipalities and Intergovernmental Relations: An Assessment. 1979
$10.95

Elliot J. Feldman &
Neil Nevitte, eds.

The Future of North America: Canada, the United States, and Quebec Nationalism. 1979 $7.95

Maximo Halty-Carrere

Technological Development Strategies for Developing Countries. 1979 $12.95

G.B. Reschenthaler

Occupational Health and Safety in Canada: The Economics and Three Case Studies. 1979 $5.00

David R. Protheroe

Imports and Politics: Trade Decision-Making in Canada, 1968-1979. 1980 $8.95

G. Bruce Doern	*Government Intervention in the Canadian Nuclear Industry.* 1980 $8.95
G. Bruce Doern & R.W. Morrison, eds.	*Canadian Nuclear Policies.* 1980 $14.95
W.T. Stanbury, ed.	*Government Regulation: Scope, Growth, Process.* 1980 $10.95
Yoshi Tsurumi with Rebecca R. Tsurumi	*Sogoshosha: Engines of Export-Based Growth.* 1980 $8.95
Allan M. Maslove & Gene Swimmer	*Wage Controls in Canada, 1975-78. A Study in Public Decision Making.* 1980 $11.95
T. Gregory Kane	*Consumers and the Regulators: Intervention in the Federal Regulatory Process.* 1980 $10.95
Réjean Lachapelle & Jacques Henripin	*La situation démolinguistique au Canada: évolution passée et prospective.* 1980 $24.95
Raymond Breton, Jeffrey G. Reitz & Victor F. Valentine	*Cultural Boundaries and the Cohesion of Canada.* 1980 $18.95

OCCASIONAL PAPERS ($3.00 per copy)

W.E. Cundiff (No. 1)	*Nodule Shock? Seabed Mining and the Future of the Canadian Nickel Industry.* 1978
IRPP/Brookings (No. 2)	*Conference on Canadian-U.S. Economic Relations.* 1978
Robert A. Russel (No. 3)	*The Electronic Briefcase: The Office of the Future.* 1978
C.C. Gotlieb (No. 4)	*Computers in the Home: What They Can Do for Us—And to Us.* 1978
Raymond Breton & Gail Grant Akian (No. 5)	*Urban Institutions and People of Indian Ancestry.* 1978
K.A. Hay (No. 6)	*Friends or Acquaintances? Canada as a Resource Supplier to the Japanese Economy.* 1978
T. Atkinson (No. 7)	*Trends in Life Satisfaction.* 1979

M. McLean (No. 8)	*The Impact of the Micro-electronics Industry on the Structure of the Canadian Economy*. 1979
Fred Thompson & W.T. Stanbury (No. 9)	*The Political Economy of Interest Groups in the Legislative Process in Canada*. 1979
Gordon B. Thompson (No. 10)	*Memo from Mercury: Information Technology* **Is** *Different*. 1979
Pierre Sormany (No. 11)	*Les micro-esclaves vers une bio-industrie canadienne*. 1979
K. Hartley, P.N. Nemetz, S. Schwartz, D. Uyeno, I. Vertinsky & J. Young (No. 12)	*Energy R & D Decision Making for Canada*. 1979
David Hoffman & Zavis P. Zeman, eds. (No. 13)	*The Dynamics of the Technological Leadership of the World*. 1980

WORKING PAPERS (No Charge)**

W.E. Cundiff (No. 1)	*Issues in Canada/U.S. Transborder Computer Data Flows*. 1978 (Out of print; in IRPP book of same title.)
John Cornwall (No. 2)	*Industrial Investment and Canadian Economic Growth: Some Scenarios for the Eighties*. 1978
Russell Wilkins (No. 3)	*L'espérance de vie par quartier à Montréal, 1976: un indicateur social pour la planification*. 1979
F.J. Fletcher & R.J. Drummond (No. 4)	*Canadian Attitude Trends, 1960–1978*. 1979

** Order Working Papers from
The Institute for Research on Public Policy
P.O. Box 3670
Halifax South
Halifax, Nova Scotia
B3J 3K6

CROSSROADS AND CONFLICT

CROSSROADS AND CONFLICT

SECURITY AND FOREIGN POLICY

IN THE CAUCASUS AND CENTRAL ASIA

Edited by
Gary K. Bertsch,
Cassady Craft,
Scott A. Jones,
and Michael Beck

Routledge
New York   London

Published in 2000 by
Routledge
29 West 35th Street
New York, NY 10001

Published in Great Britain by
Routledge
11 New Fetter Lane
London EC4P 4EE

Copyright © 2000 by Routledge

Printed in the United States of America on acid-free paper.
Design and typography: Jack Donner

Library of Congress Cataloging-in-Publication Data

Crossroads and conflict : security and foreign policy in the Caucasus and Central Asia
/ edited by Gary K. Bertsch . . . [et al.].
p.   cm.
ISBN 0-415-92273-9 (hardcover: alk. paper). — ISBN 0-415-92274-7 (pbk.: alk. paper).
1. Transcaucasia—Foreign relations—1991– .   2. National security—Transcaucasia.
3. Asia, Central—Foreign relations—1991– .   4. National security—Asia, Central.
I. Bertsch, Gary K.
DK509.C76   1999
327.475—dc21   99–20477
CIP

CONTENTS

ACRONYMS

AG	Australia Group
AIOC	Azerbaijan International Oil Consortium
BSEC	Black Sea Economic Cooperation Organization
CAU	Central Asian Union
CFE	Conventional Forces in Europe Treaty
CIS	Commonwealth of Independent States
CSO	Caspian Sea Organization
CSCE	Conference on Security and Cooperation in Europe
CTR	Cooperative Threat Reduction (Nunn-Lugar) Program
CWC	Chemical Weapons Convention
DOD	U.S. Department of Defense
DOE	U.S. Department of Energy
EBRD	European Bank for Reconstruction and Development
ECO	Economic Cooperation Organization
EU	European Union
FREEDOM	Freedom for Russia and the Emerging Eurasian Democracies and Open Markets
FSA	Freedom Support Act
FSU	Former Soviet Union
GDP	Gross Domestic Product
GUAM	Georgia, Ukraine, Azerbaijan, and Moldova
HEU	Highly Enriched Uranium
IAEA	International Atomic Energy Agency
ICBM	Inter-Continental Ballistic Missile
IMF	International Monetary Fund
MFA	Ministry of Foreign Affairs
MFER	Ministry of Foreign Economic Relations
MIC	Military Industrial Complex
MOD	Ministry of Defense

MOU	Memorandum of Understanding
MPC&A	Materials Protection, Control, and Accounting
MTCR	Missile Technology Control Regime
NATO	North Atlantic Treaty Organization
NGO	Non-Governmental Organization
NIS	New Independent States
NNWS	Non-Nuclear Weapons State
NWFZ	Nuclear Weapons Free Zone
NPT	Nuclear Nonproliferation Treaty
NSG	Nuclear Suppliers Group
OIC	Organization for the Islamic Conference
OSCE	Organization for Security and Cooperation in Europe
PFP	Partnership for Peace (NATO)
SEED	Support for East European Democracy
SNM	Special Nuclear Materials
SOCAR	State Oil Company of Azerbaijan
UN	United Nations
USSR	Union of Soviet Socialist Republics
WA	Wassenaar Arrangement
WEU	West European Union
WMD	Weapons of Mass Destruction

Introduction

Scott A. Jones

Halford Mackinder, a distinguished British geographer, suggested that there was a pivotal area "in the closed heart-land of Euro-Asia" which was most likely to become the seat of world power. He called this area—collectively known as the Southern Tier—the "Geographical Pivot of History." In many respects, Mackinder's characterization of the Southern Tier as one of the primary strategic geopolitical junctures is especially apt to the present political, social, and economic environment of the region as outside powers vie for influence amid latent and manifest instability. At the close of the twentieth century, the shape of the global arena is in many ways being determined in this region.

Nearly a decade after the collapse of the Soviet Union, many of the newly independent geopolitical entities carved from this former superpower remain largely unknown to sundry Western observers. The Southern Tier, a region including the countries of Armenia, Azerbaijan, Georgia, Kazakhstan, Kyrgyzstan, Tajikistan, Turkmenistan, and Uzbekistan, stretches from the Volga and Don estuaries into the mountains that link the Black and Caspian Seas, Europe, and Asia to the steppes of Mongolia. This area remains one of the primary examples of a region still "cloaked in mystery."

There is now only limited awareness that the emergence of several independent Southern Tier states has dramatically changed the regional balance of power and created far-reaching consequences for European, Middle Eastern, and Central and South Asian politics, economics, and security. The Southern Tier, perhaps the most ethnically and culturally diverse region in the world, continues to be affected by the tide of national revival manifesting itself in demands for secession from existing political entities, claims for autonomy, and actions aimed at creating new political divisions. Throughout the region these competing claims have resulted in a multiplicity of local conflicts from the seemingly constant struggles in Nagorno-Karabakh, Abkhazia, and the Ossetias, to the tragic civil war in Chechnya and Tajikistan. At stake in all of these battles are not simply the rights to land or the struggle to define borders, but the fundamental right of minority groups to self-determination and even independence.

In the early independence period, the optimism surrounding many of the political movements in the Southern Tier region during the Gorbachev years was destroyed as conflict swept the region. At the heart of these conflicts is the political vacuum that opened up within the republics as a result of the disintegration of the Soviet state and the elite alignments that supported it. The weakening of political authority at the center allowed a range of regional, ethnic, and political movements to challenge for power, sometimes with great success, in the case of Abkhazia, for example. Since independence, national and regional stability has remained an elusive goal.

The regions of the Caucasus and Central Asia, in particular, emerged as sites of some of the bloodiest confrontations of the *perestroika* era. In the late 1980s and early 1990s, conflicts in Alma-Ata, Fergana, Osh, Dushanbe, Baku, and Sumgait highlighted the tense situation that had developed in many regions of the Soviet Union during the previous decades. Moreover, the disproportionate number of conflicts in the Caucasus and Central Asia in comparison with other parts of the Soviet Union seemed to point to a turbulent future for these two regions.

The complex domestic, cultural, regional, and international factors underlying many of the conflicts in the area complicate any and all efforts to quell unrest. Although each situation is unique, several factors are at play in a number of disputes. Key domestic and cultural elements include the Soviet legacy, ethnic and religious differences, instability of the current transitional period, the growing problem of corruption, and increasing economic inequalities caused by the uneven distribution of wealth, which often overlaps with competition for natural resources. International factors include the contest for political and economic influence in the region by Russia, Turkey, Iran, and the West. In this volume, the authors examine these various factors with respect to regional security concerns and, consequently, political and economic stability.

In viewing the area only as the source of interethnic and interstate tensions, we may fail to understand the critical role the area could and most likely will play in international security for the twenty-first century. Not only is the area a virtual cornucopia of natural resources, including oil and gas, nonferrous and precious metals, etc., but it is the natural communications bridge between resource-rich Central and South Asia and the West. Debates today over how to build the oil and gas pipelines from the petroleum-rich Caspian Sea area to the West are but one indication of how stability in the Southern Tier has become a major international concern. For centuries the Southern Tier has endured, suffered under, and sometimes benefited from the great power struggles among its neighbors, which have often been played out on its native soil. In many ways, the future of Turkey, Iran, and Russia, and the relations among them, depend on developments in the Southern Tier. The United States and Europe clearly have serious interest in ensuring that these rivalries will be peaceful and productive and will add stability to the region. The region's future is being decided now. Will the Southern Tier be engulfed in perpetual violence and destruction as foreshadowed by the virtual annihilation of the Chechen capital of Grozny, or will it become a leading productive force in the world economy of the next century?

In addition to the sources of unrest, the authors in this volume explore mechanisms for defusing them. Regional interaction, for example, is identified as a means for resolving disputes through organizations like the OSCE Minsk Group, the United Nations observer missions, and the revitalization of the ancient trade and transportation routes of the Silk Road. Many of the authors suggest that international organizations also have a pivotal role to play. Yet they caution that despite the potential of these international bodies, their efforts often fail. Poor coordination among aid organizations and lack of cooperation with the local population have undermined many interventions. At times, however, conflicting parties are simply unwilling to compromise, saddling the international community with the blame.

Though it is acknowledged that easy solutions to the conflicts plaguing the Southern Tier are not to be found, the authors maintain that aggressive steps should be taken to address the most serious problems facing the region. Furthermore, they stress that if potential conflicts are not prevented, and existing ones continue to fester, the consequences could have implications far beyond the geographical regions involved, and subsequent intervention will be far more costly, both economically and politically. The authors agree that the international community has a responsibility to help ensure stability in the Southern Tier. However, conflict resolution can only be successful if the parties directly involved are themselves committed to resolution and prevention.

DOMESTIC FACTORS AFFECTING STABILITY IN THE SOUTHERN TIER

The Southern Tier states are multiethnic in nature with disputed borders dividing similar nationalities. They are also experiencing fundamental economic, political, and social disruption occasioned by the end of seventy years spent under the totalitarian rule of the Soviet Union. These regions, comprised of approximately sixteen million inhabitants and more than fifty different ethnic and linguistic groups, now face forces, newly unleashed, that were once contained by Soviet authoritarianism. This historic transition has resulted in the eruption of conflicts in Abkhazia, South Ossetia, Karabakh, Osh, the Fergana Valley, and Tajikistan—armed confrontations that have already produced approximately three million refugees and claimed the lives of tens of thousands.

The seeds of many of these current conflicts in the Southern Tier were sown during the Soviet era. Upon the dissolution of the Soviet Union in 1991, these new states were ill prepared for independence. Many ethnic groups found themselves living far from their ancestral homelands. Lacking the features of a strong central government, many of the new countries were in no position to control these emerging dangers.

The nascent political systems in the Southern Tier are reacting to the enormous shocks associated with transition. Each state has dealt with the post-Soviet transition in different ways, and their divergent paths have resulted in different levels of conflict. The Southern Tier broke with Soviet political tradition and the legacy of the old regime, destroying their patronage systems, whereas—by way of comparison—the Central Asian states have maintained considerable continuity with the Soviet era by preserving many of the major institutions of power.

In all of the Caucasian and most of the Central Asian states, for example, current heads of state have to some degree monopolized political power. In the short-term, this has helped to foster stability; however, this gain has often been dependent upon the personality, strength, and longevity of the regional leaders. In the Southern Tier new personalities appeared after the disintegration of the Soviet Union. Their challenges to the political order resulted in upheaval and in some cases civil war. The governments of new leaders like Zviad Gamsakhurdia in Georgia and Abulfaz Elçibey in Azerbaijan were tenuous, as they lacked both government experience and necessary connections to societal elites, law enforcement institutions, and regional powers throughout the country. Subsequent leaders, such as Azerbaijan's president, Heidar Aliev, have sought to augment central power. In effect, stability has been preserved by the personal guarantees of regional political leaders. However, many of the authors maintain that long-term stability is dependent upon enhancing political participation as well as a gradual devolution of centralized power.

In contrast, the Central Asian regimes emerged as independent states in far stronger positions than those in the Caucasus. Only in Tajikistan did the situation deteriorate into civil war. In 1992 the Soviet-era elite arrangements were challenged by a coalition of regional, Islamic, and "democratic" forces, which led to a fragmentation of the political order and a conflict that acquired a genocidal character. The failure of the Tajikistani state is, however, perhaps not surprising. Soviet state-building had been largely unsuccessful in Tajikistan. Political power in the republic came to rest on the dominance of a number of regional groupings, while the project of promoting a Tajik national consciousness to help bind the republic together failed to penetrate into many regions. In this respect, the sources of state disintegration in Tajikistan were not dissimilar to those that tore apart Georgia in the early 1990s.

In the remaining republics of Central Asia, a form of stability was established and the political regimes of the region were subsequently able to consolidate their control over their territory. In Uzbekistan, President Karimov eliminated overt internal opposition in the first years of independence, steadily destroyed the power of regional clans through aggressive personnel policies and anticorruption drives, and repressed any sign of politicized Islam. In Kazakhstan, Nazarbaev has gone a stage further and sought to remake the Kazakhstani state with the transfer of the capital from Almaty to Astana and the abolition of many of the territorial divisions established by the Soviet regime. Turkmenistan, a one-party state dominated by its president and his closest advisers, made little progress in moving from a Soviet-era authoritarian style of government to a democratic system. Saparmurad Niyazov, head of the Turkmen Communist Party since 1985 and president of Turkmenistan since its independence in October 1990, may legally remain in office until 2002. The Democratic Party, the renamed Communist Party, retained a monopoly on power; the government registered no parties in 1997 and continued to repress all opposition political activities. Emphasizing stability and gradual reform, official nation-building efforts focused on fostering Turkmen nationalism and glorification of President Niyazov. In practice the president controls the judicial system, and the fifty-member unicameral parliament (*Mejlis*) has no genuinely independent authority.[1]

Since the dissolution of the Soviet Union, a number of violent clashes, mostly stemming from separatist movements, have beset the Southern Tier. Most notably, tensions in Karabakh erupted into war in the early 1990s, about the same time secessionists in South Ossetia and Abkhazia began stridently challenging central authority in Georgia. One author from the Southern Tier notes that such instability is not a new phenomenon there. Similar separatist movements and political challenges were apparent in the earlier part of the twentieth century. National political myths and historical memories have catalyzed ethnic conflicts. Once the bonds of Soviet totalitarianism were removed, the heretofore repressed ethnic conflicts came to the fore (just as they had in the former Yugoslavia). While ethnic traditions have been helpful for cultural identity, they can be equally destructive. Simmering irredentist claims may complicate the consolidation of national sovereignty and provoke regional conflict.

Beginning in the early eighteenth century, Russia slowly asserted political domination over the northern part of Azerbaijan, while Persia retained control of southern Azerbaijan. In the nineteenth century, the division between Russian and Persian Azerbaijan was largely determined by two treaties concluded after wars between the two countries. The Treaty of Gulistan (1813) established the Russo-Persian border roughly along the Aras River, and the Treaty of Turkmanchay (1828) awarded Russia the Nakhichevan khanates (along the present-day border between Armenia and Turkey) in the region of the Talysh Mountains. The land that is now Azerbaijan was split among three Russian administrative areas: Baku and Elisavetpol provinces and part of Yerevan Province, which also extended into present-day Armenia. The majority of the Azeri nation, moreover, is resident in northern Iran, not in the Caucasian republic. Whereas the Republic of Azerbaijan contains roughly six million Azeris, between fifteen and twenty million are estimated to live in Iran. This fact has been an important reason for the ambivalence of Iran toward Azerbaijan and may complicate future amicable relations.[2]

To a large extent, Central Asia has thus far avoided acute political and social upheaval. Even Tajikistan, which has seen the region's only major violent post-Soviet conflict, has been rather well managed via Russian and international mediation. It is interesting to note how little unrest there is in Central Asia at the moment, especially in comparison to the Caucasus. This relative lack of tension is attributed to Central Asian leaders' success in developing ties of cooperation while addressing post-Soviet conflicts, but Central Asia's relative stability is still puzzling. Following independence, it was thought that Central Asia would prove to be the less stable of the two regions. The commonly held assumption was that Kazakhstan, for instance, with its large Russian population was ripe for separatism. At independence, the population of Kazhakstan was composed of almost equal shares of Kazakhs and Russians, with the Russian population concentrated in the north, along the featureless Kazakh-Russian border. Yet the predicted conflict between the two ethnic groups has not occurred. It was noted that the fear of ethnic clashes was overblown to begin with, as both Kazakhs and Russians understood the potential stakes and rejected using violence as a tool. Alternatively, the authoritarian leaders of the region may simply have been more adept at squelching political opposition.

By way of comparison, it appears that individual leaders, no matter how powerful and influential, are not sufficient to ensure long-term stability. Indeed, some authors contend that not all the Caucasian states are as strong as their leaders' ability to hold onto power might indicate. Some see these countries as coercive states based on fragile elite power structures. Although currently there is less unrest in Central Asia than in the Southern Tier, this situation will not necessarily hold true in the future. Some of the Southern Tier's marginally democratic regimes, misconstrued as stabilizing, may actually obscure underlying problems, allowing the seeds of future conflicts to germinate. If these regional issues are not addressed, these seeds will assuredly develop.

Numerous domestic and cultural factors have mingled with outside forces and external influences to cause conflicts in the Southern Tier. The dynamics that cause confrontation and violence are ever changing. The authors find it a nearly impossible task to attribute neatly defined factors as the causes of a particular conflict. Rather, it is best described as an ever evolving phenomenon. Certain variables are prominent at different stages, but there are always many underlying factors causing a particular situation to erupt. For example, when the war in Chechnya first broke out, religion was not cited as a key factor. However, Chechnya is now regarded by many as an interreligious confrontation and is frequently described as an "Islamic problem."

The authors have expressed grave doubts about the future stability of the Southern Tier region, noting that these states are trying to achieve the unprecedented task of simultaneously adopting new economic systems, building "democratic" political institutions, and creating new national identities. Whereas Western countries made these transitions gradually over decades if not centuries, the new states of the Southern Tier are trying to achieve these goals rapidly and concurrently. Compounded by the deterioration of the Soviet Union, these two regions are ripe for future conflict.

THE ROLE OF RELIGION

Regarding the role of religion as a positive or negative factor for regional stability, Central Asia seems to diverge radically from the Caucasus. In the Caucasus, historically Christian Armenia and Georgia led the way at the turn of the century in the formation of strong modern nationalisms. Other peoples of the Caucasus followed suit, not rarely under direct pressure from the more advanced nationalisms (Azeris countermobilizing against Armenians, or Abkhaz and Ossets against Georgian challenges). Smaller nationalities of the Northern Caucasus developed their respective nationalisms in relation to the loyal nationalism of the Ossets, who were cooperative with Russia, at one extreme, and the rebellious, actively defensive nationalism of the Muslim Chechens at the other.

In comparison, the peoples of Central Asia lack historical nationalisms. For a variety of reasons Central Asians missed the window of opportunity when the Russian empire broke up in 1917 and became, in the celebrated expression of Ronald Suny, "an incubator of nations."[3] Their ex post facto nation-building was conducted strictly from above and produced rather mixed results. Therefore, in Central Asia, religion—namely a more activist version of Islam—seems the only realistic opportunity for the coming popular mobilizations against the ruling regimes. It is also clear that in areas where the rural population has been growing faster than the more Europeanized urban populations, contestation of corrupt authority and the idea of "social justice" under the guise of Sharia is also likely to assume a more overtly political form.

Some of the authors note, nevertheless, that the role of religion as a variable affecting stability is often overplayed by most Western analysts. For example, the conflict in Karabakh has been variously painted as a conflict between Muslim Azerbaijan and Christian Armenia or Muslim Chechnya against Orthodox Russia. Religious affiliation is but one of many variables influencing political and social change in the Southern Tier. In and of itself, however, religion is not the critical variable deciding the future of political stability in the Southern Tier.

ETHNIC DIVERSITY

Many of the authors have identified ethnic diversity as a key domestic factor related to the rise of tensions. In several places, such as Karabakh, this has already occurred. During the Soviet era, potential catalysts of conflict, such as ethnic and religious diversity, were tightly suppressed. Relying on authoritarian control, other concepts on managing interethnic relations were never developed. The Communist Party and the Soviet government simply did not address the issue of ethnic management, leaving the regions devoid of mechanisms to cope with ethnic differences following independence. Where Party officials did address these issues, they did so in such a way to ensure internal and localized tensions that could be easily manipulated by Moscow.

In the Caucasus and Central Asia, until this century, there was perhaps no well-developed national identity among most peoples. With the exception of Armenians and Georgians, the concept of nation was largely absent among the peoples of the region. Even for the Azerbaijanis, who have a long literary tradition dating back to the sixteenth century, the main identity was either subnational (khanates, regions, or clans) or supra-national (Islam). This was equally true for the smaller mountain peoples of the north Southern Tier, whose societies were deeply permeated by a nonfeudal clan structure. With the consolidation of Soviet power in the 1920s, the leadership in Moscow was instrumental in creating not only the all-encompassing Soviet identity, but also a national identity, especially in the early years of *Korenizatsiia* (nativization) when the nonwritten languages of these peoples were written down and their use was encouraged.

The quest for identity, prompted by the new political structure of the region, has had far-reaching consequences for peace in the region. As one analyst has noted, the two prerequisites for ethnic mobilization are a strong group identity and discrimination on communal/ethnic grounds.[4] The resurgence of communal identities among the Caucasian nationalities, then, has been the decisive factor in allowing ethnic mobilization to turn into outright conflict. Discrimination, whether real or perceived, existed long before the 1980s and, in many areas, diminished over time. Hence the primary reason for the increasingly conflictual attitude of minorities is not discrimination but the strengthening of group identity. This circumstance can be observed in most of the conflicts that have raged in the post–Cold War era.

Meanwhile, the disastrous condition of the regional economies has led to scarcity of even basic goods, and as competition for scarce resources becomes more fierce, the danger is that this competition will take the form of competition between ethnic groups.[5] Regional inequalities often overlap with ethnic settlement patterns, and therefore inequalities that may not be ethnically determined are perceived as such. If in such a case populations are already mobilized around a strong communal identity, an ethnic conflict becomes a real threat. The risk of existing conflicts spilling over is not to be underestimated either. In fact, as one author notes, none of the regional conflicts have found a solution; they are merely frozen along cease-fire lines. Hence the risk of their reeruption exists.

In Central Asia, the continuity of leadership has allowed leaders essentially to contain or suppress potential ethnic disputes, much as it did in the Soviet era. The discontinuity of leadership in the Caucasus, in contrast, has hampered efforts to deal with ethnic disputes there. Furthermore, with uneven popular support, Caucasian political leaders are unable to take risks and pursue controversial initiatives for conflict resolution. For example, Armenian president Levon Ter-Petrossian was forced to resign after he came out in favor of the Minsk Group's Nagorno-Karabakh peace proposal favored by Azerbaijan.

THE PERSISTENCE OF CORRUPTION

As the states of the Southern Tier try to establish their own rule of law and national identities, corruption has become a growing problem. Several authors identify deeply ingrained corruption as the biggest obstacle to reform, and thus to long-term stability. They concur that corruption is one of the major obstacles to nation-building in the region and a major factor in distorting a fair and equitable distribution of wealth.

Political corruption has been deeply embedded in these societies prior to and since the beginning of the Soviet era, during which time corruption and bribery did not always go directly into individuals' pockets. Rather, the money was used to facilitate the functioning of the patronage political system that replaced the clan or tribal systems that preceded the Soviet system. In this sense, corruption did not play an entirely negative role. After independence, however, bribery and other corrupt practices offered a way for people to augment their incomes in these unstable economic environments.

Corruption in the post-Soviet era has taken on an insidious and pervasive form, feeding on and enlarging the growing gap between rich and poor. Of further concern, moneys from the political and criminal worlds are intermingling more and more, in ways that could fuel conflict over access to economic resources. It is evident that legal mechanisms need to be established in the Southern Tier to guard against and punish corruption. However, societies in the Southern Tier operate under very different systems that are not law-based, and there is little risk associated with being involved in corrupt or illegal activities. Until the problem of corruption is addressed, efforts to achieve stability and broader prosperity. In addition, it will have a negative impact on the effectiveness of both assistance programs and investment possibilities.

ECONOMIC INEQUALITY

The Southern Tier offers tremendous economic opportunities in the post-Soviet world, as evidenced in the recent increase in the value of Caspian Sea resources. Oil, natural gas, and associated industries are the most attractive areas for foreign investment. Furthermore, the region can serve as a potentially valuable transit corridor.

Many of the authors note, however, that uneven development patterns are a significant potential source of instability in the Southern Tier. Differences in the natural resource bases could provoke economically driven migration, polarize ethnic groups, and cause increased tensions. This combined with widespread unemployment leaves an enormous potential for conflict. Furthermore, disparities in wealth only serve to exacerbate latent and manifest social tensions. This economic transition from a centrally planned economic model to a market-oriented variant is both novel and exacting, resulting in what some analysts have referred to as "nomenklatura capitalism."[6]

Several of the authors warn that confrontations could also erupt at the regional, national, or local level as states compete for control of scarce resources, such as water. Furthermore, regional competition for control over the Caspian Sea and the oil resources that lie beneath its seabed has offered special challenges. Prior to 1991 the Caspian Sea agreements were negotiated between the Soviet Union and Iran. Since the collapse of the Soviet Union, each successor country has hoped to maximize its profit from the massive oil potential in the area. Disagreements over the legal status of the Caspian—i.e., Is it a sea or a lake?—have emerged. If the Caspian is a sea, then matters related to the exploitation of the seabed's resources would have to be resolved jointly by all littoral states. If it is a lake, then each of the countries would have sole authority over a sector of the Caspian. Russia and Iran have argued for simply extending the 1921 agreement, which divides the Caspian as a sea.

The Caspian Sea issue has generated a substantial amount of analysis and speculation throughout the world. It is clear that a decision on the legal status of the Caspian would have important implications for regional interaction, and agreements between the five states bordering the Caspian are needed. However, according to the authors specifically addressing this issue, it appears likely that no such decision will be forthcoming, and the littoral states and foreign investors will pursue a de facto division of the Caspian into national sectors.

With regard to the Caspian, the primary strategic question hinges on whether the anticipated wealth resulting from these natural resources will alleviate or aggravate problems in the regions, decreasing or increasing the potential for confrontation. Regional leaders cling to the belief that the influx of money, mainly from oil, will cure the problems they currently face. However, considerable concern exists throughout the Southern Tier that countries gaining most from this natural wealth will use it to increase their military might. This shift in power among states could be very destabilizing. The most likely such change would be between Armenia and Azerbaijan, with Azerbaijan presumably using its anticipated oil revenues to overcome its current military inferiority vis-à-vis Armenia.

The redistribution of wealth within societies is another potential source of conflict. Due to the interest of international investors, it would appear that the economic situation in the region will change dramatically over the next two decades. Some authors note that increased wealth from oil and gas has led and would continue to lead to increased elitism in various Southern Tier states, most notably Azerbaijan, along the lines of elitist societies commonly found on the Arabian Peninsula.

Wealth from natural resources can offer a means for future regional development. If mismanaged, however, it could be tremendously destabilizing. In fact, of the many factors that can cause conflict, competition over natural and economic resources (and their inequitable distribution) is most likely to lead to future antagonism. However, the countries in this region may be betting prematurely on the riches that will accrue from the extraction and transport of oil. The world oil glut and the corresponding drop in oil prices may severely limit this development. Furthermore, as one author notes, the forecasted oil and gas reserves were initially wildly inflated.

FEEBLE BOUNDARIES: DRUG SMUGGLING, WEAPONS PROLIFERATION, AND REFUGEE PROBLEMS

Throughout this volume, the authors voice unanimous concern for the inability of the central governments to control national borders against crime (i.e., drug, weapons, and other illicit smuggling), immigration, and refugees. As a potential "transshipment" point for weapons, of mass destruction, conventional weaponry, and narcotics, the Southern Tier's overall stability—let alone individual national stability—is compromised to the extent that national boundaries remain poorly policed and imprecisely demarcated.

The proliferation of conventional and mass destruction weaponry is an especially pressing factor affecting regional stability. The threat of weapons proliferation in this region, according to the authors, is high. Although the countries of the Southern Tier did not inherit a share of the former Soviet nuclear arsenal, many did inherit significant component parts (such as nuclear reactors, production facilities, military industrial enterprises, etc.), and many serve as important transit points (for legal commerce and illegal smuggling) to other regions of the world. The fact is, nonproliferation issues in this region have thus far received virtually nothing in terms of Western assistance. Unfortunately, the lack of assistance does not mean that there are no proliferation threats in the region.[7]

The Southern Tier has a small, but important, amount of industry with direct importance to the proliferation of weapons of mass destruction. Futhermore, those weapons that already exist are at risk due to the general instability of these states' political, economic, and internal conditions. Armenia has two type, 440 VVER V230 nuclear power reactors, located at a complex in Metsamor, twenty-eight kilometers outside Yerevan. This plant represents a proliferation threat by virtue of its spent fuel. Yerevan also contains a nuclear research center, and there is a possibility that a heavy water production plant exists in Armenia. And Georgia possesses an IRT-M nuclear research reactor in Tbilisi at the Institute of Physics, as well as machine tool and maraging steel production facilities. The eight-megawatt reactor at Tbilisi (which was shut down in 1988) contained approximately four kilograms of weapons-grade uranium that was only recently removed by the United States and Great Britain. There are also nuclear research and training facilities, at least two isotope-production reactors with unknown specifications located in Sukhumi, and several locations are rumored to contain radioactive wastes. Finally, according to one well-informed observer, Iranian officials have aggressively recruited Georgian weapons specialists to work for them in Iran.[8]

The Southern Tier is also a significant transit point for narcotics from Afghanistan, Pakistan, and the region itself en route to Russia and Western Europe. For example, Kyrgyzstan was once a key supplier of licit opium poppy for the Soviet Union. In addition, Kyrgyzstan's location makes it geographically convenient as a transit point, as opium and heroin traffickers seek new routes from Pakistan and Afghanistan to Russia and the West and hashish traffickers from Kyrgyzstan to Russia. Given the relatively limited resources of Kyrgyz law enforcement agencies, as well as the continuously disruptive society in neighboring Tajikistan, there is reason to believe that trafficking will continue. Officials report there are many trafficking groups operating in Kyrgyzstan, all centered in Osh, which repackage Afghan opiates and smuggle them north using a variety of transportation methods. Furthermore, arrests of government officials involved in narcotics trafficking continued to support evidence of narcotic-related corruption. For example, in February 1997, police officials in Osh were accused of providing information to drug carriers.[9]

Further undermining regional stability, criminal organizations, several authors note, have taken advantage of the weak borders. Refugees, or "internally displaced persons" (IDPs) and unregulated immigration have exacerbated national and regional political, social, and economic tensions. Displaced persons from inter- and intrastate conflicts represent a serious drain on national resources. For example, 620,000 IDPs were made homeless by the fighting in and around Nagorno-Karabakh in 1992–94. In addition, some 200,000 mainly ethnic Azeri refugees from non-Azerbaijani territory arrived in 1988 and 1989 from Armenia and later from Georgia. According to one author, migration flows are a primary security concern of the government in Kyrgyzstan.

About 12 percent of Azerbaijan's population consists of displaced people, including 10 percent of Baku's two million inhabitants. Most of them experience problems in assimilating with the Azeri population. These refugees constitute a potential time bomb for the security of the region— much like the Palestinian refugee camps in Lebanon, Gaza, and the West Bank proved over decades to be a breeding ground for the PLO and more radical organizations. Futhermore, the Azeri government has failed to provide them with anything more than moral support. They receive an equivalent of just two dollars a month in state assistance. Azerbaijan, of course, has its own problems, one of them being a 40 percent unemployment rate. This rate increases to nearly 80 percent among male refugees and almost 90 percent among female refugees. Although international organizations contribute foodstuffs, medical assistance, and some housing, large numbers of refugees and displaced persons continue to live in horrific conditions in Azerbaijan, in part because they are not being integrated.

Not all the refugees and IDPs are ethnic Azeris. Some fifty thousand are Meskhetian Turks, expelled by Joseph Stalin from Georgia to Central Asia in 1944, who returned to the Caucasus in 1989. A further five thousand are ethnic Kurds, largely from the occupied territories surrounding Nagorno-Karabakh.[10]

FOREIGN INFLUENCES AND POLICIES IN THE SOUTHERN TIER

Unlike the original nineteenth century "Great Game" between Russia and Great Britain, the twentieth-century version has a number of players, including Russia, Turkey, Iran, and the West. Also, not only governments are involved, but foreign and multinational corporations as well. Today, for the most part, the "Great Game" consists of economic competition for jobs, pipelines, new markets, and political and religious influence.

The Southern Tier region figured prominently in the foreign policies of imperial powers early this century due to the area's considerable oil and gas reserves. After the economic and, at least, political collapse of the Soviet Union, many ethnic sovereign republics of Eurasia have declared their independence from the union. Consequently, a new geopolitics of a vast area stretching from Eastern Europe to the Chinese border and from Siberia to South Asia has emerged.

The current struggle for Eurasian resources is a complex of security, geopolitical, and economic variables. Russia, as the successor of the Soviet state, is keen to maintain its economic and political influence on the former republics. The conflicts in the Southern Tier, in Chechnya, between Azerbaijan and Armenia, in Georgia, and in Tajikistan, have all been influenced or directly exacerbated by Moscow and the Russian army.

A considerably high number of foreign companies in oil, finance, and other sectors has been operating in the Southern Tier since the collapse of the Soviet Union. Turkey has close cultural, historical, and ethnic ties to this region. Four Turkic republics of Central Asia, Azerbaijan, and many other Turkic ethnic minorities in the Russian Federation speak dialects of the same language family. Iran also maintains economic and ideological interests and aims throughout Central Asia and the Caucasus.

Some authors observe that the private sector can have a positive impact on regional conflict resolution. Private investment creates employment and provides salaries, while the creation of capital markets provides an influx of much-needed money. The private sector also can help get people's minds focused on job creation and money, rather than on smoldering resentments. However, while many of the contributors agree that investment is important for the two regions, they caution against treating investment as a cure-all for conflict.

Despite the stratifying effects that private investment may cause, the process for unleashing the investment potential in the Southern Tier must start somewhere. According to one author, there is a twenty-year window of opportunity for these states to receive substantial foreign investment. They must seize these private sector opportunities soon lest the money and investment go to other areas.

RUSSIAN INFLUENCE AND POLICY

Aside from geo-strategic considerations, Russia has two primary reasons for being involved in Central Asia and the Southern Tier: one is to protect ethnic Russians in the region; another is to maintain access to important resources. However, while Russia has clear political and economic concerns, it has had problems consistently implementing policies that specifically address those concerns. This has undermined Moscow's effectiveness in securing its interests in the Southern Tier.

The connection between Russia and the newly independent states of the Southern Tier is, or at least should be, mutually beneficial. Russia clearly has important interests and will continue to play an active role in the region. However, Russia's policies have not always been evenly applied. It appears that Russia wants to maintain its presence in the area, but it is difficult to discern the exact nature of Russia's role. Russia has serious problems of its own, and it is trying to cope with its own economic and political weaknesses, compounded by internal power struggles. Until Russia is able to resolve its own internal problems, it will hardly be a beneficial influence to the republics in the Southern Tier.

At present, Russia does not have a unified concept of its proper role in the two regions. However, it remains to be seen whether other countries, such as the United States, have well-defined regional foreign policy "concepts" or approaches either. For example, in the first year after the Soviet collapse, Western countries expressed interest in developing a policy for the region, but by mid-1995 no Western state had done so. Why, therefore, should more be expected from Russia? In response, it was pointed out that the United States has outlined its regional policy, most notably in Undersecretary of State Strobe Talbott's address in the summer of 1997, albeit in blithely vague "foreign policy speak." Quite simply, geography cannot be changed, and Russia will maintain a presence in the region.

Some authors assert that Russia has played and will continue to play the role of spoiler in the region. Others believe this view exaggerates Russia's influence. While they do not see Russia as a partner always eager to cooperate, Russia will, most likely, choose a middle path. However, conditions in Russia and corresponding policies may change very quickly, and the generation of leaders to follow Yeltsin will be crucial for determining Russia's course. Who those leaders are, when they will take power, and how they will react to the region is unclear. Given the political state of flux, it is not surprising that the Russian government does not always speak with a unified voice.

Nevertheless, Russia is likely to remain engaged in the region. Throughout its history, Russia has had a tendency to compare itself to others and to compete with other nations, both in the East and the West. It seems that this tendency is still part of Russian policy-making. Ever since the United States has shown a business interest in the two regions, especially in the Caspian region, Russia's concern with the two regions has been further stirred. But Russia is limited by its inability to inject money into the regions. Russia also lacks the institutions and expertise to invest heavily. This only decreases its influence. If Russia's financial crisis continues to deepen, there will be even less money for aid and trade with the former republics, further weakening Russia's role. Russia is trying to restore its hegemony, according to some authors, and is actively competing for regional influence, yet its role continues to decrease and is constantly being undermined.

The Russian military presence in Tajikistan, for example, began in the late nineteenth century when a small Russian military unit was stationed in the Hindu Kush Mountains approaching on British India. With the coming of the Red Army and the incorporation of the territory now known as Tajikistan into the Soviet Union in 1924, the troops in Tajikistan became a branch of the Soviet defense perimeter's southern flank. The Kremlin and high-ranking officers did not view the republic's long borders with China (five-hundred kilometers) and Afghanistan (fourteen-hundred kilometers) as a matter of great concern until the deterioration of relations with China and the advent of events in Afghanistan. Historically, there have been two components to the Russian military presence in Tajikistan: border guards and military "regulars." Border troops throughout the USSR were operated by the KGB and, compared to other branches, were privileged, well supported, and highly respected. Because the defense ministry traditionally had few strategic goals contingent upon its forces in Tajikistan, regulars there merely conducted routine exercises and were on light readiness. The Soviet invasion of Afghanistan in 1979, however, changed this situation considerably. The role of the defense ministry in Tajikistan increased as the republic became a transitional area for heavy Soviet military machinery headed south.

Moscow's interests in Tajikistan are clear: the Russian political and military elite wants Russia to maintain its military presence in Tajikistan. Moscow has clearly articulated its interest in preventing instability from spreading from Tajikistan to the rest of Central Asia and to the Russian Federation itself. Moscow would also like to ensure that a friendly government, likely one in which President Rakhmonov and his Kulobi allies have a high degree of authority, controls Tajikistan. The military units stationed in Tajikistan help Russia meet those foreign policy goals. The only threat to Russian political support for their military presence in Tajikistan is the possibility of a Chechen-type scenario.

Although the "hand of Moscow" has been cited as a cause in many regional conflicts, a complete Russian withdrawal could also have a negative impact on the region. In fact, it was in the void following the collapse of the USSR that numerous disturbances arose throughout the newly independent states. For example, a Russian withdrawal from Chechnya today could have similar severe repercussions throughout the north and south Southern Tier, which are directly linked. Without the presence of Russian authority, another void would be created, which competing factions would rush to fill.

On the positive side, Russia has managed to provide security through the armed forces it maintains in Georgia. Continued and expanded political and economic contact with Russia could help to solve problems related to active conflicts. The bottom line is that Russia continues to be a key to regional peacemaking. The authors agree that Russia must be involved in regional peacemaking efforts, but not to the extent that it excludes the international community from involvement as well.

TURKISH INFLUENCE AND POLICY

Today each Southern Tier state is following its own course of political development, yet the processes of nation- and state-building are new to them. Before the Soviet period such political demarcations did not, in many cases, even exist. The history of the Southern Tier region is a chronicle of empires waxing and waning: Greek, Persian, Seljuk Turk, Mongol, Ottoman Turk, and Russian. After the collapse of the USSR, Turkey, experienced at nation-building, came onto the scene immediately. Turkish leaders made it clear that they wanted to play an influential role in both Central Asia and the Southern Tier. The conventional wisdom was that Turkey's role in the region would be to provide an "appropriate" (i.e., secular) model for the new states, many of which are Muslim, to follow.

Seeing itself as potential "big brother" to the Turkic states of Central Asia and the Southern Tier (Azerbaijan, Kazakhstan, Kyrgyzstan, Turkmenistan, and Uzbekistan), Turkey wanted to act as a window or link to the international community. Immediately following independence, many Turkish politicians, academics, and businessmen traveled to Central Asia and the Southern Tier as part of an extensive popular exchange. However, there was subsequent disillusionment among the Central Asian and Caucasian states regarding Turkey's ability to provide models for education and economic development. For instance, the Soviet educational system established throughout the region was more advanced than Turkey's.

According to one author, Turks themselves have become disillusioned with their prospects for influencing the inchoate political and economic establishments of the region. The idea of pan-Turkism in the Southern Tier, which was discussed often in the early years of independence, has been swept aside except in the area of Xinjiang, China, where the Turkic Uighur minority is continuing its struggle against Beijing. Perhaps resulting from this disappointment, Turkey has focused increasing attention on the Caucasus, a region which may show more promise for partnership than does Central Asia. Turkey shares a historical link to the Caucasus, particularly Azerbaijan. In addition, there is a symbolic value to Turkey's involvement in the Caucasus as well as to its geographic proximity. Rebuffed by the European Union, Turkey is now carving out an area of influence. The lure of the region's oil potential and the need for transit to Western markets provide added incentive for involvement. However, Turkey's influence both in Central Asia and the Southern Tier is limited by its inability to provide significant financial and technical support needed by the newly independent states.

IRANIAN INFLUENCE AND POLICY

Iran has thus far been less of a player in the geopolitical maneuverings in the Southern Tier for two main reasons: Iran is both anti-American and anti-Israeli. These positions run counter to the stances taken by the regimes of Central Asia and the Caucasus. However, Iranian policy could change, and if it does so, a moderate Iran will have a future role in affecting the political and economic shape of the region. However, particular attention needs to be paid to the further political changes in Tehran and the possible warming of relations with the United States. The direction of these political changes could provide a clue to Iran's future in the region.

Currently Iran has little to offer the Southern Tier states in terms of money and technology. However, Iran can provide convenient access to the Persian Gulf for oil and gas pipelines, an attribute that Turkey and the West cannot offer. Already in the last year, Iran and Turkmenistan made arrangements for the construction of a pipeline for natural gas.

Iran's ability to influence the region via Islam is questionable. One author notes that Tajikistan is overwhelmingly Sunni and not—contrary to popular depictions—Shiite. Furthermore, neither Tajikistan or Azerbaijan (35 percent Shiite) can be said to be under Iran's spell. On the other hand, Kyrgyzstan and Kazakhstan are not openly anti-Iranian. Only Uzbekistan qualifies as anti-Iranian because of its concerns over Tajikistan, which has close linguistic, historical, and cultural ties to Iran.

Armenia is the only part of the Southern Tier where Iran has had much influence. Of all the places in the newly independent regions, Christian Armenia was about the last place analysts expected Islamic fundamentalist Iran to be a big player. But economics, not politics or religion, dominate this mutually beneficial relationship. Armenia and Iran share an interest in seeing a north-south pipeline running from Russia to Iran. The fate of this proposed pipeline will be decided in the near future and will play a large part in determining Iran's role in the region.

U.S. INFLUENCE AND POLICY

The United States has become more active in the Southern Tier over the past several years. The United States's interest in the region revolves around four basic concepts: strengthening regional economic mechanisms, developing East-West energy and transportation processes, nonproliferation, and providing support to conflict resolution efforts. Although there are geostrategic objectives for further involvement (such as containing Iran's influence in the regions), American engagement is focused primarily on economic goals.

One author characterizes the United States's "unofficial policy" as intent on intrusively reshaping the region to suit its own economic needs. The United States currently would like to reduce its dependence on Arab sources of oil, and cultivating Caspian oil would broaden its oil-buying options. However, U.S. policy still fails to address certain regional phenomena. There is little understanding of the various reasons for conflict in the regions amongst U.S. policy makers. Furthermore, the prevalence of corruption is rarely factored into policy-making decisions, rendering numerous regional aid policies ineffective. Although the United States is one of the biggest players in the region, it is still quite uninformed regarding basic issues in these societies.

INTERNATIONAL ORGANIZATIONS

Coordinated multilateral assistance to the Southern Tier states has been inconsistent with regional independence. Wary of encroaching on the Russian "sphere of influence," international organizations have sought both to allay Russian concerns and implement viable solutions to regional problems. International organizations such as the United Nations (UN)—for example, the United Nations Observer Mission in Georgia (UNOMIG)—and the Organization for Security and Cooperation in Europe (OSCE) have sought to mediate much of the conflict besetting the Southern Tier.

The OSCE, for example, has played a mediating role in Nagorno-Karabakh, South Ossetia, and Tajikistan.[11] At its December 1994 summit in Budapest, the OSCE agreed in principle to send peacekeeping forces to maintain a cease-fire in Nagorno-Karabakh and facilitate a political solution to the war. The OSCE, moreover, is the only pan-European organization with a mandate to operate throughout the Commonwealth of Independent States (CIS). In 1992 the OSCE set up a multilateral process, known as the Minsk Group, aimed at negotiating a peaceful settlement to the Nagorno-Karabakh war. Elsewhere within the CIS, the OSCE has also established in-country missions in Georgia, Moldova, and Tajikistan to monitor and help resolve the conflicts gripping these new states. These initiatives, building up to the December 1994 decision to provide peacekeepers for Nagorno-Karabakh, have laid the groundwork for OSCE involvement in the most daunting conflict in the former Soviet South to date: the war in Chechnya. The Minsk Group of the OSCE was instrumental in securing a cease-fire in 1994, but has failed to reach a final political solution.

Regional and military cooperation efforts have received a more positive response in Central Asia and the Caucasus when initiated or supported by Western governments. In May 1997, the Georgian government proposed the creation of a Black Sea peacekeeping battalion with the participation of all the coastal states, which would, under UN auspices, participate in peacekeeping operations. NATO's Partnership for Peace already supports Baltic and Central Asian peacekeeping battalions. Furthermore, Russia's declining economic and military potential makes it increasingly difficult for Moscow to bear the costs of being a regional mediator, thereby creating an opportunity for increased Western involvement. In the last three years, monetary stability has been cared for by international financial institutions dominated by the West, such as the World Bank and International Monetary Fund.

The presence of international organizations in the area is both extremely helpful and much needed. However, the greater international community has not been sufficiently involved in efforts to resolve conflicts in the Southern Tier thus far. One author suggests that NATO represents a possible vehicle for enhancing stability. It was noted that since the end of the Cold War, the interconnectedness of Atlantic-Europe and the Southern Tier has been strengthened. As a landlocked buffer zone, the Southern Tier constitutes a vulnerable region. NATO, by working closely with Russia and by developing the Partnership for Peace program (PFP), can bring guarantees of stability which will underpin economic development and safeguard democratization. If the area is to develop as a security community, current conflicts and crises need to be addressed and confidence-building measures established. The aim for NATO must be that through PFP and in cooperation with Russia the security of the Southern Tier can be underwritten. This would represent the greatest bonus yet emanating from the end of the Cold War.

REGIONAL INTERACTION

One way for the region to help foster stability and secure economic viability is through interaction among the states of the Southern Tier. Local cooperative networks insure a diversity of foreign and security policy options for the emerging states of the region. For example, certain Pan-Caucasian organizations have sought to mediate regional conflicts. The Confederation of Peoples of the Caucasus has played an important political role in the region. This was particularly true during the Abkhaz war with Georgia, when the confederation organized the spontaneous volunteer fighters from the north Southern Tier, equipped them, and helped them get to Abkhazia.

Another emerging example of cooperation between the Southern Tier states is the establishment of the Transport Corridor Europe Southern Tier Asia (TRACECA). This European-funded project will, it is hoped, serve as a contemporary counterpart to the ancient Silk Road, facilitating the regional exchange of goods and restoring the land-based link between Europe and China. Of course, the realization of the TRACECA project is contingent upon regional stability, which can happen only through regional cooperation.

Other regional cooperative networks include: the Black Sea Economic Cooperation Zone (BSECZ), the Caspian Sea Organization (CSO), Georgia-Ukraine-Azerbaijan-Moldova Security Organization (GUAM), Economic Cooperation Organization (ECO), and the Central Asian Union (CAU).[12] Such organizations and networks will be crucial to securing long-term regional stability.

EPILOGUE

The authors of this volume represent a diverse array of regional and Western government officials, scholars, and journalists unanimous in their conviction that securing long-term stability in the Southern Tier is crucial not only to individual state-building efforts, but also to regional and international security. They have concluded that there are no universal formulas for ensuring national and regional stability. It is clear that many domestic factors and outside forces combine to cause conflicts, and each case has a unique combination of internal causes and outside influences.

The young states of the Southern Tier, struggling to emerge from the tumultuous post-Soviet transition, are searching for the keys to independence, stability, and development. One of the main contentions of this volume is that the states of the Southern Tier need to preserve their independence and should not be dictated to by outside forces. Furthermore, these new states will not survive if they attempt to chart courses separate from their neighbors. Increased cooperation is needed between the Southern Tier states as well as with the regional and international communities.

The international community needs to remain involved in helping to resolve conflicts in the region. In this increasingly interdependent world, the impact of local unrest is felt regionally, and these conflicts have repercussions felt far beyond their borders. Many of the authors believe that not enough attention has been focused on this dynamic part of the world. While outside forces need to be involved in a moderating role, direct engagement of the conflicting parties on all levels is critical in achieving resolution. And, of course, all sides must have the will to resolve the conflict. Lasting peace cannot be imposed, no matter how powerful or well funded the effort.

PART ONE

Foreign Policy
Development
in the
Southern Tier

The Evolution of the Foreign Policy of the Transcaucasian States

1

Shireen T. Hunter

INTRODUCTION

The three Transcaucasian countries—Armenia, Azerbaijan, and Georgia—that became independent states in the wake of the Soviet Union's disintegration in December 1991 previously had only a brief experience with statehood, which lasted from 1918 to 1920. By the time the Soviet Union collapsed, these countries had for nearly two centuries been under Czarist and later Communist Russian rule. Prior to falling under Russian domination during the first three decades of the nineteenth century and for most of their long history, these countries had formed part of other great empires, such as the Persian, Roman, and Ottoman.

The consequences of this past have been a relatively underdeveloped sense of national identity, a short experience with statehood, and limited aptitude for relating to the outside world and conducting relations with a large number of countries and multilateral organizations. Because for most of their ancient and modern history these countries had been part of larger political entities, their notions of what constituted their national interests and how they could best protect them had also remained underdeveloped. Thus, since eight years ago when the three Transcaucasian countries were suddenly thrust into the vortex of regional and international politics, their most important challenges have included determining what their national interests are and developing appropriate frameworks and strategies for dealing with the outside world and for affecting the policies of major regional and international actors in ways that could best serve their own interests.

When these countries first became independent, two theories regarding the future direction of their external relations were current among analysts and observers of Caucasian and post-Soviet affairs. The first maintained that, because Russia had dominated the region for such a long period, and because of its geographic proximity to and its still extensive economic, political, and cultural links with the Caucasus, it would remain the most influential actor in the region and would exercise a determining influence over the direction of the Transcaucasian states' foreign policies. The second theory maintained that, since Russia's influence would inevitably fade, the old cultural, religious, and ethnic ties between the Transcaucasian states and their two important neighbors—Iran and Turkey—would be revived and would lead to intense Turko-Iranian competition for influence in the region. Depending on the outcome of this competition, these countries would fall under the influence of either Iran or Turkey.

The last eight years have proven both of these theories incorrect. Indeed, the pattern of postindependence interaction that has developed between the Transcaucasian countries, on the one hand, and Russia, Turkey, Iran, and the rest of the world on the other, has been far more intricate and multidimensional than either of the above theories suggest. The principal reason for this outcome has been that, contrary to what was earlier expected, the foreign policies of these countries have not been unduly influenced either by ethnic or cultural affinities or by past associations. Rather, to a very large extent, the foreign policies of the Transcaucasian states have been determined by the same factors that shape the foreign policies of other countries that are in more-or-less similar geopolitical conditions.

In fact, the theoretical paradigm best suited to explain the external behavior of these countries in the postindependence period is that of small states situated in a zone of great power competition. Because they are surrounded by larger and stronger neighbors, this paradigm operates both at the regional and international levels. However, not all aspects of this geopolitical situation are detrimental to the interests of these countries. On the contrary, in some instances the fact that major regional and international actors have been interested in these countries has enabled them to pursue a relatively more independent policy and to avoid succumbing to the domination of either their excolonial master or to that of any of the other major international or regional actors. In short, they have sought to, and been relatively successful at, balancing the outside powers against one another.

Within this overall paradigm, the policies of individual Transcaucasian states have been affected by their specific geographical, ethno-linguistic, religious, political, and economic characteristics, as well as by their historical experiences. Moreover, because politics in these countries still remain highly personal, the views and preferences of their leaders have greatly influenced the course of their foreign policies. Additionally, politics of nation-building have had implications for the conduct of these countries' foreign relations, especially in the case of Azerbaijan.

Although they have been fully independent for less than a decade, their foreign policies have gone through several phases, reflecting the impact of their internal development and the evolving character of regional and international dynamics. In the future, too, the foreign policies of these countries will fluctuate under the influence of the same factors. However, as certain facts of geography, history, and culture have asserted their influence in the past several years, some of the underlying patterns of relations that have emerged in the last seven years between these countries on the one hand and their neighbors and other states on the other are likely to endure. What follows is: (1) an analysis of how three small states in a zone of great power competition have tried to define and protect their interests; (2) an assessment of their performance; and (3) a sketch of the most likely directions in which their external relations will evolve in the future. This analysis will be preceded by a brief discussion of those basic factors that, to varying degrees, have shaped the external policies of these states.

The position of the Transcaucasus as a strategically important region has to a great extent determined the context of these countries' foreign policies, in both positive and negative ways. The strategic sensitivity of the Transcaucasus primarily derives from its proximity to other highly important strategic regions, such as Russia, the Black Sea, and the Persian Gulf, all of which are of great significance to major international actors. Because the Transcaucasus borders on the Russian Federation and some of its inhabitants have close links with people of the North Caucasus, Russia has an intense interest in the Transcaucasus and views events there as important for its security and perhaps even the cohesion and the survival of the Russian Federation. In particular, Russia fears the emergence of hostile forces on its borders and believes that in order to prevent such developments it must have great influence over the external orientation of the Transcaucasian states. In the past few years, these concerns have at times led to a heavy-handed and manipulative Russian policy toward Georgia and Azerbaijan. But such policies, instead of enhancing Russian influence in the region, have reinforced these states' tendency to seek counterweights to Russia. Nor have Russian efforts ensured the stability of the Caucasian part of the Russian Federation, as evidenced by the Chechen war and the current problems in Daghestan.[1] In fact, the Russian policy of manipulating the ethnic divisions and conflicts of the Transcaucasian countries have had negative consequences for the North Caucasus.

The Transcaucasus's proximity to Russia has intensified the interest of Western powers and their allies in the region, as has the closeness of the Transcaucasus to the Black Sea and the Persian Gulf—two strategically important waterways. The latter factor has also made its politics vulnerable to the dynamics of Persian Gulf and Middle East politics. In practical terms, this situation has led major international actors, most notably the United States, to approach the Transcaucasus from the vantage point of the impact that events there might have on Middle East politics and balances of power. In this connection, of particular consequence have been the U.S.-Iranian confrontation; the declared policy of containing Iranian influence in the post-Soviet space; promoting a key role for Turkey in the region; and U.S. encouragement for the forging of close ties between the Transcaucasian states and Israel.[2]

Irrespective of the intrinsic merits of this American policy and whether it has benefited the Caucasus states, the fact is that, given the overwhelming weight of the United States within the international political and economic systems, its policies have to a great extent set the boundaries within which the Transcaucasian states could operate. The United States's policy toward Russia, notably its shift from a posture that some analysts had characterized as excessive Russocentrism to one that is aimed at preventing the reestablishment of Russian domination over the region,[3] has also affected the foreign policy options and choices of the Transcaucasian states.

The geo-economic and geo-cultural profiles of the Transcaucasus have also influenced the foreign policy context of regional countries, primarily by intensifying the interest of the outside players. From the geo-economic perspective, the vast energy resources of Azerbaijan, coupled with the difficulties involved in transporting them to consumer markets, have had the most significant impact on the politics of the region and the foreign policies of the individual countries. To illustrate, the question of how to determine the routes for the export of the region's energy resources has been more of a foreign policy question than merely that of finding the shortest and most economical route to get the oil and gas to consumers.

Nor is this situation surprising, given that oil and, increasingly, natural gas are strategic commodities; therefore, questions related to their exploitation and export are inextricably linked with political and security issues. Moreover, the question of pipelines is in reality about the political future of the Eurasian landmass and its periphery and hence cannot and will not be decided merely on its technical and economic basis.

The fact that from the geo-cultural perspective most of the Caucasus—north and south—is part of the Islamic world and thus is vulnerable to cultural and political trends, including the more extremist political ideas, has had an impact on the approach of outside players toward the region and on the foreign policy orientation of the Transcaucasian states.

Foreign policy options and orientations of the Transcaucasian states have also been affected by Russia's efforts to regroup the former Soviet republics under its own influence. This Russian drive is explained by the fact that, when Mikhail Gorbachev embarked on his program of reforming the Soviet system, his ultimate goal was to revitalize the USSR and not to dismantle it, although reform did include the granting of greater freedom of action to the constituent republics. Indeed, the purpose of the New Union Treaty, which Gorbachev presented in March 1991, was to create a freer and revitalized Soviet Union. Gorbachev's scheme failed because of infighting and power struggles within the central leadership in Moscow, notably between Gorbachev and Boris Yeltsin. It is useful to remember that it was the defection of the Russian Federation, with Yeltsin as its president, that led to the collapse of the Soviet Union, and not a massive anticolonial revolt on the part of the republics.[4]

Prior to gaining power, Yeltsin and his supporters had encouraged the nationalists and anticenter forces in the republics as a way of undermining Gorbachev's position. But once they gained power, they reverted to a policy of maintaining Russian supremacy and thus tried to regroup the former Soviet republics under Russian influence. This goal was to be achieved through the CIS, which Russia hoped—with little success so far—to turn into a close-knit economic union and a collective security system.[5] In order to ensure that all former Soviet republics join the CIS, in the past several years Russia has even resorted to the manipulation of the Transcaucasian states's interethnic conflicts.

If the CIS has thus far failed to become the close-knit institution that Russia intended it to be, it has been because of Russia's enormous economic and political difficulties and its sometimes erratic policies. Nevertheless, Russia's efforts to regroup its lost empire as a special zone of its own influence has deeply affected the shape of the postindependence political and security environment of the Transcaucasian countries, and hence their foreign policy choices. In addition to the above-noted underlying geopolitical, economic, and cultural dynamics of the Transcaucasus and Russian efforts to reassemble its old colonial empire under a new guise, the foreign policies of the Transcaucasian states have been essentially determined by the same impulses that shape the external relations of other countries: geographic location; ethnic, religious, and cultural composition, in particular the degree of national unity; historical experience; resource base and economic needs and potential; ideological tendencies and worldview of the leadership; the nature of leadership, whether it is democratic or of varying shades of authoritarianism; and personal qualities of the key leader in cases where leadership is strongly personality-based.

GENERAL DETERMINANTS OF FOREIGN POLICY IN ARMENIA

Armenia's location and its historical experience have had a determining impact on the character of its foreign policy. Indeed, it is impossible to understand how Armenia's worldview and its place in the outside world—and hence its foreign policy—have evolved without adequately taking into account its geographic location and historical experience.

Present-day Armenia is a small, landlocked country—11,620 square miles—that has been reduced to its current size and population as a result of foreign conquests and large-scale out-migration over several centuries. Armenia's landlocked nature makes it dependent on the benevolence of its neighbors for access to the outside world, a fact that gives it a sense of isolation and vulnerability. Armenia is also ethnically and religiously isolated because it is surrounded on three sides by larger and more populous Muslim neighbors (Iran, Turkey, and Azerbaijan), a fact that accentuates its sense of vulnerability. However, the relatively positive history of Armenian-Iranian relations demonstrates that religious differences have not been the main cause of strife between Armenia and its neighbors and thus are not the principal reason for its isolation and vulnerability.[6] Rather, specific incidents have been responsible for these sentiments. In this respect, Armenia's encounter with the Ottoman Empire, especially the 1915 tragedy during which close to one million Armenians perished, was particularly traumatic. The Armenians commemorate this event as the "Armenian Genocide." Turkey, however, claims that the tragedy was not the result of intentional cruelty, but of the chaotic conditions of the war of 1914–18, which was also responsible for the deaths of many Turks.

Irrespective of how this tragic event happened, it has had a tremendous impact in shaping the character of the modern collective consciousness of the Armenian people throughout the world.[7] This tragic experience has intensified Armenians' isolation and defenselessness, and has created a sense of having been abandoned by the Christian Western powers. These feelings of betrayal were intensified when, between 1918 and 1920, Great Britain sided with Azerbaijan in its war with Armenia.[8]

This historical experience has affected Armenia's post-independence foreign policy in the following ways: first, it has created serious barriers in the way of normalizing Turkish-Armenian relations; second, it has made Armenia wary of excessive Turkish influence in the Caucasus; third, it has led Armenia to balance the weight of Turkic elements and Turkish influence in the region by forging close ties with Russia and, whenever possible, by developing cooperative relations with other countries, such as Iran and Greece, that also feel uneasy about Turkish influence in the region; fourth, it has exacerbated other problems between Armenia and Azerbaijan, most notably their dispute over Nagorno-Karabakh, because Armenians often identify Azerbaijanis with Turks, thus creating an association between Azerbaijanis and the "Armenian Genocide."

Reflecting another old pattern and legacy, Armenia's doubts about the West's reliability have been reinforced because of the West's intense interest in Azerbaijan's energy resources, plus Western encouragement of a high Turkish profile in the region. Thus, although Armenia has been aware of the importance of having close and cordial ties with the West, it nevertheless has felt that it could not completely trust its fate to the Western powers. Therefore, despite Western unhappiness and Russia's growing problems and weakness, Armenia has proceeded with forging a strategic alliance with Russia. Yet, during the last years of the Soviet Union and the first two years of Armenia's independence, past experiences did not seem to exert excessive influence on Armenian thinking about the direction of the country's foreign relations. On the contrary, revisionist thinking had become current within certain intellectual circles influential within the Armenian National Movement (ANM), which assumed power in 1990 and controlled Armenia until 1997. It was the evolution of regional and international politics that caused Armenia to revert to a foreign policy greatly influenced by past memories, fears, and pathos.

The new Armenian leadership that emerged during the late 1980s and assumed power in 1990 had new ideas about Armenia's relations with the outside world, especially with its immediate neighbors. The two most significant components of this new vision were: (1) the inadequacy and unrealistic nature of the policy of relying on a third power, which traditionally has been Russia; (2) the abandonment of excessive affinity for Russia and unrealistic expectations regarding what Russia can or would be willing to do for Armenia; and (3) the need to end Turkish-Armenian animosity.[9] Because of the following considerations, the latter point was considered especially important. First, Turkey is Armenia's neighbor and a large and powerful country, a fact which meant that Armenia must eventually reach an accommodation with it. Second, present-day Turkey is a fundamentally different entity than the Ottoman Empire and has other goals and aspirations. In particular, the proponents of this view emphasized the point that modern Turkey has abandoned the late Ottoman ideas of Pan-Turkism and Pan-Islamism. Instead it has adopted a European vocation and orientation, factors which, they maintained, should facilitate Turkish-Armenian reconciliation. President Levon Ter-Petrossian and some of his key advisers largely subscribed to this revisionist thinking and believed that Turkish-Armenian relations should be cast in a new light.

Several factors, however, have prevented a rapid and substantial improvement in Turkish-Armenian relations. These included Turkey's insistence, and the Armenians' refusal, to abandon the issue of the 1915 Armenian Genocide and unequivocally relinquish Armenian territorial claims toward Turkey; Turkey's ambitions to become the dominant regional player in the Transcaucasus and Central Asia, which led it to side completely with Azerbaijan in its conflict with Armenia and to take certain punitive measures toward Armenia; the dynamics of the Nagorno-Karabakh conflict; and the resurgence of Pan-Turkist ideas in Turkey and in Azerbaijan during the early 1990s.[10] This last development rekindled the Armenians' historic fears of being surrounded by potentially hostile Turkic peoples and acted as a barrier to better Turkish-Armenian relations. In fact, the two countries still do not have official diplomatic relations. In the last two years, a change of leadership in Armenia from Levon Ter-Petrossian to Robert Kocharian (who is more responsive to the views and sentiments of Armenian nationalists), the growing strategic cooperation between Israel and Turkey (which is viewed as enhancing Turkey's regional

power), and increasing Israeli influence in Azerbaijan have further complicated Turkish-Armenian relations and dimmed prospects for their reconciliation in the near future.[11] On the contrary, these developments have led
Armenia to form its own alliances to offset this new axis. Thus one outcome of this emerging Turkish-Israeli-Azerbaijani axis has been a greater
degree of consultation and cooperation among Armenia, Iran, and Greece,
although these steps toward cooperation are thus far devoid of any military
or security dimensions.[12] In sum, the evolution of regional and international politics has undermined some of the essential arguments behind the
revisionist school of thinking about certain aspects of Armenia's traditional
views of the region, the world, and its place in it.

Unlike Turkey, the history of Armenian-Iranian relations has not been
marred by any traumatic experiences, although relations between the two
countries and their peoples have not always been easy or free of tensions.
Indeed, the overall balance of the three-thousand-year history of Armenian-Iranian interaction has been positive.[13]

In addition to the lack of any historical or psychological barriers to good
and close Armenian-Iranian relations, a number of strategic and economic
factors encouraged such cooperation: first, Iran can provide Armenia with
an outlet to the outside world and a counterweight to the Turkish power;
second, Iran can be a valuable economic partner, and most importantly it
can provide Armenia with much-needed energy; third, Iran and Armenia
share a concern over the Azerbaijan republic's ambitions of bringing about
unification between the republic and the Iranian province of Azerbaijan;
fourth, Iran and Armenia are wary of the potential emergence of a Turkic
group; fifth, the recent Turkish-Israeli alliance, coupled with close Israeli-
Azerbaijani cooperation, have intensified Iran's anxieties about its north-
western frontiers and have increased the incentive for closer cooperation
with Armenia; and sixth, there are still about two-hundred thousand Armenians in Iran.

Yet despite all of the factors in favor of closer Armenian-Iranian
relations, U.S.-Iranian hostility, active U.S. discouragement of closer
Armenian-Iranian relations, and disagreements within the Armenian
leadership about how far Armenia should go in befriending Iran have
prevented the two countries from fully realizing the cooperative potential
of their relations. In this respect, it is important to note that the ANM
government and President Ter-Petrossian were not very keen about
expanding relations with Iran beyond a certain point. Nevertheless, Ter-
Petrossian admitted that Iran had remained neutral on the Karabakh issue,
even though its Shi'a population sympathized with Azerbaijan, and characterized Iran as a friendly country. Other contributing factors have been
Russian opposition to a sharp increase in Iranian presence in its former
possessions and Iran's economic and financial limitations. Nevertheless,
because of a considerable degree of commonality of strategic interest, Iran

and Armenia have maintained good relations and are planning to expand their cooperation in areas such as transport, energy, and other economic activities. An improvement in U.S.-Iranian relations and the removal of U.S. opposition to a larger Iranian role in the Transcaucasus would facilitate the expansion of Armenian-Iranian relations.

Logically, Armenia's closest relations should be with Western countries, especially the United States. As a small Christian country on the edge of the Muslim world, with a culturally Western orientation, Armenia could be an outpost of Western cultural and political influence in a sensitive region. The existence of a large Armenian diaspora in the United States, France, and Canada also encourages close Armenian-Western relations. Moreover, Armenia's political elite, irrespective of their other political inclinations, have fully recognized the importance of having solid ties with the West for the safeguarding of Armenia's security, economic, and other interests. In fact, this realization has led Armenia to join the Council of Europe, to sign an association agreement with the European Union, and to join NATO's Partnership For Peace program (PFP).

Nevertheless, Armenia's relations with the West have not reached the level of warmth and closeness that the factors above seem to warrant. On the contrary, because of certain divergences of views and interests between Armenia and the West, and some aspects of Western policy toward the Transcaucasus—most notably toward the Nagorno-Karabakh issue— Armenia has become convinced that it cannot rely solely on the West to safeguard its security and other interests. The most important area where Armenian and Western views and interests diverge regards the fact that Armenia and the West differ on Turkey's regional role. The West sees Turkey as its main partner in the Transcaucasus and Central Asia and thus favors the expansion of Turkey's regional influence, whereas Armenia feels uneasy about an excessively high Turkish profile. Next, Armenia and the West also have diverging views of Iran and its strategic role in the region. The West, especially the United States and, until recently, Europe, have viewed Iran as a spoiler and have tried to isolate it and prevent it from expanding its influence in the region. By contrast, Armenia sees Iran as a counterweight to Turkey and to a potentially irredentist Azerbaijan. Thus it considers retaining a common border and good relations with Iran to be vital to its security and favors a more active Iranian presence in the region. Yet in the past some Western analysts had suggested a territorial swap between Azerbaijan and Armenia as a way of resolving the Nagorno-Karabakh conflict, a solution that, if realized, would have deprived Armenia of its frontier with Iran.[14] Further, the West's interest in Azerbaijan's energy reserves, plus its desire to see Azerbaijan remain aloof from Iran, has led it to adopt a posture that Armenia considers as pro-Azerbaijan. Finally, there has been disappointment with the West's stand on the Nagorno-Karabakh problem. Because the Western powers have supported the maintenance of Azerbaijan's territorial integrity, together with a large measure of autonomy for Nagorno-Karabakh, many Armenians have come to view the West's position as pro-Azerbaijan and prompted by interest in the latter's energy resources. However, this view is not held by all Armenians, including the political elite. For example, Armenia's former president Levon Ter-Petrossian had accepted the OSCE Minsk Group's proposal of November 1997 for a step-by-step resolution of the Karabakh conflict, which included the principle of safeguarding Azerbaijan's territorial integrity.[15] However, considering the fact that this acceptance contributed to his ouster from power, it becomes clear that this perspective is not shared by all Armenians.

Historically, Russia has played the role of the protecting Third Power toward Armenia; certainly, this is a view of Russia that many Armenians still hold. However, this situation has resulted more from Russia's proximity, following its southward expansion in the eighteenth and nineteenth centuries, Armenia's location as a small Christian country between two large Muslim states (Iran and the Ottoman Empire), and the lack of sustained and steady interest on the part of other great European powers in Armenia's fate, rather than from any special liking between the two peoples. On the contrary, as Ronald Suny has pointed out, Russia's view of Armenia has fluctuated between extremes of positive and negative.[16]

Nevertheless, as noted earlier, by 1990, when it became clear that the Soviet Union would not survive in its original form, traditional views regarding how to safeguard Armenia's security, including its reliance on Russia, were challenged by some Armenian intellectuals. Indeed, before the Soviet Union's disintegration, the ANM leaders had adopted harsh anti-Russian rhetoric. However, it should be noted that this attitude on the part of the ANM leadership was more the result of an overall power struggle within the Soviet Union between the conservatives, who eventually came to include Gorbachev, and the reformists led by Yeltsin, than of an upsurge of anti-Russian sentiment in Armenia. Nevertheless, the hesitant and erratic manner in which the Soviet Union had handled the Karabakh problem had generated some anti-Russian feelings. Since the ANM was pro-Yeltsin, it adopted harsh anti-Russian rhetoric. Yet even at that time, ANM leaders declared that, should Russia change into a democratic society and give up its imperial ambitions, Armenia would have no difficulty establishing close relations with it. Indeed, this is what happened after the victory of the pro-Yeltsin elements and the defeat of the coup attempt of August 1991. Developments in Azerbaijan's internal politics—notably, the coming to power in June 1992 of a pro-Turkish nationalist president, the growing Turkish profile in the region, the end of the Russo-Western honeymoon by mid-1993, Russia's efforts to reassert itself in the Transcaucasus, and Armenia's disappointment with the West—brought Armenia and Russia closer together.

The first result of this rapprochement was that Armenia joined the CIS and its collective security pact of 1992.

The rise to power of Haidar Aliev in Azerbaijan in June 1993 initially seemed to indicate a sharp improvement in Russo-Azerbaijani relations. In fact, so high was this expectation that many observers, both in the region and abroad, viewed Aliev as Moscow's man. Had this assessment been correct, it would not have augured well for Armenia.[17] Certainly, the Armenians viewed Aliev's accession to power as detrimental to their interests.[18] This view was based on the assumption that, with a pro-Moscow leader in Azerbaijan responsive to Russian demands, Russia might not value Armenia's friendship as much and thus might even adopt a pro-Azerbaijan stand on the Nagorno-Karabakh conflict.

Aliev shared Azerbaijan National Front leader Abulfaz Elçibey's excessively pro-Turkish, anti-Russian, and anti-Iranian foreign policy views and had indicated that he would restore a degree of balance to Azerbaijan's external relations. Aliev also believed that Azerbaijan could not hope to get a satisfactory resolution to the Karabakh problem without Russia's cooperation. However, after a short period under the impact of both Azerbaijan's internal realities and external influences—notably, those of the West and Turkey, coupled with the disenchantment with Russia, especially concerning the resolution of the Karabakh problem—Aliev returned to a basically pro-Western, pro-Turkish, and to some degree anti-Russian posture. This development convinced Russia that Armenia was the only country in the Transcaucasus that could be relied upon as an ally.

This Russian realization, coupled with Armenia's disappointment with the prospects of improved relations with Turkey and with the lack of Western support, led to a growing alliance between the two countries. This alliance was formalized by the signing of the Russo-Armenian Friendship Treaty in 1997. The full title of the agreement is "Treaty on Friendship Cooperation and Mutual Assistance Between the Russian Federation and the Republic of Armenia." This agreement was followed by a treaty allowing the stationing of five thousand Russian soldiers in Armenia, which was ratified by the Armenian parliament in the spring of 1997. In short, in the course of only a few years, Armenian thinking about the underlying principles of its security and foreign policy again acknowledged the need to rely on a Third Force and the importance of an alliance with Moscow for Armenia.[19]

Armenia's relations with Azerbaijan will remain tense until a solution to the Karabakh problem, acceptable to both parties, is found. Even after such an agreement, a period of reconciliation and mutual confidence-building would be necessary before the full normalization of Armenian-Azerbaijani relations.

Relations with Georgia do not present the same problem, although, historically, Georgian-Armenian relations have not always been easy.[20] A potential source of conflict between the two countries is the existence of an Armenian community in southern Georgia, descended from Armenians who went there from Erzerum after the Russo-Turkish war of 1828–29. This area has been in dispute between Armenia and Georgia since 1918, when the two countries first established independent governments.[21] However, neither Georgia nor Armenia has let these potential conflicts mar their relations, and both continue to maintain reasonable ties. Nevertheless, at times Armenia has suspected Georgia of helping Azerbaijan in the Nagorno-Karabakh dispute. For example, there was some suspicion that during 1993, when the Karabakh conflict was in an intense military phase, Georgia indirectly helped Azerbaijan by intentionally delaying the repair of a gas pipeline to Armenia.[22]

Because of strategic and economic factors, in the last two years the foreign policies of the two countries have been moving in opposite directions, with Georgia expanding and intensifying its ties with the West, Turkey, and Azerbaijan, while Armenia has become close to Russia. These different foreign policy orientations could become a potential source of discord, but thus far they have not caused serious problems in Armenia's relations with Georgia.

During the first years of independence, together with other new thinking on foreign policy, some Armenian officials and political analysts advanced the view that Armenia is part of the Middle East region and, therefore, should establish close ties with the Middle Eastern countries. However, although Armenia has established diplomatic relations with key Arab countries, its ties to the Middle East have not expanded to the level anticipated in the above-noted view. This situation is partly explained by Armenia's geographic and cultural distance from most Arab states where considerable Armenian communities have existed, with only a few exceptions, such as Lebanon and Syria. The other explanation is the Nagorno-Karabakh conflict and Azerbaijan's efforts to garner sympathy for its cause among Muslims in the Middle Eastern countries, through such means as its membership in the Organization of Islamic Conference (OIC). Because most Arab countries do not have any strategic interests in common with Armenia, they have been swayed by feelings of Islamic solidarity to favor Azerbaijan.

Relations with Israel, too, have not developed much, remaining rather cool despite similarities between the two countries in terms of their historical experience and current situation as two small, religiously and culturally isolated countries. This has been largely due to the two countries' differing perceptions of Iran and Turkey, plus the close Turkish-Israeli alliance and growing friendship between Israel and Azerbaijan.[23] During the fall of 1998, there were some efforts on the part of Armenia to improve relations with Israel, as reflected in the visit of the Armenian foreign minister to Israel.

GENERAL DETERMINANTS OF FOREIGN POLICY IN AZERBAIJAN

In the case of Azerbaijan, questions related to the development of a clear sense of national and cultural identity have had significant influence in shaping its postindependence foreign policy. Indeed, the evolution of Azerbaijan's foreign policy has been closely linked to the following issues: determining Azerbaijan's cultural identity; the construction of a history that can help sharpen the sense of national identity and enhance national cohesion; the ethno-cultural and ideological heterogeneity and fierce intraelite struggle for power; the Nagorno-Karabakh conflict; the intense interest of external powers; and the events of the last years of the Soviet period, especially the introduction of Russian troops into the republic in January 1990, which led to the killing of large numbers of Azerbaijanis. This last incident has cast a shadow over Azerbaijan's relations with Russia that will not be easily dispelled and thus, to a great extent, has determined some of the basic orientations of Azerbaijan's foreign policy.

The dimensions of Azerbaijan's identity problem becomes clear if it is remembered that the name "Azerbaijan" was affixed to the lands that constitute the current republic in 1918, when, following the collapse of the tsarist empire, the first independent government was set up with the help of the Ottomans. Historically, the lands that form the present territory of Azerbaijan were known as Arran by the Romans. By the early fifteenth century A.D., the name Arran had lost its usage as various provinces of the region were known by their individual names, such as Shirvan as Gandjch.[24]

The result of Azerbaijan's history has been a mixed ethno-cultural legacy, with a degree of polarization between the Iranian and Turkic dimensions of its identity and culture. This dichotomy has had serious implications for Azerbaijan's internal politics and the conduct of its foreign policy. Additionally, a number of myths about Azerbaijan's history, which were developed during the Soviet era and now have been accepted by all political elites, has affected many aspects of Azerbaijan's foreign policy and, in particular, has caused serious problems in its relations with Iran. The essential components of this view of its history are: (1) Azerbaijan is a five-thousand-year-old country, the birthplace of Zoroaster, and the direct descendent of the ancient kingdom of Albania; (2) Azerbaijan's Turkification began during the early centuries of the Christian era, and some ultra-Turkist nationalists even maintain that Turkic people have lived there since several thousand years B.C.;[25] (3) Azerbaijan was colonized by various empires, notably by Persia, the Arab Muslims, and, finally, Russia, a situation that led to the dilution of Azerbaijan's Turkic identity and culture and also explains why most important Azerbaijani literary works are written in Persian;[26] (4) in 1813 and 1828, in a joint conspiracy, tsarist Russia and Iran divided Azerbaijan into two parts, explaining the existence of the province of Azerbaijan in Iran (this view was further perfected during the

Communist era when the terms Southern and Northern Azerbaijan were first introduced into the country's political vocabulary);[27] and (5) the creation in 1918 of the republic of Azerbaijan—the first democracy in the East—marks the resurrection of Azerbaijan's Turkic identity and culture, as well as its political rebirth.

Despite their widespread appeal, these myths do not correspond to Azerbaijan's historic realities, including the beginning of its linguistic—but by no means complete ethnic—Turkification or the nature of its historic links with Iran. Nor does it correspond to Azerbaijan's present-day ethnic and cultural conditions. For example, even today Azerbaijan has substantial non-Turkic ethnic minorities, such as the Talesh, the Kurds, the Tats, and the Lezghis. Therefore, a policy that overemphasizes the Turkic dimensions of Azerbaijan's identity and culture, rather than recognizing its unique blend of various influences that have formed its culture, is liable to alienate these non-Turkic-speaking groups and undermine their loyalty toward the state and nation. For these reasons since 1987 there has been a debate in Azerbaijan between the Turkists, who believe in its unadulterated "Turkic-ness" and want to purify its culture and language from other influences, and those who emphasize a sense of "Azerbaijan-ness," recognizing the various influences that have shaped its identity and culture. This debate is reflected in such disagreements as what to call the language spoken in the republic. The Turkists want it to be called "Turkish" and, under Elçibey, it was so called, while the more Azerbaijani-oriented people call it Azeri-Turkish, thus distinguishing it from the Turkish spoken in Turkey.

The debate about Azerbaijan's identity has important foreign policy implications, especially in terms of its relations with two of its neighbors, Iran and Turkey. The Turkists want close relations with Turkey, going as far as perhaps some kind of political union and a more active policy to bring about the unification of what they consider the northern and southern halves of one Azerbaijan, which was divided up by Russo-Persian conspiracy. They are also very hostile to Iran. The proponents of the uniqueness of Azerbaijan's culture, by contrast, want more balanced relations with all their neighbors, although they too want unification of the so-called Northern and Southern Azerbaijans. This debate about the nature of Azerbaijan's identity and culture is unlikely to be settled soon, and thus it will continue to affect aspects of its foreign policy, depending on how this debate evolves.

Because of its long border with Iran, its substantial energy resources, and its ethno-cultural characteristics, including the fact that the vast majority of its population adheres to Shi'a Islam, in the last decade Azerbaijan has become the focus of interest of regional and international actors. This external interest has had both negative and positive implications for Azerbaijan's foreign policy choices and, especially, its ability to pursue a relatively more independent line. To illustrate, Western interest in Azerbaijan has enabled it to resist Russian pressures to become part of Moscow's zone of influence by, among other things, disallowing the stationing of Russian troops on its territory. On the negative side, the West's interest in making Azerbaijan part of a policy of encircling and isolating Iran has exacerbated other problems in Azerbaijani-Iranian relations. Meanwhile, the West's clear preference for Turkey has strengthened the existing pro-Turkish tendencies among segments of the Azerbaijani elite and overall population, thus widening the opinion gap regarding the direction of the country's external relations.

Azerbaijan, though on the Caspian Sea, has no connection to major international waterways, impeding the export of Azeri energy. This situation, coupled with the dynamics of international politics, especially Western policies toward the Middle East and the former Soviet Union, greatly affects Azerbaijan's foreign policy choices. For example, the fact that Azerbaijan cannot export its oil through Iran because of U.S. opposition has brought Azerbaijan and Georgia closer together because Georgia offers a transit route for Azeri oil through its port of Sup'sa. Similarly, the fact that the Nakhichevan autonomous republic is separated from the rest of the country by Iranian territory and often relies on Iran for the supply of energy and food means that, despite tensions in their bilateral relations, Azerbaijan has tried to prevent ties with Iran reaching a breaking point. In other words, Azerbaijan's geographical realities have to some degree counteracted the negative impact of identity-related issues on Azeri-Iranian relations.

The dynamics of the Karabakh conflict and, in particular, Azerbaijan's desire to secure a settlement that would guarantee the maintenance of its territorial integrity, have greatly influenced the direction of its foreign policy. For example, Azerbaijan's attitude toward major regional and international players has, to a great extent, been determined by its perception of their potential contribution to the resolution of this conflict in a way favorable to its interests.

All the factors discussed above have played a role in shaping Azerbaijan's foreign policy since independence. However, in certain periods the impact of cultural and identity-related factors have been stronger. Therefore, in discussing Azerbaijan's foreign policy, two distinct periods must be addressed. The first period extended from June 1992 to June 1993 and coincided with the rule of the Azerbaijan Popular Front (APF) and the presidency of Elçibey. The second period, the presidency of Haidar Aliev, began in June 1993 and has continued until now. During this latter period, Azeri foreign policy has gone through two distinct phases.

The foreign policy of the APF government was largely determined by its political and cultural ideology, especially its view of Azerbaijan's ethnic and cultural identity. The APF belonged to the Turkist school of Azeri identity. The APF's Turkism was not limited to the question of Azerbaijan's cultural identity. In politics, too, the APF and Elçibey were close to ultra-nationalist and Pan-Turkist elements in Turkey, such as the late Alpaslam Turkes's Grey Wolves (Bozkurt), and favored the eventual creation of a Turkic bloc. The APF also saw Mustafa Kemal Ataturk and his model of social and political development as the best guidelines for Azerbaijan to follow on its own process of nation building. The result of this ideological inclination was a pro-Turkish policy on the part of the APF.

The Turkist and Kemalist ideology of the APF was accompanied by an extreme anti-Iranianism, with comparatively less strong anti-Russian feelings. The intensity of the APF government's anti-Iranian sentiment derived partly from its cultural and political Turkism and partly from its revulsion toward Iran's Islamic regime, itself the result of the APF's adherence to the Kemalist form of secularism, with its anti-religious dimensions. The anti-Russian sentiment derived from the belief that Russia had conspired with Iran to divide Azerbaijan and had prevented the flourishing of its Turkic culture. Additional factors were the introduction of Soviet troops into Azerbaijan in January 1990 and Russo-Turkish rivalry for influence in the post-Soviet space. Because of its pro-Turkish and Pan-Turkist tendencies, the APF naturally was not favorably disposed toward Russia. Because of its anti-Russian sentiment, the Elçibey government refused to join the CIS and did not adhere to the CIS collective security pact. It also had an uneasy relationship with Iran. The APF government was pro-West and pro-Israel, and, during Elçibey's one-year presidency, the foundations of closer cooperation between Azerbaijan and the West and Israel were laid.

One of the principal criticisms made against Elçibey's government was that its excessively pro-Turkish, anti-Iranian, and anti-Russian foreign policy had damaged Azerbaijan's interests, especially in regard to the Nagorno-Karabakh conflict. These critics argued that Elçibey's policies had led both Russia and Iran to help Armenia and, as a result, had contributed to Azerbaijan's military reverses and losses of territory. Therefore, one of the priorities of the new Aliev government was to restore a degree of balance to Azerbaijan's foreign policy.

Within the overall context of restoring such a balance, one of the first priorities of the Aliev government was to improve relations with Moscow. As a first step in this direction, Azerbaijan joined the CIS, despite the opposition's claims that this was done under strong Russian pressure.[28] Aliev hoped that, following this gesture, Russia would help resolve the Karabakh conflict in a way favorable to Azerbaijan. However, Azerbaijan's expectations of Russia's ability to find a quick and favorable solution to the Karabakh conflict were soon disappointed.[29] Furthermore, the existence of strong anti-Russian sentiment among a large number of Azeris, partly due to the introduction of Soviet troops to Baku in January 1990, set limits on how far Aliev could go in befriending Russia without endangering his own base of popular support. Also, while Aliev wanted to maintain good relations with Russia, he did not want to make Azerbaijan subservient to Russia again. Thus, when Russia asked for the stationing of its troops on the Iranian-Azerbaijani border, Aliev refused. Azerbaijan also refused to join the CIS collective security pact. These decisions prevented significant Russo-Azeri rapprochement.

In the coming years, areas of disagreement between Russia and Azerbaijan increased. A particular bone of contention has been the legal status of the Caspian Sea and the route of the second major pipeline to carry Azeri and Central Asian energy to international markets. Finally, Azerbaijan opted for the so-called Baku-Ceyhan option that has been strongly favored by Turkey and the West, especially by the United States, a decision that Russia dislikes. However, because of negative developments in the energy markets during 1997 and 1998, notably falling oil prices and the potential high cost of the Baku-Ceyhan pipeline, its fate remains unclear. Consequently, although during Aliev's presidency relations with Russia have not reached the low levels of Elçibey's time, nevertheless Azerbaijan has not advanced much in the pro-Russian direction that was first expected from the new government. On the contrary, in the context of loose alliances that began to form among the CIS countries by early 1996, Azerbaijan has been part of the group, including Ukraine, Georgia, Moldova, and Uzbekistan, that is opposed to the strengthening of Russian influence in the post-Soviet space.

During the early 1990s, when Aliev was living in his native Nakhichevan, the Karabakh war put the province in a difficult economic situation and in dire need of all forms of assistance. Iran helped Nakhichevan by providing it with electricity, food, and other assistance. Thus Aliev was inclined to improve relations with Iran. Moreover, he initially believed that better relations with Iran would help in the favorable resolution of the Karabakh problem. Therefore, during the first year of Aliev's presidency, there was some warming up of Azerbaijani-Iranian relations.

The first indication of this improved atmosphere was the visit in October 1993 of the then Iranian president Ali Akbar Hashemi Rafsanjani to Baku. Aliev made a return visit to Tehran on June 29, 1994. However, it is important to note that Aliev made the trip to Tehran after having visited Russia, Turkey, and a number of key Western countries. This sequence of trips was intended to indicate that relations with Iran were not the highest priority of the Azeri government.

Indeed, in the following years, Iranian-Azerbaijani relations followed a downward spiral and were marred by some unpleasant diplomatic incidents. Two sets of reasons contributed to these developments: (1) those deriving from historical, cultural, and political realities of the two countries, most notably the particular Azeri view of the region's history and its irredentist tendencies toward the Iranian Azerbaijan, plus the anti-Iranian activities of

Turkist nationalists, such as former president Elçibey;[30] and (2) those related to the impact of international and regional politics. Among the latter, U.S. opposition to a significant role for Iran in the Transcaucasus and the continuation of Azerbaijan's close relations with Israel, which is also opposed to Iranian influence in the region, have had a strong influence in determining the state of Iranian-Azerbaijani relations. To illustrate, Azerbaijan was forced to withdraw its offer of a 10 percent share for Iran in the international consortium to develop part of its oil fields because of U.S. opposition. This 10 percent was divided between Turkey (3 percent) and the Exxon Corporation (7 percent).

In short, although Aliev started his presidency with the intention of improving relations with Iran, in the course of his rule the ties between the two countries have remained strained, although they are better than they were during the Elçibey presidency.[31]

The West had supported Elçibey and his policies, and thus it viewed Aliev's return to power with apprehension. One Western concern was that Aliev might adopt a different policy regarding the oil concessions. The West also was not pleased with a pro-Russian and pro-Iranian tilt in Azerbaijan's orientation, especially in light of the fact that, by late 1993, the Russian-Western honeymoon had come to an end and there were signs of a Russo-Iranian rapprochement. Additionally, the victory of ultranationalist and other conservative forces in Russia's December 1993 parliamentary elections had generated fears in the West about future political trends there.[32] As a result of these developments, the West had become much less complacent about Russian activities in the post-Soviet republics.[33]

Following this shift in Western attitude, the Russocentric character of Western policy toward the post-Soviet space greatly diminished, and Western policy increasingly became focused on nurturing ties with individual post-Soviet countries in order to prevent them from again falling under Russian domination. This change in the Western approach provided the post-Soviet republics with a viable alternative to reliance on Russia and a means of balancing Russia's proximity and influence.

These changes, coupled with other factors discussed earlier, led to a shift in Azerbaijan's orientation away from Russia and toward closer cooperation with the West. Thus by 1995, Azerbaijan had joined NATO's Partnership for Peace Program, established close ties with the European Union, and had become a key link in the EU-sponsored Central Asia-Transcaucasus-European transport and communications corridor, and is now generally viewed as part of the pro-Western coalition of post-Soviet states. However, Azerbaijan's relations with the West have not been free of tension. The West still does not fully trust Aliev, and it is also concerned about the lack of progress in regard to human rights issues.

In view of his extreme pro-Turkishness and the close relations that Elçibey had established with Turkey, his ouster from power was a severe blow to Ankara. In fact, as late as June 24, 1993, the Turkish foreign minister, Hikmat Çetin, in a letter to the Secretary General of the United Nations, stated that his country intended to support the "lawful authorities of Azerbaijan" and had described Surat Husseinov's rebellion, which catapulted Aliev into power, as an army mutiny aimed at overthrowing the lawful government.[34] Furthermore, according to press reports, Elçibey was receiving discrete counsel from high-ranking Turkish officials late into the night in his hideout. But as it gradually became clear that Aliev was there to stay, and that there was little chance of Elçibey returning to power in the foreseeable future, the Turkish government changed its attitude. Thus, the Turkish foreign minister totally reversed his government's earlier position during an interview with the dubious claim that "Aliev came to power in Azerbaijan within the democratic process."[35]

For his part, Aliev moved swiftly to reassure and befriend Turkey. There were several valid reasons why it was imperative that Azerbaijan strengthen its relations with Turkey. The first reason is the warm feelings of a significant number of Azerbaijanis toward Turkey and their promotion of close cooperation with that country. To alienate this constituency would have impeded Aliev's efforts to consolidate his power and might have led some circles in Turkey to manipulate these elements in order to undermine Aliev. Second, good relations with Turkey are important for broadening Azerbaijan's policy options and enabling it to deal with a stronger hand with Iran and with Russia. Third, because Turkey is a major Western ally and a NATO member, having good relations with it was essential for Azerbaijan's maintenance of good ties with the West.

The first major sign that Azerbaijani-Turkish relations were gradually being restored almost to their former warmth was the visit of the Turkish foreign minister to Baku on September 19, 1993. During this trip, Aliev reassured Turkey that Azerbaijan would choose the Turkish route for the export of its oil and declared that Turkey would continue to train Azerbaijani military personnel.[36] Another milestone in Turkish-Azerbaijani relations was the visit of Aliev to Turkey in February 1994. During this visit, Aliev stated that Turkey and Azerbaijan were two states but one nation.[37] Since that time, relations between the two countries have become even closer. Nevertheless, Turkey does not completely trust Aliev and would prefer the return of nationalist forces to power in Azerbaijan because they relate more instinctively and emotionally to Turkey.

In the last few years, a number of strategic and economic considerations, coupled with the fact that there is a considerable Azerbaijani minority in Georgia's Marneuli Region, have brought Georgia and Azerbaijan closer together. The facts that both countries have adopted a basically pro-Western orientation and that they are concerned about Russian intentions toward the region, plus Georgia's desire to become a transit route for the export of Azeri oil and part of the so-called East-West Eurasian corridor, have been responsible for the friendly relations that have been established between the two countries.

With the general Western trend in Azerbaijan's orientation, its relations with Israel, which were already close during Elçibey's government, also took a positive turn. This favorable trend was first indicated by the visit in 1994 of Vafa Gulizaleh, a key adviser to Aliev and a strong proponent of close Azerbaijani-Israeli ties, to Israel and his meeting with foreign minister Shimon Peres. Since then, relations between the two countries have grown closer, and Azerbaijan is considered part of the new Turkish-Israeli axis that is emerging in the Middle East and its periphery.[38] Azerbaijan has also expanded its ties with other Middle East countries, notably Saudi Arabia and Pakistan. It has also joined the OIC and ECO (Economic Cooperation Organization).

GENERAL DETERMINANTS OF FOREIGN POLICY IN GEORGIA

Georgia's foreign policy, like all aspects of its postindependence national life, has been affected by the high degree of internal strife that has bedeviled the country for a decade. This high level of strife has been partly the result of Georgia's ethnic and cultural diversity, reflected in such interethnic disputes as those of Abkhazia and South Ossetia. But it has also been due to divisions among the Georgians themselves, plus intense struggle for power among various political personalities and their supporters.[39]

In analyzing Georgia's foreign policy, two periods should be distinguished: (1) The Zviad Gamsakurdia presidency that lasted from May 26, 1991—the date of his election to presidency—to January 1992; and (2) the Eduard Shevardnadze period, which has extended from March 1992 to the present. It must be noted here that, when he returned to Georgia, Shevardnadze did not immediately become the country's president. Rather, he headed a state council and was only later elected to the presidency. Nevertheless, from the time of his return to Georgia, he was the effective leader of the country, although his authority was challenged by various opponents and rivals.

Throughout his brief presidency, Gamsakurdia was beset by ethnic conflicts and other challenges to his hold on power and did not have much time to develop a consistent foreign policy. Nevertheless, some of his views regarding the character of Georgian culture and his ultranationalism gave an inkling of what kind of policy he would have been likely to pursue had he stayed in power. For example, Gamsakurdia believed that Georgia was a natural cultural bridge between East and West and, therefore, it should act as a mediator between the two worlds. This vision of Georgia's role seems to indicate that, had he survived, he would have tried to develop extensive relations with the Middle East as well as with the West. Because of his excessive nationalism, he was anti-Russian and, as a result, he refused to join the CIS, a factor that may have contributed to Russia's efforts to bring about his removal. Meanwhile, his erratic behavior and language did not endear him to the West. Moreover, the period of Gamsakurdia's presidency coincided with the height of Russo-Western partnership. The result was that, when Russia manipulated Georgia's internal divisions in order to bring down Gamsakurdia, no help was forthcoming from the West or any other outside source.[40]

During the Shevardnadze period, too, Georgia's main foreign policy problem has been how to manage relations with Russia. Initially, Shevardnadze's coming to power had raised hopes that relations with Russia would improve and that this improvement, in turn, would lead Russia to help resolve the Abkhaz problem in Georgia's favor. This expectation was largely based on the fact that Shevardnadze had shifted his support from Gorbachev to Yeltsin during the crucial period of 1991 and thus produced the hope that the new Russian government would help him assert his authority. This view overlooked one fact: the animosity of the Russian military toward Shevardnadze due to their belief that he was responsible for the collapse of the Soviet Union. This was a major problem because when Shevardnadze returned to Georgia, much of Russian policy toward the Caucasus region was made on the ground by the military commanders rather than by authorities in Moscow. Indeed, despite repeated appeals of Shevardnadze to Russia for help against the Abkhaz rebels in the summer of 1993, there was no assistance until early November 1993, when Russia finally helped Shevardnadze to defeat the Gamsakurdia loyalists.[41]

By that time, Tbilisi had lost control over Abkhazia, and Georgia had joined the CIS. On February 3, 1994, Georgia signed an all-embracing "Framework Treaty of Friendship and Good Neighborness" with Russia. Following this agreement, Russia brokered first a ceasefire between the Abkhaz and the Georgians on December 1, 1993, and, later, an agreement in April 1994 that included provisions on how to resolve the conflict.[42] The latter agreement introduced Russian peacekeepers into Georgia. Georgia also agreed to the joint patrol of the Georgian-Turkish border by Georgian and Russian military forces and granted basing rights to Russia.

However, there has been resistance to Russian influence in Georgia, and the parliament refused to ratify the Russo-Georgian Friendship Treaty. Indeed, since 1994, Shevardnadze has been trying to reduce Russia's influence in Georgia by improving ties with the West, Turkey, and other CIS countries, such as Ukraine, which also have grievances against Russia. A major goal of Georgia has been to reduce the number of Russian troops there, which is estimated to be around twelve thousand. However, Russia has indicated that it has no intention of closing the bases, although it might be willing to hand over some of them to Georgia.[43] Nevertheless, in view of Georgia's internal vulnerabilities, there are limits to how far Georgia can go in antagonizing Russia, especially since the West has shown itself unwilling to resolve Georgia's interethnic problems or to assume a larger peacekeeping function in that country.

Despite its limitations, the Westward-looking strategy of Shevardnadze has been quite successful, partly because of a sense of gratitude on the part of the West toward Shevardnadze for the role that he played in ending the Cold War and the Soviet Union. As part of this strategy, Georgia has joined NATO's PFP program and has signed an association agreement with the EU.

Relations with Turkey have become very warm and multidimensional and have even expanded to the field of defense cooperation.[44] This policy has paid off for Georgia in terms of making it the choice of Western oil companies and governments as one of the transit routes for Azerbaijani oil and in terms of increased economic assistance.

Georgia has been able to maintain good relations with Azerbaijan and Armenia, despite some areas of potential tensions with both countries, mainly related to the existence of Azerbaijani and Armenian minorities in Georgia. However, as noted earlier, Georgian-Azerbaijani relations have become much closer in the last few years, reflecting the impact of economic consideration, common concerns over Russian intentions toward the region, and a pro-Western shift in their policies. The choice of Georgia as a transit route for Azerbaijani oil has been particularly important in bringing the two countries together. Georgia has also been promoting the idea of regional cooperation among the three Transcaucasian states in the context of Shevardnadze's "Peaceful Caucasus" concept.

Initially Shevardnadze looked to Iran as a potentially important economic partner and a counterweight to Russia. Aware of U.S.-Iranian hostility, he even tried to mediate between the two countries.[45] But he soon realized that, because of U.S. hostility, the Iran option was not realistic. Thus, although Georgia maintains good relations with Iran, it has had to look elsewhere for partners. The country that has emerged as Georgia's primary partner in the Middle East is Israel. Israel is the largest foreign investor in Georgia, and its prime minister was to visit Georgia in September 1998 in order to attend the celebration of the 2,600th anniversary of the Jews first settling in Georgia, but his visit was postponed for health reasons.[46] Georgia's relations with other Middle Eastern countries have not developed to any considerable degree.

CONCLUSIONS AND OUTLOOK

This chapter has illustrated that the foreign policies of the Transcaucasian states have been determined by the same factors that influence those of other countries that face similar geopolitical conditions. As small states in a zone of great power rivalry, the foreign policies of these countries have been greatly influenced by the impact of systemic factors. These factors have at times narrowed these countries' policy options, while at other times they have offered them an opportunity to widen their margin of independence. For instance, until 1993, the West's willingness to allow Russia a relatively free hand in the post-Soviet space limited their options. However, since 1994, greater Western interest has allowed them a larger degree of maneuverability, especially by enabling them better to resist Russian pressures. Rivalry among major regional countries for influence in the region has had a similar contradictory effect on the Transcaucasian countries' foreign policies.

In addition to the pressures emanating from the regional and international systems, these countries' foreign policy–making processes have been made more difficult by their internal characteristics, notably their ethnic and cultural heterogeneity (with the exception of Armenia), their interethnic disputes, their historical experience, the legacy of Russian-Soviet domination, and Russia's efforts to reestablish its influence in the post-Soviet space. However, the relative impact of each of these factors has differed in the case of each country. For example, in the case of Armenia, its historical experience, especially the 1915 tragedy, has been most influential. In the case of Azerbaijan, identity-related and cultural issues have had a great impact. And in Georgia's case, the country's internal divisions and conflicts have to a large extent determined its foreign policy choices. These influences have also led to the establishment of certain patterns of relations that, in their basic characteristics, are likely to survive.

Considering their limited economic and military resources, their unfavorable geographic conditions (all are effectively landlocked states, with the exception of Georgia), and their internal conflicts, the three Transcaucasian states have done relatively well in trying to expand their international ties, achieve a modicum of independence, and resist total domination by their larger neighbors.

2 | Regional Security Prospects in the Caucasus

Alexander Rondeli

The Caucasus is a region of new states facing many uncertainties. Several great powers are involved in the region, which complicates the overall situation in the Caucasus. But the absence of real nation-states, let alone democracies, is a key problem that persists in the Caucasus and is the main obstacle to regional security.

All three states of the Caucasus are not only weak powers but also weak states; they are essentially no more than quasistates, with a very fragile statehood. One can even argue that, amid the ruins of the Soviet Union, a type of small state not seen in quite some time on the Eurasian landmass has emerged—the protostate. The protostate is characterized by societies that lack democratic traditions and civil elements in their political and economic culture, and by economies in deep crisis as they undergo a painful transition to the market from central direction and away from a one-sided dependence on Russia. Finally, these newly independent states have yet to develop their own strategic culture to support the formation and realization of an independent foreign policy.

The reorientation of post-Soviet states involves a partial, or even a major, revision of the pattern of their individual relations with their regional neighbors. Amidst this state of flux, the process of establishing new security relations is, however, gaining momentum.

STATE-BUILDING AND NATIONAL SECURITY

The states of the Caucasus tend to exaggerate the external threats to their national security. Although there are certain external security threats for all three Caucasian states, the main security problems stem from these countries' own internal weaknesses. Among them, one could say *primus inter pares*, is their fragile statehood.[1] There are numerous obstacles standing in the way of building nation-states and in creating new and effective social orders. Certain interrelated factors stand out as the main impediments of state-building in the Caucasus. Ethnic nationalism, insufficient socio-economic cohesion of the population, parochialism, familism, lack of democratic traditions, corruption, and preference for a strong, even caudillo-type, leader are factors that significantly hinder the process of formation of a modern democratic state. One can argue that the obstacles to state-building in the Caucasus are not only interrelated, but also participate in a viscious circle in that one causes the next which contributes to another and on around until the "last" helps to cause the "first." This is a particularly pernicious spiral for the Caucasus states due to the extremity of their political, military, and economic weaknesses. The new Caucasian states also face an acute problem of political and ideological integrity. In two of them (Azerbaijan and Georgia) the jurisdiction of the central government is not yet fully established over the whole country. In these two states, the strategic goal is to promote national unification and an awareness of nationhood as a value important for the country's citizens. Otherwise, they will fail to develop and to conduct an effective national security policy. Finally, there is very little experience in strategic thinking in Caucasian independent states, which makes the formation and development of a national strategic culture a top priority for a newly independent nation.

DIFFERENT SECURITY CONCERNS

The main obstacles standing in the way of creating a stable security environment and stimulating regional cooperation are the different security visions and concerns among the three Caucasian states and the irresponsible, negative role of some regional powers.

All three states seek security, but their perception of threats and security concerns greatly differ.[2] Azerbaijan and Georgia perceive their roles in the region more in geoeconomic terms, and see their future security based on regional economic cooperation. Armenia, because of its specific threat perception and its conflict with Azerbaijan over Karabakh relies heavily on its relationship with Russia. Basically, Armenia's security perception is mainly based on a geopolitical interpretation of the region's political and economic reality.

The Commonwealth of Independent States (CIS) was created in 1991 as an attempt by Russia to reintegrate the post-Soviet space and to maintain a common security and economic space. The Caucasus states joined the CIS under different conditions, and continue to participate in it to different degrees and for different reasons. Georgia, for example, joined the CIS under heavy pressure from Russia, but many people in Georgia believed that the CIS would provide Georgia with security and bring economic benefits. Such expectations quite quickly proved unrealistic because of centrifugal processes within the CIS itself. Most disappointing of all, membership in the CIS could not rescue Azerbaijan and Georgia from outside interference in their internal affairs and violation of their territorial integrity, which constitutes one of the major threats to any country's national security.

It has to be stressed that all three Caucasus states' national interests lie somewhere between the CIS (or some other regional concept) and independent development with the ultimate goal of integration into Europe. This dualism adds to the uncertainty of their foreign policy and security priorities. The CIS is in a deep crisis, and there is widespread disillusionment with the commonwealth, which is mainly seen as a tool for the reconstruction of a unified post-Soviet entity on the territory of the former Soviet Union that will be under Russian domination.[3]

The situation is aggravated not only by Russia's efforts to dominate the CIS to the greatest extent possible and the insufficient Russian regard for the security interests of other CIS members, but also because of the fear of political uncertainty within Russia and the possible coming to power of more neoimperialist forces. Finally, there is the fear of the further disintegration of Russia itself. Russia is still uncertain about its own security priorities and, after creating a collective security treaty within the CIS, it is building networks of bilateral agreements and introducing significant amounts of weaponry into certain regions and countries (as was the case with Armenia in the Caucasus).

Regional security in the Caucasus is increasingly complex and operates with concentric security dilemmas. Using the term "revisionist" or "unsatisfied" state, one can conclude that if in 1991 there was only one revisionist state (Armenia) in the Caucasus, all three of the region's states can now be so identified. This situation is aggravated by the presence of certain ethnic groups and state-claiming nationalities who are revisionist themselves. This results in ethnic tensions, claims to self-determination, separatist and irredentist agitation, and intrastate and interstate tensions and conflicts. In some cases external forces support such revisionist ethnic groups and states, which compounds regional insecurity.

It is generally accepted that a small state's foreign policy is a response to external conditions, such as the degree of competition between great powers and the demands made upon small states by great powers. In the Caucasus the situation includes such powerful regional actors as Russia, Turkey, and Iran, as well as the added twist that all of them are simultaneously struggling to preserve their self-perceived superpower status via their traditional dominance in the region. Domestic determinants of foreign policy are less salient in the case of the Caucasian states and, in any event, we are dealing with a neorealist kind of security. It has to be stressed that this differs from the very early years of independence, when domestic policy concerns significantly influenced foreign policy. In that period, the foreign policy behavior of Caucasian states was more a function of pressures from domestic groups. Even now, pressures from domestic groups significantly influence the foreign policy behavior of the Caucasian states, but the decisive factor is their position in the regional and global hierarchy of power. When the internal political situation is uncertain and the dominant faction of the political elite does not feel secure and fully in control, domestic emotions may prevail in directing foreign-policy. Domestic instability within the Caucasian states creates problems for foreign-policy makers, who are forced to make strategic decisions that are not always rational and "long-term."

Outside powers meddling in the Caucasian states' internal affairs contribute paradoxically to both external and also internal influences on the foreign policy of the small Caucasian states. The security problems the Caucasian states have faced "on the inside" make them not only extremely vulnerable to domestic unrest but also to threats from the outside.

The national interest, foreign policy, and security priorities of small states have regional, rather than global, dimensions. But certain regions sometimes attract the attention of world powers and become the focus of great power interests, as is the case with the Caucasus because of the region's significance to world energy markets and its potential role as a transit route between Europe and Asia. The Caucasus, traditionally described in geopolitical terms, is now gaining geoeconomic importance. Historically, however, the Caucasian states have lost rather than gained when they occupied positions of importance in global terms. They have sought Western aid to secure their independence in the past but, despite promises, it has never been dependable. Is this to be the pattern at the end of this century? The answer to this partly depends on the state-building skills and the economic progress within the new states, as well as on other variables, such as political culture, leadership, and luck. However, just as important as economic fortune or effective political leadership are the policies of the neighboring states, Russia, Turkey, and Iran, and the reaction to these policies by Western powers.

A new phenomenon, whose influence is steadily growing and giving a new dimension to the region, is international business—primarily oil multinationals. Their growing role is difficult to overestimate. However, while discussing the Caucasus, one can not avoid consideration of its geopolitical problems. Looking at the Caucasus strictly from the geopolitical point of view, one can find here certain elements of the regional security complex "in formation": the operation of the "security dilemma" mechanism; the revival of the "great game" between Russia and Turkey, and Russia and Western powers; and the involvement and even meddling of the regional powers. The region is also characterized by ethnic tensions, claims to self-determination, and interstate and intrastate tensions and conflicts. In some cases external forces support revisionist ethnic groups and states. This increases common insecurity and hinders the state-building process, the most important factor which can create favorable conditions not only for intrastate but also for regional security and cooperation.[4] Regional powers, acting responsibly, could not only contribute positively to state-building processes in the region, but also to regional cooperation and security.[5] Unfortunately this is not always the case.

THE CAUCASUS: A BUFFER REGION?

Despite a widespread view that geopolitical factors nowadays play a lesser role in world politics and that the global forces promoting economic integration are taking the lead, the Caucasus represents a clear case where small states became the object of great power struggles, and where all the features of realpolitik are exposed.

An attractive potential future for the Caucasus is to become a buffer zone.[6] Martin Wight defined a buffer zone as "a region occupied by one or more weaker powers between two or more stronger powers; it is sometimes described as a 'power vacuum.'"[7] For the Caucasian states the role of buffer would be an ideal solution at the moment because the stronger neighboring powers perceive that they have vital interests in the region and try to prevent others from controlling the possible buffer zone, yet none are strong enough to control it themselves. One of the regional powers, Russia, considers its presence in the Caucasus as a vital factor for its national security and cannot accept that the region could be anything other than a totally subordinate zone of influence. Russia fears that a power vacuum in the Caucasus would be filled by powers hostile to Russia and perceives as the ideal solution the Caucasus states remaining as impotent satellites of Russia—a kind of "frontier province."

The growing political and especially economic weakness of Russia, however, does not permit her to preserve the dominance she once had or wants to have in the region. As a result, there is insecurity in the Caucasus, unresolved conflicts, and an extremely uncertain political and economic future for the region's nations. Russia's old-fashioned power politics do not bring her the expected political and economic dividends and only contribute to regional tensions and instability. Russia has been "fighting above its weight" since at least 1992. With an economy smaller than that of the Netherlands, it does not have the resources to achieve the dominant position it craves, nor to maintain such a position were it to be achieved. As a result, Russia has utterly lost the capacity to play the dominant role of benevolent hegemon in the region. Recognition of its status as a "great power" can only come from its willingness and future ability to cooperate in the development of open markets and democratic societies in the region.

If not, its future is as the regional "dog in the manger," doomed to wreak havoc and, possibly, to undermine its own internal stability and security considering its own troubles in Chechnya and elsewhere.

Because of their vulnerability and sensitivity to Russian security perceptions, the ideal role and function for the three Caucasian states would be as a buffer zone, which, despite all the security problems of buffer states, gives them the possibility of maneuvering and provides more flexibility and bargaining ability in advancing their own interests. To be a buffer is not a blessing for small countries, but in the Caucasus context the "bufferization" of the region under the "responsible supervision" of all interested parties (Russia, Iran, Turkey, and the West) would be a serious step toward regional stability and cooperation.

WILL THE UNCERTAINTY LAST LONG?

As previously mentioned, the security dilemma mechanism is active in the region, especially with the participation of outside powers. With regional economic cooperation still quite weak and security cooperation almost absent, the future of the Caucasus does not seem very attractive. The big oil of the Caspian basin and emerging East-West transportation corridor contribute not only to the economic growth potential of the region's states but could also contribute to regional cooperation and security. At the same time these factors, until now, also contributed to tensions between Russia and Georgia and Russia and Azerbaijan, and to confrontation between Russia and the West, namely with the United States and Turkey. The uncertainty in the Caucasus cannot last forever. There must certainly be a solution that will lead the Caucasian states toward cooperation and a better future. But a better future for the region is not and cannot be guaranteed by anyone from the outside. Caucasian states themselves have to start a more active economic and security cooperation if they wish to resurrect themselves as dynamic and democratic modern states. If they do not, there are—as there have always been—outside powers ready to "assimilate" them, with tanks and soldiers if necessary.

What are the prospects for regional security in the Caucasus? What are the factors that could significantly influence the current situation in the region? I close by pointing out six factors capable of changing the current situation in the Caucasus:

1. Drastic changes within Russia; the coming to power of a "qualitatively" different leadership (outright dictatorship, authoritarian democracy, democratic reformers, corporate statism in the service of the leading economic interest groups)
2. A solution to the Nagorno-Karabakh conflict
3. A rapid and successful state-building process within Caucasian states themselves

4. A deal between Russia and Western powers on their interests and rights in the Caucasus; setting a certain and clear framework for their cooperation and the economic development of the region
5. Dramatic increase in the proven quantity of oil reserves in the Caspian Sea and/or significant rise of oil prices
6. A definitive decision on the construction of a main export pipeline from Baku to Ceyhan

Whether and how these six factors come to pass, and whether they will play a positive or destabilizing role in the Caucasus will have to be left to the laboratory of future history to figure out. For the small, weak Caucasus state, though, the answers are of paramount importance. It is argued here that the particular regional dynamics of the Caucasus make the answers important in a global sense, as well. Truly, the Great Game is afoot for the Caucasus states.

Turkish Strategic Interests in the Transcaucasus

3

Scott A. Jones

INTRODUCTION

> The central stage of the next millennium, many observers agree, will be Eurasia, defined as the territory stretching from Western Europe to Western China.... The post cold-war political framework witnessed the reappearance of several independent states. Out of the multitude of those "new" states, almost all—in the Balkans, in the Caucasus or in Central Asia—are those with whom Turkey shares a mutual history, religion or language. This provides Turkey with a new international environment of historical and cultural dimensions. This strategic change corresponds with a new consciousness in Turkey. The role of a shared history and of parallel cultural characteristics is highlighted and put into practice in all spheres of our foreign policy.
>
> —Ismail Cem, Foreign Minister, Republic of Turkey[1]

The dissolution of the Soviet Union in 1991 and the chronic membership deferrals from the European Union (EU) led some analysts to the qualified conclusion that Turkey would seek a more independent, regionally hegemonic role, competing with Russia and Iran for spheres of influence in the Turkic newly-independent states (NIS).[2] Increased Turkish involvement in the Southern Tier (the Transcaucasus and Central Asia) can be seen as complementary to purported Western objectives in the region, insofar as Kemalist Turkey could serve as a developmental model for the Turkic former Soviet republics. By late 1996, however, many of the same analysts were stating that Russia was now in a dominant position in its "near abroad" and that Turkey's economic, political, and diplomatic resources had proved insufficient to allow it to play a major role in the region. Turkish policy toward Azerbaijan, the most strategically located NIS for Turkey, also appeared to have failed to secure direct political influence and economic benefits. For instance, even during the pro-Turkish administration of Azerbaijani president Abulfaz Elçibey (1992–93), Turkey was unable to procure a consistent and stable presence in Azerbaijan.

Despite initial Turkish plans for greater involvement in the Turkic republics of the former Soviet Union generally, and in the Transcaucasus specifically, Ankara's Transcaucasus policy has been inconsistent and episodic. Given the geopolitical complexities of the region, the somewhat measured Turkish response is both pragmatic and victim to circumstances. First, the Caucasus republics have been independent for only eight years, thereby allowing little time for the maturation of policies, let alone of governments. Furthermore, domestic political and economic developments—which have directly affected the shape of Turkey's NIS policies— and the significant legacy of Russian/Soviet rule are factors which mitigate against the easy realization of policy objectives that are themselves subject to the same post–Cold War acclimation processes. Second, Turkey's Caucasus policy has actually been surprisingly reserved. More importantly, despite Ankara's rhetorical flourishes, Turkey's even and measured policy in the Transcaucasus has secured against directly antagonizing Russia or Iran.[3]

This chapter will examine Ankara's policy toward the Transcaucasus republics in general and Azerbaijan in particular, taking into account the fact that Turkish initiatives toward Azerbaijan began only in 1991, and that Turkish goals in the region were relatively modest.[4] With regards to Turco-Azeri relations, Ankara considers Azerbaijan the most strategically located Turkic state in terms of access to petroleum resources and access to Central Asia.[5] Since 1991, Turkey's policy toward Azerbaijan has been composed of a number of objectives, including: securing Azerbaijan's independence; the creation of an accommodating administration in Baku; procuring Azerbaijani sovereignty over Nagorno-Karabakh; limiting Russian presence in the Transcaucasus; and participating in Azerbaijani petroleum production and the export of a significant portion of Azerbaijani oil through Turkish territory.[6]

REALIZING TURKISH REGIONAL POLICY GOALS

To accomplish the above objectives, Ankara's regional policy—especially vis-à-vis Azerbaijan—has sought primarily to assuage Russian fears of Turkish expansionism while pursuing policies that would secure a firmer Turkish presence.[7] Azerbaijan, the winning of which is considered by Ankara as the sine qua non of a successful regional policy, illustrates the diverging nature of Turkish and Russian regional interests.[8] Specifically, Russia would prefer a pro-Moscow government in Baku that could provide military bases for Russia and accept its troops as peacekeepers in Karabakh.

Ideally, Moscow would be able to encourage Azerbaijani dependency on Russia by becoming the sole outlet for Azerbaijani oil exports and by forcing Azerbaijan to accept a partnership with Russia in the production of offshore Azerbaijani oil in the Caspian Sea.[9] Furthermore, Russia has openly and variously expressed its concerns about Turkish presence in the Southern Tier, a region viewed in Moscow as exclusively within its strategic orbit.[10]

In addition to addressing Russian sensitivities, Turkish regional policy has sought stable relations with Armenia and Georgia. However, Armenian involvement in an undeclared war with Azerbaijan over Nagorno-Karabakh, the occupation of almost 20 percent of Azerbaijani territory by the Karabakh Armenians, and the presence in Nagorno-Karabakh of an Armenian paramilitary militia have conspired to make relations between Turkey and Armenia extremely difficult.[11] Moreover, Ankara refuses to normalize ties with Armenia while the latter is informally occupying Azerbaijani territory.[12] For example, Turkey has closed its border with Armenia in response to the ongoing occupation by ethnic Armenian forces of Nagorno-Karabakh and surrounding Azerbaijani territory. For its part, Yerevan—especially under the current Kocharian administration—has also found it difficult to normalize relations with Turkey because of the latter's failure to admit responsibility for the 1915 Ottoman army genocide of the Armenian population in eastern Anatolia. Relations between Ankara and Yerevan are also strained by Russian-Armenian military cooperation. For example, Russian Air Force commander Anatoly Kornukov said that Russia has begun delivering the components of an S-300 Zenith air defense system to its Gyumri military base in Armenia, in addition to MiG-29 aircraft deployed in Armenia last December. Both Ankara and Baku view such transfers as fundamentally undermining the regional balance of power. Kornukov is the first Russian official to confirm that S-300s are being deployed in Armenia.[13]

Turco-Georgian relations have by all accounts been positive. Initial neglect on behalf of Ankara was quickly reversed when it became clear, in 1994, that the most likely export route for Azerbaijan's Caspian oil was through Georgia.[14] Thus, until recently, Ankara's economic and political overtures were minimal. Georgia, for its part, has had to cope with secessionist rebellions in South Ossetia since late 1990, and in Abkhazia since July 1992. Unable to successfully manage these conflicts, Georgia turned to Russia in an effort to prevent its dismemberment. In June 1992, Russian president Boris Yeltsin brokered a cease-fire in South Ossetia, and since then a predominantly Russian Commonwealth of Independent States (CIS) force has been stationed there under an umbrella of the Organization of Security and Cooperation in Europe (OSCE).[15] In Abkhazia, between 1,500 and 2,500 Russian troops have been deployed since June 1994 after the United Nations, the OSCE, and Russia managed to impose a cease-fire

agreement.[16] Post-independence Georgian presidents Zviad Gamsakhurdia and Eduard Shevardnadze have variously accused Russia of perpetuat-
ing these conflicts, implying that Russia manipulates regional conflicts so as
to justify maintaining a military presence in Georgia and influencing its
policies.[17] Nevertheless, under the Shevardnadze administration, Georgia
has sought to distance itself from Russian influence and augment relations
with Ankara.

Georgia, joining NATO's Partnership for Peace (PFP) program in 1994,
also signed its first defense cooperation agreement with Turkey in June
1997, whereby Ankara undertook to provide training for Georgian officers.
Moreover, since Vardiko Nadibaidze, a career Soviet army officer, was
replaced as Georgian defense minister in 1998 by West Point graduate
Davit Tevzadze, bilateral defense cooperation with the United States and
Turkey has increased. Yet, military cooperation is only one facet of what
Georgian President Eduard Shevardnadze referred to during his visit to
Turkey in February 1999 as a "strategic partnership" between the two
countries. A major component of that partnership is the U.S.-backed plan
for an east-west energy corridor through Georgia, which is paralleled by
the EU-sponsored TRACECA program to create a road, rail, and ferry network linking Central Asia with Turkey and Europe. However, acutely
aware of Tbilisi's vulnerability to Russian influence, Shevardnadze added
that "strategic partnership" is not intended to damage any third party.[18]
Ankara and Tbilisi share a common interest in preserving domestic political stability and stability throughout the South Caucasus as the precondition for economic prosperity. Georgia has a 114-kilometer land border
with Turkey (unlike Azerbaijan, whose exclave of Nakhichevan has a mere
10-kilometer stretch of contiguous border with Turkey). The Georgian-
Turkish frontier and expanding network of transport links facilitates not
only military but economic cooperation. Furthermore, Turkey has replaced
Russia as Georgia's main trading partner.[19]

The post-Soviet role prescribed for Turkey in the Southern Tier invariably tended toward the extreme. Feted as the most likely regional
power to hold sway in its former Ottoman satraps, Ankara's initial eupho-
ria quickly gave way to the complex realities of the Caucasus and to its own
internal limitations. In the final analysis, Ankara's relations with the Transcaucasus states are, despite this early Pan-Turkish rhetoric, predicated fundamentally on Turkey's economic objectives: namely, the creation and
expansion of markets for Turkish goods and services and the securing of
energy resources in the Southern Tier.[20] Yet there are several factors
inhibiting these regional objectives.

FACTORS AFFECTING TURKISH REGIONAL POLICY

In addition to the war between Armenia and Azerbaijan over Nagorno-
Karabakh, there is a restrained yet chronic regional conflict between Turk-

ish ambitions to construct a zone of influence in the Southern Tier generally—the Transcaucasus specifically—and Russian determination to remain in its traditional spheres of influence.[21] Upon the dissolution of the Soviet Union, Turkey was exemplified by the Western powers as the developmental model for the Muslim republics: secular, democratic and market-oriented. To that end, Turkish regional policy has received, for example, explicit U.S. support. The Bush and Clinton administrations openly encouraged Turkey to proclaim itself a Westernizing model for the former Soviet republics so as to limit Russian revanchism and to arrest Iranian influence in the Southern Tier.[22]

Turkey's geographical position—astride a critical nexus linking Asia, the Middle East, and Europe—prevents undue concentration on any one area lest it lose influence in the others.[23] Because Turkey also acts in the Balkans, the Aegean, and the Middle East and faces a long-standing Kurdish insurgency at home, it cannot refrain from strategic engagement in those areas to concentrate exclusively in Transcaucasia. Turkey must claim a presence in all four areas.[24] Furthermore, Turkish relations with regional states are, in many instances, strained and openly hostile. In 1993, Foreign Minister Hikmet Çetin observed: "Because its geopolitical and geostrategic location places Turkey in the neighborhood of the most unstable, uncertain, and unpredictable region in the world, it has turned into a frontline state faced with multiple fronts. It is at all times possible for the crises and conflicts in these regions to spread and engulf Turkey."[25]

Domestic economic factors also affect Turkey's regional policies and ability to play the role of a model in the former Soviet southern states. In July 1993, Turkey had a 73 percent annual inflation rate, and its state budget is operating at the limits of its capacity. Its capital resources are also heavily engaged in the mammoth Ataturk Dam and hydroelectric project and a substantial military modernization program. In addition, 30 percent of its expanding military budget goes to contain the Kurds, who appear to be a growing burden.[26] According to the International Monetary Fund (IMF), Turkey's economy has grown at a real rate of 7–8 percent since 1995, with annual wholesale inflation of 82–89 percent. In 1997, Turkey's real Gross Domestic Product (GDP) grew 7.1 percent. This is expected to slow to 4.7–6.4 percent in 1998. High inflation remains a serious problem for Turkey, although it is below the triple-digit levels that Turkey experienced earlier in the decade. Turkey also has a high foreign debt burden and an inefficient tax collection system, while privatization has lagged far behind target.[27]

The United Nations (UN) embargo on Iraq is estimated to have cost Turkey $30–$60 billion in lost trade and forgone business opportunities through 1997. Prior to the UN embargo, Iraq was Turkey's top oil source, supplying Turkish refineries with around 250,000 barrels per day (bbl/d) of oil. Iraq also utilized the 1.6-million-bbl/d-capacity twin pipeline system from its northern Kirkuk fields to export oil via the Turkish port of Ceyhan, but the pipeline was closed in August 1990, following Iraq's invasion of Kuwait.[28]

Another factor affecting Turkey's regional strategy is Turkish defense policy. Turkey is undergoing large-scale/long-term defense modernization. The military's high status in policy making and society, the impact of Desert Storm, and the violence in Kurdistan and the Transcaucasus are invoked to justify this program.[29] The program aims to build modern forces needed to ensure Turkish security and gain self-sufficiency in military production. Turkey is also restructuring its forces to make missile defense a high priority against proliferation threats from its neighbors. The program evidently will cost $12 billion, a 20-percent increase over original estimates.[30] Turkey's inflation rate, military modernization, and the socio-economic costs of the Kurdish insurgency all suggest a broad unfinished domestic agenda that constrains Turkey fiscally and economically from playing a leading or dominating role in the Southern Tier. These constraints also suggest the high importance of economic goals in Turkey's overall foreign strategic engagement especially in the Transcaucasus. Furthermore, the Kurdish threat to Turkey's territorial integrity is the military's first priority.[31] The Kemalist doctrine against foreign "adventurism" all but rules out serious consideration of military action on behalf of Azerbaijan. This position not only reflects an inward looking military policy that rejects foreign activity, it also reflects the limits that Turkey's economy and military modernization program place on Turkey's war-fighting capabilities.[32]

These factors evince Turkey's strategic dilemma. The post-Soviet strategic vacuum in the Transcaucasus has provided Turkey with an immediate opportunity to enhance its regional interests. However, domestic economic factors mean Turkey cannot afford to conduct an activist regional policy. Nor can Ankara escape the fact that efforts to play this role will inevitably increase tensions with Russia and Iran and could lead to military challenges that it cannot or will not accept: for example, intervention on behalf of Azerbaijan. Indeed, to reach a level where it can play a prominent role abroad based on a flourishing domestic economy, Turkey's primary objective throughout the Southern Tier apparently is access to economic markets, particularly in energy. To protect its energy sources from interruptions by Iran, Iraq, or Russia, Turkey seeks a continuous pipeline linking it, through Azerbaijan and the Caspian Sea, with Kazakhstan and Central Asia. A prime strategic objective is a leading position in the transport, if not exploration, extraction, and refining, of Azerbaijani and Central Asian oil and gas to the West. Attaining these objectives would make Turkey the principal intermediary in an extremely lucrative East-West energy business and offer it an enormous windfall.[33] Pan-Turkic rhetoric notwithstanding, such are Turkey's real stakes in the Southern

Tier and—attendant and necessary thereunto—in a peaceful resolution of the Nagorno-Karabakh war.

NAGORNO-KARABAKH: TEST FOR TURKISH POLICY IN THE CAUCASUS

The variable most affecting the scope of Ankara's Caucasus policy in general, and Azerbaijani policy specifically, is Nagorno-Karabakh. In 1991, Turkey embarked on a policy of neutrality, which simultaneously enabled it to present itself as an impartial mediator between the parties. Although Armenia was wary of Turkish involvement from the beginning, it did not immediately denounce Ankara's efforts. Thereafter, Turkish diplomats embarked on several rounds of shuttle diplomacy to the region and to European capitals, and were instrumental in bringing the issue to the agenda of the OSCE. Then Prime Minister Demirel defended his cautious policy by arguing that there was no legal basis for a Turkish intervention, and that, in any case, the Azeris never requested such assistance.[34]

The initial period of neutral mediation, however, was exacerbated by events surrounding an intensification of the conflict. After the massacre of Azeri civilians in the Karabakh town of Khojaly in late February 1992, huge anti-Armenian demonstrations were held in Turkey, with hundreds of thousands of people demonstrating in favor of an intervention on Azerbaijan's behalf.[35] The government found it increasingly difficult to disregard public demands. In particular, President Özal on several occasions stated that the Armenians should be "frightened a little," and statements of the like, which sent shock waves through Armenians in Armenia and in the diaspora community, and enabled them to discredit Turkey as planning a "new" genocide on Armenians.[36] In any case, Turkey soon adopted a more pro-Azerbaijani stance, as Armenian military advances on Azerbaijani territory intensified.[37]

Domestic political squabbles complicated Ankara's early attempt at forging a neutral Karabakh policy. Criticism for standing idle while their "Azeri brethren" were being massacred came from virtually all political directions. Foremost among the government's critics was the leader of the Nationalist Movement Party (MHP), Alparslan Türkes, who at a very early date argued for Turkish military intervention in the war, arguing that "Turkey cannot stand idly by while Azerbaijan's territory is being occupied."[38] Former prime minister and leader of the Democratic Left Party, Bulent Eçevit, argued that Turkey's failure to demonstrate unambiguous support for Azerbaijan might undermine Turkey's prestige there and in Central Asia. Perhaps the most significant challenge to the government came from main opposition leader and head of the Motherland Party, Mesut Yilmaz, who argued for troops to be deployed along the Armenian border and reminded the public that Turkey retains a guarantor status over Nagorno-Karabakh. On several later occasions, he reiterated his belief that Turkey should deploy troops near the Armenian border and Nakhichevan to make explicit the seriousness of its opposition to Armenia's behavior. Straying from its initial neutral position on Karabakh, the government eventually began taking on an explicitly pro-Azeri hue. For example, Turkey helped enforce Azerbaijan's economic blockade of Armenia, refusing to allow aid for that country to pass through Turkey.[39]

Nevertheless, Ankara has always remained receptive to a more moderate position vis-à-vis its Armenia policy. Turkey has refused to establish full diplomatic relations partly because of Armenian support for the Karabakh separatists,[40] but also because the Armenian government did not recognize its borders with Turkey, thus keeping potential territorial claims on Kars and other regions of Northeastern Turkey open—in addition to Turkish claims that Armenia had assisted PKK rebels in staging terrorist acts from Armenian territory.[41] In spite of that, both Ankara and Ter-Petrossian's moderate government attempted to create positive bilateral relations.[42] Hence, on certain occasions Turkey did open its border with Armenia, thus allowing humanitarian aid to pass through. In November 1992, for example, Turkey even signed a deal by which it would have supplied 300 million kilowatt hours of electricity to Armenia, which at the time was suffering from a severe energy shortage that threatened to leave thousands of people without heating in the winter. This deal received vehement criticism from the opposition and Baku. Thus, in January 1993, Turkey rescinded the deal before it had even begun to be implemented.[43]

The explicitly pro-Turkish Elçibey government was ousted in June 1993 by a coup that, although orchestrated by Colonel Surat Husseinov, brought Heydar Aliyev, Azerbaijan's leader in the Brezhnev era, to power. This development was seen as a loss for Turkey and a gain for Russia. Indeed, voices both in Turkey and in the West saw in the power shift Turkey's inability to maintain a friendly regime and to keep its position in Azerbaijan. In Turkey itself, voices were heard that Elçibey's fall would herald the end of the Turkish model.[44] Aliyev's replacing Elçibey was initially seen as a victory for Moscow; however, Aliyev has subsequently shown himself to be a formidable political player, manipulating various sides for Baku's ultimate benefit.[45] For although Aliyev made some accommodating moves toward Moscow, by joining the CIS for example, he staunchly refused to accept the stationing of Russian troops in Azerbaijan.[46]

With respect to Turkey, it is clear that unlike Elçibey, who gave priority to Turkey, Aliyev plays the Turkish card whenever it suits his purposes, but can turn his back to Ankara as well if necessary.[47] In September 1993, for example, he annulled many agreements signed between the Elçibey administration and Turkey, ordered Turkish nationals to seek visas before entering Azerbaijan, and dismissed 1,600 Turkish military experts serving in the country. Only a year later, Aliyev courted Ankara and expressed his confidence in the "brotherhood" existing between the two countries. Furthermore, Aliyev attempted to broaden Azerbaijan's links with the Muslim world, courting Iran and Saudi Arabia in particular, thereby attempting to legitimize and promote his Islamic credentials.[48] Thus, clearly for Turkey, the replacement of Elçibey with Aliyev meant a less reliable and more unpredictable regime in Baku.

Overall, the benefits of a Turkish-mediated peace settlement was to be a postwar Azerbaijan that showcased the Turkish model and provided Turkey with an uninterrupted supply of Central Asian and Azerbaijani gas and oil. In 1992 Turkey proposed a territorial realignment as part of a peace settlement that would attain those very goals. The proposal called for a cease-fire and the immediate creation of a pure Armenian state out of Armenia and Nagorno-Karabakh, and a continuous, purely Muslim, Turkic state of Azerbaijan incorporating the formerly detached area of Nakhichevan. Naturally, this territorial exchange would allow construction of a pipeline whose path conformed to Turkey's objectives.[49]

Under this plan, Azerbaijan would remain intact, but it and Armenia would be dependent on Turkey while Turkey obtained its cherished pipeline. The plan cuts off Iran and Russia from those energy routes and Russia from Transcaucasia as Central Asian oil and gas go directly to Turkey and Europe, making Turkey a major player in the energy game.[50] This plan also would effectively reorient much of Central Asia's economy from Russia to Turkey and the West since energy is that region's main source of foreign exchange. Turkey could then lead Central Asia and Transcaucasia into overall economic integration and even alliance. But Turkey's support for that solution and its potential future ramifications, in turn, have led Iran and Russia to counter Turkish efforts for leverage over the region's energy sources and its overall economy. For example, Iran at various times blocked Turkey's TIR (Transit Highway International) trucks from its highways, effectively obstructing overland trade with Azerbaijan and Central Asia. This has forced Turkey to retaliate in kind for what it believes are politically dictated actions.[51] Such actions indicate the value that rival regional actors place upon economic relationships in the former Soviet republics.

Utilization of the rich energy potential of the region in a manner whereby the needs of all the countries of the region are satisfied and extension to international markets becomes possible is an issue of special importance that leads to the establishment of lasting ties. Turkey's economic limitations already cast doubt upon this endeavor's success; but its chronic inability to effectively influence events surrounding Nagorno-Karabakh and maintain consistent relations with Baku throws Turkey's entire strategic profile as a model and leader into question.[52]

PRAGMATISM AND RESTRAINT: TURKISH TRANSCAUCASIA POLICY OVER TIME

The conflict in Nagorno-Karabakh at an early stage dispersed the illusions of Turkish policy makers about the capacities of their country with regard to its relations with its Turkic counterparts in the Southern Tier. Domestic factors—including changes in governments—and a complicated regional environment in which to formulate its foreign policy prevented Turkey from pursuing an activist policy in the region. In view of the difficult conditions to which it was subjected, Turkey in fact managed to keep its relations with all involved powers, avoiding compromising its position in any center where that would have been to its detriment. The price Turkey had to pay for this was a popular dissatisfaction in Azerbaijan and a manageable loss of prestige in the Muslim republics of the former Soviet Union, who, in any event, were not eager to exchange Moscow's tutelage for Ankara's.

Despite the rhetoric of the early 1990s of a "Turkic twenty-first century," Turkey quickly overcame any illusions of its own power and capacities. Although in the longer term Turkey certainly intends to expand its relations with the Southern Tier republics, it has no illusion of replacing Russia as the dominant power in the region. Rather, Turkey's interest for the time being lies in expanding economic, cultural, and scientific relations with the Transcaucasian states.[53] Thus, although momentarily Turkey has not shown its ability to assert its influence in the Southern Tier, it still maintains a pivotal role in the region, being the main link between these countries and the West, and poses a developmental model for these countries. Simultaneously, Turkey has ensured that it keeps at least working relations with the Russian Federation, which for the foreseeable future will remain an indispensable regional factor.

Ankara's relations with Georgia have been slow to develop. While Ankara was able to co-opt Shevardnadze into supporting the Baku-Supsa-Ceyhan oil pipeline to carry early Azerbaijani oil to Turkey, Tbilisi's dependence on Moscow for economic and military aid has limited Georgia's cooperation with Turkey. However, Turkey has recently proposed military cooperation with Georgia. Some analysts contend that a military presence in the Caucasus for Turkey, which belongs to NATO, is not out of the question in the future. Russia is supposed to retain three military bases in Georgia under an accord signed last fall, but Georgia's president Eduard Shevardnadze has declared that parliament will not ratify the agreement until Moscow helps to return the breakaway region of Abkhazia to Georgian control—something that the Russian government is unlikely to agree to. Senior officials from the Turkish armed forces have signed a five-year military cooperation agreement with Georgia. The pact will enable Georgian officers to undergo training in Turkey and also includes financial assistance to help modernize Tbilisi's military.[54] Nevertheless, Moscow's presence in Georgia could foil developing and future Turco-Georgian relations, for example in Russian manipulation of the South Ossetian and Abkhazian disputes.[55]

Despite the realization on the part of both Yerevan and Ankara that normalization of relations is in their national interests, they have failed to achieve this goal. The persistence of the Nagorno-Karabakh dispute prevents Ankara from improving relations with Yerevan. This is not because the Turkish people are against such an improvement per se, but because the Turkish government knows that strengthening its ties with Armenia would strain relations with Baku and potentially discredit any Turkish government in the eyes of Turkish public opinion. Furthermore, Azerbaijani-Armenian antagonism has led to the discarding of the optimum pipeline route, the Baku-Armenia-Ceyhan route, for the export of Azerbaijani oil. This option would have dramatically reduced Baku and Yerevan dependence on Moscow, and contributed to better relations between the three neighboring countries. The continuation of the Karabakh dispute has not only prevented this from happening, it has also forced Yerevan to ask for the return of Russian military forces, for the most part to guard the Turkish border.

Recently, Turkish minister of state Ahad Andican recently articulated the Turkish government's priorities with regard to the Turkic Soviet successor states as follows: first, to fortify the independence of these countries and thus enable them "to stand on their own feet"; and second, to develop "a system of relations based on equality," abjuring what Andican described as the "sentimental" approach of the early 1990s.[56] Having now abandoned the patina of a vaguely Pan-Turkist Southern Tier policy masking primarily economic motives, Ankara will now perhaps be better placed to respond positively and effectively in this still-unfolding and complex region.

4 | Trends of Strategic Thinking in Georgia
Achievements, Problems, and Prospects

David Darchiashvili

INTRODUCTION

The level of internal and external security largely determines the stability and overall outlook of a state. A national security system is a unity of state mechanisms aimed to neutralize threats and risk factors. To evaluate the level of security and stability of a country, it is necessary to analyze the structure responsible for its maintenance—a system to defend national interests. The viability of a state depends on international agreements endorsed by its political elite, implementation of approved legislation, the effectiveness of structures created for the state's protection (the military, police, and other governmental agencies), and the amount of material resources allocated to the functioning of the whole system. Other indicators of a country's viability include its per capita gross domestic product, its ability to defend the basic rights of its citizens, the existence of frontier control, the amount of corruption in state agencies, and accession to or ratification of relevant international agreements. All these are material, objective aspects of a national security system.

However, it is also important to find out what perceptions the country's sociopolitical elite or the society have of their own country: what they consider threats to the state; what the people's attitudes are toward the government on the whole and the structures responsible for national security in particular; how well the importance of various components of national security are understood and articulated; the effectiveness of their strategic thinking; how intent the political elite and society are on achieving their own ends; and how strongly they believe in their own capabilities. These are the subjective aspects of a national security system, and they are critical factors for newly emerged states. Georgia is such a state, and this chapter attempts to assess perceptions, views, strategic priorities, and intentions of its sociopolitical elite rather than analyze its material resources or military and political tools.

To evaluate subjective aspects of the Georgian national security system one must determine whether there are official statements outlining the country's security and strategy and how a national security concept is being developed. One must also analyze the contents of such documents for their true sociopolitical weight, as well as their relevance to practical politics, on the one hand, and to those concerns that are widely shared among the population or informally expressed by the politicians themselves on the other. Finally, one must analyze the possible future developments of the Georgian national security system.

STRATEGIC THOUGHT IN GEORGIA:
A CASE STUDY OF A DEVELOPING, TRANSITIONAL, POST-COMMUNIST STATE

National/state security, as a necessary component of the state itself, has figured in Georgian state acts and general political statements since independence. It is outlined by the constitution, defence legislation, and foreign policy agreements and declarations. The theme of national strategy—or the avenues through which Georgia has sought to guarantee its national security—has been high on the agenda of its three parliamentary and two presidential elections to date. The Shevardnadze government perceived the need for a statement of strategic views at the end of 1993. At first, the state was to draft developmental programs on the one hand, and the military doctrine on the other. The second stage of understanding the problem is reflected in the government's attempts to draft a more encompassing national security strategy, efforts that have been in progress since 1995.

An important turning point in these efforts occurred when several conferences on the issue, initiated by local nongovernment organizations (NGOs) and sponsored by NATO, were followed by the creation of an ad hoc state commission in the autumn of 1996. In 1997, the first results of the Shevardnadze government's and Georgian parliament's strategic orientation became known. In April 1997, the parliament made its views known by approving "Basic Principles of Sustainability of Social Life, Strengthening of State Sovereignty and Security, and Restoration of the Territorial Integrity of Georgia," a national security strategy proposed by a multiparty parliamentary group. Other parliamentary views are expressed in the Parliamentary Group for Developing Basic Conceptual Principles of National Security's draft "Bases of Maintaining National Security of Georgia," and the Parliamentary Foreign Relations Committee's "About Conceptual Issues of Foreign Policy of Georgia." The Shevardnadze government has been even less cohesive, with no less than three governmental agencies presenting their views: the Ministry of Foreign Affairs' (MFA) military-political department, a state commission led by the foreign minister, and the Georgian Department of State Border Forces. The Academy of Science; the Center of Strategic Studies; the Caucasian Institute for Peace, Democracy, and Development; several NGOs; and others are also involved in the process.

The existence of so many various drafts indicate the recent progress, and confusion, of Georgian strategic thinking. The main achievement of these activities is that the political elite and the public are gradually growing aware of the necessity of state-building and of the consequent need for consensus on national security issues.

These draft security concepts present a range of security problems and concerns. Special attention is given to the following: separatism; external interference in domestic affairs; the relative strength of ethnic self-identification (lack of nationalist feeling); corruption and lack of respect for the law-enforcement authorities; violations of human rights on the part of the police and military; and the lack of coordination in the activities of security-related executive agencies. There is also concern over the widening income gap and the unique problem of the sociopolitical transformation from communism and centralized rule to a democratic form of government. In the foreign policy arena these drafts highlight the Caucasus region's vulnerability to conflicts, Georgia's relatively weak military potential in comparison with neighboring countries, and its unprotected frontiers. Such problems as uncontrolled transits of drugs and weapons and the role of organized crime in society are spotlighted in the national security concerns of other countries, including the United States, and are also reflected in these draft national security strategies.

There is some evidence to suggest that the values and notions of Western political culture have entered Georgian strategic thinking. These drafts underline the necessity to protect basic human rights and impose democratic control over the "power structures" of the government. They also assert the importance of political pluralism and self-government, and acknowledge the rights of ethnic minorities (some of the drafts even speak about a multiethnic Georgian population). Distinguishing the strategic threats and risks of the Georgian state by underlining the dissolution of a clear-cut line between external and internal security relationships in the modern era, some of the drafts suggest that their authors are attempting to be more pragmatic and have a relatively sophisticated view of such issues. Speaking about the legal basis of national security, some of the drafts encourage concrete constitutional provisions, adoption of UN regulations, OSCE participation, and adherence to international legal acts on human rights.

The drafts propose other ideas about creating and developing a national security strategy that are analagous with strategic thinking in the West: the definition of component parts of the national security system; the importance of a regional dialogue against the background of closer cooperation with European structures; the necessity of creating regional security structures; the priority of peaceful political solutions to conflicts; and the refusal to claim neighboring territories or consider the neighboring countries hostile. None of these are necessarily "left over" from the Soviet past, and many fly in the face of the current Russian practices. Most strikingly, almost all the Georgian draft national security concepts regard the ideas of liberal democracy, the rule of law, a democratic and civil society, and the progress of economic reforms as the main guarantees of security.

However, it is obvious that the Georgian drafts of a national security strategy are unique when compared with developed countries and post-Communist republics. The Georgian public is mainly concerned about territorial integrity, ethnic separatism, the low level of popular civic awareness, the lack of social security, inefficiency of executive structures, and lack of respect for the law and government. The need to develop the most basic concepts of statehood remains urgent. Terrorism, the existence of criminal organizations, and illegal transportation of drugs and armaments all pose direct threats to the government's sovereignty. Most of the drafts underline these problems in light of the absence of independent frontier control. While such circumstances are not unique to Georgia, they create a truly unique security environment in combination with unique geopolitical factors, such as Georgia's access to the Black Sea, its location in the center of the Caucasus region, and the importance to the country's stability of developing a Europe-Asia transport corridor.

It must be mentioned that although many themes and provisions are repeated in these drafts, they do display some individual traits. For instance, the draft created under the aegis of the state commission grapples at length with the essence of such notions as the state, civil society, and security, and examines the role of social solidarity, civic initiative, and the importance and direction of economic reforms. There are also passages analyzing how significant the legitimacy of the state authority is for stability and national security. At the same time, this draft pays little attention to military and foreign policy aspects. The draft of the Parliamentary Group for Developing Basic Conceptual Principles of National Security is distinguished by its extraordinary emphasis on the military. It gives priority to combating guerrilla warfare and civil disobedience in the country's defense and attempts to define all the threats and risk factors (expected and hypothetical) for the state. The draft of the MFA military-political department seeks to create a complete list of general issues and problems facing the country.

The document "About Conceptual Issues of Foreign Policy" prepared by the parliamentary foreign relations committee is especially worth mentioning due to its specific structure and essence. It is distinguished by the analysis of the interests of neighboring states, and makes an attempt from this analysis to chart a general course for Georgian foreign policy. Its main conclusion is that a balance must be struck between the interests of regional powers that incorporates and emphasizes areas of common Caucasian cooperation and builds closer contacts with the West.

The fact that the government has not adopted the final version of a national security strategy indicates that some confusion still remains. Much of the confusion revolves around basic contradictions in priorities, obscurity in the meaning of basic terms, and the tendency to drift when defining which elements of social, political, and economic intercourse are security related.

INCONSISTENCY IN GEORGIAN NATIONAL SECURITY STRATEGY

The Georgian National Security Doctrine contains a mix of incompatible priorities and contradicitions. For example, the draft of the state commission emphasizes the need for strengthening civil society, respect for the universal declaration of human rights, the dangers of ethnic factionalism, and the necessity of cultural integration. But at the same time the commission shows concerns that globalization threatens national identity and that individualism—without establishing social responsibilities—can damage the country's territorial integrity. The same document says that a small country cannot defend itself by military means, but it emphasizes the necessity of strengthening the army. The draft of the MFA military-political department at times specifies the citizen as the supreme object of security, but also defines the state as the main object of security. It says also that Orthodox Christian traditions need promoting and regards the "negative influence" of mass culture as a threat, despite claiming to respect liberal democratic traditions. The draft of the Parliamentary Group for Developing Basic Conceptual Principles of National Security and the Border Guards' Guidelines reflect similar confusion and inconsistency between the needs of the state and the rights of the individual.

The drafts do not clarify the meaning of "the weakening of national immunity," a family's social "responsibility," or a citizen as "the subject of the security system." Speaking about national interests and the problems of security policy the authors often use the term "etc." Also unclear are the underlying meanings of such phrases as "traditions should be preserved" and citizens must "defend national values." The draft of the MFA prioritizes the task of "applying industrial potential" without explanation of how that is defined; the document prepared by the border guards mentions but does not clarify the intent to integrate with "not only CIS countries." There are no answers to the ambiguities triggered by the draft of the parliamentary group when it struggles with "attempts to enforce double citizenship."

Press reports, parliamentary debates, and politicians' informal statements often cite the assumption that the Georgian people and political elite consider Russia a threat. At the same time, Georgia has formally participated in the creation of the CIS security system since 1993, and Russian military bases are still deployed in the country. Curiously, most of the various drafts of the prospective Georgian security strategy say nothing about this contradiction. However, the theme of the Russian threat is presented in the draft of the parliamentary group, which states that "proximity to a militarized state with undeveloped democracy and a highly unpredictable development course is an essential factor of the geopolitical environment of Georgia's security." Readers, however, are left to guess which "militarized state" is meant, as Russia, Iran, Turkey, Azerbaijan, and Armenia are all in proximity and all meet that description to varying degrees. Finally, does this "militarized state" pose a particular, intentional threat or is it only a potential threat?

Most of the drafts are based on the principle that the notion of national security has substantially expanded in the modern world, no longer confined to traditional military and foreign policy. They pay more attention to organized crime; ecological, informational, and economic threats to the state; and to nonmilitary means to maintain security. At the same time, the drafts show that Georgian strategic thinking goes beyond the Western approach, introducing educational and cultural issues into the national security dialogue. On the one hand, this may be explained by prioritizing civil relationships and the rule of law in a newly emerged state. But if one declares educational, cultural, and national traditions to be the domain of security policy, some risk arises: (1) the state structures responsible for national security would have grounds to invade one's privacy; (2) security policy would be viewed as a field that is complex, comprehensive, and, therefore, hard to understand or control; (3) the list of most urgent tasks or priorities may become vague—or worse, impossible to construct. Most of the draft national security documents give the impression of a complex, eclectic collection of problems, and thus fall short of their main function, which is to show Georgian citizens and the international community a concrete list of concerns and measures aimed to deal with these concerns.

At the same time, practically none of these documents provide any clear division between risk potential and intentional threats. At first sight such a treatment is apparently provided by the draft of the parliamentary group, but this document does not define which of the threats (for instance, "dictate of foreign states," attempts to "enforce alarming agreements," "transit of weapons," "financial panic," "huge foreign debt," "the flow of refugees," etc.) are real or hypothetical.

PROBLEMS REMAINING IN GEORGIAN STRATEGIC THOUGHT

All of the above-mentioned aspects show fluctuations in Georgian strategic thinking. Although the authors of the drafts have often expressed their commitment to human rights, the market economy, democracy, and national sovereignty, the concrete meaning of these principles remains unclear. Against the background of the entrenched Soviet mentality in society, some passages of the drafts may be perceived as restrictions of human rights and individual freedom. Fluctuations of the Georgian strategic thought is the reason that, despite eight years of independence, the government has not formulated a clear strategic message.

At the same time, as stated earlier, there are also the military doctrines adopted by the parliament, as well as the "Basic Principles of Sustainability of Social Life, Strengthening of State Sovereignty and Security, and Restoration of Territorial Integrity of Georgia." Unlike the previously discussed drafts of views of national security strategies, these two documents have a formal status and, therefore, may be regarded as reflecting the real position of the government. The contradictory spirit of these two documents, however, indicates that their authors have rather shaky convictions.

The military doctrine approved in the autumn of 1997 specifies every country of the world as Georgia's partner and considers "intentions of a group of countries to obtain hegemony in the world" and deployment of military units of "some countries" along the frontiers a threat. These general phrases may be illuminated somewhat by noting that the 1993 version of the Russian military doctrine contains a very similar passage. It is unclear why the Georgian military doctrine reiterates the Russian military's concerns, which were based on the threat of NATO expansion into Central and Eastern Europe and the Baltics.

The "Basic Principles" adopted by the parliament in April 1997 seem to be closer to Georgian politicians' real attitudes when confronted by the Russian threat. They specify that some Russian moves are remnants of the old strain of Russian imperialism, while the Russian military presence in the country is regarded as the residual consequence of the 1921 occupation of Georgia by Bolshevik Russia. However, it is interesting that the same document does not oppose any aid that Russia might provide Georgia in its military operations against the Abkhaz separatists. At the same time, the story of how these "principles" were adopted indicates the tenuous nature of Georgian politics. The document received parliamentary approval due to the pressure of the opposition and against the background of protest rallies of refugees from Abkhazia. The executive powers, which carry out practical policies, neither took part in the process of creating this document, nor have they implemented it. It is also noteworthy that these "principles" have not been officially published yet. Was the creation of such a document only due to hard times and the need to let off steam?

Until recently, Georgia, on the one hand, has tried to escape Russian control, and utilize Russian influence and power on the other. As early as 1993 the president of Georgia declared that it was necessary to take into account Russian interests in order to neutralize their negative influence. In 1995, Georgia endorsed the CIS declaration of collective security and made some moves toward closer military cooperation with Russia. In 1996,

Georgia demanded that Russian peacekeeping forces disarm Abkhaz separatists and requested that the Russian Federation impose temporary military rule on this breakaway region. From 1995 to 1997 the president many times specified Russia as Georgia's strategic partner.

However, at the same time Georgia refuses to ratify the 1995 agreement on Russian military bases in the country. In its April 1996 resolution, the Georgian parliament blamed Russian peacekeeprs in Abkhazia for supporting Abkhaz separatists. The same year that Georgia joined the CIS collective security declaration, the government expressed concern that Russia wanted to revise its quotas on conventional armaments set by the Conventional Forces in Europe (CFE) agreement. By spring 1998, the double nature of the Georgian military and foreign policy clearly revealed itself in the pro-Russian orientation of the Ministry of Defense (MOD) on the one hand, and the pro-Western orientation of the Border Guards on the other.

One final problem created by Georgia's underdeveloped strategic thinking is the legal vacuum in the field of defense law and crisis management. There is still no law to regulate responsibilities and missions of the MOD and armed forces. The law "on defense" says little about these problems. There are elements of contradiction and obscurity in the division of responsibilities between the president and parliament in defense policy. According to the constitution, the structure of the armed forces is approved by the president. This is also stated in Article 9 of the law on defense. However, the same law says that the structure of the armed forces shall be stated by law (i.e., parliament). At the same time, listing the parliament's responsibilities, the law on defense does not credit parliament with such a function. Crisis management maintains features of voluntarism; consider, for example, the participation of the former minister for mail and communication and some MPs in the May 1998 fighting between Abkhaz and Georgian forces in Gali.

CONCLUSION

It may be said that the Georgian political elite recognizes the need for developing a cohesive and stable national security strategy. Some steps have been made in this direction, and several versions of a national security strategy have been drafted. Certain events have happened in Georgian politics since 1998 that suggest the Georgian political will to provide national security has increased. A new defense minister has taken office, the International Security Advisory Board (ISAB) started its functions, and in July 1998 the parliament passed a law on the state frontier, according to which Russia is no longer legally responsible for the control of Georgia's borders.

At the same time, many urgent political and economic problems are left, and the prevailing political culture and the norms of behavior of the ruling elite suggest that Georgian strategic thinking will continue to develop in a halting and hesitant manner. By their eclecticism and attempts to match contradictory provisions, the Georgian strategic documents can be likened to the newly approved Russian security concept as a style of traditionalist thinking favored by some developing countries. Concerns about the danger of losing cultural identity and about "fundamental" traditions of the nation are understandable. But their presence in the documents determining national security policy can hardly be considered compatible with intentions toward closer European integration.

Georgian society has never been fanatical. The current ruling elite acknowledges the necessity to respect modern democratic values. But given the poor living conditions of the people, more attention should be given to the popularization of liberal democratic values. The development of a clear-cut national security strategy must play a decisive role in this respect. This strategy is the country's internal and foreign visiting card and must clearly define the state's policy and intentions toward its neighbors and its own citizens. History has shown that it is in everyone's interests if the state's national security strategy is overseen by civilian control over the military and democratic supervision of the government. However, for such controls to be said to exist, the government must create a sound and coherent national security strategy that is agreed upon by all branches and agencies of the government.

U.S. Political Activism in Central Asia

The Case of Kyrgyzstan and Uzbekistan

5

Liam Anderson and Michael Beck

Increasingly, the United States and other Western countries are turning their attention to Central Asia as a zone of strategic significance. They recognize that the Central Asian region has a wealth of resources, including oil, natural gas, gold, and uranium. They also recognize that Central Asia could serve as a conduit for drugs reaching Europe, small arms to conflicts in the region, and strategic missile and nuclear technologies bound for Iran. Finally, they understand that the region could become a battleground of competing cultures and ideas.

In a 1996 *Foreign Affairs* article, Frederick Starr, a leading scholar on the region, rightly called attention to the strategic import of the region.[1] Starr argued that Central Asia could fall under the influence of outside powers or "lapse into chaos" unless stability was insured by Uzbekistan, which he identified as a potential "anchor state" for the region.[2] This idea of a secular, pro-Western Uzbekistan acting as a bulwark against instability, Islamic fundamentalism, and Russian hegemony gained attention in U.S. policy circles. Some U.S. policymakers praised Uzbekistan as "an island of stability" and recognized Uzbekistan's staunch willingness to back U.S. policies in the region.[3] It seems evident, therefore, that in the case of Uzbekistan, the U.S. government's approach is driven by short-term strategic interests at the expense of other goals, such as the promotion of political and economic reforms, or the establishment of basic human rights. In neighboring Kyrgyzstan, meanwhile, President Akayev has made a sincere and concerted effort to push his country through the painful process of political and economic reform, and yet has managed to maintain reasonable stability throughout. At the rhetorical level, the U.S. government seems to recognize the importance of the divergent paths taken by the two countries. The Department of State in particular has been a frequent and vocal critic of Uzbekistan's human rights record, while Akayev has been widely praised within government circles for his reform efforts. At the material level, however, U.S. policy toward the two has been largely indistinguishable. We argue that this policy is misguided for a number of reasons. First, the United States' approach sends troubling signals to other states in the region, and throughout the former Soviet Union as a whole, concerning the sincerity of the United States' committment to support and promote political and economic reforms. Authoritarian and repressive regimes will apparently be tolerated, or even supported, in order to ensure the maintenance of stability. Second, there are increasing signs that the policies adopted by President Karimov in Uzbekistan to maintain his cherished "island of stability" may be in serious danger of provoking precisely the opposite outcome. Hence, the much-vaunted Uzbek "stability" may prove to be more illusory than real. Finally, while the promotion of democratic reforms is often viewed as the "moral dimension" of post–Cold War U.S. foreign policy, this policy can also yield important economic, political, and strategic benefits for the United States, both from a broad perspective, and in the specific context of Central Asia.

We argue that the United States should do more to support Kyrgyzstan, the one state in the region that has made a sincere effort at embracing democratic and market reforms and the one state best equipped to serve as a model for others in the region. Drawing support from a number of empirical studies, we demonstrate that democratic reforms in Central Asia promise to bring greater stability and peace to the region, additional U.S. trade partners, and an alternative to Islamic fundamentalism. Despite the benefits that would come from a region of democratic states with open economies, we find that the United States has sometimes shown less interest in promoting democracy than in securing the short-term stability that is achieved by supporting more authoritarian regimes.

WHY PROMOTE DEMOCRACY?

Regardless of any moral justification for a policy of promoting democracy and market reforms, there are a number of reasons why this policy serves the long-term economic, security, and foreign policy interests of the U.S. First, there is now an overwhelming body of empirical evdience to suggest that democratic states rarely or never fight against each other.[4] According to Levy, the so-called democratic peace phenomenon is "as close as anything we have to an empirical law in international relations."[5] It is also one of the few findings that has sucessfully made the transition from academic to policymaking communities. President Clinton has proclaimed "democracies rarely wage war on one another," a sentiment echoed by a number of key players in the policymaking community. From a U.S. perspective, the lessons of the democratic peace are clear. If democracies do not fight each other, then each new democracy equals one fewer potential adversary. Additionally, the logic of the democratic peace suggests that as the number of democratic dyads in the system increases relative to democratic/nondemocratic and nondemocratic dyads, so the system should become less conflict-prone. While at times the United States has been reluctant to embrace the role of "global policeman," the rest of the world still looks to it to provide leadership in conflict resolution. Bloody conflicts in Somalia, Rwanda, the former Yugoslavia, and Kosovo have confronted the United States with a series of difficult decisions about where, when, and on what scale to intervene. A less conflictual world means fewer such decisions for U.S. policymakers.

The spread of democracy also promises to yield economic payoffs for the United States. Empirically, demonstrating the link between democracy and capitalism is straightforward. Using data drawn from the "Freedom House Index" as a measure of "democraticness," and the "Index of Economic Freedom" as a measure of economic openness, we ran a simple bivariate analysis to examine the relationship between the two variables.[6] The resultant correlation coefficient of .65 indicates what is conventionally considered a "very strong" relationship between democracy and economic openness. The only remaining question surrounds the direction of causal arrows. Does democracy promote economic openness, or vice versa? There is no categorical answer to this question, and in all probability there is an interactive relationship between the two. Nonetheless, while it continues to be relatively commonplace for authoritarian states to operate capitalist economies, it is almost unknown for a democratic state not to embrace free-market capitalism. In turn, as one of the world's most open economies, the United States stands to benefit disproportionately from the opening up of markets on a global scale.

Promoting the diffusion of democratic institutions can also serve the broader foreign policy interests of the United States. An example of this is provided by considering the pattern of support for the United States in the General Assembly of the United Nations. Empirically, even after controlling for potentially confounding factors, a robust relationship emerges between the "democraticness" of a state and the percentage of the time the state votes with the United States in the General Assembly.[7] In simple terms, the more democratic a state, the more supportive it is of U.S. positions in the UN. From a broad perspective, it is reasonable to view General Assembly votes as a way of gauging the opinion of the international community on any particular issue. At a minimum, votes that go against the United States in the UN seriously undermine the credibility of any U.S. claim to be acting on behalf of the international community. While this leaves open the option of acting unilaterally, many of the most pertinent foreign policy issues confronting the United States in the 1990s are very difficult to resolve without concerted, multilateral action. The war against drugs, the spread of terrorism, and the proliferation of weapons of mass destruction are problems that transcend national borders and are thus not amenable to unilateral action.

To summarize briefly, we need make no assumptions about the United States perceiving the promotion of democracy around the world as some form of moral crusade. Regardless of any moral dimension to the U.S. policy of encouraging the spread of democracy around the world, this policy can provide important, tangible benefits to the United States in economic, strategic, and security terms.

THE CENTRAL ASIAN CONTEXT

Aside from the general arguments outlined above, there are a number of context-specific reasons why the promotion of democracy in Central Asia is of particular importance to U.S. national interests. In a July 1997 speech at the Central Asia Institute in Washington, D.C., Acting Secretary of State Strobe Talbott succinctly summarized the importance of democratic and economic reforms in the region:

> If reform in the nations of the Caucasus and Central Asia continues and ulti-mately succeeds, it will encourage similar progress in the other newly inde-pendent states of the former Soviet Union, including in Russia and Ukraine. It will contribute to stability in a strategically vital region that borders China, Turkey, Iran, and Afghanistan, and that has growing economic and social ties with Pakistan and India. The consolidation of free societies, at peace with themselves and with each other, stretching from the Black Sea to the Pamir Mountains, will open up a valuable trade and transport corridor along the old Silk Road, between Europe and Asia.[8]

Moreover, according to Talbott, the failure of reforms in this region could have potentially devastating consequences:

> If economic and political reform . . . does not succeed, if internal and cross-border conflicts simmer and flare, the region could become a breeding ground of terrorism, a hotbed of religious and political extremism, and a bat-tleground for outright war. It would matter profoundly to the United States if that were to happen in an area that sits on as much as 200 billion barrels of oil.[9]

This represents a strikingly unambiguous statement of the magnitude of the stakes involved for the United States in the Southern Tier region of the former Soviet Union. It also highlights the U.S. commitment (at least at the rhetorical level) to support political and economic reforms throughout the region. Examined more closely, however, the critical assumption under-lying these statements is that reforms will "contribute to stability." The experience of most former Soviet states since 1991, however, suggests pre-cisely the reverse. Aside from the Baltic states, reforms elsewhere in the former Soviet Union have generally been accompanied by severe eco-nomic, social, and political upheaval. In Russia and Ukraine for example, it would be difficult to conclude that economic reforms have not contributed to economic and political unrest. Georgia has struggled to maintain a functioning democratic system, but the country's post-independence existence has been fraught with internal strife. The people of Georgia have been ravaged by a brutal civil war pitting Georgian government troops against supporters of an independent Abkhazia (a conflict which resurfaced in May 1998 in the Gali district). Relations are also tense between the central government and both the Muslim-dominated autonomous region of Ajaria and the ethnic Armenian–populated region of Javakheti. While these represent latent rather than actual conflicts, it is clear that central government authority in these regions is, at best, tenuous. The most tragic example of failed political reform is Tajikistan, where the implementation of multi-party democracy soon after independence very rapidly degenerated into a highly destructive civil war that is estimated to have cost over one hundred thousand lives, and that has almost totally demolished the Tajik economy. Aside from Kyrgyzstan in Central Asia, few other former Soviet states have launched serious reform efforts.

Whether the economic, political, and social turmoil that has afflicted most of the states of the former Soviet Union can be causally attributed to attempts at political and economic reform is a debatable question. In a sense, however, it is also an irrelevant question. What may matter more is the growing perception in much of the region that instability and reform are causally linked. This perception in turn, can be used to justify (legitimately or otherwise) the absence of progress toward economic and political reform. This strategy has been used to great effect by President Karimov of Uzbekistan, who has managed to reap the benefits of significant gains from the West while making minimal efforts to advance reforms in his country. By emphasizing the threat posed by Islamic fundamentalism in the region, and by highlighting the instabilities generated by reforms elsewhere in the former Soviet Union, Karimov has succeeded in projecting a powerful image of Uzbekistan as an "island of stability" in the Central Asian region.[10] "Stability" has thus become Uzbekistan's major selling point to the United States and the West, and has provided a convenient excuse for the maintenance of an authoritarian political regime. By framing the debate as a trade-off between stability and reform, Karimov has been largely successful in getting Western policymakers to mute their criticism of Uzbekistan's bleak human rights record and Uzbekistan's failure to introduce meaningful economic and political reforms. Referring to relations between the West and the Central Asian region as a whole, one analyst notes, "The interest of outside powers in the region's wealth and strategic importance means that the rulers receive some scrutiny, but it also means that foreign governments and companies have incentives to flatter rather than pressure them."[11] The Uzbek government also benefits from its "secularism" and portrays itself as a bulwark against a largely nonexistent fundamentalist threat.[12] In a similar vein, one analyst noted that, "In recent years Western countries and organizations have supported the Uzbek government, preferring to take on trust its pro-democracy protestations rather than its determinedly anti-democratic behavior."[13]

It is in this context that the survival of democracy and market reforms in Kyrgyzstan must be judged. On a superficial level Kyrgyzstan constitutes merely one more, rather than one less, democracy in the world. Symbolically, however, the survival of reforms in Kyrgyzstan is of critical importance to the West. The relative degree of social, political, and economic stability enjoyed by Kyrgyzstan as of 1998, despite the significant progress made on reforms, provides a powerful counterexample to the negative experiences with reforms elsewhere in the former Soviet Union. Moreover, the collapse of democracy in Kyrgyzstan would provide regional leaders such as Karimov with important ammunition in the fight to justify to the West their own lack of progress on reforms. Habitually, when offering such justifications, Karimov draws on the example of Tajikistan. In August 1996, for example, in a speech before the Uzbek Supreme Council, Karimov referred to democratic experiments in neighboring states as "pseudo-democracies" and used their negative experiences to excuse his own lack of commitment to political reforms, stating, "This path could have led us to political, social, ethnic, and religious confrontation; to disorder and chaos; and to losing control over the state ... there is no need to look for examples. Neighboring Tajikistan ... and certain other newly independent states speak for themselves. Thank God that He saved us from this path, and prevented us from taking this path."[14] Most observers doubt the sincerity of Karimov's commitment to political reform and view such statements as little more than convenient pretexts for maintaining tight personal control over the levers of state power. As the *Economist Intelligence Unit* notes, "Whether the Tajik civil war ends or not, the very fact that it has happened at all will continue to provide an excuse for the lack of political freedom in Uzbekistan."[15]

The survival of democracy in Kyrgyzstan is, therefore, of immense symbolic value, not least because according to most criteria Kyrgyzstan seems less well-equipped than most to sustain democracy. Unlike neighboring Uzbekistan and Turkmenistan, Kyrgyzstan is virtually devoid of hard-currency-generating natural resources. The Kyrgyz population is also significantly more ethnically heterogeneous than that of Uzbekistan, and is further fragmented along lines of clan affiliation and geographical region. Viewed from the perspective of 1991, there would have been few grounds for predicting the establishment and sustenance of multiparty democracy in such apparently inhospitable terrain. In defiance of the odds, as of 1998, Kyrgyzstan remains among the most democratic and most economically liberal of the former Soviet republics. In contrast, the more ethnically homogeneous and resource-rich Uzbekistan has made next to no progress on economic and political reforms.

COMPARING REFORM IN KYRGYZSTAN AND UZBEKISTAN

Kyrgyzstan

Immediately following the Soviet collapse, Kyrgyz president Akayev set forth a broad program of political and economic reforms. In a region of heavy-handed authoritarianism, Kyrgyzstan has emerged as a relative model of democracy. According to the Freedom House Survey on Political Rights and Civil Liberties, Kyrgyzstan falls into the partly free category, with a score of four, which is among the highest of the post-Soviet states.[16] In 1991, President Akayev moved his country toward multiparty democracy and economic reforms. Despite Communist resistance, Akayev managed to dissolve the legislature and establish a bicameral legislature with a thirty-five-member lower chamber and a seventy-member upper chamber. Since 1994, parliamentary elections and presidential elections have been held. Akayev has also worked with international organizations and the parliament in reforming the electoral system.[17] Akayev, in fact, is the only Central Asian leader to be elected to a second term in a contested election.[18] Several political parties compete for seats in the Kenesh, including the Communist Party, Social Democrats, the Republicans, the Agrarians, Erkin (Freedom), Asaba, and some smaller parties. Unlike his counterparts elsewhere in the former Soviet Union, Akayev views debate with his political foes as a sign of a healthy democracy, not a sign of a government that is teetering on collapse. The willingness to tolerate opposition, criticism, and the creation of a multiparty system led Strobe Talbott to call Akayev "a true democrat" and "about the only man in that part of the world who is not reconstructed of the old regime."[19] Akayev has also spoken of the need for democratic values, such as tolerance and "civic spirit."[20] The notion that political parties should recognize one another as legitimate while engaging in political competition is foreign in much of the former Soviet Union, where those parties or individuals in power prefer to squelch all opposition.

Kyrgyzstan's constitution recognizes the country as a secular state, even though most of the population is Muslim. The country has been open to a wide array of religious denominations, and most Kyrgyz citizens enjoy the freedom of assembly and worship. Religious groups, including Christians and Jews, worship openly without fear of persecution. The only requirement is that groups register with authorities. There are around thirty-five different religious groups that have registered with the government, from Baptist churches to Baha'i and Krishna communities.[21] The government has also been relatively tolerant of Christian missionaries, despite concerns among the Islamic and Orthodox clergy that Christians are winning converts.

Economic Reforms

Among the new independent states of the former Soviet Union, Kyrgyzstan has introduced some of the most significant economic reforms. The government has freed prices, established an independent central bank, and lifted financial restrictions. Despite resistance from Communists in the parliament, Akayev also privatized land and key industries. As of 1998, the government had privatized five thousand enterprises or about 62 percent of all enterprises and 90 percent of all land. Moreover, nearly 70 percent of Kyrgyzstan's GDP came from the private sector.

Akayev has also sought to prompt economic growth by initiating legislation that would attract private investment, promote entrepreneurship, and increase exports.[22] Moreover, his team recognized the need for an independent judicial authority that is capable of building a law-based state that will provide the necessary order for bringing about economic reforms. Akayev argued that land reform and policies to increase investment would favor the emergence of a middle-class.

Uzbekistan

In contrast to the bold reform effort in Kyrgyzstan, Uzbekistan is a one-party state rigidly controlled by President Islam Karimov, who has shown little willingness to relinquish his tight grip on power.[23] An examination of the Freedom House survey on Political Rights and Civil Liberties finds Uzbekistan in the category of "not free" states, which also includes such states as Iran, Kenya, and Liberia. Uzbekistan has a score of 6.5 on a 7-point scale.[24] In many ways, Uzbekistan is less democratic in the 1990s than it was at the end of the 1980s.

Karimov was elected president in a 1991 election that was neither free nor fair, and had his term extended to the year 2000 by holding a referendum in 1995. This referendum to cancel elections and extend Karimov's rule was also suspect because in order to oppose the measure one had to request a special ballot from government officials monitoring elections and then cast the ballot in a specially designated booth. Not surprsingly, few Uzbeks chose to voice dissent. Karimov has also silenced opposition parties. During past elections, the largest opposition group (Birlik) was not allowed to register, and the Islamic Renaissance Party was banned.[25]

Karimov's grip on power is unchecked by the legislative and judicial branches, and the rule of law is virtually nonexistent despite "democratic" rhetoric coming from the government. The Oliy Majlis, Uzbekistan's parliament, simply rubber-stamps initiatives from the president rather than introducing new legislation. Karimov contends that tough policies are necessary, stating, "In historic periods, especially when a people attains statehood or in transition periods from one system to another, a strong executive power is indispensable. It is necessary to avoid confrontations and bloodshed."[26] Karimov insists that a strong hand is needed to build an environment in which a "democratic state" can function.[27] Karimov even rationalizes human rights abuses in Uzbekistan by pointing to racial problems in the United States, noting that "ten to fifteen years ago black people were shot and were treated like dirt."[28]

Not surprisingly, basic human rights in Uzbekistan are in short supply. While the human rights record of Kyrgyzstan is by no means perfect, it is without question superior to Uzbekistan's performance. The annual U.S. State Department human rights report notes several abuses of human rights by Uzbek authorities.[29] The report chronicles cases of police torture, and the arbitrary detention of citizens, human rights workers, and political opponents. Authorities are known to detain and arrest opposition and religious figures for offenses such as drug possession, illegal possession of arms, and narcotics.[30] Karimov released eighty political prisoners in 1996 in an effort to win support from Washington, but according to human rights organizations, there are still some twenty to thirty political prisoners held by Uzbek authorities.[31]

Freedom of speech and press are also notably lacking in Uzbekistan. The government has shown great intolerance of criticism in the press. All publications must register with state authorities. In 1991 a law was issued that prohibits "offending the honor and dignity of the President." This law limits the ability or willingness of journalists and ordinary citizens to criticize President Karimov. Newspapers are subject to government censorship.[32] The last of all opposition newspapers, that of the Erk party, was banned in 1993.[33] In addition, those who speak out about the lack of this freedom may be removed from their jobs. In 1994 a U.S. professor from the University of Indiana visiting Uzbekistan to examine freedom of the press was deported.

As noted above, opposition parties have found Uzbekistan to be a hostile environment. The Birlik movement and the Erk party were denied the right to register, and most legitimate opposition group leaders have gone into exile.[34] The Uzbek constitution and a 1991 amendment ban all parties that are of a religious nature. In the past several years, Karimov has allowed several parties to form, but these parties—which include the Fatherland Party, the Peasants' Party, and the Communist Party—do not present any serious challenge to Karimov.

Uzbek authorities have also been intolerant of some Islamic groups in the country. The government has sought to regulate the Islamic hierarchy and censor Islamic publications. Uzbek authorities have also used the pretext of Islamic extremism to keep political activists imprisoned.[35] Imams who fail to tow the government line may be removed from their positions. Moreover, there has been no progress in the investigation of the kidnapping of former vice president Shukrullo Mirsaidov and his sons or in the disappearance of Abdullah Utaev, leader of a chapter of the Islamic Renaissance Party. Security agencies are also known to wiretap telephone calls of opposition party members.[36] Despite attempts in 1996 and 1997 to affirm Uzbekistan's commitment to human rights, 1998 brought increased repression of Islamic activists and harassment of Islamic dissidents as Karimov continued to make claims that foreign-financed extremists were seeking to topple the government.[37] In the Fergana Valley region, Uzbek authorities launched a major crackdown against "Islamic extremism," targeting in particular men with beards and women in veils and arresting them on trumped-up charges after evidence was planted. In particular, the crackdown has targeted those who subscribe to Wahhabism, which refers to a Saudi Islamic movement bent on purifying the faith.[38]

Karimov has defended his crackdown on fundamentalism, contending that to allow fundamentalism to take hold would be to spawn civil unrest. Karimov once declared that a hundred persons arrested are better than a thousand killed.[39] Some outside observers and opposition activists claim that this attempt to clamp down on Islam is designed to divert public attention from economic stagnation in the country.[40] According to Mikhail Ardzinov, president of the Independent Human Rights Association of Uzbekistan, "The government itself is creating fundamentalism."[41]

Economic Reforms

President Karimov has chosen to introduce economic reforms slowly, opting for a very gradual easing of government reigns on the economy. He has rejected any "shock" programs and has pursued what many have argued parallels the Chinese model of reform.[42] The argument of the Karimov government is that market reforms should not be pursued at the expense of social stability. To that end, the government continues to subsidize inefficient state enterprises and to provide large credits to agriculture. President Karimov has also opposed implementation of reform measures called for by international lending institutions. In Uzbekistan, the state still dominates most of the economy aside from some small businesses. As of 1998, only about 12 percent of small-scale, state-owned enterprises were privatized. The lack of a convertible currency coupled with burdensome foreign investment regulations began to discourage foreign investors in the late 1990s. The government placed barriers on the import of consumer goods despite opposition from Western governments and investors. Furthermore, the government does not provide reliable economic data. Uzbek data conflicts sharply with projections of growth by the IMF and other international groups.

While Karimov's proposal of introducing market reforms slowly may bear fruit, his argument that stability is the precondition of political and economic development begs further examination. Is Karimov most interested in guaranteeing stability for the good of the country, or are demands for stability little more than a pretext for his political ambitions? Is a strong hand in Uzbekistan a necessary condition for ensuring Uzbekistan's sovereignty and a move toward a more democratic society? Despite grounds for criticism, Karimov's policies are popular among the majority of the populace. Karimov has been credited with stabilizing Uzbekistan. He succeeded in building a state while civil war raged in Afghanistan and Tajikistan. He managed to build an Uzbek military and to de-Russify the officer corps. Finally, Karimov has pursued economic policies that have ensured greater independence in the realms of agriculture and energy. While Karimov had initial success, his unwillingness to loosen control of the economy and government are gradually proving to sow discontent and economic stagnation.

U.S. POLICY IN CENTRAL ASIA

Although the United States' stated policy in the region is to support those governments that pursue democratic and market reforms, it is not clear that Kyrgyzstan has seen benefits corresponding to its willingness to pursue reforms. Instead, it appears that Uzbekistan initially gained as much or more political and financial support from the United States as Kyrgyzstan, despite Karimov's poor human rights record and authoritarian grip on almost all sectors of Uzbek society.

U.S. policy was in part dictated by the defense establishment in the United States, which promulgated the view that Uzbekistan had a key role to play as an anti-Russian and anti-Iranian buffer. This approach meant that the United States had little political leverage to use against Uzbekistan and was willing to continue providing financial assistance despite Karimov's harsh policies. The United States also on occasion softened its criticism of Karimov and Uzbekistan's human rights record because Uzbekistan is seen as a key player in efforts to exploit Central Asia's resources. Most observers saw occasional moves by Karimov to release political prisoners or to otherwise improve human rights as token gestures to ensure that the West would not withhold support. For example, prior to his 1996 visit to the United States, Karimov released a group of opposition activists.

Karimov's political gestures seemed to win friends in Washington. Despite Uzbekistan's unwillingness to adopt political and economic changes, the United States provided roughly $144 million in humanitarian aid, technical assistance, and investment support to Uzbekistan.[43] The United States formed a joint commission on economic cooperation for strengthening bilateral economic relations and for encouraging Uzbekistan's integration into international economic structures. In January 1994 the United States entered a bilateral agreement with Uzbekistan providing for Most Favored Nation (MFN) status for products from both countries.[44] In 1998 the United States allocated $19 million to further market reforms and bilateral economic ties. The U.S. government has also provided support for U.S. companies seeking to invest in Uzbekistan, securing over $400 million in U.S. investments. The United States Overseas Private Investment Corporation also provided a $200-million insurance policy for a U.S.-Uzbek joint venture, Zarafshan-Newmont, to expand gold production.[45] The U.S. Export Import Bank has provided over $500 million in direct loans, guarantees, and export credit insurance policies since 1992.

Uzbekistan has been a major beneficiary of other sources of Western foreign aid. Prior to 1998 the World Bank commitments to Uzbekistan totaled $327 million for five projects.[46] In 1998 the Asian Development Bank approved a $70-million-dollar loan for enhancing railroad repairs along the old Silk Route.[47] Also, Japan is helping to finance a project that will modernize airports in Samarkand, Bukhara, and Urgench.

The European Union has also decided to overlook Uzbekistan's human rights record and failure to introduce democratic and market reforms. Hans van den Broek, the European commissioner responsible for relations with Uzbekistan, has downplayed Uzbekistan's unwillingness to make crucial reforms and continued to call for implementation of a trade deal between the EC and Uzbekistan, the Partnership and Cooperation Agreement (PCA). Within the European Commission, there has been support for pushing this partnership through the European parliament given the ability of Uzbekistan to play a key geopolitical role in Central Asia as an anti-Russian ally. The Commission has pushed for ratification despite the fact that Uzbekistan was to have shown improvement in human rights and made the som (Uzbek currency) convertible prior to the agreement.

Kyrgyzstan too has received Western aid as a reward for its willingness to follow the prescriptions set forth by the West. In fact, Kyrgyzstan has received more per capita aid from the United States and Europe than any other former Soviet republic.[48] Nonetheless, in raw money terms, the quantity of aid disbursed to Kyrgyzstan by the United States annually is meager. In 1997, for example, U.S. foreign aid to Kyrgyzstan totalled just over $20 million, a figure similar in magnitude to that received by states such as Ireland, Benin, Madagascar, and Guinea, and significantly smaller than that granted to Senegal, Malawi, and Liberia.

Kyrgyzstan has also received recognition from multilateral lending institutions for the structural reforms to its economy carried out since 1991. By the end of the 1990s, for example, Kyrgyzstan had received loans from the World Bank totalling over $300 million, while the IMF approved $44 million in loans in 1997 and nearly $30 million in 1998. However, while Kyrgyzstan's reform efforts have enabled it to access loans, the much-needed influx of foreign investment has been slow to materialize, despite strenuous efforts on the part of Akayev to create a hospitable climate for foreign investors. The little foreign investment that has been made in the Kyrgyz economy has not come from the West, but primarily from Russia, China,

Kazakhstan, and other CIS countries. U.S. foreign direct investment in Kyrgyzstan is roughly equal to that of Iran, one of principal foes of the United States in the region. Clearly, the U.S. government cannot compel the private sector to invest in specific economies, but there are several institional mechanisms available, such as the Ex-Im Bank or OPIC, which could be used to encourage and promote American investment in Kyrgyzstan. Kyrgyzstan lacks the kind of resources that offer short-term opportunities for large returns on capital investment, but in several areas, for example agriculture or tourism, there is considerable potential over the long term for a return on investment.

AN ASSESSMENT OF U.S. POLICY IN CENTRAL ASIA

However well conceived in its broad outlines, U.S. policy toward Uzbekistan has been poorly executed. By providing political and economic support to President Karimov, the United States has sought to sustain an island of stability in a strategically important and highly volatile region. A stable, pro-Western Uzbekistan would, in turn, provide a crucial front line of defense against the spread of Islamic fundamentalism and the threat of revived Russian expansionism. As a trade-off for preserving stability, the United States accepted Karimov's argument that the political and economic reform process in Uzbekistan should be gradual rather than sudden. As of 1999, however, there is growing evidence that none of the key U.S. policy goals have been achieved.

Economically, following initial successes, the failure to implement meaningful reforms has begun to affect the Uzbek economy detrimentally. Prior to 1997, Uzbekistan's conservative policies seemed to be working as inflation was down and foreign investment, production, and wages seemed to be on the rise. Karimov's opposition to "shock-therapy"and attempts to shield Uzbeks from inflation won widespread domestic support. After a relatively slow rate of decline in GDP prior to 1994, soaring inflation forced the government to institute a number of genuine economic reforms, including stricter fiscal policy, cooperation with international lending institutions, and greater effort to attract private investment. This effort to attract investment met with relative success. The number of U.S. and other Western companies registered in Uzbekistan grew rapidly. U.S.-Uzbek trade more than doubled in the first half of 1996.[49] However, as imports grew, Uzbekistan erected import barriers that frightened away investors.[50] Problems with currency convertibility have also deterred some investors. In addition, the European Bank for Reconstruction and Development is threatening to curtail its support of Uzbekistan because of the barriers to free trade that have not been removed. It now appears that Uzbekistan will be unable to avoid many of the economic troubles that initially plagued those states that chose to introduce changes rapidly. In fact, Uzbekistan may find itself now trying to catch up to its neighbors that have gained greater experience in attracting Western investment and are more comfortable in free-market practices.

Politically, a veneer of stability has been sustained through the use of repressive policies to silence opposition to the regime. Karimov has been particularly harsh in recent treatment of suspected fundamentalist groups; indeed, in a parliamentary speech of May 1998 Karimov asserted, "Such people should be shot in the head. If necessary, I'll shoot them myself."[51] There is a broad consensus among observers, however, both that the Islamic threat has been deliberately exaggerated by Karimov for political purposes and that, ironically, the real danger is that Karimov's repressive policies may help to create a threat where none had previously existed.

Strategically, the reliability of Uzbekistan as a U.S. ally in the region is becoming questionable. One example of evidence is provided by the changing pattern of Uzbek voting practices in the United Nations over the course of the 1990s. From 1994 to 1997 Uzbekistan engaged in classic real politik by voting with the United States in the United Nations on almost all issues. Analysts from Uzbekistan agreed that this was largely a political move designed to earn goodwill at no cost, attract U.S. investment and assistance, and to prompt the United States to tone down criticism of human rights problems in Uzbekistan.[52] Uzbekistan was one of only two states in the United Nations that did not condemn the U.S. blockade of Cuba and sanctions against Iran. However, in 1998, as U.S.-Uzbek relations deteriorated, Uzbekistan reversed its decision and refused to support the United States in the vote against the Cuban blockade and also became critical of U.S. sanctions against Iran. Uzbek media also condemned U.S. missile attacks on Iraq, marking the first time in several years that U.S. foreign policy had been criticized by Uzbekistan.[53] The deterioration in U.S.-Uzbek relations confirms the danger of pursuing a policy that seeks to promote stability by supporting "friendly" regional hegemons or authoritarian regimes. Regardless of how friendly or how willing Central Asian leaders are to combat fundamentalism, to counter Russian designs, or to vote with the United States in the United Nations, if they are not "democratic," their support may rest on shallow foundations.

Overall, therefore, the United States policy of extending political and economic support to the Karimov regime has failed to yield the expected dividends. One problem is that U.S. policy is premised on the dubious assumption that an authoritarian regime at the heart of Central Asia is preferable to an Islamic fundamentalist regime. Yet these are not the only alternatives; indeed, neighboring Kyrgyzstan offers a powerful reminder that reforms and stability are not mutually exclusive, as Kyrgyzstan clearly lacks the resources and population to play an "anchor" role in the heartland of Central Asia. Its importance to the United States is therefore largely symbolic. What the relative success of the reform process in Kyrgyzstan provides is a compelling and positive alternative to the authoritarian and fundamentalist models. Conversely, if the democratic experiment in Kyrgyzstan is allowed to fail, then this failure will be taken by other states in the region as further confirmation of the incompatibility of stability and reforms. The United States, therefore, has a great deal at stake in ensuring the continued survival of democracy in Kyrgyzstan, yet U.S. policy has failed to reflect this for most of the 1990s.

Although the United States has assisted Kyrgyzstan in some important ways, more must be done to ensure that the reform effort sees its way through a very difficult period. First, the United States must do more to ensure that the agricultural sector is reformed. Now that collective farms have been sold off, individual farmers need capital, modern farm equipment, education in modern farming, and assistance in marketing.[54] Some 60 percent of Kyrgyzstan's adults are employed in the agricultural sector. The United States can also help Kyrgyzstan by ensuring that it has the distribution infrastructure, storage capability, and packaging equipment needed to sell its agricultural products on the international marketplace. The United States could also assist Kyrgyzstan in building the infrastructure needed to attract tourism, which might also provide the country with an influx of capital and jobs. The United States should also do more to encourage investment in Kyrgyzstan. If institutions are not in place for attracting major investors, the United States should invest greater resources in upgrading infrastructure in an effort to attract capital to Kyrgyzstan. While it is true that the United States cannot coerce U.S. or other businesses to invest where they do not wish, they can help put in place institutions that will attract outside investment. Finally, the United States should also invest additional resources toward building viable political institutions and NGOs. Fortunately for Kyrgyzstan, and unlike most other states of Central Asia, a large body of NGOs are working to turn the tide and to further reform efforts. The United States can intensify its support of a civil society promoted by NGOs in Kyrgyzstan. Together, these U.S. efforts will offer insurance that Kyrgyzstan's reform efforts will not be viewed in the former Soviet Union as yet another example of the dangers of pursuing a Western-inspired democratic path.

6

Emerging Political Order in the New Caspian States

Azerbaijan, Kazakhstan, and Turkmenistan

Shirin Akiner

INTRODUCTION

In the early nineteenth century Russia, having annexed most of Trans-caucasia and much of western Kazakhstan, became the dominant power in the Caspian Sea. The Gulistan Pact of 1813 and the Treaty of Turkman-chai of 1828 allowed Iran some rights of access to the Caspian Sea, but gave Russia the exclusive right to maintain a fleet of warships. After the Bolshevik revolution of 1917 these unequal arrangements (always much resented in Iran) were abrogated, to be replaced in 1921 by the Iran-Soviet Friendship Treaty. In theory this gave equal rights of access to the two sig-natories, but in practice Russia, and subsequently the Soviet Union, con-tinued to play the dominant role. In Transcaucasia and Central Asia there were brief struggles for national independence, but by the early 1920s Soviet rule had been established in these regions. Hence, from this period until the collapse of the Soviet Union at the end of 1991, there were only two state entities bordering the Caspian Sea: the Soviet Union and Iran.

With the disintegration of the Soviet Union three new littoral states came into existence: Azerbaijan, Kazakhstan, and Turkmenistan. Today, they are grappling with the complexities of rapid economic and social tran-sition. They are also faced with the need to construct a new political order. The responses of these new states to the challenges of the post-Soviet era have many common features. This is not surprising, since they have had similar experiences over the past seven decades of Soviet rule. Moreover, the titular peoples in each of these states are ethnically Turkic and by reli-gion (at least nominally) Muslim. Yet increasingly, there is a divergence in the pace and style of reform. This is partly rooted in different historical experiences. Partly, too, it is the result of geographic location, which in turn determines in large measure the opportunities for contact with the global community, and hence exposure to external influences and pressures. There are also significant differences in size of territory and population, likewise in social and ethnic composition. All of these elements are currently interacting in dynamic fusion, and mediating—often erratically—the process of change.

The problems of transition are not of course unique to this region. However, here they attract particular attention because these countries, as well as the Caspian Sea itself, possess world-class reserves of hydrocarbons. Foreign oil and gas companies have already made large-scale investments in research and development. Competing export pipeline projects are the focus of fierce lobbying at national and international levels. Whether it will be possible to continue to attract the foreign investment that is required in order to exploit fully the economic potential of the region will depend to some extent on the level of political risk. This in turn will largely be determined by internal developments in these new countries. This chapter examines the principal features of the emergent post-Soviet political systems in Azerbaijan, Kazakhstan, and Turkmenistan and attempts to draw some conclusions about likely future trends. Some background information is given in Appendix 1 (basic data) and Appendix 2 (historical outline).

INDEPENDENCE

In order to set post-Soviet developments in Azerbaijan, Kazakhstan, and Turkmenistan in context it is necessary to bear in mind the situation at the time of the collapse of the Soviet Union. In August 1991 conservative forces in Moscow staged a coup d'état to remove President Gorbachev from power. The attempt failed, but it accelerated the process of disintegration that culminated in the formal dissolution of the Soviet Union a few months later. Several Soviet republics declared their independence during this period, including Azerbaijan (August30)[1] and Turkmenistan (October 27); Kazakhstan was the last to follow suit (December 16), but only after it became clear that the Soviet Union had effectively ceased to exist.[2]

In Turkmenistan and Kazakhstan, prior to the events of August 1991, there had been no liberation movements or demands for autonomy. On the contrary, there was considerable support for remaining within the Soviet Union.[3] Consequently, these countries were in no way prepared for independence when it came. They were still bound to the "center" psychologically, as well as by a myriad of formal and informal links. The suddenness with which the Union collapsed could well have led to turmoil. In fact, the constitutional transition from Soviet republic to independent state took place almost imperceptibly. This was chiefly because the leadership in these republics remained unaltered and firmly in control. In the political sphere there was thus continuity, which mitigated the sense of shock and uncertainty.

The situation in Azerbaijan was very different. Here a sense of national awareness, and concomitantly of anti-Soviet sentiment, had crystallized before the collapse of the Soviet Union. It was prompted by the war over Karabakh (also known as Nagorno-Karabakh).[4] The train of events that led to the outbreak of hostilities gathered momentum in 1987, when the Armenian population of Karabakh, an autonomous province within Azerbaijan, began actively to demand unification with Armenia. This provoked a furious reaction from the Azeris and in 1989 led to a massacre of Armenians in Azerbaijan (nearly half a million Armenians were domiciled in Azerbaijan at this time). The Armenian government retaliated by expelling thousands of Azeris from its territory. There were further attacks on the Armenian population in Baku, the Azeri capital, in early 1990. The central government sent in troops to restore law and order and reinstate Soviet rule. In the ensuing clashes many Azeris were killed. On January 6, 1992, Karabakh declared its independence. A full-scale war broke out between Azerbaijan and the Karabakh Armenians. The latter made rapid gains. The newly formed Azeri army achieved some successes, but by early 1993 the Karabakh Armenians were once more in the ascendancy and before the end of the year had taken control of the entire southwest of Azerbaijan (approximately 20 percent of the territory of the state). By May 1994 an estimated twenty-five thousand people had been killed in the war. A cease-fire was declared and international peacekeeping initiatives were launched. At the time of writing, the cease-fire remains in place, but there has been no final resolution of the conflict.[5]

Anti-Armenian feeling, as well as anger over Russia's perceived support for the Karabakh Armenians, precipitated a wave of nationalism in Azerbaijan. The Popular Front movement emerged as a powerful political force in the late 1980s. Fervently anti-Communist in outlook, it began to reassert ideas of Azeri identity and to lead the struggle against Soviet domination. Other nationalist groups also took shape at this time, some consciously drawing on the legacy of the brief era of pre-Soviet national independence. However, Communist Party officials continued to dominate the government. It was only after the defeat of Azeri troops in 1992 that the leader of the Popular Front, Abulfaz Elçibey, was able to make a bid for power. He was elected president in June of that year on an anti-Russian, pro-Turkish platform. He promised democratic reforms within the country and victory in Karabakh. He did not succeed in delivering either, finally, and the country began to slip into chaos. By 1993 he had lost control of the situation and was forced from office, to be succeeded by a former Communist leader, Heidar Aliev. Aliev restored law and order domestically and in his foreign policy pursued a more evenhanded approach in relations with neighboring countries. A cordial attitude was adopted toward Russia and Iran, though strategic distance continued to be retained; relations with Turkey remained good, but were given less prominence than under the previous leader.

The economic consequences of the disintegration of the Soviet Union were severe in all three countries. Previously they had formed part of a single economic space, a single economic system. As other Soviet republics, they did not have separate national economies. When the Soviet Union collapsed, budgetary transfers from the central government suddenly ceased, causing serious shortfalls in the funding of social welfare services. Trade and transport links were also abruptly dislocated, leading to massive bottlenecks and shortages. Hasty and ill-prepared attempts at economic reform exacerbated the problems. There was soon hyperinflation and soaring unemployment. Manufacturing industries ground to a halt and the agricultural sector was devastated. Poverty and deprivation became widespread.[6] In Azerbaijan, the cost of the war with Karabakh and the influx of nearly a million refugees imposed crippling additional burdens.

However, there was general optimism about the future as it was believed at the government as well as the popular level that exploitation of the region's rich hydrocarbon resources would provide a solution to its economic woes. After independence several major oil and gas deals were concluded with international consortiums, but to date revenues have fallen far short of local expectations. Reasons for this include such factors as problems over export routes; lack of clarity over the legal status of the Caspian Sea, hampering offshore developments; and unprecedentedly low world prices for hydrocarbons.[7] These difficulties will no doubt be overcome eventually, hence the long-term economic outlook for these countries remains favorable. In the short term, however, the rate of recovery is likely to be slow. Consequently, there will probably not be a significant improvement in the living standards of the population at large in the near future.

LEADERSHIP

Since the collapse of the Soviet Union the dominant feature of the political systems in Azerbaijan, Kazakhstan, and Turkmenistan has undoubtedly been the role of the leader. Power today is overwhelmingly concentrated in the hands of the incumbent presidents—Heidar Aliev, Nursultan Nazarbaev, and Saparmurad Niyazov, respectively. All three came to prominence during the Soviet period. They were groomed within the Communist Party hierarchy and acquired legitimacy and authority as they rose through the ranks. Equally importantly, they honed their survival skills in the harsh school of intrigue and competing interests that characterized the Soviet system. Their career paths during this period are superficially similar in that they held important posts both within their own republics as well as in Moscow, but the focuses of their activities were somewhat different.

Heidar Aliev (b. 1923) spent his early career in the KGB, eventually becoming the first Azeri to head the KGB of Azerbaijan (a post previously reserved for Slavs). A Brezhnev protégé, he served as first secretary of the Communist party of Azerbaijan from 1969 until 1982 and thereafter, under

Yuri Andropov, was elevated to the central party leadership as a full member of the Politburo.[8] In 1987, under Gorbachev, he fell from favor and was removed from this post. His political prospects looked bleak. He subsequently returned to Azerbaijan and for a time headed the local parliament in his home province of Nakhichevan. During this period, however, far from withdrawing from the national scene, he consolidated his power base within the republic. The turmoil that ensued following the collapse of the Soviet Union and the Azeri military fiasco in Karabakh provided him with the opportunity to return to power. In 1993, he was elected president of Azerbaijan with a majority of just under 100 percent.[9] He was re-elected in 1998. (See section on "Elections and Referendums" below.)

Nursultan Nazarbaev (b. 1940) worked in industry for several years before turning to full-time employment in the Communist party administration. In 1984 he became chairman of the Council of Ministers of Kazakhstan. His real rise to prominence, however, came under Mikhail Gorbachev. In 1986 he was made a member of the Central Committee of the Communist Party of the Soviet Union, based in Moscow. Concurrently, from 1989 to 1991, he served as first secretary of the Communist Party of Kazakhstan. In 1990 he became the first president of Kazakhstan (still part of the Soviet Union), elected unopposed to this post by the Supreme Soviet of the republic. In early 1991 it was widely thought that he might be elevated to some prominent all-Union role, possibly as deputy to President Gorbachev. Before the end of the year, however, the Soviet Union had ceased to exist. In December 1991 he was reconfirmed as president of Kazakhstan by a nationwide (though uncontested) general election for five years.[10] His term of office has since been extended first by referendum, then by a somewhat questionable election in January 1999. (See section on "Elections and Referendums" below.)

Saparmurad Niyazov (b. 1940) spent most of his early career working in the Communist Party apparatus in Leningrad (where he had studied) and in Turkmenistan. From the mid-1980s he concentrated on accumulating power in Turkmenistan. Like Nazarbaev, he was a Gorbachev protégé. In 1985 he became chairman of the Council of Ministers and from 1986 to 1991 was first secretary of the Communist Party of Turkmenistan; in 1990 he also became chairman of the Supreme Soviet of Turkmenistan and a few months later president. He was reelected in an uncontested poll in 1992. In January 1994 his term of office was extended by referendum to the year 2002.[11] (See section on "Elections and Referendums" below.)

After the collapse of the Soviet Union, Aliev, Nazarbaev, and Niyazov skillfully transformed themselves from Soviet officials to national heroes. They had not been freedom fighters, but rather, passive observers of a chain of events over which they had little control. Nevertheless, they soon succeeded in constructing images of themselves as "founding fathers" of the new states, and moreover, as the unique guarantors of independence, stability, and communal harmony. There has certainly been a notable degree of civic order and an impressive lack of friction under their rule. Detractors claim that this would have been the case whether or not these individuals had been in power. It is impossible to know, but it seems likely that the strong leadership that they have exercised has helped to maintain equilibrium.

Their record on political reform has been less positive. All have vociferously proclaimed their commitment to democratization and pluralism. However, there has to date been little real movement toward creating more liberal societies. The constitutions of these countries originally gave the president wide powers, but also set certain limitations, including constraints on age and on number of terms of office. These have been gradually removed by decrees and referendums. At the same time, the incumbents have established personal control over virtually every sphere of public life in their respective states. All have promoted members of their family and "clan" (friends, relations, and clients) to key positions in the state apparatus, the legal system, the economy, and the media. They have also stacked the bureaucracy and the provincial governments with their supporters. Thus, they have created a core network of loyal henchmen.[12] A massive personality cult has been orchestrated around each of them, marked by numerous portraits in public places and adulatory commentaries in the official media. This phenomenon is most pronounced in Turkmenistan,[13] but is also evident in the other two countries.

Opponents and critics have sometimes described the presidents of Azerbaijan, Kazakhstan, and Turkmenistan as dictators. They have certainly established authoritarian monocracies. The concept of collective leadership, which was embedded in every level of the Soviet political hierarchy, has been abandoned. Consequently, the opportunities that were formerly provided by the politburos at republican and all-Union levels for discussion, consultation, and mediation of conflicting group interests have been greatly narrowed. Policy-making—insofar as it is possible to identify how and where this process takes place—now appears to be solely in the hands of the leader. Coercion is used to maintain public support for the incumbent regimes, though this generally takes an indirect form, for example, through manipulation of the media and the selective use of the law as a means of curbing incipient opposition.[14] Undoubtedly these leaders resemble the absolutist heads of state that are found in many parts of the developing world rather more than they do the constitution-bound presidents of Western countries. Nevertheless, compared with the brutal rulers that have come to power in some countries in Asia and Africa, they conduct relatively restrained regimes. There are reasonably sound legal systems in place and the rights of the individual are more often than not respected.

The security services remain, as during the Soviet period, an important tool for checking and controlling social behavior. Fear of reprisals—often an imagined threat rather than an actual danger (a legacy of the random terror of the Soviet past)—acts as a powerful incentive to concur with official policies and to accept unquestioningly the explanations provided by the authorities. Instances of violations of human rights, most frequently in connection with the suppression of political opposition, are widespread in all three countries. However, they do not extend to gross abuses such as the systematic use of torture or arbitrary executions.[15] The presidents do recognize, if only as a matter of political expediency, the need to work with international organizations in order to establish standards that are in line with commonly accepted norms. Progress is certainly slow, but in each of the three countries there has been some improvement in this area over the past few years.

The personal style of the presidents is sometimes likened to that of the autocratic khans of the precolonial period. It is a colorful metaphor and certainly similarities in attitude and conduct can be traced. However, closer and more recent parallels may be found in the political elites of the Soviet period. Leonid Brezhnev in particular has been an influential role model. A less terrifying figure than Stalin, he nevertheless wielded huge power and was surrounded by a personality cult on a grandiose scale. He drew his support from the formal state/party organs, as well as from extensive informal patronage networks. This pattern of leadership has been replicated in the newly independent states (and not only in the Caspian region, but also elsewhere in the former Soviet Union). Brezhnev's behavior toward his subordinates—jovial informality alternating with excoriating rudeness—is also characteristic of the style of the present leaders. Likewise in the opulence of his personal tastes (which reputedly included a liking for foreign cars), he set a trend that has been maintained by the presidents of today, most notably in Turkmenistan. The imprint of other Soviet leaders is less immediately apparent. Yet there are striking similarities (even if coincidental) between the persona of Mikhail Gorbachev in the late 1980s, exuding charm and self-confidence in the international arena, and that of Nursultan Nazarbaev in the early 1990s. Likewise, the intellectual control of Heidar Aliev is reminiscent of the austere style of Yuri Andropov.

On a more abstract plane, a formative influence on the style of leadership of the new presidents has been the Communist Party, no longer as a source of doctrine, but rather as a mode of government. Yet whereas in the past they were constituent parts of the Party apparatus, today they have subsumed and personalized the role of the Party. Hence, it is they who are now "the guiding force of society," formerly the prerogative of the Party. Similarly, those who disagree with the presidents are treated with the same intolerance as were dissidents during the Soviet era. This sense of having a monopoly on wisdom has been translated, in rhetorical terms, into a paternalistic discourse, with the president cast in the role of sage father to the young nation. This approach is most strongly articulated in Turkmenistan, but is also evident in Kazakhstan and Azerbaijan.

INSTITUTION-BUILDING

Post-Soviet institution-building has been largely driven and shaped by the incumbent leaders. There are two main strands to the process. One has focused on the consolidation of new state and national identities through the creation of symbols, rituals, and histories. The other has sought to create new constitutional frameworks and organs of state management. In Turkmenistan, President Niyazov has been the guiding force in both areas. In Kazakhstan likewise, President Nazarbaev has played an influential, though generally lower-profile, role in developing new institutions. In Azerbaijan, the process of national rebirth began before President Aliev came to power and to some extent occurred spontaneously. In the shaping of the present constitution and state organs, however, he has had considerable influence. In Azerbaijan and Kazakhstan, Western democratic institutions have provided the theoretical model for constitutional and parliamentary reforms; the way in which those models are applied in practice, though, still owes much to the Soviet past. In Turkmenistan, native precedents have been used as the inspiration for new institutions. Other institutions (for example, political parties, independent media) are emerging far more slowly.

Symbols and Historicization

Azerbaijan was the first of these three countries to reject the Soviet-era state symbols. In their stead, the flag, emblem, and national anthem of the first independent Azerbaijan republic (1918–20) were reinstated. The nationalizing project included the renaming of cities, streets, public buildings, institutions, and titles, where possible reverting to pre-Soviet designations. An analogous process took place, though more gradually and starting slightly later, in Kazakhstan and Turkmenistan. New flags, emblems, and anthems were devised in both countries, aimed at encapsulating the nation's cultural heritage.[16] There was also extensive renaming of places and institutions.[17] National currencies were adopted in 1992–93.[18] In all three countries artists and scholars have provided the intellectual validation for the new identities. In particular, there has been a proliferation of revisionist histories that reinterpret the past in a more nationalistic manner, particularly episodes demonstrating resistance to tsarist or Soviet rule.

Language

During the Soviet era Russian, though not officially the state language, was widely used in public statements. In urban areas, it was common for people of all ethnic origins to use this language in place of their native tongue. Toward the end of the 1980s, under the more liberal regime of Gorbachev, there was a reaction against this. The languages of the respective titular peoples were given the formal status of "state language," and efforts were made to promote their use in the public sphere. This campaign continued after independence with renewed vigor and greater legal and administrative backing.

It met with most success in Azerbaijan, where, in the wake of resentment over Moscow's perceived support for the Armenians, there was a move to reject the Russian language at all levels of society. This was particularly striking in Baku, which had long been a predominantly Russian-speaking city. The influx of Azeri refugees further boosted the use of the language. In Turkmenistan and Kazakhstan efforts to increase the use of Turkmen and Kazakh, respectively, have been haphazard and have made only a limited impact. There is undoubtedly greater public use of these languages than was the case at the time of independence, but Russian continues to be widely used, particularly in urban areas.

An important symbolic step has been the decision, adopted by all three countries, to shift to the Latin script in place of the Cyrillic script, which was introduced during the Soviet period as the medium for writing Azeri, Kazakh, and Turkmen. (Before the Soviet period and for the first decade of Soviet rule these languages were written in the Arabic script; the Latin script was used c. 1930–40, then was replaced by the Cyrillic script.) Azerbaijan has been implementing the change quite rapidly, while Turkmenistan has favored a more gradualist approach; in Kazakhstan, however, it has been quietly dropped from the current agenda.

Islam and "National Ideologies"

In the Soviet era Marxism-Leninism, the official ideology, was ever present, an integral feature of the very fabric of society. It shaped societal values and lent legitimacy to the regime; it explained the past, gave meaning to the present, and set goals for the future. When the Soviet Union collapsed, the ideology, too, was discredited in the eyes of all but the staunchest Communists. For society at large, this left a sudden vacuum—a loss of a sense of purpose and direction. Intellectuals and government officials soon came to regard the fashioning of post-Soviet "national ideologies" as a real and important challenge. In the absence of a clear political doctrine, there was a tendency to look to history and culture for defining features.

In all three countries, given that the titular people were Muslim, Islam was regarded as an essential component of a new "national ideology." Under Soviet rule, Islam, like all other religions, had been severely persecuted. Consequently, by the 1980s knowledge of the faith was very rudimentary; for the great majority, it was more of a cultural identity than an active commitment. Moreover, it had been mainly relegated to the private sphere, to the celebration of life-cycle rituals.[19] Now, as one of the symbols of independence, the state authorities are giving greater public prominence to the religion. Senior clerics are invited to take part in state events, and there is substantial consultation between government and religious authorities. Many new mosques and *madrassah* (Islamic colleges) have been opened. Restrictions on making the *haj* (prescribed pilgrimage to Mecca) have been relaxed. Also, it is now relatively simple to get official permission and funding to study in Muslim institutions abroad.

However, the intention is certainly not to create Islamic theocracies. The constitutions of these countries stress the separation of religion and state. If that position can be said to have been eroded, it is because of the level of control that the state exercises over all official religious establishments and functionaries. Moreover, Muslim communities are kept under strict observation, and activities (such as informal prayer meetings) that are not sanctioned in advance by the authorities are liable to incur severe penalties. Although Islam is given particular prominence, other established religions (such as Orthodox Christianity) are also treated with respect, and on occasion, senior representatives of these religions are invited to participate in public ceremonies alongside Muslim clerics.

Other elements that have been co-opted into the national ideologies include mythologized histories that illustrate such features as national unity and indigenous forms of democracy. Thus, for example, in Turkmenistan much emphasis is given to Maghtumkuli, an eighteenth-century poet who called on the Turkmen tribes to abandon internecine strife and to unite; in Kazakhstan, several dissertations have been devoted to tracing the roots of Kazakh democracy, delving some two thousand years or more into the past. Ceremonies and rituals have been devised, especially in Turkmenistan, to replace the parades, rallies, and other displays of public loyalty of the Soviet era.[20]

These efforts are at an early stage, however, and the themes are still being elaborated. One problem that has emerged is how to balance the desire to create an ideology that is distinctively national, which draws on the culture and history of the titular people, but at the same time does not exclude those who belong to other ethnic groups. In Azerbaijan and Turkmenistan this is less of a problem, since the majority of the population are Azeri and Turkmen, respectively. Also, in Turkmenistan in particular, positive efforts have been made to give national ceremonies an inclusive, multiethnic character. In Kazakhstan, however, where the Kazakhs constitute less than half the population, the situation is more complicated. The very designations used for the population raise questions: "Kazakh" for example, may be understood as referring to a specific ethnic group, while "Kazakhstani" is more inclusive. In the immediate aftermath of independence there was some enthusiasm for using the term "Kazakhstani," but this soon faded and "Kazakh" is now more commonly used. President Nazarbaev emphasizes the need to create a civic identity that embraces all the republic's citizens, but Kazakh nationalists favor a more discriminatory policy, and in questions relating to the symbolic aspect of state-building they generally succeed in imposing their views.

Constitutions and Government Systems

Turkmenistan was the first of the three countries to adopt a new constitution and a new system of government. The new constitution, adopted in 1992 to replace the Soviet constitution, specifies a secular democracy with a presidential system of government. There is a symbolic separation of powers, but the strong emphasis on the executive role of the president makes this little more than a formality. The legislative body (the *Majlis)* has fifty seats. The role of the deputies is primarily to confirm decisions made by the president; there is no opposition faction.

An innovative institution created after independence is the People's Council (*Khalk maslakhaty*). Its members include senior ministers, senior judges, provincial governors (all appointed by the president), deputies from each region of the country, and the president himself. The People's Council has among its formal powers the right to declare war and to amend the constitution.[21] Another new institution is the Council of Elders (*Yashulyl-arling maslakhaty*). The members of this body are respected members of society, chosen from all parts of the country. The intention is that they should provide wise guidance in affairs of state, and also ensure a regional balance of interests. This council has among its powers the exclusive right to nominate presidential candidates. The objectivity and independence of the council may, however, be questioned, since the president personally selects all the members. The judicial system, which comprises a supreme court, an economic court, provincial courts, and district courts, is likewise firmly under presidential patronage.

Constitutional and parliamentary reform in Kazakhstan was instituted slightly later. The state is now officially described as a "parliamentary republic." However, over the past few years the Kazakh parliament has seen a steady diminution of its authority, and a corresponding growth in presidential power. In 1993 the parliament that had been inherited from the Soviet era was dissolved, ostensibly as a prelude to institutional reform though more probably because the deputies had obstructed some of the president's attempts at reform. A new parliament was elected in 1994. A year later, however, this parliament, too, was disbanded, on the grounds of a procedural irregularity. Opposition deputies believed that this was because the legislative body was still not compliant enough. The president ruled alone, by decree, for the next nine months. A new, bicameral structure for parliament was approved in October 1995; this provided for the *Majlis*, a forty-seven-seat upper chamber (seven seats of which were reserved for presidential nominees), and the Senate, a sixty-seven-seat lower chamber. The elections, held at the end of the year, produced a parliament that was heavily weighted in favor of the president in both houses.[22] At this time, too, the president's personal staff was enlarged, while some of the ministries and state committees were pared down. Thus, within four years of independence a style of government had been instituted in Kazakhstan that, though structurally different from the Turkmen model, had nevertheless resulted in almost as high a degree of presidential control.

Azerbaijan initially seemed set to follow a different trajectory from the other two states. This was chiefly a consequence of the turmoil caused by the war over Karabakh, which brought about two presidential elections within a year and several changes of policy direction. On the one hand this created uncertainty and instability, but on the other, it did allow a certain political dialogue to emerge. There appeared to be the beginnings of a genuinely pluralistic system. In August 1995 a new electoral law was passed. It stipulated the provisions for elections to the reformed unicameral, hundred-seat parliament that had been created to replace the fifty-seat legislative body (*Milli mejlis*) set up after independence. Later that year a new constitution was introduced, replacing the 1978 Soviet Azerbaijan constitution. It owed much to the influence of Western, particularly U.S., constitutional models, embodying fundamental democratic ideals. It contained articles on human and civil rights that seemed to promise a fresh start. However, hopes of reform were soon dashed. The parliamentary elections that were held later that year were seriously flawed and many violations were reported.[23] Almost three quarters of the candidates who represented opposition groups were denied registration. The outcome, as in Kazakhstan, was a parliament that was overwhelmingly propresident in composition.

Parties and Other Groups

Political Parties

Contemporary political life in Azerbaijan, Kazakhstan, and Turkmenistan is marked by profound apathy on the part of the majority of the population. This is to some extent a reaction to the enforced politicization of the Soviet era. It is also a result of the disillusionment with the Communist Party that followed the collapse of the Soviet Union; this has engendered a sense of cynicism and distrust toward all forms of political activity. In addition, preoccupation with the problems of everyday life—for many, the sheer struggle to make a living—allows little time or energy for political issues.

Nevertheless, embryonic multiparty systems have begun to emerge in Kazakhstan and Azerbaijan. Parties tend to be centered around an individual who has a strong personality and/or sufficient wealth to establish a power base. Programs and party platforms, insofar as they are discussed at all, are generally vague, consisting of little more than idealistic platitudes. Party membership is almost always very small and restricted in its social range, drawing predominantly on a network of personal contacts and acquaintances.

Party politics do not play a significant role in either parliamentary or presidential elections: candidates at both levels are elected as individuals rather than as representatives of a particular party. In all three states, most parties have either been created by the incumbent leaders, or profess support for him. All parties and other types of political groupings (movements, unions, associations, etc.) must be officially registered, otherwise they are declared illegal and liable to prosecution.[24] The preconditions for registration are onerous, and in Azerbaijan and Kazakhstan they are difficult to fulfill without government backing. In Turkmenistan, registration without official support is impossible.

Azerbaijan has, comparatively speaking, the most developed political system and the largest number of parties. In mid-1995, in preparation for the parliamentary elections that were to be held later that year, all political parties had to apply for reregistration. Registration was granted to thirty-one parties.[25] Of these, only eight qualified to take part in the elections. The party that eventually gained the overwhelming majority of seats was New Azerbaijan, founded by Heidar Aliev in December 1992. Other progovernment parties included the Azerbaijan Democratic Independence Party, the Motherland Party, the Democratic Entrepreneurs Party, the Alliance in the Name of Azerbaijan, and the Azerbaijan National Statehood Party. The Popular Front (the party of Abulfaz Elçibey) in tandem with the Musavat Party, and the Azerbaijan National Independence Party provided the main opposition. By early 1998 there were over sixty parties, of which more than thirty were registered. However, apart from progovernment parties, very few new groups have been registered since Aliev came to power. There is a reformed Communist Party, but it plays an insignificant role.[26]

In Kazakhstan there are currently some ten to fifteen political parties, but most are very small. Almost all of the parties that have secured registration are progovernment. Insofar as they have programs at all, these are generally vague statements in support of health and happiness for all. The main party (since March 1999) is the Otan-Fatherland Party, which is an amalgamation of several other parties, including the Party of People's Unity of Kazakhstan. The revived Communist Party has had some success, but remains relatively small.[27]

In Turkmenistan there have been only two registered parties: the current Democratic Party of Turkmenistan (formerly the Communist Party but renamed in November 1991), and the apparently stillborn Peasant Justice Party. Both were sponsored by the government. In 1990, while still under Soviet rule, there was an attempt to create an independent Democratic Party. In 1991, however, the then Communist Party appropriated this designation. Consequently, the original Democratic Party changed its name to the Party of Democratic Development; it was never allowed to register and its leaders were harassed (two were reportedly incarcerated in psychiatric hospitals for a time).[28] This party is now moribund. There are a number of Turkmen opposition groups abroad, mostly in Scandinavia, Russia, and the the United States, but they have very little influence within the country.[29]

Other Groups and Movements

Some signs of an emergent civil society in these countries might be seen in the recent proliferation of various types of semiformal associations, unions, and movements. Several nongovernmental groups have now been registered in Azerbaijan and Kazakhstan, and some in even Turkmenistan. Most are concerned with such issues as human rights, gender rights, and ecological problems. In general they are closely supervised by the authorities. Their activities are hampered by the fact that they have limited and often short-term funding. Like the formal political parties, they attract very little public support and are frequently regarded with suspicion, as though they were believed to be motivated by subversive intent. Nonetheless, especially in Azerbaijan and Kazakhstan, they have begun to raise public awareness and to make some contribution to policy debates.[30]

Religious organizations in Azerbaijan and Kazakhstan, like political parties, have to be registered. The faiths that receive particular support from the state authorities are the established confessions of the main ethnic groups, namely Islam and Russian Orthodox Christianity. In recent years Muslim and Christian missionaries of many different sects (and funded from a wide array of sources) have made an appearance in these states; representatives of New Age faiths have also been active. Such newcomers are often subjected to considerable restrictions and even harassment. Unsanctioned activities, particularly among Muslims, are treated as criminal offences because the state authorities fear the emergence of Islamic fundamentalist groups. In general, however, such fears appear to be exaggerated. It is difficult to know quite how many such groups might be in existence, but the level of religious observance among the population at large is still at a comparatively low level. The registration of religious parties is banned in both states, as also in Turkmenistan. In Turkmenistan, moreover, only the official religious organs (Muslim and Christian) are allowed to function.

Ethnic relations in these countries are, at least on the surface, amicable. In Azerbaijan, apart from the crisis with the Karabakh Armenians, there was a period of tension in the early 1990s, and some ethnically based organizations, notably those of the Lezghi and Talysh minorities, made bids for autonomy. Since 1994, however, they have been quiescent.[31] In Kazakhstan there are several national cultural associations (e.g., Korean, German), but only the Russians based in the north of the country have, through their organization *Lad* (Harmony), sought specific ethnic political representation in parliament; up until about 1995 they were quite active, but over the last few years have taken a more low-key stance.[32] In Azerbaijan and Kazakhstan there are a handful of xenophobic, ultranationalistic movements among the titular peoples. They are in favor of the exodus of all other ethnic groups from their territories, but enjoy little popular support. However, in Kazakhstan they have succeeded in exerting some influence on the government and have thereby gained a degree of preferential treatment for the

Kazakh language and culture. The 1992 Turkmen Constitution bans political parties based on ethnic affiliation.

Military

In many parts of the developing world the armed forces play a significant role in the political process, acting as power brokers and at times taking power into their own hands. It is, however, unlikely that this will happen in Azerbaijan, Kazakhstan, and Turkmenistan in the near future. The military and other armed forces in these states are relatively small and still at an early stage of development.[33] They were formed on the basis of the Soviet personnel and equipment stationed on their respective territories at the time of the breakup of the Union. None of these countries possess nuclear weapons. Kazakhstan, which did have a significant part of the Soviet arsenal located on its territory, voluntarily renounced this in 1995.[34]

All the new armed forces are in need of modernization, reorganization, reequipment, and retraining. There is currently recruitment of professional servicemen, as well as compulsory conscription. There are some training facilities in these countries, but also several bilateral agreements that provide for training abroad (e.g., in Turkey and some European countries). There are some high-ranking former Soviet officers of national ethnic origin (i.e., Azeri, Kazakh, and Turkmen), but they are too few in numbers for present needs. Consequently, in Turkmenistan and Kazakhstan some Russian officers have been retained on contract while the fledgling national armed forces are being developed. Azerbaijan has taken a determined stand on the immediate nationalization of its armed forces and no longer has any Russian officers.

The only army to have seen active service since the collapse of the Soviet Union is the Azeri. It has not to date acquitted itself with great distinction. It has lacked effective leadership and there have been numerous allegations of corruption and internal rivalries. Numerous changes of senior personnel do not appear to have improved the situation.[35] In Kazakhstan, too, there have been allegations of corruption in the armed forces. In both countries there are problems with draft dodging and desertion. Little is known of the situation in Turkmenistan. In theory, all three countries support the principle of parliamentary control over the new national armed forces; parliamentary deputies in Azerbaijan and Kazakhstan, for example, have been quite active in raising questions relating to the welfare of the troops. Nevertheless, there is still much secrecy regarding policy, budget, and organizational matters. Real control appears to lie in the hands of the heads of state: it is they who appoint and dismiss senior officers to positions of responsibility and thus are able to monitor and reinforce ties of personal loyalty.

Communication Media

The constitutions of Azerbaijan and Kazakhstan guarantee freedom of word, thought, and information.[36] The constitution of Turkmenistan does not specify such freedoms; on the contrary, it is enshrined in law that those who disseminate material that might be considered critical of official policies "commit criminal deeds" and are therefore liable to prosecution.[37] The situation in Azerbaijan and Kazakhstan, would, on this basis appear to be more liberal than in Turkmenistan. This impression is further enhanced by the fact that there are far more media structures—newspapers, magazines, television and radio companies, and information agencies—in Azerbaijan and Kazakhstan than in Turkmenistan.[38] However, when actual output is examined, the differences are not so great as the provisions of the legal framework would imply.

First, in both Azerbaijan and Kazakhstan, a large proportion of the communication media, electronic and print, is either state-owned or state-run. Consequently, as a matter of policy, they support the government and restrict themselves to reflecting official views. Second, although independent media outlets do exist, these bodies encounter a number of problems. One is the sheer operational cost of these ventures; commercial rates (leaving aside questions of availability) for such items as equipment, premises, and paper are often exceedingly high. Another problem is harassment. This can take a number of forms. It ranges from physical assault (recent examples include the firebombing of the offices of an independent newspaper in Kazakhstan, and the beating of a newspaper editor who published material sympathetic to the opposition in Azerbaijan), to indirect methods, such as pressure on printing houses not to accept opposition material, the use of the tax inspectorate to impose sudden fines, interference with distribution systems, and withholding of necessary licenses and accreditation.[39] Such pressures combine to create yet another obstacle, one that is perhaps the most effective of all: self-censorship. In order to avoid difficulties with the authorities, virtually all independent media organizations prefer to mimic the state sector in their coverage of news and information. Thus they do not provide an alternative source of information, but rather reinforce the official line. Under these circumstances, it is perhaps not surprising that the general public tends to regard the national media, state or independent, with a considerable degree of cynicism, as a source of government propaganda rather than of objective news.

Broadcast and print media from abroad do penetrate these countries, but to a limited extent. Russian television channels are quite widely watched and are generally regarded with respect. However, in Turkmenistan and Kazakhstan the state authorities prerecord programs, then rebroadcast them: this allows for editing and censorship, when deemed necessary. In Azerbaijan, Russian and also Turkish channels can be received directly. The BBC World Service, Voice of America, and other such foreign stations are available on radio, though not always without interference. In all three countries cable television provides access to Western channels; however, such facilities are beyond the reach of most ordinary citizens. The same is true of the internet: opposition groups abroad, especially Turkmen, make active use of this means of communication, but very few members of the general public have access to it.

The restrictions on the formal channels of communication may give the impression that the population in these countries has little access to uncensored information. There is, however, a source of information that is both powerful and very largely beyond official control, namely, private communication between individuals—the informal news, rumor, and gossip that circulates freely and over great distances. The Kazakhs call this mode of communication *uzun qulaq* (the long ear). The relatively small size of the populations concerned, and the strong social and family networks in the region, enable this system to function quite effectively. It is a potent tool for forming public opinion, establishing or destroying a reputation, validating or rejecting an official statement. However, informal communication of this type is highly selective and is by no means always accurate. It creates—or confirms—certain assumptions that may in broad outline be grounded in reality, but the factual details of which are not necessarily reliable.[40] Under "normal" circumstances, gossip of this type acts as a safety valve, mocking authority but not undermining it. In times of crisis, however, it could readily be transformed into a means for spreading disaffection.

Elections and Referendums

In Azerbaijan, Kazakhstan, and Turkmenistan several bouts of elections (presidential and parliamentary) and referendums have been held since independence. As member states of bodies such as the OSCE (Organization for Security and Cooperation in Europe), all three countries are committed to conducting free and fair elections and referendums in line with international standards. To date, they have all fallen far short of this goal. Referendums have been used to give the stamp of legitimacy to constitutional reforms and to reconfirm the mandate of the incumbent president. Presidential elections have also been used to reconfirm the mandate of the leader, while parliamentary elections have served to select docile legislative bodies.

There are three main obstacles to the holding of "free and fair" ballots. One is the lack of genuinely free print and electronic media; as discussed above, directly or indirectly the formal channels of communication are controlled by the state and act as a support system for the incumbent. Another obstacle is that there is no concept of a loyal opposition; dissent is regarded as potentially subversive, and officials, whether acting on orders from higher authority or on their own initiative, regard it as their duty to stifle any incipient signs of pluralism. A third obstacle is that the present leaders are averse to any form of power sharing; they are still in thrall to the idea of a monolithic polity that gives total allegiance to a sole and undisputed chief. In Azerbaijan and Kazakhstan there has been some slight shift away from the unanimous endorsements of the Soviet era (i.e., recent elections have produced votes in favor of the leader of 75 to 80 percent, instead of over 95 percent). In Turkmenistan, however, there has been little change.

So far as the general public is concerned, the experience of participating in elections has changed little since independence. In the Soviet Union elections were held at regular intervals.[41] Candidates, however, stood unopposed. Nevertheless, universal participation in the poll was expected: the aim was not to exercise choice but rather to demonstrate support for the regime and thereby to bestow legitimacy. Polling day was a national holiday and there was a general air of festivity to encourage the electorate to turn out to vote. Much of this tradition has been retained today, despite attempts to give the proceedings a more democratic veneer. Election days are still regarded primarily as a time for family outings and celebrations. The business of voting is seen as a formality, a chore to be avoided if at all possible. In rural areas, proxy voting and block voting are common; even in urban areas, it is not uncommon to find that one member of a family is detailed to vote on behalf of all its members.

The constitutions adopted in Turkmenistan in 1992, Kazakhstan in 1993, and Azerbaijan in 1995 set forth new electoral procedures. Thereafter, amendments were introduced that either reduced the opportunity for competition or completely eliminated such a possibility. The first such move occurred in Turkmenistan. Saparmurad Niyazov, the incumbent president (originally elected in uncontested elections in 1992 for a five-year period) had his term of office extended to the year 2002 by a referendum held in January 1994;[42] virtually 100 percent support from the electorate was recorded for this motion. The previous year the title *Turkmenbashi* (Leader of the Turkmens) had already been bestowed on him, and his birthday had been declared a national holiday. There are now calls from the public and the parliamentary deputies that he be confirmed as president for life.

Parliamentary elections were held in Turkmenistan in 1994; all the candidates stood unopposed. However, there has been some change of attitude since then. In January 1999 the president announced that the parliamentary elections scheduled for December of that year would be conducted on a multiparty basis. New rules for the establishment of parties were to be introduced before that time, including a reduction in the number of founder members deemed necessary in order to register a party, from 1,000 to between 300 to 500. However, it was stressed that the manifesto of new parties must be "in keeping with Turkmen habits and traditions."[43]

In the immediate aftermath of the collapse of the Soviet Union, foreign analysts were for the most part enthusiastic about the Kazakh leadership's commitment to democratic reform. By the end of 1993, though, doubts were beginning to surface, nationally and internationally. In November of that year President Nazarbaev announced plans for a reform of the *Zho-gharghy Kenges* (Supreme Council), the legislative body that had been inherited from the Soviet period. It thereupon agreed to dissolve itself. On March 7, 1994, elections to a reformed parliament were held. However, foreign observers declared that the elections had not corresponded to international standards of democracy. There had been numerous violations of the electoral law, including ballot stuffing, blocking of media access to polling stations, and hindering publicity for antigovernment candidates. Moreover, up to a third of the votes were cast by proxy and should have been disallowed. Of the 177 seats in the new parliament, 42 had to be chosen from a specially selected list of presidential nominees. Deputies who were critical of government policies won only 23 seats. The ethnic mix of the new legislative body was tilted in favor of the Kazakh population, with some two thirds of the new deputies being drawn from the titular people, although within the population as a whole the Kazakhs represented less than half the total.

When the new parliament convened in April 1994, President Nazarbaev promised that more constitutional safeguards would be introduced, presumably in order to avoid a repetition of the electoral violations noted by the CSCE (precursor to OSCE) observers during the March elections. He indicated that there was to be a clearer definition of the conditions under which the president could be impeached or parliament dissolved. Yet in March 1995 parliament was again dissolved. The ostensible cause was that the constitutional court found in favor of a defeated candidate who had instituted proceedings against the central electoral committee on the grounds that there had been many shortcomings in the electoral procedures. President Nazarbaev at first appeared to reject the decision of the constitutional court but later changed his mind. The elections as a whole were declared invalid and the mandate of the current parliament cancelled.

International observers were invited to monitor a new round of parliamentary elections held in December 1995. The voter turnout was good (78 percent), though somewhat lower than for previous elections and referendums. Seats were contested by several candidates. Nevertheless, there was a widespread sense of apathy, especially in the northern provinces, where the population was predominantly composed of ethnic Russians. Foreign observers again noted a number of electoral violations, including multiple voting. The final results of the elections were not announced until January 24, 1996, more than six weeks after the event.

A referendum was held in April 1995 on extending the term of office of Nazarbaev (originally elected to the post of president for a five-year period, in uncontested elections in 1991). An overwhelming majority of the population voted in favor of his remaining in office until the year 2000. Nevertheless, there were some who condemned the referendum; Kazakh nationalists as well as representatives of the ethnic Russian minority protested that it amounted to a Soviet-style uncontested election.[44] In August of that same year another referendum was held, this time on a new constitution. The new constitution considerably broadened the powers of the president. Rule by presidential decree was formally sanctioned; also, the president was given the right to call a state of emergency and to dissolve parliament if it passed a motion of no confidence in the government, or twice rejected the presidential nominee for the post of prime minister.

In October 1998, well over a year before the term of office of the president expired, it was suddenly announced that the next round of presidential elections would be brought forward to January 1999. Other amendments to the election law were announced at the same time: these included the extension of the presidential term of office from five to seven years; the abolition of the maximum age limit for presidential candidates (previously set at sixty-five years of age); and the abolition of a minimum turnout of 50 percent of the electorate for the poll to be considered valid. Reasons for advancing the date of the elections were not given. However, it was widely suggested that the move had been prompted at least in part by fears of a further downturn in the economic situation and the negative effect this might have on the electorate.[45]

Three alternative candidates stood against Nazarbaev, but it was generally agreed that they were not serious contestants. The only person who posed any real threat to the incumbent was the former prime minister, Akezhan Kazhegeldin. However, he was barred from the race on a minor technicality. It is very unlikely that he would actually have won the elections, but the fact that he was not allowed to participate undermined the credibility of the proceedings.[46] Nazarbaev gained a substantial mandate, winning just under 80 percent of the votes (some 10 percent less than in 1991). Foreign observers were for the most part highly critical of the elections.[47]

In Azerbaijan, parliamentary elections were held in 1995. Most candidates stood primarily as individuals, not as representatives of a party. As in Kazakhstan, there were allegations of major violations of the electoral law. The outcome produced a legislature that was heavily weighted in favor of the incumbent president. Presidential elections were held, as scheduled, in 1998 (i.e., five years after the previous poll). However, there were again many procedural shortcomings. Five prominent opposition figures boycotted the elections in protest against what they regarded as the lack of free and fair conditions. There was little surprise when the incumbent president, Heidar Aliev, won. He gained 76.11 percent of the vote. Members of the opposition disputed the official election tally. It was claimed that one of the other candidates, Etibar Mamedov of the Azerbaijan National Independence Party, had gained over 35 percent of the vote.[48]

FOREIGN INFLUENCES ON DOMESTIC POLICIES

Turkey, Iran, and Russia

Foreign influences on the development of the post-Soviet political systems in Azerbaijan, Kazakhstan, and Turkmenistan have been relatively small. In the immediate aftermath of the collapse of the Soviet Union it was assumed by some foreign commentators that the region would seek to follow either the so-called Turkish model of Western-style democracy, or the Iranian model of Islamic fundamentalism. In fact, this issue was never a matter of debate in these former Soviet states. The main priority for both the leaders and the population at large was to preserve stability. Far from radical attempts to abandon the Soviet political legacy, the principal innovations were cosmetic changes to the terminology of government. Azerbaijan, embroiled in the war over Karabakh, did for a while, under President Elçibey, seek a closer relationship with Turkey, but this did not result in political reforms in the domestic sphere.[49] Relations between Iran and Azerbaijan were strained at this time, since Azerbaijan regarded Iran as pro-Armenian. Also, Elçibey favored the creation of a "greater Azerbaijan," to be achieved by the annexation of northern Iran (home to an estimated 10 million ethnic Azeris).[50] Under President Aliev relations with Iran have improved, but are mostly restricted to trade and cultural exchanges. Turkmenistan and Kazakhstan have cordial relations with both Turkey and Iran.

There were also concerns that Russia would try to reassert control over these countries. This has not happened in any direct sense, but undoubtedly Russia continues to be an important influence. Proximity, coupled with sheer size of territory, population, and military strength render it an intimidating presence in regional politics, especially for neighboring Azerbaijan and Kazakhstan.[51] Moreover, Russia has many channels through which leverage can be exerted. Whether it will choose to use them will depend on the leadership in the Kremlin. Relations with President Yeltsin are cordial; he is, to some extent at least, a known quantity. Who will succeed him is inevitably a question that is of very pressing concern to the governments of Azerbaijan, Kazakhstan, and Turkmenistan. If the next president were to espouse aggressively expansionist ambitions, it would constitute a real threat to the independence of these new states.

One set of levers that Russia has at its disposal relates to the economic sphere. The new states have made considerable strides in diversifying foreign trading links in recent years, but nevertheless Russia remains an important economic partner.[52] Furthermore, in the development of the hydrocarbon resources of the Caspian Sea, Russia is a key player. As a littoral state it can block efforts to resolve the legal status of the Caspian Sea, thereby jeopardizing the aims of these new states to exploit offshore oil and gas fields.[53] Russia also has the power to facilitate or delay the export of oil and gas from these countries across its territory.[54]

Another set of levers relates to the Russian diaspora in these countries. Kazakhstan has some six million ethnic Russians, mostly settled in compact groups in the northeast near the Russian border. The Russian populations in Azerbaijan and Turkmenistan are far smaller (350,000 or less), but they are mainly concentrated in cities and occupy important niches in the administrative and professional structures. In the early 1990s the Russian government seemed eager to assume the role of extraterritorial protector of these communities. This raised fears in the region that ethnic clashes might be manufactured in order to give Russia a chance to intervene. This did not happen, and in recent years Russia appears to have been too preoccupied with its internal affairs to pay much attention to such matters. It is not impossible, however, that this issue could be revived in the future.

There are several other channels through which Russia could influence events in the region, including the media and personal contacts at many levels. One potentially useful card is the fact that a considerable number of political dissidents from these countries have established a base in Moscow. They do not necessarily have the support of the Russian government, but they do present the opportunity for intrigue and covert meddling.[55] This inevitably creates a certain element of distrust. For Azerbaijan, an additional reason to suspect Russia's motives is the political and material support that the latter is believed to have given the Armenians over the Karabakh issue.

Western Countries

Securing foreign investment in order to develop their oil and gas industries has been a policy priority for all three countries. They have looked primarily to the West for this, and have met with considerable success. Concomitants of the investment flows from the West have been aid and technical assistance programs. Donor agencies include governmental and nongovernmental organizations, foundations, and institutions. Many of the assistance programs are aimed at democratization, with special emphasis on institutional capacity building, improving human rights, and establishing legal structures. Turkmenistan has been reluctant to accept training programs aimed at influencing its political development. However, several projects have been implemented in Azerbaijan and Kazakhstan, and some progress has been made in these countries in raising awareness of democracy-building issues. Nevertheless, in terms of concrete achievements, results to date have been limited. This is hardly surprising, given the short period of time that such programs have been in operation. Also, problems have sometimes arisen owing to the donors' lack of familiarity with regional conditions, as well as to an obstructive attitude on the part of the local bureaucracy. There is, too, a lack of responsiveness on the part of the general public, who often find such undertakings of little direct relevance to their lives. In sum, the attempts of Western countries to accelerate political reform at the grassroots level in these former Soviet republics have scarcely begun to make an impact.

International Organizations

Since independence Azerbaijan, Kazakhstan, and Turkmenistan have joined an array of international organizations. A survey of the spread of these organizations reveals a desire to balance the influence of different political and regional groupings. Apart from United Nations organizations, the three countries have joined, amongst others, the Commonwealth of Independent States,[56] the European Bank for Reconstruction and Development, the Organization of Islamic Conference, the Economic Cooperation Organization (other members include Pakistan, Turkey, and Iran), the NATO Partnership for Peace program, and the Organization for Security and Cooperation in Europe (OSCE). These last two organizations lay particular emphasis on democracy building.

The OSCE has been actively involved in commenting on human rights issues in Azerbaijan, Kazakhstan, and Turkmenistan, and in assessing the way in which elections are conducted in these member states. OSCE monitors were sent to observe the Kazakh parliamentary elections of 1995 and the Azeri presidential elections in 1998. In both cases the monitors found that there were serious shortcomings.[57] No official monitors were sent to the Kazakh presidential elections in January 1999 since it was clear from the outset that the contest would not be fair and open; the OSCE took the position that if they sent monitors, this in itself would be used as a way of legitimizing the elections, even if the actual verdict was negative. They did, however, send a small team of assessors; their stringent criticisms of the proceedings were subsequently made public.[58] Human rights activists within these countries welcome these indictments, but also note that such statements appear to have very little effect on their governments.

THREATS TO SOCIAL AND NATIONAL COHESION

To date, Kazakhstan and Turkmenistan have been free of major civil disorders. In Azerbaijan, too, despite the continuing problems caused by the war over Karabakh, there has been a marked improvement since 1993, when terrorism was rife. Thus today, the security situation appears to be relatively stable. However, there are a number of factors that could precipitate serious unrest during certain conditions of stress (for example, prolonged bouts of bad weather resulting in disastrous harvests, or turmoil in neighboring states). The issues that seem most likely to cause or contribute to instability are listed below. They are not ranked in order of seriousness, not only because it is impossible to assign an objective weighting to them, but also because they are interrelated and feed off one another.[59]

Fragmentation of Society

During the Soviet period there were many differentials in society. However, the popular perception, reinforced by the official ideology, was that there was social equality and solidarity. Since independence, rifts between different groups have begun to open up. Some of these have historical roots, such as clan-tribal divisions. There are also other cleavages along regional, ethnic, religious, and urban/rural lines. It is possible that such differences could eventually be activated to create hostile factions. For the present, however, although there are perceptible tensions between these groups, they do not represent a serious problem.

A potentially more dangerous divide is that which is emerging between the "haves" and the "have-nots." A small but extremely affluent elite has emerged in these countries. Some individuals have no doubt accumulated their wealth by legitimate means, but many are suspected of having enriched themselves illicitly. The new rich indulge in a lifestyle of ostentatious opulence. Typically, their clothes and cars will be expensive foreign imports, while their children will be sent to private schools or educated abroad in prestigious Western establishments. By contrast, large sectors of the population have seen a drastic decline in their standard of living. The situation is exacerbated by high birthrates, especially in rural areas, and large numbers of elderly dependents. Unemployment is widespread (local observers claim that it is far higher than official estimates).[60] The social services that used to be provided free of charge during the Soviet period are now either no longer available or have become prohibitively expensive. The numbers of those falling below the poverty line are steadily increasing.[61]

Education is one of the areas that has been catastrophically affected by the economic crisis. In poor families with many children, which is the rule rather than the exception in much of the region, a choice sometimes has to be made as to whom should be educated; invariably it is the sons who are favored. Thus, universal education for both sexes, one of the major achievements of the Soviet regime, is rapidly being eroded. Health care, too, has suffered: there are many that can no longer afford to pay for medical treatment, and health standards are falling.[62] As a result of these and similar downward trends in social welfare, an underclass is being created. In effect, parallel societies are emerging: physically they inhabit the same country, but in economic status, social organization, and cultural environment they belong to different worlds. In time, this could lead to a bitter clash of values and aspirations.

Corruption

Corruption—bribery, fraud, misappropriation of public property, covert "levies," nepotism, cronyism, and other such forms of malpractice—is endemic in the region (as elsewhere in the former Soviet Union). It existed during the Soviet period but has increased dramatically in recent years. This decline in standards of public ethics is to some extent the product of the uncertainties of life today. Those who are employed, at whatever level and in whatever sphere, have little expectation that they will remain at their post for long; consequently, they milk the system as much as possible while they still have access to it. However, corruption on such a scale is not simply a moral issue: it has practical implications for policy implementation. It subverts attempts to press forward administrative and economic reforms. This in turn increases social divisions by giving hidden privileges to the favored few, while excluding those who do not have the right contacts and "pull."

There is scarcely any area of public life that is not affected by this evil. In the educational sphere, for example, it has undermined the credibility of academic qualifications, since it is well known that good results and degrees can be bought. Such a situation breeds cynicism and lack of respect for authority. All three presidents have spoken firmly of the need to eradicate corruption; campaigns to clean up government have been launched, and many senior officials and ministers have been summarily dismissed. Nevertheless, there has been little noticeable improvement. Local gossip ascribes this to the fact that the tentacles of corruption reach to the very highest echelons of government. Whether this is so or not, it is generally acknowledged that current levels of corruption are a serious obstacle to the efficient functioning of the state in these countries.

Organized Crime

Organized criminal networks, known colloquially as mafia,[63] have long been active in this region, but they have mushroomed since the end of the Soviet regime. They are particularly active in Azerbaijan, but are also well entrenched in Kazakhstan. Too little is known about the situation in Turkmenistan for it to be possible to judge the strength of such groups there, but it is probable that they do exist. The main spheres of activity of these crime syndicates include illegal trafficking in high-value goods, especially drugs;[64] protection rackets; contract killings; black marketeering; gambling rings; and money laundering. Their leaders are reputed to have close links with high-ranking members of the police force and national and local government officials, and thus to enjoy covert official protection.

War and Secession

Azerbaijan is the only country for which war and secession present immediate threats. The seven-year-long conflict over Karabakh is still unresolved, although the Armenian population has established de facto independence. The Azeris continue to believe that they will eventually win back this territory. This could only conceivably be achieved if Azerbaijan's future oil revenues were sufficient to enable the army to be fundamentally overhauled and reequipped. Even if this were to happen, the Armenian diaspora would very likely succeed in mobilizing international opinion to such an extent that oil companies involved in the region would find it difficult to continue working with Azerbaijan in the face of a bloody campaign in Karabakh.

In the wake of the collapse of the Soviet Union other ethnic minorities (Lezghis, Talysh) also began to fight for autonomy from Azerbaijan. After Aliev came to power, however, these movements were crushed. In Kazakhstan, likewise, in the early 1990s it seemed possible that the Russian and Cossack communities in the northeast might attempt to secede. This danger, too, has subsided as many Slavs have now emigrated; the majority of those who remain appear to prefer an accommodation with the Kazakhs rather than confrontation. In both Kazakhstan and Azerbaijan the possibility of divisive tendencies emerging among the ethnic minorities, especially those situated in border areas, cannot be excluded, but there are no indications that this will happen in the near future.

CONCLUSIONS AND OUTLOOK

Azerbaijan, albeit within very limited terms of reference, has moved furthest toward establishing an open society. There is some competition of ideas rather than merely of personalities; the Azeri mass media, though by no means free, is slightly more pluralistic than elsewhere. One reason for this greater level of political maturity is the experience of the Karabakh war: this brought a succession of leaders to power and diversified the forces in society. Relatively intensive exposure to Western commercial and political norms has also accelerated the process of articulating demands and accepting the need for discussion and compromise. A third, more distant, spur toward democratization has been the inspiration drawn from the first era of political awakening in Azerbaijan over a century ago (see Appendix 2); under Soviet rule this episode was denounced, but in the 1980s it became a source of legitimization for the nationalist movement.

Kazakhstan at first seemed the most eager of the three countries to embark on political liberalization. However, the leadership, perhaps unnerved by the enthusiasm with which Kazakh intellectuals embraced the new freedom, soon began to falter in its commitment to democratization. The dissolution of parliament in 1993, and again in 1994, signaled a steady augmentation of presidential control. Since then it has become increasingly difficult to express in public any criticism of the current regime. The media, under growing pressure to support official views, has turned to self-censorship in order to survive. Human rights activists in Kazakhstan[65] and abroad have noted with concern recent moves to curb such basic freedoms as the right to peaceful assembly and likewise the onerous conditions placed on the formation of political groups.

In Turkmenistan, the explicit aim since independence has been to construct a political order that accords with the culture and history of the Turkmen people. Western-style political institutions are regarded by the leadership as inappropriate since they reflect different societal values and aspirations. The concept of indigenous approaches to democracy and human rights is being promoted. It is based on an idealized official interpretation of Turkmen traditions. The intention is to build consensus and minimize group competition. This is of no small importance in a country where regional and clan-tribal factions continue to play an important role in public life. The idea of a genuine opposition, putting forward alternative views, is seen as unnecessary obfuscation. The president, as signified by the title *Turkmenbashi*, symbolizes and personifies national unity and oneness of purpose. The external image of this society is thus one of monolithic conformity. Yet the system is not quite as rigid as it seems: there is in private more diversity of opinion than surfaces in the public domain. Whether this will in the foreseeable future be incorporated into an open political debate or will lead to confrontation and resistance is impossible to tell.

The leaders of the three states are now so firmly established in office that, barring sudden and unforeseeable events (a danger that should not be underestimated),[66] they will remain in power as long as they wish, or as long as vigor and mortality permit. In making their way to the higher ranks of the Soviet system, they acquired an extraordinarily acute instinct for survival. President Aliev, already in his mid-seventies, is the most vulnerable to health problems.[67] The other two, both just under sixty, could have long careers ahead of them.[68] The crucial problem, however, is precisely that the skills they learned in the preindependence era are today of limited value in the positions in which they find themselves. Their strengths were firstly to be able to secure their own positions within an established system; and secondly to organize the implementation of directives handed down from higher authority.

Since the dissolution of the Soviet Union these leaders have continued to show an impressive ability to enhance their personal standing. In making the transition from subordinate executive to chief policy maker, however, they have been less surefooted. Initially, it seemed as though all three were intent on introducing radical reforms. In the economic sphere they have implemented some important changes (though often inconsistently and without adequate preparation). In the political sphere, their main goal has been the maintenance of stability. They have accomplished this by preserving the most conservative aspects of the Soviet system. Given their backgrounds, and the fact that they inherited legitimacy rather than making an independent bid for power, this is perhaps not surprising. However, the result is that they have come to appear more as caretakers rather than as mold-breaking reformers such as a Mao or an Ataturk.[69]

This situation will probably continue as long as they remain at the helm, but not beyond that. After they leave the scene (however that may come about), certain issues will inevitably arise. First, there is the question of succession. The transfer of power has to be accomplished with at least a facade of legality. In the precolonial past, the new leader would be confirmed by some nominal form of election; in the Soviet period, the choice was made in Moscow. Today, according to the constitutions of these countries, the issue ought to be decided through the ballot box. Yet given the experience of these first seven years, it seems unlikely that this procedure will present the electorate with a genuine choice of candidates.

It is more probable that the successor will be preselected; a vigorous political campaign will then be mounted to give the candidate validity. It is possible that the "heir" will be chosen from within the incumbent leader's family, creating embryonic presidential dynasties. There are already hints and popular rumors that the sons of the Azeri and Turkmen presidents, and the eldest daughter (in fact, stepdaughter) of the Kazakh president are being groomed for such a role.[70] It cannot be excluded, though, that a contender from outside the family—possibly an erstwhile member of the present leader's entourage—might seek to gain power. Such an attempt has already been made, though unsuccessfully, in Kazakhstan (by former prime minister Kazhegeldin). Without the blessing of the incumbent president, however, it would be difficult to build up the necessary organizational base.

The next presidents will almost certainly not be as powerful as those of today. There are a number of reasons for this. First, the post-Soviet generation of leaders will not have had the administrative and organizational preparation of the present incumbents, and consequently will almost certainly not be able to dominate the state apparatus to the same extent. Second, the Soviet system encouraged the formation of personal patronage: Aliev, Nazarbaev, and Niyazov have all benefited from the support of the networks that they established earlier in their careers. Present conditions are inimical to the creation of such alliances; hence the next generation will not have the same staunch power base. Third, the caliber of the bureaucracy is rapidly deteriorating. Remuneration is so low that it attracts only those who cannot make a better living in any other way; also, the prestige of state employment has been eroded. The law enforcement agencies, of crucial importance in maintaining coercive control, have been badly affected by this trend. The result is a loss of professionalism and dubious loyalties.

There are several challenges that the new leaders will have to contend with. One is the likely increase in the power of crime syndicates. Today they are not very visible, but the experience of Azerbaijan in 1992–93 showed that as soon as the leadership weakens, the "mafia bosses" swiftly extend their reach. Private militias mushroomed during those years, and the situation rapidly descended into anarchy. Hydra-headed, it is very probable that these mafia groups will reemerge as soon as they sense a new opportunity to flex their strength. As the experience of other countries has shown, such crime syndicates could come to play a significant role in the politics of the future by securing a weak candidate's election—and then dictating terms. This would fatally undermine a leader's ability to make rational, independent decisions.

There is no "legitimate" political opposition of any substance in these countries at present. Those who identify themselves as opponents of the current regimes are for the most part from a background and generation similar to that of the incumbent leaders and thus share a common Soviet legacy. There are a few idealists among them (e.g., Elçibey), but the majority offers little that is fundamentally different from current policies. Consequently, were they to come to power (which does not seem very likely), they would probably introduce new faces rather than a qualitative change in style of government. A more fundamental challenge to the authority of the new leaders could emerge from among the younger generation (roughly speaking, those born from the 1970s onwards). The bright young technocrats who are now going abroad for training and work experience may acquire a more independent outlook than those who have grown up within the system. Eventually it is possible that they will press for a more transparent, accountable style of government. The emerging business community may also come to feel that its best interests are served by a more orderly, open political system, and this, too, could be a force for democratic change.

A more dangerous and unmanageable challenge is likely to come from the alienated, deprived sections of the population. A post-Soviet generation is growing up, many of whom are poorly educated; unless there is a dramatic improvement in the economy they will very likely experience long-term unemployment. At present the overwhelming majority is politically apathetic. However, if the gulf between rich and poor continues to widen—a gulf that is not only one of material wealth, but also of a contrast between the "decadent" cosmopolitanism of the rich and the conservative "traditionalism" of the poor—it is very likely that this will trigger acute instability, as has happened in many other developing countries. Such conditions would favor the emergence of a populist leader preaching a radical ideology based on nationalism and/or religion (specifically, some form of politized Islam). Given the huge quantities of arms that are circulating in the region (overspill from the wars in the Caucasus, as well as weapons acquired illicitly from poorly guarded military bases), this could very soon turn into a bloody confrontation.

External influences on the emerging political order in these new countries have to date, as commented above, been very limited. In the future this could change, and clearer political-ideological alignments could emerge. At present, though, the situation is still too fluid for long-term predictions. All that can be done is to point to possible poles of attraction. Of these, Iran and Turkey, for reasons of proximity as well as historical and cultural ties, are likely to prove influential for Azerbaijan and Turkmenistan, though probably to a lesser extent for more distant Kazakhstan. Russia, too, will almost certainly continue to exert an influence; one or more of these three newly independent countries, either voluntarily or under compulsion, may gravitate back into the political, cultural, and economic orbit of the former "center." Yet it is also possible that these states will seek to develop a different set of linkages. In Azerbaijan, for example, there is a strong pro-Europe faction; in some political and intellectual circles this extends to a desire to seek membership of the European Union.[71] In Kazakhstan, although there was initial enthusiasm for stressing the country's European credentials (and some hopes of seeking membership of the European Union), this shifted first to a concept of Kazakhstan as part of Eurasia, and then as part of Asia. If China remains stable and continues its economic growth, it is possible that it will become the dominant influence in Kazakhstan.

These and other such permutations provide plentiful material for speculation. This merely underlines the fact that these new states have as yet no clearly defined orientation. As of now they are struggling to come to terms with the cataclysmic upheavals of the last decade. The emerging political orders are still in flux. The process of transition from Soviet republics to independent statehood, far from nearing the end, has hardly commenced. Today these young countries are stable and comparatively low in political risk. This position may be maintained and improved, but, equally, it could deteriorate, and the risks could escalate very rapidly. This uncertainty does not inspire confidence among foreign investors. Yet unless there is significant foreign investment there is little hope that the economic situation will improve; and unless this does improve, and the benefits trickle down to the population at large, the political situation will become increasingly volatile.

APPENDIX 1

Basic Data

Kazakhstan

Kazakhstan, by far the largest of the newly independent Caspian littoral states, has an area of 2.7 million square kilometers. It lies to the northeast of the Caspian Sea, with a coastline of some 1,890 kilometers. It is bordered by the Russian Federation to the north; China to the east; Kyrgyzstan, Turkmenistan, and Uzbekistan (all former Soviet republics) to the south. The capital was until recently Almaty, in the southeast of the country; in 1998, it was moved to Astana, which is located more centrally. Kazakhstan has a population of approximately 15 million, comprising over a hundred different ethnic groups.[72] The main ethnic groups are the Kazakhs, who constitute some 45 percent (about 7.5 million) of the total population, and the Russians, who constitute some 35 percent; other groups of significant size include Ukrainians (about 6 percent), Uzbeks, Uighurs, Tatars, Koreans, and Germans.

Kazakhstan has rich resources of hydrocarbons, minerals, and coal. It also has good agricultural land (for grain and cattle production) and a broad manufacturing base (though this is urgently in need of modernization). The economy declined dramatically in the early 1990s; by 1995 real domestic product had contracted to below half the 1990 level. However, since 1996 there has been some growth. Inflation is currently below the CIS average. Kazakhstan has attracted more foreign direct investment per capita than any other CIS member. Most of this investment has been directed toward the oil industry. Some analysts predict that it will become one of the world's ten largest producers of oil early in the next century. The estimated GDP per capita is $1,372 (1997).[73]

Turkmenistan

Turkmenistan, located along the southeast of the Caspian Sea, with a coastline of 1,768 kilometers, has an area of 488,100 square kilometers. It is adjoined by Kazakhstan and Uzbekistan to the north (both former Soviet republics), Afghanistan to the southeast, and Iran to the south. The capital is Ashkhabad. The country has a population of some 5 million, of whom 77 percent are Turkmens. Other ethnic groups include Russians, Uzbeks and Kazakhs.

Turkmenistan has the world's fourth largest gas reserves. It also has rich deposits of oil and other minerals. The agricultural sector is dominated by cotton, of which Turkmenistan is one of the largest producers in the world. An economic reform program was launched in 1995, including liberalization of prices and tighter monetary and fiscal policies. There has been some improvement. The inflation rate was reduced from 1,748 percent in 1994 to 20 percent in 1997. Economic recovery, however, has been hampered by difficulties with gas export routes and markets (particularly the failure of CIS members to pay in full for supplies), as well as bouts of bad weather that adversely affected the cotton harvest. The estimated GDP per capita is $426 (1997).[74]

Azerbaijan

The smallest of these three states as regards size of territory is Azerbaijan, which has an area of 86,600 square kilometers. It borders the southwest of the Caspian Sea with a coastline of some 800 kilometers. Azerbaijan's neighbors are the Russian Federation to the north, Iran to the south, and Georgia and Armenia to the west. The capital is Baku. Azerbaijan includes Nakhichevan, a small Azerbaijani exclave (5,500 square kilometers), which lies to the southwest and is separated from the rest of the country by a strip of Armenian territory; to the south Nakhichevan abuts Iran, and in the west shares a short border (about 9 kilometers) with Turkey. During the Soviet period Azerbaijan also included Nagorno-Karabakh (4,400 square kilometers), a province situated in the southwest of the country. Since the late 1980s the Armenian population of Karabakh (as Nagorno-Karabakh is now more generally known) has been seeking secession from Azerbaijan. It declared its independence in 1992, but has not been recognized internationally.

The population of Azerbaijan numbers approximately 7.6 million. The Azeris (also known as Azerbaijanis) are the main ethnic group, constituting over 80 percent of the total; other groups include the Russians (about 5 percent) and small numbers of mountain peoples. Since the early 1990s some 800,000 refugees and displaced persons have swelled the Azeri population.

Azerbaijan has extensive oil reserves. It has been a major oil producer since the middle of the last century. Since independence several deals have been signed with foreign oil companies. In 1994 an agreement that has been called the "deal of the century" was concluded with an international consortium to develop three offshore fields, with estimated total reserves of 3 billion barrels. Azerbaijan has a well-developed industrial sector, including a downstream petroleum industry. It also has a diverse agricultural sector (fruits, cotton, tobacco, etc.), which accounts for more than 25 percent of its GDP. As elsewhere in the CIS, Azerbaijan experienced a dramatic fall in output in the early 1990s; since 1996, however, this trend has been reversed, and GDP has started to increase. Inflation was brought down from 1,664 percent in 1994 to less than 4 percent in 1997. There is optimism over anticipated oil revenues from the Caspian Sea; based on this, a growth rate of 8.5 percent is projected for 1999. The estimated GDP per capita is $506 (1997).[75]

APPENDIX 2

Historical Background

Kazakhstan

The territory of modern Kazakhstan was integrated into the tsarist empire in the eighteenth century. The Kazakhs who inhabited this region followed a nomadic way of life, traveling hundreds of kilometers during their annual round of seasonal migration. They had a complex system of clan and tribal groupings, based mainly on ties of kinship. The main political formations were three "Hordes" (*zhuz*), which had their own specific territories: the Large (*ulu*) Horde controlled the southeast, the Middle (*orta*) Horde the central steppe, and the Little (*kishi*) Horde the region between the Aral Sea and the Caspian. Each Horde was headed by a *khan* (leader). In theory, the *khans* were elected, but in practice the choice was restricted to those of a particular lineage and moreover, usually predetermined by factional interests. A Supreme Khan was chosen from amongst the three leaders. His status was that of *primus inter pares*, and his main role was to encourage unity of action between the hordes; generally, however, the Supreme Khans were very weak and little more than figureheads.

From the mid-seventeenth century the Kazakhs suffered devastating attacks from the Oirats, a Mongol people from the east. It was primarily in response to this menace that first the khan of the Little Horde, then of the Middle Horde, and finally of the Big Horde sought protection from the Russian crown. (However, a section of the Big Horde looked to China for help, and eventually these Kazakhs, along with the eastern margin of traditional Kazakh territory, were incorporated into the Manchu empire; approximately 1 million Kazakhs still live on the Chinese side of the border.) Once the Russians had established a presence in the region, they began to build up a strong administrative and military infrastructure. Subsequently, in the first half of the nineteenth century the khans were deposed, and the entire region was brought under direct Russian rule.

Colonial rule contributed to a fragmentation of Kazakh society. Members of the Kazakh aristocracy acquired a Russian education, and some joined the imperial army. They adopted a Europeanized lifestyle and largely lost contact with the rank-and-file nomads. Another development was the emergence of wealthy Kazakh entrepreneurs whose success derived not from privileged birth, but from innate talent. A third trend was the sedentarization of impoverished nomads who sought paid employment in the newly established factories, mines, construction projects, and other industrial enterprises. The influx of thousands of Slav settlers further undermined traditional Kazakh society. Changes such as these eventually led to an awakening of a national consciousness and the first stirrings of political awareness among the aristocracy and the emerging middle class. There were two main groups: one was ideologically close to the Russian liberals of the day; the other was Marxist in orientation. A tiny number of Kazakh-language newspapers began to appear at this time, but they had very limited influence among the population at large owing to the very low level of literacy (about 7 percent).

Kazakh resentment over Slav immigration and other aspects of colonial rule led to a major uprising in many parts of Kazakhstan in 1916. This was brutally suppressed by tsarist troops, but before it had been entirely crushed it merged into the civil war that broke out after the 1917 Revolution between the White Army, the Red Army, foreign interventionists, and nationalists. Soviet rule was established in 1920.[76]

Azerbaijan

The territory of modern Azerbaijan first attracted Russian interest at approximately the same period as Kazakhstan. Peter the Great regarded this region as the gateway to the East and was eager to acquire a base on the Caspian coast. In 1722–23 Russian troops occupied Derbent and Baku.

Subsequently, pressure from the Ottomans, and later from the Persians (under Nadir Shah), forced them to relinquish their conquests. However, neither the Ottomans nor the Persians succeeded in establishing a permanent presence in the area, and by the mid-eighteenth century the dominant powers here were independent local rulers such as the khans of Baku, Gandja, Karabakh, Nakhichevan, and Talysh. At the end of the eighteenth century the Russians again occupied Baku and Derbent and this time were able to consolidate their position sufficiently to expand their rule into the hinterland. The local ruling elites were rapidly deposed, and the region was brought under Russian military control.

As in Kazakhstan, Russian influence set in motion a number of changes in society. By the second half of the nineteenth century Azeri scholars, writers, and educationalists were seeking to modernize and reform Islam by creating a synthesis of the best elements of Muslim and Russian culture. Questions such as the introduction of the Latin script for the Azeri language in place of the Arabic script were discussed; progressive, European-style schools were opened; and a vernacular theater and opera were created.

The first Azeri-language newspaper appeared in 1875. The development of the oil industry in the early twentieth century made Baku one of the largest industrial centers in the Russian empire. It attracted a multiethnic urban proletariat and proved fertile ground for revolutionary ideas. Stalin, one of the leaders of Bolshevik activities in Baku at that time, described the city as the revolutionary center of the Caucasus. A nationalist Azeri party, *Musavat* (Equality) was founded in 1911. In 1918, this party succeeded in setting up an independent government in Azerbaijan. It lasted until the spring of 1920, when it was overthrown by the Bolsheviks, aided by the Red Army.[77]

Turkmenistan

The territory of modern Turkmenistan was annexed by the tsarist empire in the last quarter of the nineteenth century. The Turkmens, formerly nomads, were by this period semisedentary; the majority were located in the vicinity of the oases and rivers of southern Transcaspia. They were divided into six main clan-tribal formations, each with control over a particular territory. The tribes were headed by khans; these were supposedly elected, but in fact they were put forward by various clan factions and in general were drawn from the family of the incumbent ruler. There was frequent internecine fighting between these groups, as also between the Turkmens and their neighbors. When Russian troops invaded this region, some of the Turkmens offered a valiant resistance, notably at the battle of Geok Tepe in 1881. However, they were unable to stem the tsarist advance.

In comparison with Kazakhstan and Azerbaijan, the Russian presence had little effect on Turkmen society. Traditional social structures were weakened, but not destroyed. The influence of European culture was almost entirely restricted to the environs of the small Russian military settlements. In 1916 there was some spillover from the uprising in Kazakhstan, and in 1917 civil war broke out. A nationalist faction, aided by a British mission from Meshed, briefly succeeded in establishing an independent state. However, this soon fell and the Red Army took possession of the region.

Soviet Era

After Soviet rule had been established Central Asia was divided into five main administrative units. One of these was the Turkmen Soviet Socialist Republic (Turkmen SSR), another (created somewhat later) the Kazakh SSR.[78] On the other side of the Caspian Sea, in Transcaucasus, new administrative units were likewise being formed, among them the Azerbaijan SSR (created in 1920). The borders that were drawn in the 1920s were internal, administrative demarcations within the larger territorial entity of the Soviet Union. The only international frontier at that time was that which separated the Soviet Union from surrounding states (e.g., Iran, Afghanistan, and China). After the collapse of the union, the internal borders between the Soviet republics (which had remained largely unchanged throughout the Soviet period) became international borders between the now independent states.

During the Soviet era a radical and far-reaching program of modernization was undertaken. This included mass education (literacy levels were raised from under 10 percent in 1926 to virtually 100 percent by the 1960s), the emancipation of women (including abandoning the veil in those areas where it had been customarily worn), secularization, collectivization of agriculture, sedentarization of the nomads (completing the process that had started in the late nineteenth century), and industrialization. Modern bureaucracies were created, as well as modern systems of transport and communication.

Slav (mainly Russian) immigration into the region had commenced in the nineteenth century, but increased vastly during the years of Soviet rule. Kazakhstan was most severely affected, with the combined Russian and Ukrainian population rising from approximately two million in 1926 to nearly seven million in 1979 (i.e., from 20 percent to almost 47 percent of the total population). Representatives of many other ethnic groups also came to these republics at this time. Some were volunteers, others political deportees; the majority of the latter were sent to Kazakhstan, with a much smaller proportion going to Turkmenistan and the other Central Asian republics.

Throughout the Soviet period there was intensive political indoctrination of the population. The official ideology of the regime, Marxism-Leninism, was inculcated by both formal and informal means. The educational system, from nursery school upward, was saturated with ideological content. The message was continually reinforced in the media, as well as through the arts (paintings, plays, operas, films, etc). Sociopolitical organizations amplified this ideological work. These included the Young Octobrist and Young Pioneer movements (7–14-year-olds), and the Young Communist League (14–28-year-olds), as well as trade and professional unions.

The core of the political system, underpinning the state apparatus, was the Communist Party. The organization of the party was highly centralized. Grassroots control and mobilization were carried out through local "primary party organizations"; these in turn were responsible to a hierarchy of administrative-geographic levels of organization (regional, provincial, etc). Each republic had its own Communist Party (e.g., the Communist Party of Azerbaijan), headed by a first party secretary. These republican institutions were in turn affiliated with the Communist Party of the Soviet Union (CPSU). The head of the CPSU was the general secretary, who in real terms was the most powerful individual in the Soviet Union. The central organs of the CPSU were situated in Moscow. Members were drawn from all over the Soviet Union, though there was always a great preponderance of Slavs. The Politburo of the Central Committee of the CPSU was the body that exercised power over the day-to-day decision-making process. It convened under the chairmanship of the general secretary and acted somewhat like a parliamentary cabinet. The numbers of members varied, with up to about fifteen full members and some eight non-voting members.[79]

Membership of the Communist Party was regarded as an honor, and admission procedures were long and painstaking. For successful applicants there were privileges as well as obligations. Party membership was all but indispensable for advancement in the state apparatus, the armed forces, or the other professions. Consequently, the large native elites that were created during this period in all spheres—political, administrative, military, intellectual, sports, and the arts—were overwhelmingly members of the Party. They were not necessarily actively committed to the doctrines of the Party, but, as members of an exclusive institution, they shared a common ethic. Also, bonds of friendship and loyalty were created that often cut across other ties such as, for example, those of ethnic origin.

When the Soviet Union disintegrated, the Communist parties of the newly independent states were either renamed, as in Turkmenistan, or recreated on a much smaller scale, as in Kazakhstan and Azerbaijan. There are virtually no government officials in these countries that would today claim to be Communists. However, the overwhelming majority of those who are over thirty years of age are former Party members, and in their attitudes and outlook the imprint of the Party experience is still very strong. Also, many of the informal networks and alliances of today are founded on links formed within the ranks of the Party. Thus, though the Communist Party no longer has any real power in these countries, nevertheless, it continues to exert an indirect influence on the way in which they function.

PART TWO

Conflict in the Caucasus and Central Asian Regions:

Oil, Secession, and Questions of Outside Intervention

NATO Expansion and Implications for Southern Tier Stability

7

Ewan W. Anderson

The Southern Tier states are located on either side of the eastern boundary of Europe in the middle of the World Island. In the center is the Caspian Sea and on either side are two groups of states. To the west of the Caspian are the three states of the southern Caucasus and to the east the five states that are generally grouped under the term Central Asia. They have in common locational factors but, more important, until the early 1990s they had been for seventy years an integral part of the Soviet Union. As a result, they are both geographically and politically relatively isolated. Although the peoples can all trace very long histories, the states are in essence "new." Their boundaries remain those dictated by the former Soviet Union and, like the boundaries of Africa, they tend not to accord with either ethnic or perceived reality. Thus, there remains a range of actual and potential flashpoints, many focused upon boundaries.

Economically, the region is as yet poorly developed, but there is hope for future improvement centered upon the oil and natural gas deposits of the Caspian Basin. The scale of these has probably been exaggerated, but their full extent is as yet unknown. Ideally, the resource-rich states should benefit and those without oil or natural gas would gain indirectly through the enhanced prosperity of the region and, perhaps, directly through the transboundary movement of the resources. However, issues such as pipelines in international law and the security of pipelines require further study.

Two key geopolitical factors will govern the future development and prosperity of the Southern Tier. First, with the exception of Georgia, all the states are landlocked. Therefore, links with the global trading system have to be negotiated with neighboring states. In addition, there need to be long-term guarantees so that it remains in the interests of all states involved to keep trade routes open. Trade security can be further enhanced by developing a multiplicity of routes so that alternatives are always available. Second, the region is a classic buffer zone, in some senses as it was during the period of the "Great Game." However, this analogy should not be pressed too far in that all the territory is now within the boundaries of states, whereas at the earlier period, the "Great Powers" involved delimited the boundaries for their own purposes.[1] Also, the exponential development in technology has rendered obsolete such devices as the Wakhan Panhandle, intended to insulate the Indian Subcontinent from the powers of Central and Eastern Asia.[2]

Today Russia, Turkey, and Iran, each an intrinsic part of the region, compete to extend their influence. However, whereas Turkey and Iran are regional powers, Russia remains a global power. It is therefore in competition with China, from the east; India and Pakistan together with various Middle Eastern States, particularly Saudi Arabia and Israel, from the south; and the United States and Western Europe in various guises including that of the North Atlantic Treaty Organization (NATO), from the west.

Thus, as a buffer zone, there is an ever-present danger of fragmentation and either collaboration with or more likely subservience to a regional or outside power. It can be argued, however, that there are potential advantages in being part of a buffer zone, but these must surely depend upon cooperation among the states of the Southern Tier. They require guarantees of security that will allow them to nurture their fledgling democracies and improve their economies. The only possible guarantors are Russia and the Western powers. This is why a consideration of the possible role for NATO and, in the context of the region, the relationship between NATO and Russia, is so significant.

HISTORICAL BACKGROUND

In the aftermath of World War II, the United States identified two areas as being vital to its security interests: Western Europe and Asia Pacific, specifically Japan and South Korea. In 1947 Marshall Aid was initiated, and it was realized that effective economic rejuvenation required political and military security. As NATO has developed, these two key interests have remained intertwined.[3]

To the two areas of security concerned was later added a third, focused upon the Gulf region of the Middle East. This was formalized by 1980 under President Carter with the inauguration of the Rapid Deployment Force (RDF) and the delimitation of the area of operation for Central Command (CENTCOM). It is arguable that the security provided by these interlocking blocs has allowed the ensuing economic and political cooperation and development.[4] Furthermore, this remains the key economic pattern given that more than 80 percent of world trade occurs between the three major blocs: North America, the European Union, and Asia Pacific. Thus, the security architecture developed during the post–World War II period is still in place, and concerns over the Southern Tier merely represent an extension of the central area.

With the conception of NATO in 1948, the security interests of North America, the core states of Western Europe, and a number of other disparate states such as Norway, Denmark, and Portugal were formalized. With the onset of the Korean War, it was realized that pledges were insufficient, and NATO became essentially a defensive/military alliance.[5] At the same time, Turkey and Greece acceded to NATO, becoming full members in 1952. Two states, mutually hostile, with a range of major disagreements including the future of Cyprus and the delimitation of the Aegean Sea, had been accommodated. Despite periods of great tension, they have not actually confronted each other in war, and this must be attributed in no small measure to their common membership of NATO. It is of interest that the economic counterpart, membership in the European Union, has not been accorded to Turkey, and this rejection could irreparably damage the relations between Turkey and the West so assiduously nurtured in NATO.

In 1955, despite much foreboding, the Federal Republic of Germany became a member of NATO. This not only added German resources to the alliance but allowed constraints to be placed upon its military. Further, it eliminated the unlikely possibility that Germany might have seen itself as in a bargaining position between East and West. Certainly, accommodation within NATO dissolved French fears of a resurgent neighbor. Membership of an alliance allows a degree of control over the states involved that would not otherwise be possible. There are several instances in which the United States has been constrained or encouraged in its activities by pressure from other NATO members. Thus, it is tempting to see the offer of NATO membership to Russia as, in a measure, paralleling the offer made to Germany in 1955.

In 1982 the third enlargement of NATO occurred when Spain was admitted. Within NATO, aside from the obvious strategic considerations, there was concern to support a recently established democracy, and Spain saw membership as a stepping-stone to inclusion within the European Economic Community (EEC). This accession provides close analogies with the situation today. The states of Eastern Europe and the Southern Tier require support for their democratic institutions and assistance in the development of their economies.

The fourth enlargement of NATO occurred in 1990 with the unification of Germany and the effective accession of the former East Germany. Understandably, given the undertakings which had been articulated, this move began the process by which relations between Russia and NATO have been increasingly soured. However, it is the fifth enlargement, in which Poland, Hungary, and the Czech Republic will become full NATO members in 1999, that has generated the most political controversy despite the general lack of public discussion.

This brief history illustrates the point that NATO has always been pragmatic in its selection of alliance members. While every enlargement can be related to security concerns, there was on each occasion at least one other reason for the particular accession. In phase with developments in Western Europe, NATO has constantly changed. The focus has remained the same, but the breadth of alliance aims has increased. The major changes have, of course, occurred since 1990 with the perceived need for the maintenance of what had been an extremely successful alliance.

NATO CHANGES

With the end of the Cold War and the dissolution of the Warsaw Pact it appeared, superficially, that NATO was without a role. However, at the very least, there remained the need for a body to supervise and monitor the various arms limitation agreements such as Conventional Forces Europe (CFE) and Strategic Arms Reduction (START II). The only organization with the experience and expertise for such activities was NATO. Furthermore, whatever European-based security alliances might arise, NATO remains the official link between North America and Western Europe. With the range of missions developed over its forty-year history and with a tried and tested structure, NATO was well-placed to change its focus to more broadly based defense management. While the historical precedents for such a transformation may not be particularly good, NATO does possess the characteristics which best suit it for survival.[6]

In the event, to maintain what it has already achieved and to give confidence to the emerging democracies of Central and Eastern Europe, NATO has diversified its role. While remaining at core a security alliance, NATO has developed two other related but clearly discernible roles: (1) the management of crisis, and (2) the projection of stability.[7]

The most obvious indicators of preparations for crisis management are the new command structure, the agreements on the European Security and Defence Identity (ESDI), and the Combined Joint Task Forces (CJTF).[8] While this role may be of significance in the Caucasus and Central Asia because of the numerous potential flashpoints and also because troops from NATO-associated countries may be included in the task forces, the main interest for the region must be the projection of stability. If the countries of the Southern Tier are to develop politically and economically as independent democracies, there is a basic requirement for stability. This may be achieved in a number of ways, but one would be through the various guarantees that could be provided by NATO. To project stability, NATO has fashioned three approaches: enlargement, the Partnership for Peace (PFP), and the two special relationships formed with the Founding Act with Russia and the Charter Agreement with Ukraine.[9]

It is contended that the PFP and the development of a workable relationship with Russia are the key potential contributions of NATO toward stability in Central Asia. In 1997 the alliance enhanced the PFP concept, increasing the possible roles for participants in both operations and policy making. National delegations at NATO headquarters may be accredited to the new Euro-Atlantic Partnership Council (EAPC) at the diplomatic level. Indeed, the differences between full membership of NATO and participation in PFP are becoming increasingly indistinguishable.[10] As NATO moves from being an alliance of necessity to an alliance of choice, NATO operations are likely to be undertaken by both member and non-member PFP participants under the CJTF concept.

THREATS IN THE SOUTHERN TIER

In the post–Cold War period, the security architecture fashioned by the West has not changed. Concerns for the security of the Caucasus and Central Asia have merely resulted in an enlargement of the central area of concern, originally focused only upon the Persian-Arabian Gulf region.

The main threats to the continuing political and economic development of the Southern Tier, which could be nullified by the projection of a stability program, are: disruptions to the exploitation and distribution of oil and natural gas resources which are crucial for the future economic prosperity of the region, instabilities on a local scale, and competing strategic interests of relatively more powerful states both within and outside the region. If the Southern Tier is compared with the Persian-Arabian Gulf, it is clear that the two have much in common and that, despite the obvious instabilities generated by two Gulf conflicts, Western guarantees have at least ensured that no power, either internal or external, has been able to impose itself upon the region.

OIL AND NATURAL GAS

The energy resources of the Caspian Basin have been envisaged as alternatives to Gulf supplies for Europe and North America in particular and also as potentially significant in the development of China and the Indian Subcontinent. However, it appears that expectations have leapt ahead of reality in that current proved oil reserves are relatively limited, particularly when compared with those of the Middle East (Table 7.1). The point is enhanced by the R/P ratio, the number of years the reserves will last at present rates of production.

Although the combined proved reserves for Azerbaijan and Kazakhstan combined equal only 1.5 percent of the global total, each exceeds various significant Middle Eastern producers, including Oman and Qatar. The main point, however, is that exploration is still taking place, and there are clear indications that the total proved reserves will be significantly enhanced.

With regard to natural gas, the situation is very different in that the

Table 7.1: Proved Oil Reserves at End of 1997

Country	Share of Global Total	Reserves/Production (R/P) Ratio
Azerbaijan	0.7%	100+
Kazakhstan	0.8%	42.5
Russian Federation	4.7%	21.7
Uzbekistan	0.1%	8.0
Other Former Soviet Republics	0.1%	15.4
Total Former Soviet Republics	**6.4%**	**24.7**
Iran	9.0%	69.0
Iraq	10.8%	100+
Kuwait	9.3%	100+
Oman	0.5%	15.8
Qatar	0.4%	15.1
Saudi Arabia	25.2%	79.5
Syria	0.2%	12.0
United Arab Emirates	9.4%	100+
Yemen	0.4%	28.9
Other Middle East Nations	Less than 0.05 %	9.4
Total Middle East Nations	**65.2%**	**87.7**

Source: *BP Statistical Review of World Energy 1998*

states of the former Soviet Union have greater proved reserves than are located in the Middle East (Table 7.2). Turkmenistan, Uzbekistan, and Kazakhstan all have, by world standards, important reserves, and these are likely to be increased as a result of further exploration.

The major question regarding the energy resources of the region concerns the extent of exploitable reserves. There are both political and economic reasons why a complete assessment for the Basin will take some time. Many of the potential sources are located either in areas of the Caspian Sea yet to be delimited or are near disputed territorial boundaries.[11] Technology is therefore ahead of the law, and the situation is exacerbated by the relatively low current price of oil on the world market. Thus, for many potential wells, the lead times for the start of production are impossible to forecast. Given favorable conditions, five years would be a reasonable figure. In this case, it must be considered a minimum estimate.

The unknowns of proved reserves, world prices, and lead times must be added to the problems of distribution. This region has generated the concept of pipeline geopolitics. Factors range from the physical to the geopolitical and include distance; difficulty of terrain; the desire to avoid the territories of Russia, Iran, or possibly Afghanistan; the tanker capacity of the

Table 7.2: Proved Natural Gas Reserves at End of 1997

Country	Share of Global Total	Reserves/Production (R/P) Ratio
Azerbaijan	0.6%	100+
Kazakhstan	1.3%	100+
Russian Federation	33.2%	85.9
Turkmenistan	2.0%	100+
Ukraine	0.8%	65.1
Uzbekistan	1.3%	38.7
Other Former Soviet Republics	Less than 0.05%	76.6
Total Former Soviet Union	**39.2%**	**86.2**
Bahrain	0.1%	18.6
Iran	15.8%	100+
Iraq	2.2%	100+
Kuwait	1.0%	100+
Oman	0.5%	100+
Qatar	5.9%	100+
Saudi Arabia	3.7%	100+
United Arab Emirates	4.0%	100+
Yemen	0.3%	100+
Other Middle East Nations	0.2%	100+
Total Middle East Nations	**33.7%**	**100+**

Source: *BP Statistical Review of World Energy 1998*

Bosporus; and the desirability of further outlets in the Persian-Arabian Gulf.[12] Since all the potential producer states are landlocked, at least one stage of export must be through pipelines, but these lack the flexibility of tanker transport and can be damaged or switched off. Pipelines are permanent trade links and may be of symbolical significance, but they do not provide any guarantee of permanence: the Middle East is replete with pipelines that have been closed, partially destroyed, or temporarily switched off. Pipelines have a potential to enhance the security of an international relationship, but there needs to be a reasonable level of security before a pipeline can be built. There is also the question of cost, particularly at a time of downturn in oil prices. Under the most benign environmental conditions, the installation of a pipeline costs approximately $1 million per mile.[13]

In the Southern Tier the production and export of oil and natural gas, which is the chief hope for the future prosperity of the region, is beset with potential physical, political, and economic problems. Some degree of regional stability must be ensured so that effective exploitation can occur and a secure pipeline network can be constructed.

LOCAL INSTABILITIES

The competition for oil and natural gas sources, as well as for pipeline routes, provides one obvious source of instability in the region. This may result from domestic sources, interstate activity, or rivalry among outside countries, including many from NATO, competing for the resource. Already within the region there are numerous flashpoints, as well as continuing conflicts in Afghanistan, Tajikistan, and the various parts of Kurdistan. Among the more obvious flashpoints are Nagorno-Karabakh and Abkhazia in the Transcaucasus and the Fergana Valley in Central Asia.[14] However, of potentially greater significance are transboundary movements on a macropolitical scale involving, for instance, drugs, nuclear material, arms, and refugees. No state individually has the power to eliminate such activity, and regional, if not global, cooperation is required

COMPETING STRATEGIC INTERESTS

Competing powers within the region are normally identified as Russia, Turkey, and Iran, but these three are by no means equal. Russia remains a global power, and therefore its potential influence must be viewed as not only internal but also as opposed to external great powers such as China, India, and the West.[15]

Following the breakup of the Soviet Union it was generally thought that Turkey and Iran would compete for influence in the Southern Tier; to a degree this has happened. The efforts of Turkey, bolstered by the commonality of Turkic languages, have made significant progress in gaining influence, but such gains have been largely offset by turbulence within Turkey and by its serious Mediterranean problems. Also, in general the countries that might have responded most strongly to Turkish advances have preferred to develop stronger contacts with the United States and Western Europe. However, Turkey remains of great significance in the development of export routes for the energy resources of the region.

Iran has adopted a relatively low-profile approach, which has largely excluded the expected export of Islamic militancy. Major problems affecting the spread of Iranian influence have been the ongoing dispute with Azerbaijan over the Azeri minority in northern Iran and the virtually continuous conflict in Tajikistan, the only Farsi-speaking member of the Central Asian states. The direct influence of Iran in the region may therefore appear somewhat limited, but its main impact is likely to be seen in the future as a result of its relationship with the great powers. Already Russia and Iran have worked closely together, particularly in the field of energy cooperation, but relationships with the United States exhibit continuing mutual hostility.[16] With an apparently more moderate regime in Iran, there are a few signs that the U.S. approach may be undergoing a degree of moderation, but as yet U.S. commercial activity is constrained by foreign policy.

For many reasons Russia remains critical to the security of the Southern Tier, and it already provides the protection of most of its neighbors' boundaries. Furthermore, the major issue in the pipeline conundrum concerns routes through Russia and the control that would therefore be bestowed. The question has to be posed as to whether there are any incentives or desires to attempt to restore hegemony. The argument regarding the Russian position has been simplistically characterized as either empire or democracy. For stability in the region, which must be in the long-term interests of Russia, it would appear important that the independence of the eight states is maintained. Economically, it would seem highly desirable that there are multiple pipelines to guard against external manipulation of the system.

Within the Southern Tier, relations with Russia vary, being particularly warm in the case of Armenia and Kazakhstan. Among the internal powers, Russia has generated strong links with Iran, providing thereby something of counterbalance against the more severe effects of U.S. influence in the region. Most significantly, Russia has been nurturing contacts with China, India, and Japan in what might be viewed as a new, embryonic alignment for Asia. It is obvious that whatever the influence of NATO and the West, Russia will remain a key player in the region.

Despite the remoteness of Central Asia from its core area, China has had a long-term involvement in at least the eastern side of the Southern Tier. In particular there have been ethnic and boundary considerations, but there is now renewed interest due to the potential for energy supplies. Indeed, there are already well-advanced plans for the construction of a gas pipeline from Turkmenistan to China. Questions remain concerning the export of arms and nuclear materials from China, and relationships with the United States and Western Europe have fluctuated. In the longer term, it seems probable that Western Europe will wish to cultivate stronger ties with China for economic reasons and also as a safeguard against any renewed large-scale hostility from Russia.

In the south, nuclear weapons testing by India and Pakistan has focused world attention on their uneasy relationship. While any outcome from this is unlikely to be projected into Central Asia, both countries have an interest in the region. India is generally perceived as a global power of the future and has looked favorably upon overtures from Russia. Pakistan, like India, has concern for the energy resources of the Southern Tier, but in addition has a cultural link to the region through Islam. Of potentially greater significance in the short-term to the region are the relationships with Southwest Asia and particularly Israel and Saudi Arabia. Saudi Arabia has sufficient financial resources to influence events, but at present its chief concern is with the reestablishment and entrenchment of Islam. Israel appears to be totally pragmatic in seeking cooperation, although there is a common theme of deep hostility toward Iran. Close collaboration, as yet chiefly in the defense field, has been established with Turkey, and links are being fostered with Azerbaijan, Uzbekistan, and most recently Afghanistan. Since Israel appears to have the uncritical support of the United States for its foreign policy, it must be considered an increasingly important actor in the region.

RUSSIA

The key to success in any projection of stability by NATO would appear to be the relationship between the alliance and Russia.[17] The NATO-Russia Founding Act, signed in 1997, was a start, but the legitimate sensitivities of Russia must be continuously addressed. If NATO is to retain an open-door policy, it would seem illogical to exclude Russia.[18] This point has been made forcibly by experts ranging from Brzezinski to Talbott.[19] A more realistic strategy may be the development of PFP to dispel unease about any apparent encirclement of Moscow and to reassure non-NATO members that they do not inhabit a "gray zone." As a result of either membership or an enhanced PFP, Russia would be included in a security community in which problems are not resolved by force.[20] Russia's membership would mean that NATO would address problems in Eastern Asia, but the advantage of a group of states committed to peaceful resolution of problems covering the entire Northern Hemisphere is surely a highly desirable and not totally over-optimistic goal.

The major point must be that the continuing improvement of NATO-Russian relations must parallel any enlargement of NATO and should, if anything, precede it. Potential Russian alienation is not so much a military as a political issue, and the resulting actions could well set back and possibly, in some cases, abort political and economic reform within the region. There is also the important question of the continuation of the START II and CFE processes.[21] If NATO continues to be perceived as a threat, Russia may have little option but to renew its emphasis upon nuclear strategy and even first use.[22]

Russia's isolation outside the European security structure runs counter to the interests of NATO and the Southern Tier in particular. Russian relationships must not be a pawn in the security debate and must be treated entirely separately from any issues of enlargement. Russia needs to complete the process of political reform alongside economic growth and social development, but it must always be remembered that Russia is a major autonomous actor within the region. The most realistic option for ensuring Russian cooperation in the Southern Tier would seem to be through a twin-track approach of developing stronger, more consistent links with the West through PFP and the European Union. Indeed, as the largest trade and investment partner with Russia, the European Union may prove in the long term to be a more important body than NATO.

CONCLUSION

Since the end of the Cold War, the interconnectedness of Europe and the Southern Tier has been strengthened. As a landlocked buffer zone, the Transcaucasus and Central Asia constitute a vulnerable region. NATO, by working closely with Russia and by developing PFP, can bring guarantees of stability that will underpin economic development and safeguard democratization. If the area is to develop as a security community, current conflicts and crises need to be addressed and confidence-building measures established. The aim for NATO must be to underwrite the security of the Southern Tier through PFP and in cooperation with Russia. This would represent the greatest bonus yet emanating from the end of the Cold War.

Conflicts, Caspian Oil, and NATO

8

Major Pieces
of the Caucasus Puzzle

Elkhan E. Nuriyev

There are currently many serious concerns about broad strategic issues in the Caucasus, including oil and pipeline politics in the Caspian Basin, the ongoing conflicts in the geopolitical setting of the Caucasus, and, of course, increasing U.S. engagement in the region, especially via the NATO alliance. Add in the Russian responses to the above and the emergence of Iran and Turkey as players in the region, and you have a potential—and all too often an actual—political, military, and economic flashpoint. So, what is going on in the Caucasus? What are the difficulties and problems for regional cooperation? And finally, what are the prospects of maintaining and consolidating stability, security, and peace in the region? This chapter attempts to provide an answer to these questions.

The Caucasus is a vital link between Asia and Europe, between East and West. The region is also the land bridge between the Caspian and Black Seas. The Caucasus certainly deserves special attention as it cradles many civilizations. The area in and of itself has a great potential both in terms of trained, skilled human power and abundant, natural resources. It is an area rich in history, culture, and tradition. Most importantly, what happens here has implications for the region and the world.[1]

The Caspian Sea, bordered by Russia, Azerbaijan, Iran, and the Central Asian states of Kazakhstan and Turkmenistan, has been a major commercial oil producing area since 1871. From its beginning the region's oil industry has been dependent on foreign capital and technology. The Swedish Nobels and French Rothschilds built considerable fortunes drilling wells and constructing railroads to carry oil from the Azerbaijani capital, Baku, to Georgian ports on the Black Sea. During World War I control of Baku's oil fields was the goal of fierce competition among German, Turkish, and British forces after the collapse of the Russian Empire. During World War II the oil fields were a strategic objective in Nazi Germany's campaign against the Soviet Union.[2]

Analysis of the history of the region reveals an extremely complicated and problematic historical and political inheritance that has made the Caucasus one of the most unstable world regions, even during the age of the great empires. The present military and political situation in the region indicates that the Caucasus has been attractive to imperial powers since early in this century due to its large gas and crude oil reserves. Control over these energy resources and export routes out of the Eurasian hinterland is quickly becoming one of the central issues in post–Cold War politics. Similar to the "Great Game" of the late nineteenth and early twentieth centuries, which pitted British interests against those of the Russian empire and Germany, a new geopolitical game in the Transcaucasus and Eurasia has emerged after the collapse of the Soviet Union in 1991. Today's struggle involves oil and geopolitics as well as many state and nonstate actors. Consequently, the region is again in the news due to its unstable transition period following the breakup of the USSR and, most importantly, its abundant, unexploited natural resources.[3]

In fact the collapse of the Soviet Union has created a unique opportunity for the countries of the Caucasus—Azerbaijan, Georgia, and Armenia—to play a new and significant role as independent forces between the dominant Eurasian power in the north, Russia, and the rival powers in the south, Turkey and Iran. With the disintegration of the Soviet Union and the founding of the new independent states in the region, the three most powerful countries—Russia, Iran, and Turkey—gained vast opportunities for cooperation and partnership with their new neighbors. At the same time, they faced new challenges as several armed conflicts erupted in the region. Inevitably these affected regional powers and the geopolitical situation in the CIS space.

Regional conflicts in the Caucasus threaten to deny Western access to the vital oil and gas reserves the world will need in the twenty-first century.[4] Some analysts believe that the current conflicts in the Caucasus were started or exacerbated by the Russian military, and are tied to control over the pipeline routes. At times these violent conflicts blocked the transit routes to the West for Caspian and Central Asian oil and gas. Consequently, regional conflicts in the geopolitical setting of the CIS are affecting oil politics and transit routes to the world market. Moreover, today's instability in the Caucasus has a direct impact on neighboring areas, and these conflicts prevent the Caucasian states from engaging in mutually beneficial processes of interaction and economic cooperation.

History has now given the countries of the Caucasus a chance to act as a bridge between north and south and as a major transportation and com-

munication link between east and west. Whether these countries will succeed as an independent force will depend heavily on the capabilities and
ingenuity of their leaders. Success will also depend on the role that Russia,
Turkey, and Iran will play. If these powerful neighbors pursue constructive
policies toward the region and contribute to its development, the countries
of the Caucasus will have a good chance of success. If, however, traditional
hegemonic policies predominate, the region may succumb again to domination by its powerful neighbors.

RUSSIAN MANIPULATION OF REGIONAL CONFLICTS AND ITS AFFECT ON OIL PIPELINE ROUTES

Political science scholars are interested in learning more about how and
why ongoing conflicts affecting oil pipeline routes continue to pose the
most serious obstacle to the long-term stability and development of the
Caucasus region. For centuries the Caucasus was a frontier between
Europe and Asia, and between Islam and Christendom. Russia has protected its strategic interests in the Caucasus for three centuries. Long a
hotbed of ethnic warfare, the region was ripe for Russia to find and exploit
dissatisfied ethnic minorities such as the Abkhaz, Karabakh Armenians, and
others. Since 1991, however, Moscow has seen its position in the region
progressively decline. The independence of the Caucasian countries, and
specifically Azerbaijan's reorientation toward the West, have been accompanied by cultural, economic, and political incursions by Turkey and Iran.
Traditional geopolitical rivalries with Turkey and Iran and competition for
Caspian oil were two of a number of compelling factors that focused
Moscow's attention on reestablishing its dominance over the Caucasus.
From the very beginning of the founding of the CIS, Georgia and Azerbaijan took strict centrifugal positions and tried to leave the Russian sphere of
influence. Although they possessed strong liberation movements akin to
those in the Baltic states, Azerbaijan and Georgia, unlike the Baltic countries, did not gain any political support from the West and were left alone
in their struggle for independence. Unlike Armenia, which rapidly turned
to its traditional historical ally, Russia, both Georgia and Azerbaijan suffered invasion by Russian troops, whose aim was to repress the democratic
movements in both countries. Both suffered bloody wars with more powerful adversaries as well as coups d'état that overthrew legally elected leaders and brought to power former Communist leaders. These conflict
developments made the fates of these two Transcaucasian countries very
similar.

One of the main goals of the Russian occupation of Chechnya and the
Caucasus as a whole is to ensure control of the pipeline that goes from
Baku, via Grozny, the Chechen capital, to the Russian Black Sea port of
Novorossiysk, which is designed by Russia to be the terminal for both the
Kazakh (Tengiz) and Azerbaijani pipelines. Unlike Armenia, which became
the most homogeneous former Soviet republic after the departure of the

Azeri minorities, Georgia and Azerbaijan are multinational states that are vulnerable to Russian manipulation. The bitter war in Abkhazia claimed thousands of lives and was precipitated by Russian military involvement authorized by former defense minister Grachev. The Russian move was aimed at weakening Georgia, undermining Turkish and Western influence in the region, and controlling access to its oil. Gaining control over the long Black Sea coastline in Abkhazia, protecting the Russian ports of Novorossiysk and Tuapse, and moving closer to the Georgian oil-exporting ports in Poti, Supsa, and Batumi perfectly suited Russia's plans. In addition to the above, the conflict in Chechnya and, generally speaking, the southern border region of the Russian Federation increasingly resembles Lebanon or former Yugoslavia, complete with hostages, refugees, and vendettas. Chechnya is still an acute problem and a source of instability for Russia. Since 1996, neither Russia nor Chechnya has been able to find a creative middle ground that can reconcile the Chechen desire for independence with Russian fears of a "domino effect" and the rupture of the territorial integrity of the Russian Federation.[5] Therefore, the outlook for oil transportation through Chechnya looks questionable in the absence of a settlement of this conflict. As Russia became entangled in Chechnya and word about Chechen commando training camps being operated from Abkhazia spread, Moscow started to show less support of the Chechen allies, the Abkhaz. But despite Georgian acquiescence on military basing rights, Russia refused to effectively cooperate in restoring Georgian territorial integrity.

In 1995 Armenia and Georgia signed agreements allowing Russia to post its military on their soil. Georgia permitted four bases, Armenia three. But while Armenia signed the agreements voluntarily (as a precaution against its historic foe, Turkey), Georgia did not. In Georgia civil war and military collapse forced Tbilisi to end its assault on Abkhazia in 1993, but neither Moscow nor a United Nations mission has since been able to bring the two sides together.[6] There are at least twenty thousand Russian troops in Armenia, concentrated around three major bases.[7] Azerbaijan came under severe pressure from Moscow to allow Russian bases on its territory, but thus far has refused to do so. Moscow still continues to influence Azerbaijan and its pro-Western leader, Heydar Aliev, to establish Russian military bases on the Azeri territory, and on very many occasions there has been pressure to bring Russian troops back to Azerbaijan. Aliev has been able to conduct a foreign policy that is more balanced between Russia, Iran, and Turkey. Many Western politicians had expected that Aliev would turn and move close to Russia. Although he brought Azerbaijan back into CIS, he nevertheless did not go far beyond establishing dialogue with Russia. In fact, Moscow considers Aliev's foreign policy too independent.

Moscow has interfered in the internal affairs of the countries of the Caucasus with the purpose of destabilizing the military and political situation in the region. Indeed, Russia tries to play a trump card against Azerbaijan, supporting not only the Karabakh Armenians but also the Lezgin national movement in the north of the country and the Talish one in the south. Moscow incited local pro-Russian factions, such as Abkhazians in Georgia, Armenians in Karabakh, and hard-line Communist pro-Russian clans in Tajikistan, to challenge the independence and territorial integrity of these nascent states. As a result, hundreds of thousands were left dead, wounded, and homeless.[8]

Turning to the conflicts in the region, another example of Russian military involvement in the Caucasus is the Armenia-Azerbaijanian conflict over Nagorno-Karabakh, which is situated in a possible strategic oil route from the Caspian Sea to Turkey. The strife between Armenia and Azerbaijan escalated in 1988, and full-scale war broke out in 1992. As is well known, in 1993 Armenian forces launched a series of offensives against Azerbaijan that resulted in the deaths of thousands of innocent civilians, the military occupation of 20 percent of Azerbaijan, and the creation of about one million refugees. These Azerbaijani refugees are crammed into miserably inadequate camps. The 1994 truce ended the war, which killed over fifteen thousand people and was the first serious ethnic conflict in the former Soviet Union space. A fragile cease-fire halted the fighting, but efforts to resolve the conflict have not produced results. The sides remain far apart, and peace talks are deadlocked. Although both Armenia and Azerbaijan have gradually moved toward a compromise solution proposed by the Organization for Security and Cooperation in Europe (OSCE), the Karabakh Armenians are holding out for a result that gives them de jure, as well as de facto, independence.[9]

These wars, which until recently have devastated the Caucasus, took a heavy toll in terms of human lives. Many refugees still live in squalid conditions, especially in Azerbaijan. At present, Georgians and Abkhazians have a significant interest in avoiding another war. For the Georgians, renewed fighting in Abkhazia would threaten the dramatic political and economic progress the country has made under Shevardnadze's leadership. The anarchy that prevailed in 1992 and 1993 is now a memory, and Georgia had the fastest growing economy in the CIS in 1996 and one of the fastest in 1997. To sustain this recovery, however, it needs substantial foreign investment. Particularly important is the completion of a pipeline bringing the so-called early oil from Azerbaijan's Caspian oil fields to the Georgian port of Supsa. If this project proves successful, Georgia may benefit in the future from the construction of larger-capacity pipelines for delivering the enormous reserves of oil and gas in the Caspian Basin to the international marketplace. All this, and indeed foreign investment in general, would be jeopardized by a resumption of the Abkhaz war.[10]

In February 1998 domestic disagreement in Armenia over the prospect of a compromise solution for Karabakh resulted in the resignation of

President Levon Ter-Petrossian.[11] After new presidential elections in Armenia, the party headed by Robert Kocharian, former Armenian prime-minister and former leader of Nagorno-Karabakh, came to power in Yere-van. Having become the new Armenian president, Kocharian stated that "we Armenians should gain international recognition for Karabakh—national self-determination—guaranteeing its development toward perma-nent geographical connection with Armenia."[12] In Azerbaijan there is widespread concern about the possibility of new destabilization in the region after the recent change of power in Armenia. There is the possibil-ity of a renewed war over Karabakh—one that can complicate the general situation not only in Azerbaijan but in the Caucasus as a whole. If no agree-ment on Karabakh is reached by the end of 1998, Western governments and businesses engaged in the Caucasus will likely begin to reconsider their plans regarding oil deals and pipeline systems for the region.

Competition between the West and Russia over mediation of the con-flict creates serious geopolitical difficulties for stability and development of the region. Russia does not want to see the United States as a major arbi-trator in the Caucasus. The Russians do not want to leave the Caucasus. All Moscow wants is to dominate in the region and always keep the Caucasus in its own sphere of influence. Thus, the solutions to the conflicts depend not only on the warring parties but also on whether the great powers can resolve conflict between themselves. It would be a mistake to believe that the Kremlin will work closely with the United States, OSCE, and the UN to settle conflicts in order to bring about lasting peace and stability in the region, which is absolutely essential for the Caucasus and Central Asia. Events both in Daghestan and Chechnya, as well as the military and polit-ical situation in the Caucasus, clearly attest to this fact. In short, there are many serious obstacles to the long-term stability and development of the Caucasus states.

RUSSIA, TURKEY, IRAN, AND THE UNITED STATES: OIL PIPELINE ROUTES AND THE NEW GEOPOLITICS OF GREAT POWERS

Any discussion of conflict resolution in the Caucasus would be remiss if it did not discuss oil developments in the Caspian Basin and this new source of energy supply in the twenty-first century. Since the dissolution of the USSR, hydrocarbon resources—specifically, oil and gas reserves—have been identified as perhaps the most important source of economic revival for the NIS countries. This has been especially true for Azerbaijan, whose population is dwarfed by its massive energy reserves. In the past several years a series of events on the energy front has contributed to a palpable shift in Azerbaijan's prospects for realizing substantial energy revenues in the near future as well as in its respective strategic orientation.[13]

September 1994 brought the signing of the oil agreement, which is known now as the "contract of the century." This agreement opened the doors for Azerbaijan to join the international community and made foreign investment more attractive. The Azerbaijani government signed an $8 billion agreement with an international oil consortium, the Azerbaijan International Operating Company (AIOC), to exploit the Caspian Sea oil fields. Since then, Azerbaijan has begun wide-scale cooperation with the major oil companies of the world. Amoco, UNOCAL, Pennzoil, Exxon, Mobil, Chevron, British Petroleum, Statoil, Lukoil, Turkish Petroleum, Itochu, Delta, Ramco, OIEC, Petrofina, Deminex, Total, Elf Aquitaine, and Agip are all working in Azerbaijan within the framework of the oil consortium.

By the middle of 1998 Azerbaijan had signed eleven agreements with foreign partners. All of these oil contracts underscored the historic strategic significance of Azerbaijan and the Caucasus as a whole. Almost all of the major U.S. oil companies are involved, and five major international consortia have been established in the past several years to explore for oil and gas in the Azerbaijan sector of the Caspian Sea. By the year 2010, the AIOC is projected to be producing 700,000 to 800,000 barrels of oil per day. In developing this project, the AIOC will spend over $8 billion. Furthermore, for every dollar invested in the oil industry, an additional three dollars will be spent on infrastructure and services. Japan is about to undertake major investment in Azerbaijan, with estimates running as high as $3 billion. British and French companies are establishing a prominent presence and are also committing large financial resources to Azerbaijan. According to the U.S. Department of Commerce, foreign direct investment in Azerbaijan increased from $15 million in 1993 to $545.5 million in 1996. That is an increase of almost 3,700 percent. By 2010 total investment in the oil and gas industry is estimated to reach $25 billion.[14]

In October 1995 the AIOC announced that the early oil (approximately 80,000 barrels a month) would be split between two pipelines. The first, a northern pipeline that goes through Russian territory to the Black Sea port of Novorossiysk via Chechnya, is quite unsafe. The second line goes to the Georgian port of Supsa in two separate pipelines. For the AIOC the priority is to transport the main oil, the peak of which will be reached in the year 2004, to the Mediterranean Sea. The Azerbaijani government is thinking now about having a system of several pipelines, which may be very useful because both Azeri officials and their foreign partners clearly understand that security issues are crucial in the region. In other words, it is better to have an alternative not depending on one single route.

Because of its geopolitical location, abundant natural resources, and political circumstances Azerbaijan will be at the very center of international politics and diplomacy for years to come. All of its neighbors maintain strong interest in what happens to Azerbaijan. Russia claims the Caucasus as her legitimate sphere of influence and has concerns about security on her southern border and the possible spread of Islamic fundamentalism (i.e., Iranian influence) and the potential alliance of Turkey and new secular

Islamic states in the region. Finally, the Russians are deeply suspicious and resentful of U.S. "encroachments" that promote democracy and development in the "near abroad." Russia also has economic interests and claims regarding the energy resources of the Caspian. Needless to say, Russia would like to see pipelines transport these resources to or through Russia. Much of what happens in Russia will have a significant impact on Azerbaijan as well as on the Caucasus and on the whole NIS.

Today Russia benefits from the state of "frozen instability" in the Caucasus, which effectively denies independence and economic development to the states in the region. It also hinders viable and lucrative exporting routes to the oil consortia in the area. Moscow has gone beyond words in establishing its power in the Caucasus. Russia is pursuing a policy of military basing in the Caucasus aimed at placing Moscow in a position of exclusive control over all future pipelines in the region. Russia, as the successor state of much of the government apparatus and mindset of the Soviet Union, might in the future become a more developed democracy or a huge empire again. In any case, and despite which of these outcomes occur, it can be said with certainty that the Russian Federation wants to ensure its economic and political influence in the NIS. Russian politicians know well that the natural resources of the Caspian Sea and Azerbaijan make it a geopolitically important region.

Turkey is another important player in this game because much of the Caspian oil will probably go through the Bosporus Straits, or possibly because of the economic benefits from the oil lines that could come to them through its Mediterranean port of Ceyhan. Turkey wants to limit the amount of oil passing through the Bosporus for ecological reasons and is positioning itself to build a pipeline from the Caucasus to Ceyhan. Besides the political and economic interests, strong cultural and linguistic ties link the Caucasian republics, especially Azerbaijan, to Turkey. Turkey sees Azerbaijan and the new Central Asian countries as its natural allies in a loose confederation of secular Muslim republics. But Turkey is presently too weak because of its serious internal economic and political problems to carry out major power responsibilities in the region. However, its geopolitical location as well as cultural and historical ties with the Turkic societies of the Caucasus represent the hope of neo-Ottomans and the great fear of the Russians.

Iran as a historic player of the "Great Game" has economic and ideological interests and aims throughout Central Asia and the Transcaucasus. Iran is in a geostrategically sensitive and significant position between Central Asia, the Indian Ocean, the Transcaucasus, and Turkey. In regard to the latter, Iran sees itself in a competitive position because a strong, politically independent, secular, pro-Western, and pro-American Azerbaijan is not in the interests of Iran. In addition, Azerbaijan will become a competitor to Iran by developing its energy resources and emerging as a strong petroleum country. A recovered and developed Azerbaijan may also be seen as attractive to some twenty million Azeris living in Iran and could ultimately threaten Iran's territorial integrity. Azerbaijan's emerging relationships with the United States, Turkey, and Israel will significantly decrease Iranian influence in the Caucasus. However, Iran is a powerful neighbor that cannot be ignored easily. By isolating Iran, Azerbaijan is nourishing a strategic alliance between that country and Russia—an alliance that may ultimately threaten Azerbaijan's existence as an independent country. It may also bring about an enhancement in the rapprochement between Iran and Armenia that has been developing over the last few years. Because of the danger inherent in such a policy, Azerbaijan should pursue cooperation with Iran.

It should be noted that the transportation of Caspian oil is an issue which neither Turkey nor Russia can monopolize. Attempts to do so will undoubtedly leave the region as unstable as it has always been when such rivalries have existed unchecked. Compromise must replace competition in the pipeline interests, otherwise a more agitated Caucasus will bring poverty and bloodshed to everyone in the region, with no clear winner. Therefore, the dual-pipeline solution remains the only strategy for a prosperous "compromise" between Turkey and Russia.

The United States is the final important player in the region, despite its remoteness. Questions related to oil supplies, gas reserves, and the security of energy supplies are of vital national, economic, and geostrategic interest to the United States. Azerbaijan is, therefore, an important country, and the Southern Tier of the NIS a crucial geopolitical location.

Being the leading world power today, the United States has become one of Azerbaijan's main partners in the international political system. Considering the geostrategic location of Azerbaijan, this partnership is a good precursor for long-term stability and security in the region. Being the cochair of the OSCE Minsk Group, and having great abilities to influence the positions of the parties to the Armenia-Azerbaijanian conflict, the United States can become the guarantor of the just solution of the conflict. To be just, this solution must be based on the OSCE Lisbon summit principles that were supported by all OSCE member-states except the Republic of Armenia.

Besides the above, the United States needs to ensure free and fair access for all interested parties to the oil fields of the Caucasus and Central Asia. Of course reasonable Russian interests, such as access for Russian companies to bid for the exploration and transport of oil and gas in the region, must be respected. However, the West has a paramount interest in assuring that the Caucasian states as well as Central Asian countries maintain their independence and remain mostly secular and reasonably pro-Western. The United States sees its objectives in the region as promoting the economic independence and autonomy of the former Soviet republics from Moscow and ensuring that Caspian oil does not come under the sole control of Russia. Moscow, however, sees the American policy as an attempt to limit its influence in the Caucasus. Russia also sees such an attempt in the Western policy of "destabilization" in the Caucasus together with the expansion of the North Atlantic Treaty Organization (NATO) closer to its Western frontiers.[15]

Some analysts in the United States believe that Moscow is manipulating many of the conflicts in the Caucasus to prevent the states in the region from moving out of the Russian orbit. Russia is also seen as using the ethnic unrest to block the development of the pipelines through Caucasus as an alternative to the current Russian network.[16] If this were not enough fuel for the U.S./Russian "post–Cold War" rivalry, there is the highly politicized relationship between Russia and Iran. Russia is responsible for pursuing a number of policies in this relationship that conflict directly with U.S. interests. These include supplying nuclear reactors and sensitive technology to Iran; selling modern nuclear weapons technology, military aircraft, and warships to China; pressuring Azerbaijan for Russian control of the Caspian Sea; and, perhaps, purposeful ineffectiveness in its efforts to control organized crime and corruption.[17]

There are at present two crucial issues which need a lot of attention. One is that Russian domination and possible expansionist ambitions must be contained. The ties of Russia with an increasingly more pragmatic Iranian regime, due to its own economic and social distress, may not be so welcome by the West and even contradictory to its crucial interests. Consequently, the United States and its allies could be better off upon a rapprochement and cooperation between Turkey and Russia in the future rather than an alliance between Russia and Iran. The second issue at stake is the internal stability of all the countries involved in this Transcaucasian/Eurasian game. As discussed above, Russia and Turkey may pay more attention to their own domestic conflicts and have extra incentives to solve them because the Chechens and Kurds may endanger Russian and Turkish pipeline dreams. For Azerbaijan, in addition to enormous economic benefits, the oil deal also represents a major political gain. Economic considerations prompted the West, and particularly the United States, to insert itself into the Transcaucasian picture and play an important part—not only in negotiating the petroleum accord, but also in making efforts to block Russia from assuming the dominant role in attempts to resolve the Nagorno-Karabakh conflict. Only through U.S. and Western intervention—and Russian cooperation—can Azerbaijan's internal struggles be resolved.

THE CAUCASUS AND NATO ENLARGEMENT: FUTURE PROSPECTS FOR REGIONAL SECURITY

The present enlarging of NATO is a requisite part of achieving lasting peace and security in the Caucasus and in Eurasia as a whole. Three years ago NATO launched one of its most successful ventures, the Partnership for Peace (PFP). This has brought within the compass of NATO effort and activity some twenty-seven countries, from Central Europe through Ukraine and Russia into Central Asia. For those few countries seeking to join NATO, Partnership for Peace is the way station to membership, the training ground for the alliance, the transition that takes place before joining rather than afterward—so that when the U.S. senate asks whether a a nation is ready for membership the answer will yes.[18] And for those countries that do not join NATO, at least not at first, Partnership for Peace offers them a permanent engagement with the NATO structures, doing virtually everything that an ally can do. At the same time, NATO has given greater political meaning to Partnership for Peace by creating a new Euro-Atlantic Partnership Council that enables its forty-three members to help direct the course of PFP and to bring their security concerns to the heart of the alliance.[19]

Today we face an important question: Are future NATO interests confined to Central Europe, or should we also talk about possible NATO enlargement to the NIS? The Transcaucasian region has been visited by many representatives of various NATO structures, even by Secretary-General Javier Solana. A review of NATO officials' visits to the Caucasus reveals that their diplomatic mission has shown unequal interests in the three Transcaucasian countries. NATO officials' talks to Armenian and Georgian leaders were substantively different from their intensive negotiations with the Azerbaijani president.

For instance, while U.S. Ambassador Robert Hunter was in Armenia and Georgia the main topics of his talks were based around the issue of broadening and deepening cooperation between the above countries and NATO in the Partnership for Peace program. Azerbaijan is, however, seeking a special partnership with NATO and is eager to promote its own cooperation with the alliance. In bringing up the issue on a special partnership with NATO, Azerbaijan uses as political leverage its position on the Caspian coast and the existing level of the republic's cooperation with the Western world.

Today ongoing uncertainty about regional peace is indeed something to be considered very carefully by all countries involved in the pipeline debate and NATO expansion.[20] A huge market of more than 200 million people and an array of countries with large natural resources and security needs could develop the region so that it enjoys welfare and peace. It could also create a huge area of economic and political instability whose warfare and turmoil could easily spill across borders and have negative effects on the future of the region and the entire world.

CONCLUSION

The Western democracies and regional powers should work more closely on creating a balanced interplay of international competition in the Caucasus and in Eurasia as a whole. In addition, the United States has to strengthen cooperation with the Caucasian states, more fully employ the

OSCE to settle ethnic conflicts, and help Turkey to broaden cooperation with its allies. Regional powers should do their best to bring about lasting peace and stability in the region, which is absolutely essential for increasing economic integration.

It is time for all parties involved in the present struggle for Caspian oil to recognize that they need to combine efforts with the purpose of solving conflicts and promoting economic development in the Caucasus region. They should do all that is necessary so that history does not repeat itself again. At present, one can see how many nations in the Caucasus are still trapped in disputes and conflicts that prevent them from realizing their economic potential. It is very sad that the peoples of the Caucasus have still not experienced lasting peace, stability, and economic prosperity in the region.[21] The resolution of the conflicts in the Caucasus depends on how successfully the great powers seek to end the competitions for primacy and control in the region, and also whether the Caucasus peoples can choose conciliation over confrontation. The future of the region and the character of the next century's international relations are at stake, for the ongoing geopolitical game is quickly becoming a paramount challenge for great powers' policy making for the twenty-first century.

No War, No Peace in the Caucasus

9

Contested Sovereignty
in Chechnya, Abkhazia, and Karabakh

Edward Walker

INTRODUCTION*

After the implosion of the Soviet Union in December 1991, the USSR's fifteen republics quickly won international recognition as independent states. Seats at the UN's General Assembly, however, did not mean that sovereignty for the successor states was uncontested. Along with various border disputes between and within the new states, Azerbaijan, Moldova, Georgia, and Russia found themselves confronting armed challenges from secessionists demanding independence for Nagorno-Karabakh (or simply Karabakh), Trans-Dniestria, South Ossetia, Abkhazia, and Chechnya.

Strikingly, the outcomes of these five conflicts, at least for the moment, have been similar. Without exception, secessionists have triumphed on the battlefield and control their respective territories (and, in the case of Karabakh, a considerable piece of Azerbaijani territory beyond the borders of Karabakh as well). Despite their military success, however, the secessionists have failed to win international recognition—indeed, not one secessionist movement has been recognized by a single state, no matter how sympathetic.[1]

There are other similarities as well. In all five cases, cease-fires have ended most of the violence, but settlements on legal status remain elusive. Instead, national governments continue to insist on their territorial integrity, while secessionists assert their right to national self-determination. Nevertheless, it has become increasingly clear that the international community will deny diplomatic recognition as long as national governments refuse to accept the demands of the separatists. Foreign governments and international organizations (IOs) may condemn the use of excessive force and the violation of human rights by national governments; they may try to promote dialogue and compromise; and individual states or IOs may agree to help monitor or enforce cease-fires or peace settlements. But, fearful of promoting secessionist wars around the globe, the international community will not accept the unilateral secession of a territory from an existing state with recognized external borders. Having won on the battlefield but not at the negotiating table, the secessionists therefore find themselves in a state of "no peace, no war."

This is not to say that the likelihood that "no peace, no war" will persist is equal between cases. On the contrary, the risks of both renewed fighting and opportunities for a political settlement vary considerably. What follows is an assessment of those risks and opportunities in three of the five cases—Chechnya, Abkhazia, and Karabakh. I argue that the stand-off between Russia and Chechnya is very likely to endure because Moscow has no interest in renewed fighting, but legal and political obstacles to an agreement on status are great. In contrast, "no peace, no war" in Abkhazia is quite unstable—while there is a substantial risk of renewed fighting, there is also an opportunity for a political agreement in the foreseeable future. Finally, I argue that that the parties to the conflict in Karabakh are unlikely to reach agreement on status in the foreseeable future. On the other hand, there is still a possibility that a "first-stage" agreement over Karabakh can be reached, although the deepening rift between the Karabakh and Armenian governments, as well as growing political turmoil within the Armenian government, make a first-stage agreement in 1998 unlikely. If no such agreement is reached, the risks of renewed fighting will be significant and likely to increase over time, particularly after Azerbaijan's presidential elections the fall of 1998.

OBSTACLES TO WAR AND PEACE IN CHECHNYA

The cease-fire currently in effect in Chechnya dates from an August 1996 agreement signed by then Russian security council secretary Aleksandr Lebed and Chechen Chief of Staff (now President) Aslan Maskhadov. With presidential elections approaching in the summer of 1996, Yeltsin apparently concluded early that spring that he needed to convince the Russian electorate that an end to the war in Chechnya was in sight. On March 31, 1996, he issued an order to the Russian military to cease offensive military operations, and on May 27, 1996 acting Chechen President Zelikhan Yandarbiev and Russian Prime Minister Viktor Chernomyrdin signed a cease-fire agreement that provided for an exchange of prisoners and a Russian troop withdrawal.

While it is doubtless that the cease-fire contributed to Yeltsin's victory in the second round of Russia's presidential elections that July, the agreement broke down immediately thereafter. The Chechens quickly took the offensive and launched a daring and shockingly successful attack on Grozny on

August 6, 1996. The humiliating defeat induced Yeltsin to appoint Lebed, who had come in a close third in the first round of the presidential elections and subsequently agreed to support Yeltsin in exchange for a position in the administration, as his special envoy to Chechnya. Lebed took on his new charge with characteristic gusto, and after visiting Grozny announced that Russia was no longer in a position to win the war by military means and that a withdrawal of Russian troops and negotiations with Chechen resistance leaders were therefore unavoidable.

Despite opposition from Russian military commanders and the hard-line Interior Minister Anatolii Kulikov, Lebed arranged a ceasefire agreement on August 31, 1996. The text of this so-called Khasavyurt agreement included the following important provision:

> An agreement on the basics of mutual relations between the Russian Federation and the Chechen Republic, defined in accordance with universally recognized principles and norms of international law, must be reached by 31 December 2001.[2]

The agreement also called for the formation of a special commission to bring about an end to "combat operations," the gradual withdrawal of Russian troops from the republic, an exchange of prisoners, and cooperative efforts to reconstruct Chechnya's devastated economy.

Unlike earlier cease-fires, the Khasavyurt agreement held and was followed by the withdrawal of Russian troops from the republic. By the beginning of 1997, resistance forces had assumed uncontested control of Chechnya. To consolidate their political position, the new authorities in Grozny held presidential elections on January 27, 1997. Maskhadov, who had directed Chechen military operations during the war and then negotiated the cease-fire agreement with Lebed, won the election handily.[3]

While negotiations over the implementation of the Khasavyurt agreement began soon after its signing, both Yeltsin and Chernomyrdin were careful not to endorse the agreement formally. Only in early October did Yeltsin indicate his approval of Lebed's undertakings in Chechnya, and he then distanced himself from the agreement by firing Lebed in late October. And while Chernomyrdin signed an agreement with the Chechens on October 3 establishing a joint commission to implement the Khasavyurt agreement, he took the opportunity to emphasize the "inviolability of Russia's territorial integrity" and later made clear that the government did not consider the Khasavyurt agreement to be legally binding.

Not until May 12, 1997, did Yeltsin put his signature on an agreement with Grozny. Entitled "Treaty on Peace and the Principles of Mutual Relations between the Russian Federation and the Chechen Republic of Ichkeria," the terse agreement included only three provisions: the first stipulated that both sides had "renounced forever the use of force and the threat to use force in resolving all disputed issues"; the second affirmed that they both agreed "to construct relations in accordance with the generally-recognized principles and norms of international law, and to deal with one another on the basis of specific agreements"; while the third indicated that the treaty would "serve as the basis for additional treaties and agreements on the entire complex of mutual relations."[4]

Having won a military victory against improbable odds, and having suffered enormous losses in defeating an invading army, the Chechens have understandably concluded that their republic is now de facto, if not yet de jure, independent. Accordingly, they have refused, and will continue to refuse for the foreseeable future, to accept any compromise with Moscow over the republic's status—defending independence is now a matter of honor for Chechen politicians. Moreover, Chechen officials believe that both the Khasavyurt and May 12, 1997, agreements are tantamount to recognition of Chechen independence, particularly in view of the provisions stipulating that future relations between Moscow and Grozny are to be governed by "generally-recognized principles and norms of international law." They have therefore refused to take any steps, including symbolic ones such as carrying Russian passports abroad, that might compromise Chechen sovereignty. The five-year delay provided in the Khasavyurt agreement, they believe, is simply a face-saving device designed to allow Russia's leaders to prepare the Russian electorate for Chechen independence.

Accordingly, Grozny is taking every opportunity to remind Moscow of its powerlessness. It has refused to send representatives to Russia's Council of the Federation or State Duma or to participate in any way in the Russian government. Chechen officials are being dispatched to foreign countries in search of political and economic support, while the republic has begun issuing its own passport.[5] The Chechens have also refused to allow Russian police officials on Chechen soil to investigate the many kidnappings that have taken place inside the republic. In addition, Chechnya has proven to be a tough negotiator regarding an agreement on transit fees for "early oil" from Azerbaijan that is to pass through Chechnya en route to the Russian Black Sea port of Novorossysk. In addition, President Maskhadov has indicated that Chechnya will soon declare itself an Islamic republic, renaming itself "the Islamic Republic of Chechnya." Meanwhile, the government has begun to post street signs in Chechen using Arabic scripts (which few Chechens can read), and it has announced plans to establish a system of Islamic banks, to replace the ruble with its own currency, and to force female students and government employees to wear Islamic clothing. Finally, border clashes have continued between Russian and Chechen forces, particularly in western Daghestan, the most recent of which led the hard-line Russian interior minister Anatolii Kulikov to threaten preemptive strikes into Chechen territory to "destroy" Chechen "bandits."[6]

The war was an unmitigated disaster for Yeltsin personally and for Russia generally. Politically, the war only deepened Chechen enmity toward

Moscow, making it all but inconceivable that Chechnya will ever become a normal "subject of the federation." It also dealt a severe blow to Russia's international prestige, placed additional burdens on an already strained federal budget, and badly damaged Yeltsin's approval ratings. Finally, it laid bare the weakness of the Russian military, undermining military morale and prestige as well as the credibility of the federal government's ability to impose its will on recalcitrant regional governments elsewhere. Demoralized, underfunded, and on the political defensive, the Russian military would be inviting yet another disaster were it to resume war in Chechnya.

Unfortunately, neither recognition of Chechen independence nor some form of associated status is politically possible for Moscow. This is not because the Russian people are deeply opposed to Chechen independence. On the contrary, the war was extremely unpopular, and while most Russians are not particularly sympathetic to the Chechens, they have been angered and humiliated by Russia's military ineptitude and by the decision to wage a brutal and devastating war that proved unwinnable. Nor do Russians believe that Chechnya is "sacred" Russian territory, and most would readily accept Chechen secession if it meant greater stability and prosperity for Russia. Finally, unlike President Shevardnadze of Georgia or President Aliev of Azerbaijan, Yeltsin does not have to deal with a large community of displaced persons (DPs) demanding repatriation and the restoration of lost property. While many ethnic Russians have indeed fled the republic, they represent only a tiny portion of the Russian electorate and remain scattered and politically weak. It is not, therefore, Russian public opinion that stands in the way of Chechen independence or associated status—rather, it is the Russian constitution, on the one hand, and the dynamics of Russian elite politics on the other.

The constitutional obstacles to Chechen independence or associated status are considerable.[7] Article 65.1 of the Russian constitution unequivocally identifies "the Chechen Republic" as one of Russia's twenty-one republics. Nor does the constitution include provisions for secession—on the contrary, Article 4.1 specifies that the "sovereignty of the Russian Federation extends to its entire territory," while Article 4.3 requires that the Russian Federation "ensure the integrity and inviolability of its territory." Even associated status for Chechnya, let alone independence, would be unconstitutional without a host of amendments.

While Yeltsin may not be a stickler for the observation of constitutional niceties, neither can he openly flaunt the constitution or accept its amendment to accommodate a deal with the Chechens. It is, of course, very much *his* constitution, having been ratified only after the bloodshed of November 1993 and by an extremely narrow (and disputed) margin in the referendum of December 12, 1993. Moreover, Article 80.2 charges the president with being the "guarantor" of the constitution, and as such he is obligated to take "measures to protect the sovereignty, independence, and state integrity of the Russian Federation and to ensure the coordinated action and interaction of bodies of state authority." Should Yeltsin move to grant Chechnya its independence, he would therefore be vulnerable to impeachment unless he were to call simultaneously for the amendment of the constitution.[8] It is, however, extremely difficult to amend the Russian constitution.[9]

Amending the constitution would allow Yeltsin's opponents to reopen fundamental questions about Russia's precarious democracy and the extensive powers of the president. And while many factions of the Russian political elite have demanded that the constitution be amended, they are very far from agreeing on the substance of any amendments. Moreover, although Yeltsin does not have the right to veto an amendment, he can effectively block any amendments by provoking a crisis with the Duma and disbanding it if it appears intent upon initiating the amendment process. Yeltsin also has low approval ratings and few allies in a conservative parliament that is very opposed to Chechen independence, and he also confronts a foreign policy establishment that would be quick to attack him for undermining Russia's position in the Caucasus by allowing the Chechens to secede. In particular, many Russian officials fear that recognizing Chechen independence would have a domino effect, inducing other Russian republics, and perhaps even some of its non-ethnically defined regions, to press for independence, thereby threatening the disintegration of the federation.[10]

Yeltsin's preferred solution to his Chechen dilemma is to postpone negotiations regarding status until after the end of his second, and presumably final, term in office. The hope in Grozny that Yeltsin is preparing the Russian people for de jure recognition before the five-year deadline provided for in the Khasavyurt agreement is therefore unrealistic. In fact, even most of the accord's Moscow supporters accept that the agreement has no status under Russian law. It was signed by Lebed, who at the time was secretary of the Security Council, and neither the council itself nor the position of secretary is provided for in the constitution or federal law (both the council and its secretary were established by presidential decree). Nor does the position of secretary require approval by parliament, which means that the Khasavyurt accord is not even an intergovernmental "agreement" signed by heads of government (e.g., the Russian prime minister) or government ministers, or an "interstate treaty" between federal and regional executives on the mutual delegation of powers, as provided for by the constitution.[11] Even less is it an international treaty, which the constitution specifies must be ratified by the Federation Council. In short, the agreement has only political, not legal, significance, and even this political significance is limited—neither Yeltsin nor Chernomyrdin ever officially endorsed it, and Lebed was fired shortly after signing it.

Yeltsin is thus under no real political pressure to reach an agreement with the Chechens on status. On the contrary, an agreement formally recognizing Chechen independence would give his opponents yet another opportunity to attack him by challenging his legal authority for doing so, thereby reminding the Russian electorate of who was responsible for the war. It is therefore very unlikely that Yeltsin will push for an agreement on status with the Chechens during his remaining years in office. Instead, the Russian government will try to find common ground on more immediate economic and political issues, signing bilateral agreements on specific issues. If the Chechens prove irreconcilable, as appears increasingly likely, or if the political situation inside the republic continues to deteriorate, Moscow will then intensify its efforts to isolate the republic by routing transportation routes, communications, and pipelines around it.

It is far from clear that Yeltsin's successor will actually prove more sympathetic to the Chechens.[12] On the other hand, neither is Russia about to launch another invasion of the republic, regardless of the saber rattling of some politicians, and it will be a very long time indeed, if ever, before the Chechens consider any compromise on independence. As a result, today's "no war, no real peace" is likely to last for the foreseeable future, and Chechnya will remain an acute problem and a source of instability for Russia's fledgling democracy for years to come.

RISKS OF WAR AND PRESSURES FOR PEACE IN ABKHAZIA

In September 1993, Georgian troops suffered a humiliating defeat in Abkhazia at the hands of a curious coalition of Abkhaz, North Caucasian (particularly Chechen), and Russian irregular forces supported by elements of the Russian military.[13] The Georgian defeat and the flight of its troops from Sukhumi, the Abkhaz capital, prompted the exodus of virtually the entire population of ethnic Georgians from the republic. Taking advantage of the chaos that ensued, troops loyal to Zviad Gamsakhurdia, the former Georgian president who had been ousted in a coup in December 1991, launched an uprising in western Georgia. By mid-October, Gamsakhurdia's forces were advancing on Kutaisi in central Georgia and threatening to move on to Tbilisi. To deal with the threat, the Georgian government was forced to call upon Russian troops to repress the rebellion, in exchange for which Tbilisi promised to comply with Russian insistence that it join the CIS. Shortly thereafter, talks began over a treaty providing Russia with military bases on Georgian territory.

UN-sponsored talks between Abkhazia and Georgia got underway in Geneva that November, and a formal cease-fire was signed on December 1, 1993. Additional rounds of talks led to a April 4, 1994, agreement to deploy a peacekeeping force (PKF) to separate the combatants and help repatriate the estimated 180,000 to 240,000 "displaced persons" (DPs) who had fled the fighting and were now being housed in horrific conditions in Tbilisi and elsewhere in Georgia.[14] However, disagreements over which international organizations would sponsor the PKF (the United Nations or the CIS), which countries would contribute troops, and where the PKF would be deployed prevented implementation of the April accord.[15] It was therefore not until May 14, 1994 that an agreement was reached on the specifics of the PKF deployment. The agreement called for the establishment of a demilitarized zone (referred to as "the Security Zone") stretching for twelve kilometers on each side of the Inguri River. In addition, heavy weapons would be withdrawn from a Restricted Weapons Zone extending for another twelve kilometers on each side of the Security Zone. The PKF would operate under a CIS mandate, and troops were to come from a number of CIS states. The PKF was charged not only with monitoring the cease-fire but also with helping to ensure "the safe return of refugees and displaced persons, especially in the Gali District," by policing the Security and Restricted Weapons Zones as well as "other areas" subject to the agreement of all parties.

To support the PKF, the UN Security Council subsequently agreed to expand the mandate of the UN Observer Mission in Georgia (UNOMIG) to include monitoring the activities of the CIS PKF.[16] The mandates of the PKF and UNOMIG were repeatedly extended, and by early 1997 some 1,500 peacekeeping troops and 136 UNOMIG observers were stationed in Abkhazia. The UNHCR also established a small mission in the republic, headquartered in Sukhumi, while the OSCE has had a limited role in providing humanitarian assistance and contributing to efforts to reach a political settlement.[17]

As it turned out, however, a number of the key provisions of the May 1994 agreement were never implemented. First, Russia ended up contributing the overwhelming majority of troops for the PKF, and indeed all 1,500 PKF troops in Abkhazia today are Russian military personnel.[18] Second, the Abkhaz allowed only a very limited number of Georgians to return to their homes, arguing that they had a right to screen returning DPs to prevent the repatriation of war criminals, that economic conditions in Abkhazia did not allow for the rapid return of such a large number of refugees, and that they could not provide for the safety of the returnees in view of Abkhaz enmity toward Georgians in the wake of the war.[19]

Prior to the PKF's deployment, Tbilisi had been very concerned that the PKF not entrench the status quo, becoming in effect an Abkhaz border guard that did nothing to reverse what Tbilisi characterized as "ethnic cleansing" of Georgians from the republic. Georgian president Eduard Shevardnadze repeatedly insisted that the April 1994 agreement on repatriation be implemented and that the PKF police all of Gali as well as the southern Ochamchire district. The Abkhaz refused, however, arguing that the May 1994 agreement had specified that all parties had to agree to any expansion of the PKF's mandate.

Nevertheless, while Abkhazia's officially sponsored repatriation program proceeded at a snail's pace, a significant number of DPs began to return quietly to the Gali district, where in 1989 the region's population had been 93.8 percent Georgian and only 0.8 percent Abkhaz.[20] The exodus of ethnic Georgians had left Gali largely depopulated immediately after the war, but by mid-1997 an estimated fifty to sixty thousand Georgian villagers had returned to the district under a low-profile repatriation program run by the UNHCR.[21] In many respects the program was a considerable success, with conditions in Gali improving as villagers returned to farm their land under the informal protection of the UNHCR. Unfortunately, the program also increased tensions in the district. Returned Georgian villagers were harassed by the Abkhaz militia, who undertook frequent patrols into Gali to demonstrate Abkhaz sovereignty over the district. The often unruly Abkhaz militiamen conducted document checks and forced villagers to "register" with the Abkhaz government and pay "taxes." In addition, Georgian villagers feared that the Abkhaz would attempt to enforce conscription in the district, coercing young Georgians to serve in the Abkhaz militia. As a result, the patrols led to frequent violence. To defend themselves, Georgian villagers placed antipersonnel mines around their villages, which helped to deter Abkhaz raids but also constituted a substantial hazard to neighboring villagers as well as to PKF and UNOMIG personnel.

Adding to the tension in Gali was the activity of a Georgian irregular force known as the White Legion. White Legion guerrillas were attacking not only the Abkhaz militia and sabotaging economic targets in Abkhazia, but they were also targeting Russian PKF troops on the grounds that the PKF was preventing Georgia from exercising its right to use force to preserve its territorial integrity.[22] The White Legion also objected to the fact that PKF troops had been escorting Abkhaz militia on their patrols, apparently in an effort to minimize violence. While UNOMIG observers reported that the Abkhaz militia were indeed better behaved when escorted by PKF troops, the White Legion argued that Russian troops were siding with the Abkhaz, just as they had in 1992–93, and that they were therefore legitimate military targets. Raids into Gali by the White Legion's well-trained guerrillas, who were equipped with sophisticated weapons including remote-controlled antitank and antipersonnel mines, had led to the deaths of over 40 Russian soldiers by the summer of 1997. Their military proficiency convinced the Abkhaz, as well as many Western observers, that the White Legion was being trained, equipped, and otherwise supported by the Georgian government, the latter's denials notwithstanding.

By the summer of 1997, Georgian-Abkhaz relations were extremely tense, to the point where many observers were predicting an imminent resumption of hostilities. In particular, it was feared that an expansion of the Security Zone, as demanded by Georgia, would lead to new violence. Sukhumi was adamantly opposed to a PKF redeployment, and were the PKF to begin to redeploy without Sukhumi's permission, the Abkhaz militia might intensify their raids on Georgian villages and begin attacking the PKF. Alternatively, Tbilisi might insist on the PKF's withdrawal because of its refusal, or inability, to fulfill its mandate. In either case, Georgian villagers in Gali would be even more vulnerable to Abkhaz harassment, and in the event of a massacre of Georgian villagers by the Abkhaz militia, or of a major clash between Abkhaz and White Legion forces, Shevardnadze might have no choice but to order an invasion. Indeed, this was the case during the "Six Day War" in 1998.

Fortunately, both the Georgians and the Abkhaz have a significant interest in avoiding another major war. For the Georgians, renewed fighting in Abkhazia would threaten the dramatic political and economic progress the country has made under Shevardnadze's leadership. The anarchy that prevailed in 1992–93 is now a memory, and Georgia had the fastest growing economy in the CIS in 1996 and one of the fastest in 1997 (although it faltered in 1998). To sustain this recovery, however, it needs substantial foreign investment. Particularly important is the completion of a pipeline bringing the so-called early oil from Azerbaijan's Caspian fields to the Georgian port of Supsa. If this project proves successful, Georgia may benefit in the future from the construction of larger capacity pipelines for delivering the enormous reserves of oil and gas in the Caspian Basin to the international marketplace. All this, and indeed foreign investment in general, would be jeopardized by a resumption of the Abkhaz war.

Nor could Georgia be confident that it would win such a war. The Abkhaz reportedly have some four to five thousand regular troops and claim to be able to mobilize another thirty thousand reservists, most of whom participated in the 1992–93 war. The Georgian military, on the other hand, has an estimated fifty thousand troops in uniform, most of whom have had limited, if any, combat experience, and who reportedly remain poorly trained. The Georgians also have a limited number of tanks and armored vehicles to carry out an offensive into enemy-held territory. Neither can Tbilisi be confident that Moscow, or factions of Russia's security apparatus acting independently, would not once again provide material support, intelligence, advice, or more to the Abkhaz in the event of war, while the Muslim peoples in Russia's North Caucasus might again provide arms and irregular troops. And even if the Georgian army managed to occupy Sukhumi, the Abkhaz would likely retreat to the north, as they did in 1992, and wage a guerrilla war that would sap the strength of Georgia's military and destabilize Georgia politically. It is with good reason, then, that Shevardnadze has repeatedly asserted that it is imperative that Tbilisi's conflict with the Abkhaz be resolved by peaceful means.[23]

The Abkhaz, too, have a considerable incentive to avoid another round of fighting. The fighting in Abkhazia in 1992–93 caused some six to eight thousand deaths and destroyed much of the republic's infrastructure, industrial capacity, and housing stock.[24] More fighting would only lead to greater devastation and increased emigration. Moreover, while the Georgian military is still underfunded, internal order and a rapidly improving Georgian economy have allowed Tbilisi to improve its military capabilities. As a result, the Georgians would likely prove a more formidable foe than in 1992–93, when the "army" was little more than a cluster of paramilitary forces and other irregular troops.

Moreover, conditions inside Abkhazia are very bad. After Georgia joined the CIS and signed its military-basing treaty with Moscow, Russia agreed to implement a CIS-mandated blockade of Abkhazia, which it did relatively conscientiously by imposing restrictions on frontier crossings and inspecting vessels entering Abkhaz waters to prevent anything other than food and consumer goods from entering the republic.[25] Even before Moscow began to enforce the blockade, however, Abkhazia's economy had been devastated by the war. Its tourist industry had been destroyed (tourism had been a major part of Abkhazia's economy before the war—the republic's beautiful and mountainous coastline and excellent beaches made it one of the Soviet Union's most desirable vacation spots), while the interruption of rail service from Russia had isolated the republic and interrupted trade not only with Georgia but with its large neighbor to the north as well. In addition, war and deteriorating living conditions caused the republic's population to fall by 70 percent, from 535,061 in 1989 to an estimated 145,000 today.[26] Losses of skilled labor and white-collar workers have been particularly acute. Economic activity inside the republic, with the exception of mostly subsistence agriculture and petty smuggling, has come to a virtual standstill, while the absence of legitimate employment together with new smuggling opportunities help account for a significant increase in crime in the republic.[27]

Perhaps most importantly, Abkhazia's ability to defend itself has been undermined by its loss of support from abroad. The Chechen debacle has made Moscow far more chary of supporting secessionists elsewhere, particularly along Russia's volatile North Caucasus border. While some Russian officials doubtless still hope that continuing instability in Georgia will increase Tbilisi's dependence on Moscow, thereby making it more likely that pipelines carrying Caspian oil and gas will be routed through Russia, more liberal-minded officials in Moscow argue that Russian interests have been ill served by heavy-handedness in the Caucasus and hope for a stabilization of the region. Accordingly, Moscow has been attempting to improve its relations with Georgia and Azerbaijan in an effort to enhance Russia's political position and economic penetration of the region. Even Russian conservatives have cause to be concerned about a possible deterioration of relations with Tbilisi, which might lead to Georgian renunciation of the still unratified military-basing agreement with Russia; the replacement of a CIS-mandated PKF by a UN- or OSCE-mandated force with non-Russian troops; Georgian withdrawal from the CIS and closer relations between Georgia and Ukraine or between Georgia and the West; or increased Georgian support for the Chechens.[28]

Finally, the Abkhaz can no longer count on substantial support from Muslim sympathizers in the North Caucasus.[29] Relations with the Chechens in particular have soured dramatically. The Chechens deeply resent the fact that the Abkhaz failed to support them during their war with Russia, particularly in view of the critical role Chechen fighters played in the Abkhaz victory in 1993.[30] Moreover, Grozny has been attempting to improve relations with Tbilisi in an effort to reduce its dependency on Russia, and it will therefore think twice before encouraging its fighters to once again leave the still-vulnerable republic to support the Abkhaz in another war with Georgia.

On the other hand, while both parties have a considerable interest in avoiding war, the Georgians have also been very unhappy with the status quo. In an effort to overcome the impasse in negotiations that had been reached by late 1996, Tbilisi pressed its demand that the PKF begin patrolling areas beyond the currently defined Security and Weapons Exclusion Zones to provide security for returning DPs in Gali and the southern Ochamchire district.[31] The Georgians made clear that, should the CIS refuse to order a redeployment, they would veto the extension of the PKF mandate past its expiration date of January 31, 1997. Although a withdrawal of the PKF might destabilize the situation, officials in Tbilisi argued that it would not lead to a full-blown war but would put pressure on the Abkhaz to speed up the repatriation process and be more flexible at the negotiating table.[32] Failing that, Tbilisi hoped that a UN- or OSCE-mandated PKF would replace the Russian force that has been unwilling, or unable, to ensure repatriation. And if the OSCE or NATO refused to provide such a force, Tbilisi might even accept an outstanding offer from Ukraine to provide peacekeepers.

A UN- or OSCE-mandated PKF, or a PKF with Ukrainian troops, was unacceptable to Moscow, which has attempted to monopolize peacekeeping operations in the CIS and fears a further loss of influence in the Caucasus. As a result, Moscow finally agreed to Tbilisi's insistence on a redeployment, and with Russian backing a decision was made at the CIS summit of March 28, 1997, to order the PKF to begin patrolling Gali and southern Ochamchire up to the Galidzga River. The PKF's mandate was also extended for another six months, to July 31, 1997, while a plan for implementing the expanded mandate was to be prepared by the end of April.

To Tbilisi's disappointment, however, the March 28 decision was never implemented. In part this was because the PKF lacked the capability to expand its responsibilities—its Russian troops are poorly equipped and ill trained for peacekeeping duties, let alone for policing a large and volatile area such as Gali and southern Ochamchire.[33] The principal obstacle to implementation, however, was vehement opposition to the plan from the Abkhaz, who argued that a redeployment would force them to abandon a strategically important defensive line in northern Gali and undermine their ability to resist a Georgian invasion or to protect Abkhaz living in Ocham-chire district.[34] As a result, they made clear that they would demand the PKF's withdrawal before allowing a redeployment to proceed. And this, the Abkhaz minister of defense asserted, might well lead to war.

To head off a diplomatic debacle, the Russian government intensified efforts to broker a compromise. On June 8, President Ardzinba arrived in Moscow for a series of meetings with senior Russian officials, the Georgian foreign minister, and Tbilisi's ambassador to Moscow. After almost two weeks of talks, Ardzinba announced that an agreement had been reached on a "possible formula" for a political settlement.

While the details of the agreement were not made public, it reportedly consisted of a seven-point "interim protocol" drafted by the Russian foreign ministry. The protocol specified that the two parties agreed "to live within the confines of a shared state within the boundaries of the Georgian SSR as of 21 December 1991." Georgia and Abkhazia would each "preserve its constitution, and relations between them will be regulated by a special treaty, which both sides agree to invest with the status of constitutional law." In addition, the Abkhaz would provide for the repatriation of Georgian DPs. They would, however, be allowed to continue to screen returnees, as the agreement failed to provide for a repatriation schedule. Finally, Tbilisi was required to prevent White Legion and other irregulars from launching raids into Abkhazia.

Unfortunately, hopes that the protocol constituted a breakthrough went unrealized. Georgian constitutional experts reportedly objected that it implied the subordination of the Georgian constitution to a future Abkhaz-Georgian treaty, which would be a violation of the Georgian constitution, the highest law of the land. At the same time, Georgian hard-liners and representatives of Georgian DPs from Abkhazia insisted on a timetable for repatriation. Hard-liners in Abkhazia, on the other hand, objected to the agreement because a redeployment of the PKF would compromise Ab-khazia's ability to defend itself and because repatriation threatened to again make the Abkhaz a minority in their own republic.[35]

To overcome this opposition, Russian security council deputy Boris Berezovsky undertook three days of shuttle diplomacy with Shevardnadze and Ardzinba in early July, but to no avail. A week later, a major clash in Kodori Gorge reportedly led to the deaths of some twenty White Legion guerrillas. With tensions rising once again, Shevardnadze left for a visit to the United States, where he tried to convince President Clinton and UN secretary general Kofi Annan to provide UN-mandated PKF to replace the current force. But with both the UN and the Clinton administration already under fire for overcommitting to peacekeeping operations elsewhere and reluctant to provoke a possible crisis with Moscow, Clinton and Annan refused.

Both Tbilisi and Sukhumi seem to have been sobered by the crisis atmosphere of late July 1997.[36] As a result, in early August Shevardnadze and Ardzinba met with Yeltsin in Moscow. However, during preparations for this meeting, Primakov and Ardzinba flew to Tbilisi (Ardzinba's first visit to the Georgian capital since the war began) for a meeting with Shevardnadze. The next day—August 15, 1997—it was announced that the two presidents had signed a no-use-of-force agreement that specified that both sides would use peaceful means only to overcome their differences.

The no-use-of-force agreement, which was similar to the May 12 agreement between Moscow and Grozny, was received by many as a major breakthrough. However, while it made renewed fighting less likely in the event of a withdrawal of the PKF, it did not resolve the fundamental issues of repatriation and status. It therefore came under immediate attack in Tbilisi, with critics arguing that it amounted to Georgian acceptance of the status quo and that it provided Moscow with an excuse to lift its blockade of Abkhazia. On November 7 a Chernomyrdin decree lifted restrictions on Russian imports of agricultural products from Abkhazia, a decision that Shevardnadze argued created "hot-house conditions" for Abkhaz separatism.[37]

Nevertheless, the August 15 agreement was followed by a series of low-profile meetings between Abkhaz and Georgian officials that reportedly led to significant progress on specific issues, particularly restoring economic links. Despite the improvement in atmosphere, however, Georgia continued to insist that the March 1997 CIS resolution on expanding the PKF's zone of operation be implemented, which again led to speculation that Shevardnadze would demand its withdrawal at the CIS summit in Chisinau, Moldova, on October 22–23. Once again, however, Shevardnadze agreed to allow the CIS to extend the mandate for yet another six months, this time to December 31, 1997, explaining his reluctance to veto the decision on the grounds that the PKF was facilitating the return of Georgians to Abkhazia.

With Georgia continuing to complain about the inability or unwillingness of Russia to engineer a political settlement, a second round of the talks got underway in Geneva on November 17–19. Again, the talks led to unexpected progress. Agreement was reached to establish a permanent "Coordinating Council," chaired by a UN special representative, to oversee the negotiating process. Three separate working groups were also established to address repatriation, security issues, and economic cooperation. Delegates to the negotiations reported that Moscow seemed to have become more supportive of the Geneva talks and that the atmosphere at the discussions had improved substantially.

Nevertheless, tensions between Abkhazia and Georgia remain high. Acts of sabotage in Abkhazia and attacks on the PKF by the White Legion, as well as clashes between White Legion and Abkhaz forces, continued in and around Gali, as did harassment by the Abkhaz militia of Georgian villagers in Gali and the Kodori Gorge. At the same time, militants in Tbilisi pressured Shevardnadze to take whatever steps were necessary to accelerate repatriation and restore Georgian sovereignty, including resorting to force if necessary. In early October, the Georgian military conducted large-scale maneuvers in western Georgia near the border with Abkhazia, prompting protests not only from the Abkhaz defense minister and the commander of the CIS PKF but from UNOMIG observers in Abkhazia as well.

Obstacles to a compromise over status are somewhat less daunting than in Chechnya or Karabakh due to the fact that the Georgian constitution, unlike the Russian constitution, is not a major barrier to a settlement. Therefore, the principal obstacle to Georgian recognition of Abkhaz independence is not the constitution, but rather the extent to which both the Georgian political elite and the Georgian electorate believe that Abkhazia is an alienable part of Georgia. Unlike Yeltsin, who could doubtless convince the Russian people to accept Chechen independence with little difficulty, Shevardnadze would find it all but impossible to persuade members of parliament or the Georgian electorate to reconcile themselves to an independent Abkhazia. Any public figure in Georgia who would dare to make the recommendation that Abkhazia be allowed to secede would be jeopardizing his or her career and even life. Moreover, the 180,000 to 240,000 DPs are well organized and represent a significant electoral bloc. They have formed a government-in-exile, the leader of which, Tamaz Nadareishvili, is an influential member of parliament and deputy prime minister who is militant about the restoration of Georgian sovereignty in Abkhazia.[38]

Nevertheless, it is conceivable that the Georgians and Abkhaz could eventually agree to some kind of compromise arrangement on status. The Abkhaz have indicated that they would accept a status that falls short of full independence entailing a "confederal" arrangement of equal partners, entered into on a purely voluntary basis, whereby neither Georgia nor Abkhazia would be subordinate to the other but with a common defense and foreign policy. Each party to the confederation would have its own constitution, with the confederation itself defined by treaty alone. Accordingly, the Abkhaz have been generally supportive of the agreement drafted by the Russian Foreign Ministry that was initialed in June 1997. On the other hand, Tbilisi continues to insist on the applicability of the Georgian constitution to Abkhazia (hence its rejection of the June agreement). Nevertheless, it has also indicated a willingness to grant Abkhazia "the highest level of autonomy" and a special status within an "asymmetrical" Georgian federation accompanied by security guarantees, including a commitment not to deploy Georgian troops within the republic except (presumably) for a modest force along the Abkhaz-Russian border.

Even if it were possible to reach a compromise on status, the two sides would still need to deal with the even more intractable problem of DP repatriation. Were it not for the fact that there are 180,000 to 240,000 Georgians who wish to return to their homes in the republic, Tbilisi and Sukhumi could postpone a resolution of the status question and focus on more prosaic topics such as trade, the restoration of telecommunication links, and the resumption of railroad service between Russia and Georgia across Abkhaz territory. This in turn could help to build trust and make possible a compromise on status. The need to repatriate the DPs, however, makes a staged approach to a settlement extremely difficult. Given the extent to which they distrust Georgian intentions, the Abkhaz will almost certainly reject a repatriation program that threatens to make them an electoral minority in the republic once again. Even preferential policies, such as parliamentary quotas or reserved positions in government, would do nothing to alleviate their fears that, once a majority, the Georgians would move to eliminate those preferential policies and insist on the full restoration of Georgian sovereignty over the republic, including policing powers. This, the Abkhaz fear, would lead either to "ethnic cleansing" by the Georgians or to more subtle forms of discrimination or cultural pressure that would force them to emigrate, a prospect that is all the more horrifying because, unlike the Karabakh Armenians or the Russians who have fled Chechnya, the Abkhaz have no titular state to escape to should they be driven from Abkhazia.

It is therefore very unlikely that the Abkhaz will accept a repatriation program that restores the demographic balance of 1989. As a result, any settlement will likely require a redrawing of Abkhazia's borders to remove areas with large prewar Georgian majorities (e.g., Gali District, southern Ochamchire, and the Kodori Gorge) from Sukhumi's jurisdiction. In addition, a multilateral PKF would have to be deployed to separate Georgian and Abkhaz troops and to provide Sukhumi with the security needed to induce it to trade territory for peace, and it would be better if that PKF operated under a UN or (less likely) an OSCE mandate in view of Georgian distrust of Russian intentions.[39]

While possible, reaching such an agreement is by no means probable. It would inevitably leave many grievances unsatisfied—most notably, many Georgian DPs would be unwilling to return to territory controlled by the Abkhaz, while others would be unable to return because the rate and extent of repatriation would be limited. At the same time, the Abkhaz would likely continue to resist repatriation in the areas under their administrative control.

On the other hand, today's "no peace, no war" impasse is also unlikely to persist. Shevardnadze may find that his political credibility is dependent upon his ability to make some progress over Abkhazia, and he may therefore decide to insist on the PKF's withdrawal, gambling that the international community would ultimately step in and provide a replacement force. Alternatively, Moscow may decide to withdraw its troops either because it no longer wishes to incur losses suffered at the hands of the White Legion or other irregular forces, or because it wishes to precipitate a crisis in the region.

Shevardnadze's current strategy for resolving the current impasse is to improve political and economic conditions in Georgia while persuading the international community to take a more active role in mediating a political solution. He has concluded that there is little prospect for solving the Abkhaz conflict simply by appeasing Moscow. Joining the CIS and allowing Russian military bases on Georgian territory did not, contrary to the hopes and expectations of many Georgians, lead Sukhumi to capitulate to Tbilisi's demands, in part because Moscow has been unwilling to apply full pressure on Abkhazia and in part because Sukhumi is not, in fact, a puppet of Moscow. However, despite Shevardnadze's recent appeals for a "Bosnia style" peace enforcement intervention by the Western powers in Abkhazia, the international community is extremely unlikely to enter into such an operation. Shevardnadze doubtless understands this. Instead of peace enforcement, he is hoping for a political settlement and that a UN- or OSCE-mandated PKF can help entrench the peace and implement the provisions of any agreement.

Thus the situation in Abkhazia is unstable—the risks of new fighting, and even small wars like that in 1998, are significant, even though the parties to the conflict are under considerable pressure to reach a settlement. If no agreement is reached in the next several years, Shevardnadze or the future leader of Georgia may decide to order the Georgian army to occupy Gali or even to take Sukhumi, thereby precipitating another full-scale war.

KARABAKH: AN IRRESISTIBLE FORCE MEETS AN IMMOVABLE OBJECT

A relatively effective cease-fire has been in effect in Karabakh since May 1994. Early that month, talks between Armenian, Azeri, and Karabakh officials under CIS auspices in Bishkek, Kyrgyzstan, led to the signing of the so-called Bishkek Protocol, which provided for a cease-fire and the deployment of a CIS PKF. The agreement was viewed at the time as a victory for Russian diplomacy, which as noted earlier was directed at monopolizing peacekeeping operations in the CIS. Moscow's particular concern in Karabakh was to exclude the CSCE from the peace process, or at least significantly limit its role. In early 1992, the CSCE called for the convening of a "Conference on Nagorno-Karabakh" to be held in Minsk, Belarus. In addition, it established a group of member-states to organize the event (referred to as the "Minsk Conference"). As it became clear that the conference would be more difficult to arrange than expected, the same group of countries renamed themselves the "Minsk Group," a subgroup of which, meeting separately, managed in late 1992 to agree to a methodology for negotiation, on the basis of three documents. The first defined the mandate of the group itself; the second outlined the basic principles for a resolution of the conflict; and the third—the so-called military-technical document—addressed the war's immediate consequences, including security issues, and provided for the deployment of a CSCE-mandated observer mission in Karabakh. The understanding at the time was that each issue would be addressed separately and that there would be no general settlement until agreement had been reached on each of the three documents. In early 1993, agreement was reached on the first document. However, Russian efforts to undermine the initiative, the reluctance of other OSCE member-states to provide troops or financing, and an Azeri summer offensive prevented the agreement from being implemented.

When it signed the Bishkek Protocol in early May 1994, Baku made clear that it did so only on the condition that a cease-fire would be followed by the withdrawal of Karabakh and Armenian forces from districts in Azerbaijan outside Karabakh's borders. It also insisted on a prisoner exchange, the repatriation of DPs, restoration of communications between Azerbaijan and Karabakh, and negotiations on Karabakh's status. Karabakh, on the other hand, made clear that it was not prepared to withdraw from occupied areas prior to an agreement on status because doing so would compromise its security. As a result, while a ninety-day cease-fire took effect on May 12, 1994, Azerbaijan refused to sign an agreement that had been drafted by Moscow setting out the terms for the PKF's deployment. Only after considerable diplomatic maneuvering would both sides sign a permanent cease-fire, which finally occurred on July 27, 1994.

Azerbaijan's refusal to sign Moscow's proposal and its delay in signing a formal cease-fire was indicative of a general hardening of Baku's position. Azeri hard-liners opposed any agreement, including a cease-fire, to which the Karabakh Armenians were cosignatories on the grounds that doing so would help legitimize a government that represented only the Karabakh Armenians, not the Karabakh Azeris, who had made up some 25 percent of the republic's population prior to the war. Cosigning an agreement with Stepanakert would also imply that Karabakh was an independent actor and not a mere pawn of the Armenian government, whose involvement in the war was said to account for Azerbaijan's defeat. Baku therefore took the position that the conflict was ultimately an international one between the independent states of Azerbaijan and Armenia. As a result, while Baku accepted that Stepanakert was a party to the fighting and could thus be involved in negotiations over a cease-fire or certain "military-technical" issues, it could not be a party to negotiations over a final resolution of the conflict and Karabakh's future legal status. Finally, objections were raised to the presence of Russian troops on Azerbaijani territory as many Azeris feared that a Russian-dominated PKF in Karabakh would open the door to further Russian interference.

As a result of these objections, Moscow's hopes for deploying a CIS-mandated PKF of mostly Russian troops under Russian command were never realized. Nevertheless, the 1994 cease-fire has remained in effect, despite occasional artillery duels, sniper fire, and minor border skirmishes. But as in Abkhazia, the cease-fire not only brought an end to the fighting but helped freeze the status quo, in this case entrenching the territorial gains of the victorious Karabakh army. By mid-1994, Karabakh forces controlled almost all of what had been the Nagorno-Karabakh Autonomous Oblast, as well as seven districts of Azerbaijan proper (henceforth, "the occupied districts"), which together represented some 14 to 15 percent of Azerbaijan's Soviet-era territory.[40]

Of particular importance to any future political settlement was Stepanakert's control of two districts outside Karabakh, Lachin and Kelbajar, which had separated the former autonomous oblast from Armenia and had been populated mostly by Azeris and Kurds before the war. In addition, the Karabakh army controlled the strategic heights to the south of Stepanakert, including the town of Shusha, where again the population had been predominately Azeri before the war. At the same time, however, Shusha had been the traditional capital of Karabakh, and both Azeris and Armenians consider it of cultural and historical significance. Moreover, its location and strength as a fortress make it of great military value, as evidenced by the fact that Azeri forces subjected Stepanakert to sustained shelling from Shusha during the war, thereby forcing the evacuation of much of the city's population.[41] Control of Lachin, Shusha, and Kelbajar therefore became a critical issue in negotiations.

While less appalling than in Chechnya, the costs of the Karabakh war, along with related fighting between Azeris and Armenians beginning in early 1988, were substantially greater than those in Abkhazia. Some 15,000 to 25,000 people were killed and 50,000 were wounded, while many towns and villages in the region were completely destroyed.[42] In addition, Armenia suffered acutely from an economic blockade imposed by Azerbaijan and, later, Turkey.[43] It has also contributed to political instability in Azerbaijan, which has suffered numerous coup attempts and four leadership changes since 1988, and also in Armenia, where Levon Ter-Petrossian won reelection in late 1996 in tainted elections that international observers characterized as "free but not fair" and that were followed by anti-government demonstrations and street violence in Yerevan. Ter-Petrossian later resigned because of his unpopular stance on peace in Karabakh and was replaced by Robert Kocharian, the former president of Karabakh and a Karabakh citizen at the time of his taking the office as Armenia's president.

The conflict has also been responsible for the former USSR's largest DP crisis. While figures are controversial, the vast majority of the estimated 345,000 Armenians who lived in Azerbaijan prior to 1988 have fled the country, with some 280,000 of them now in Armenia and Karabakh and another 45,000 in Russia.[44] In addition, virtually all of the estimated

185,000 Azeris who lived in Armenia and the estimated 47,000 Azeris who lived in Karabakh (out of a total Karabakh population of approximately 190,000) have fled. The largest number of DPs—over 500,000—come from the occupied districts bordering on Karabakh (most of whom are ethnic Azeris, although some are ethnic Kurds from Lachin and Kelbajar). Not all of these 500,000, however, are still in Azerbaijan—UN officials estimate that the population of Azerbaijan has fallen by approximately one million since 1989, which suggests that many DPs have since left the country. Together with the estimated 48,000 Meskhetian Turk refugees from Central Asia now in Azerbaijan, the DP population in Azerbaijan is therefore estimated at between 600,000 and 800,000 (although government sources claim that there are over one million).[45] The DPs in both Azerbaijan and Armenia continue to experience extreme hardship, although Armenia has made an effort to integrate its significantly smaller DP population into Armenian society while the Azeri DPs continue to live for the most part in appalling conditions in refugee camps or homes abandoned by Armenians or others.

Between May 1994 and late 1996, international efforts to mediate a settlement to the conflict continued episodically. Nevertheless, no agreement was reached on the withdrawal of Karabakh forces from the occupied territories, repatriation, the deployment of a PKF, or status. Three factors in particular blocked a compromise. First, Baku was unwilling to accept the Karabakh Armenians as a party to negotiations on status, insisting instead that it would negotiate this fundamental question with Yerevan only. Yerevan, on the other hand, argued that the government in Stepanakert was an independent actor not under its control, and that Yerevan could not agree to anything that was unacceptable to Stepanakert.[46] Nor would the Armenians agree to treat representatives of the Karabakh Azeris as a party to the conflict with equal status to the Karabakh Armenians. Second, Baku insisted that negotiations on status and other issues could begin only after the Karabakh army had withdrawn from the areas beyond Karabakh's borders. Stepanakert, however, refused to give up hard-won territory and undermine its security in the absence of an agreement on status and international security guarantees. Finally, a Vienna-based OSCE High Level Planning Group (HLPG) failed to reach agreement on the composition and command of a PKF.[47] While Baku opposed the deployment of a Russian-dominated PKF, insisting that Russian troops constitute no more that 30 percent of any peacekeeping contingent and that the PKF be answerable to the OSCE and not Moscow, Armenia objected to Turkish military involvement. The OSCE, on the other hand, refused to deploy either an observer mission or a PKF until a settlement had been reached on force separation and repatriation. Finally, Moscow pressed for a Russian-dominated "separation force" that would be under Moscow's command and deployed prior to a broad political settlement, as in Abkhazia.

Other factors contributed to the stalemate as well. The Western powers, particularly the United States, were reluctant to become involved in what was seen as a remote and irreconcilable conflict nor did they wish to encroach upon what was perceived as Yeltsin's sphere of influence. Finally, the international community was already committed to difficult peace-keeping operations elsewhere, particularly in Bosnia, and had been sobered by the peacekeeping operation in Somalia. As a result, it was initially some-what sympathetic to Moscow's demands that Russia be afforded a leading role in conflict mediation in the CIS, including Karabakh.[48]

In an effort to reconcile Russia's advocacy of "sphere of influence" peacekeeping in the CIS with the OSCE-led mediation effort, an agreement was reached at an OSCE summit in Budapest on December 5, 1994, to increase Moscow's weight within the Minsk Group. The group would henceforth have two chairmen, with Russia being a permanent cochair. It was also agreed that any future PKF in Karabakh would be a joint OSCE-Russian force operating under a UN mandate. The deployment of a PKF, however, would have to wait for a political settlement, at which point its composition, financing, and chain of command would be determined. Finally, the OSCE expressed its support for UN Security Council Resolutions 822, 853, 874, and 884, which had called for the withdrawal of Karabakh and "local Armenian forces" from the occupied districts and affirmed the territorial integrity of Azerbaijan. While papering over differences between the West and Russia regarding peacekeeping in the CIS, the Budapest summit therefore effectively postponed the deployment of a PKF while relieving pressure on the conflicting parties to reach a settlement.

As a result, negotiations achieved little by late 1996. Instead, both sides dug in along the Line of Contact, improved their defensive positions, and built up their military capabilities. Azerbaijan received significant military support and training from Turkey, signing a military cooperation treaty with Ankara on May 5, 1997. It also reportedly purchased some 150 tanks and ten warplanes from Ukraine. Nevertheless, morale in Azerbaijan's armed forces has been poor, its soldiers are paid little if at all, and the government has had difficulty enforcing conscription. Moreover, while President Aliev had managed to stabilize the country politically, the economy continued to contract, making a sustained commitment to improving Azerbaijani military capability difficult. As a result, Azerbaijan had done little to improve its near-term prospects for resolving the Karabakh conflict by force by late 1996.

Armenia, on the other hand, moved to cement its already close ties with Russia. Prior to 1997 a series of bilateral agreements provided the legal framework for a Russian military base in Armenia. In addition, Russian officers have helped train the Armenian military, and Russian and Armenian units have conducted regular joint maneuvers. The extent of Russian military support for Armenia was highlighted in early 1997 when Moscow newspapers reported that Russia had delivered some $1 billion in military hardware, including eighty-four T-72 tanks, fifty BMP2 armored person-nel carriers, eight SCUD-B ballistic missile launchers, and thirty-two SCUD-B missiles to Yerevan despite a Yeltsin directive of September 1993 banning arms sales to either Armenia or Azerbaijan pending a settlement in Karabakh.[49] Many of the weapons had allegedly been deployed in Karabakh.[50] Although an Armenian official denied having received any ille-gal arms transfers, Armenian defense minister Vazgen Sarksian later boasted that Armenia's defense capability had doubled in the past two years at no cost to the budget. This was followed in September 1997 by the sign-ing of a "Treaty on Friendship, Cooperation and Mutual Assistance" that provides for further military and economic cooperation, including a requirement that each country assist the other in the event of armed aggression by a third party.[51] Baku has claimed that the treaty represents a full-blown military alliance that requires Russia to intervene on Armenia's behalf should Baku try to take Karabakh by force. While Moscow has denied this, the treaty will deter the Azeris from undertaking any military operations inside Armenia should they decide to attack Karabakh.[52]

Karabakh, too, used the cease-fire to improve its military capabilities. In contrast to Chechnya and Abkhazia, Stepanakert has managed to maintain a high degree of internal order, to the point where its economy has report-edly begun to improve. Militarily, Karabakh forces control most of the strategic heights along the Line of Contact, and they have fortified their defensive positions and mined and concentrated artillery fire along possible routes for an Azeri offensive. The republic's popular president, Robert Kocharian, was reelected in November 1996, despite international con-cerns that the election would destabilize the region. He was later named prime minister in Armenia and when Ter-Petrossian resigned became pres-ident there. And unlike Abkhazia and Chechnya, which have received little support from the outside world since the fighting has ended in each repub-lic, Karabakh has received extensive material and political support from Armenia, and through Armenia, from the relatively wealthy Armenian Diaspora in the West and Middle East.

Ties between Karabakh and Armenia are not limited to trade, however. There are virtually no border controls along the Lachin road except for a tiny "customs station" that does little except check the documents of Iran-ian truck drivers on their way to Stepanakert. The Armenian dram is the sole legal tender in Karabakh, while Karabakh Armenians use Armenian passports when traveling abroad. Nor do they need visas to cross the bor-der, just as Armenians do not need visas to visit Karabakh.

By late 1996, then, little progress had been made toward a settlement despite the best efforts of the Minsk Group and periodic bilateral meetings between Vafa Gulazade, a senior adviser to Aliev, and his Armenian coun-terpart, Gerard Libaridian.[53] While this impasse may have been acceptable to Stepanakert and (less so) to Yerevan, it was not acceptable to Baku.

Indeed, like Shevardnadze, Aliev frequently asserted that while Baku would prefer a political solution to the conflict, it would eventually use force to defend its territorial integrity in the absence of a settlement.[54]

While similar threats had been made before, what was different in late 1996 was the intensifying international pressure on the warring parties to reach an agreement. For Moscow, the withdrawal of its troops from Chechnya in mid-1996, Yeltsin's reelection, and Yeltsin's decision to rid his administration of hard-liners in the so-called party of war had led to a change of policy toward conflict zones in the former Soviet Union generally and the Caucasus particularly. Yevgenii Primakov, the Russian foreign minister and a specialist on the Middle East and former Soviet Union's "southern tier," was engineering a shift in focus for Russian foreign policy from the West toward the south. As a result, Moscow began to abandon its clumsy divide-and-rule tactics of 1993–94 and committed more unequivocally to the pursuit of regional stabilization and the promotion of Russian economic interests in the Caucasus.

At the same time, the international community generally and Russia and the United States particularly were becoming increasingly interested in the Caucasus and the Caspian littoral as the extent of the region's oil and gas reserves became clear. Both U.S. and Russian oil and gas companies were committing huge sums of money to the development of these resources, and renewed fighting over Karabakh seemed likely to sabotage investment projects and complicate plans to build the pipelines needed to bring the Caspian's energy reserves to market. Renewed fighting might even lead to a full-blown showdown between Azerbaijan and Armenia (Armenia's involvement in the fighting during 1992–94 had been substantial but covert), in which case Karabakh and Armenian forces might carry the war even deeper into Azerbaijani territory, threatening Gyandzha (Azerbaijan's second largest city, which lies only thirty to forty kilometers to the north of the Line of Contact) or even Baku. Nor could attacks by Armenian and Karabakh forces on Azeri oil production facilities and pipelines be ruled out. At the least, renewed fighting could lead to renewed political chaos in Baku. As a result, Moscow and Washington decided in late 1996 that the time had come to launch a diplomatic offensive to promote a settlement in Karabakh.

Baku, too, had come to the conclusion that it needed to switch tactics. Apparently convinced that Ter-Petrossian had been weakened by his disputed election victory in late 1996 and that the international community was now more sympathetic to its position on Karabakh, Baku decided to abandon the quiet diplomacy being carried out by Gulazade and Libaridian. Instead, it managed to convince the Minsk Group cochairs to submit a proposal establishing a broad framework for a settlement to the OSCE at its Lisbon summit scheduled for early December 1996. The proposal was based on three broad principles: the preservation of Azerbaijan's and Armenia's territorial integrity; the realization of the right of the Karabakh people to self-determination through the provision of the "highest degree" of autonomy within Azerbaijan; and security guarantees for all parties.

Armenia, however, proved unwilling to accept the proposal, particularly the language on the preservation of Azerbaijan's territorial integrity. Doing so, they argued, would predetermine Karabakh's status even before negotiations had begun. Moreover, they argued that it constituted an OSCE effort to impose a solution on Karabakh, which was not even represented at Lisbon. Yerevan therefore vetoed the inclusion of the principles in the summit's final communiqué. Instead, under a U.S.-sponsored compromise, the proposal was read as a "chair-in-office" statement that affirmed all three of the principles entailed in the proposal, including the provision that Karabakh should have the "highest degree" of autonomy *within* Azerbaijan. The chair also affirmed that the statement had been approved by all member-states except Armenia

Predictably, the Armenians were furious at the summit's outcome. They were convinced that Baku was using its oil weapon to force the West, and particularly the United States, to take Baku's side, and that as a result Armenia and Karabakh were becoming increasingly isolated. They also felt they had been blindsided by the rapid change in tactics in Baku and by the Minsk Group's willingness to succumb to Azeri pressure. Accordingly, Ter-Petrossian promptly issued a formal objection to the statement, Karabakh's parliament threatened to withdraw from the Minsk process, and Libaridian announced that he would no longer engage in bilateral meetings with Gulazade unless representatives from Karabakh were present. Gulazade responded that Baku would reject any direct talks with the Karabakh Armenians until Stepanakert formally accepted the principles outlined in the Lisbon statement.

Although the Armenians asserted that the Lisbon statement had set back the peace process, the OSCE nevertheless continued its diplomatic offensive into the new year. When Baku objected to France succeeding Finland as the new cochair of the Minsk Group in January (Baku considers both Russia and France to be traditional allies of Armenia), and after Washington indicated that it was now interested in the position, it was agreed that the United States would join Russia and France as the group's third chair. The three cochairs then met in Copenhagen in late February and decided to send a French fact-finding mission to the region. In late March the cochairs reconvened in Paris and announced that they had agreed to "a common approach" to a new round of negotiations that would begin in April with a visit to the region by the cochairs.

The April round took place as planned but did not lead to a substantive breakthrough. Instead, tensions mounted as a series of military clashes broke out along the Line of Contact. In addition, the appointment of Kocharian as Armenia's prime minister was vigorously objected to by

Baku, as were the reports of Russian arms transfers to Armenia in 1995–96. Baku responded by asserting that Russia could no longer be an impartial mediator, that the terms of the 1994 cease-fire had been broken, and that Armenia was now in violation of the CFE treaty. Adding to tensions was a speech by Kocharian before the Armenian parliament, his first as Armenia's new prime minister, in which he suggested that Armenia give serious consideration to annexing Karabakh, a statement that Azerbaijan's foreign minister claimed was confirmation that "Armenia is waging war on Azerbaijan."

Amidst these rising tensions, an OSCE delegation that included U.S. deputy secretary of state Strobe Talbott and his Russian and French counterparts arrived in the region at the end of May to present a proposal for a resolution of the conflict.[55] While the exact wording of the plan was not made public, it reportedly consisted of two parts, the first of which dealt with the conflict's immediate "consequential issues" and the second with status. The first part of the proposal provided for Karabakh's withdrawal from all the occupied districts (that is, including Lachin), and an OSCE-mandated PKF that would patrol a buffer zone separating the two armies.[56] Azeri DPs would be repatriated in the occupied districts. Finally, the blockade of Armenia by Azerbaijan (and presumably by Turkey as well—Turkey indicated its approval of the plan on June 2) would be lifted. As for status, the second part of the proposal provided that Azerbaijan's territorial integrity would be formally preserved but that Karabakh would become fully self-governing and a free economic zone with a right to its own currency, government budget, and tax-raising powers. It would also be allowed to keep its own "national guard" and police force, but at the "minimum necessary level." Finally, it was to be a "multinational" society, thereby implying that Azeris would eventually be repatriated to Shusha and other parts of Karabakh.[57]

The intent of the Minsk cochairs was not that the proposal be immediately accepted as a rigid blueprint for a final settlement; rather, it was to serve as "the basis for negotiations." Negotiations on both parts of the proposal would proceed simultaneously, and while it was assumed that an agreement on consequential issues would likely precede agreement on status, agreement and implementation in one forum was not contingent upon an agreement in the other. The proposal was therefore neither strictly a step-by-step nor a package one—rather, it left both possibilities open.

While Azeri officials had some objections (in particular, they wanted explicit jurisdiction over the towns of Lachin and Susha), Baku was generally pleased by the proposal.[58] Yerevan was less so, although it indicated that it was willing to accept it as a basis for negotiation with "serious reservations."[59] Stepanakert, however, made clear that it would not withdraw from Lachin nor agree to repatriation in the absence of ironclad security guarantees from the international community, including Armenia. Neither would it accept any preconditions, particularly the preservation of Karabakh's territorial integrity, before entering into negotiations over status.

After the extent of Karabakh's objections to the May proposal were made clear, the cochairs returned to the region in July with a modified version of the May proposal. This time, however, the cochairs proposed a step-by-step, or "staged," approach that would address consequential issues first and leave negotiations over status to the future. At Yerevan's suggestion, they also removed the question of Lachin from the consequential issues stage and placed it instead on the agenda for the second stage negotiations. In addition, repatriation of Azeri DPs within Karabakh (including Shusha) and Lachin, and Armenian repatriation in Shaumian or other neighboring districts in Azerbaijan, would be left to the second-stage. The first-stage negotiations would thus address the withdrawal of Karabakh forces from the six occupied districts other than Lachin; repatriation within these six districts; the deployment of a PKF to separate the two armies, and the lifting of the blockade. Meanwhile, Lachin would remain under Karabakh's control, while Karabakh would retain full control of its existing armed forces.

Diplomatic efforts to broker an agreement resumed in the wake of the elections in Stepanakert on September 1. On September 20–22, the Minsk Group cochairs returned to the region and met with officials in Baku, Yerevan, and Stepanakert. They presented a slightly modified version of the May proposal, this time placing all security issues, including the right of Armenia to intervene on Karabakh's behalf in the event of an Azerbaijani invasion, in the first stage in an effort to allay Stepanakert's security concerns.

Two weeks later, Ter-Petrossian and Aliev attended a Council of Europe summit in Strasbourg. Addressing the assembled heads of state, Ter-Petrossian reiterated his government's commitment to a peaceful resolution of the conflict, while Aliev claimed that Azerbaijan hoped to establish "firm and longlasting relations with Armenia." In a face-to-face meeting, Aliev and Ter-Petrossian reportedly agreed to the terms of the Minsk Group's first-stage provisions, after which they issued a joint statement calling for a new round of negotiations in which all parties to the conflict, including Stepanakert, would participate.[60] Yeltsin and Chirac, who were also in Strasbourg for the summit, then publicly invited Ter-Petrossian and Aliev to Moscow for talks under their auspices. While Yeltsin added that the United States would be welcome to participate, clearly there had been no prior agreement that Clinton would attend, and neither was there any likelihood that he would be willing to do so. Nor did Yeltsin specifically invite Ghukasian (the newly elected president of Karabakh) to Moscow, despite a statement by Aliev and Ter-Petrossian that the next round of talks should include representatives from all parties.[61]

The Yeltsin and Chirac invitation suggested that divisions were emerging once again inside the Minsk Group. Russian complaints about the

excessive influence of the United States in the international arena generally and its involvement in the Caucasus particularly had been increasing
over the summer. In August Yeltsin had asserted that "the Americans
already are starting to infiltrate [the Caucasus], openly calling it a zone of
their interests," while Primakov, in a September address to the UN General
Assembly, argued that no single country can be responsible for settling all
conflicts, an obvious reference to the United States. Russia may be concerned about U.S. involvement in the region, but it also has an interest in
cooperating with Washington to stabilize the region. Indeed, Primakov
singled out the joint efforts of Russia, France, and the United States in the
Minsk Group for praise in his September speech to the United Nations,
while U.S. officials reported late last year that Moscow was continuing to
take a constructive approach to the Minsk process.

Indeed, Washington remained optimistic about the possibility of an
agreement to begin first-stage negotiations by the end of the year.[62] Unfortunately, these expectations proved unwarranted. Stepanakert remained
adamant in rejecting the Minsk Group plan, again making clear its objections during a meeting with the group's cochairs in Stepanakert on December 3–4, 1997. Karabakh has continued to insist on either a comprehensive
settlement or a staged agreement that would address status first, determine
borders second, and provide for a troop withdrawal third. It also wants to
be recognized as a party to the conflict throughout the negotiating
process—that is, even after a possible first-stage agreement. Finally, it
insists that negotiations begin between Baku and Stepanakert without preconditions, particularly ones that would predetermine the republic's status.

As a result, the OSCE was unable to announce a breakthrough at its foreign ministers' meeting in Copenhagen on December 18–19, 1997. Neither did it reaffirm the 1996 Lisbon declaration, as Baku had hoped, or
rescind it, as Yerevan and Stepanakert had hoped. Finally, it denied
Karabakh's request that it be recognized as a permanent party in the negotiating process. Baku and Yerevan expressed their satisfaction with the
results of the meeting. Stepanakert, however, complained that it had done
nothing to reinvigorate the peace process.

For Azerbaijan, a first-stage settlement would contribute to the government's efforts to improve Azerbaijan's economy. In the short run, it would
lead to the lifting of Section 907 of the U.S. Freedom Support Act, which
limits U.S. government-to-government aid to Azerbaijan as long as the
blockade remains in place. In addition, shuttle trade with Armenia across
the Armenian-Azerbaijani border in the north would likely pick up. Most
importantly, foreign investment, including but not limited to foreign
investment in Azerbaijan's energy sector, would be given a significant boost.
Finally, a settlement would improve the prospects for diversifying pipeline
routes to bring Azerbaijan's hydrocarbon reserves to the international
marketplace.

Popular sentiment within Azerbaijan also seems to be amenable to a compromise. The conflict began earlier than those in Abkhazia and Chechnya, and war weariness has had ample opportunity to set in and temper extremist sentiments. The Azeris have already suffered one military defeat in their effort to preserve Baku's authority over a relatively remote and mostly Armenian-populated area, and they are not anxious to risk more casualties and territorial losses in another round of fighting, at least for now. While the Azeris will continue to reject out-of-hand full independence for Karabakh, they would very likely accept a face-saving arrangement under which Karabakh forces withdraw from the occupied districts, the 500,000 DPs from the occupied territories are allowed to return to their homes, and Azerbaijan preserves its territorial integrity de jure but accords the Karabakh Armenians self-government in practice.

Kocharian appears to be secure in his intransigence on the Karabakh issue, at least in the short term. Armenian defense minister Vazgen Sarksian, has called on Armenians to "fight our last war to the finish" and asserted that a withdrawal from Shusha, Lachin, and Kelbajar districts is impossible under any circumstance, even if Karabakh's independence were accepted by Baku. Armenian interior and national security minister Serzh Sarkisian likewise opposes a compromise with Baku and has called for the permanent annexation of some Azerbaijan territories.[63] Kocharian rejected Ter-Petrossian's claim that economic prosperity for Armenia was impossible in the absence of a Karabakh settlement and has asserted, "No decision adopted in Armenia will be implemented without Karabakh's consent, irrespective of who is in power in Yerevan."[64] Finally, he has expressed his opposition to a staged settlement and, like Ghukasian, has rejected any kind of "vertical" arrangement that would subordinate Stepanakert to Baku.

It has become increasingly clear that Armenia's poor relations with its neighbors and its inaccessibility to international markets have been major impediments to improved economic performance. While Armenia's peak-to-trough decline in output was substantially greater than Azerbaijan's, it began to recover earlier (indeed, it was the first CIS economy to do so after the Soviet collapse), growing at a rate of 5 to 7 percent per annum in 1994–96.[65] However, Armenia's GDP grew by only 1.4 percent in the first six months of 1997, down from 5.8 percent in 1996, while its annualized inflation rate rose from 5.7 percent to 16 percent, and exports shrank by some 30 percent. This slowdown augurs poorly for an economy that has yet to return to 1989 levels of output, particularly given the government's earlier success in reducing inflation and privatizing most of agriculture and much of industry.

Armenia's long-term security is, however, threatened by a continuation of the impasse over Karabakh. Support for Armenia from the international community may well deteriorate in the coming years. Iran is currently the only neighboring country with which Armenia has both reasonably good relations and significant trade.[66] Iran, however, can provide Armenia with only limited diplomatic, financial, or military support, in part because closer ties with Tehran would give offense to Washington. Since gaining its independence, Armenia has relied primarily on Russia and the United States to be its international benefactors. This awkward collection of friends—Iran, Russia, and the United States—is unlikely to last given Moscow's and Washington's interest in Azerbaijan's energy reserves and Washington's hostility to Iran. Nor can Yerevan continue to count on unqualified support from Moscow, which already has been trying to improve its relations with Baku and has repeatedly expressed its unequivocal support for the preservation of Azerbaijan's territorial integrity.[67] Finally, the Clinton administration has made the resolution of the Karabakh conflict a top foreign policy priority.[68] To this end, it has argued for evenhandedness in U.S. relations with Azerbaijan and Armenia, which it feels requires the lifting of Section 907 restrictions on U.S. government-to-government aid to Azerbaijan. To date, Armenia's supporters in Congress have been able to block these plans. However, were Yerevan and/or Stepanakert to prove unreasonably obdurate, pressure to lift Section 907—a move that has been vigorously advocated by the U.S. oil lobby—as well as pressure to reduce aid to Yerevan would increase significantly.

Armenia also has cause to worry about increased Azerbaijani military spending, particularly after oil revenues begin flowing into the country. The U.S. Arms Control and Disarmament Agency (ACDA) estimates that Azerbaijan's military expenditures increased by 46 percent between 1992 and 1995. Armenia and Karabakh, on the other hand, are already heavily burdened by their defense expenditures, and this burden is likely to increase if Russia's clandestine arms transfers of 1995–96 have indeed halted. Finally, the Armenians cannot be confident that the balance of military power is clearly in their favor even today, despite an imbalance of military hardware in their favor. Azerbaijan has some 87,000 men and women in arms, compared to Armenia's 60,000 and Karabakh's 20,000–25,000.[69]

Stepanakert has officially rejected the Minsk Group proposal and continues to express its preference for a package rather than a staged settlement. A phased agreement, it argues, would force it to withdraw from the occupied districts without guaranteeing that Baku would not later launch an offensive to retake Karabakh if it did not get its way on status. As noted earlier, it has also indicated that it could accept a phased settlement in which agreement was reached first on status and then on "consequential issues," a position doubtless intended for public relations purposes given the improbability of an agreement on status before trust is restored by more modest measures. Karabakh is also very reluctant to place its security in the hands of a multilateral PKF, preferring instead that Armenia, and/or possibly some other regional power, act as a guarantor of any settlement, presumably by means of a commitment to come to the republic's aid in the event of an Azerbaijani attack. It also continues to object vigorously to the Lisbon principles and its "predetermination" of status, and it has indicated that it will not sign any agreement that does not formally retract the Lisbon statement in support of Azerbaijan's territorial integrity. Finally, it has made clear that any first-stage agreement will have to specify not only that Karabakh is an equal party with Azerbaijan and Armenia in the first-stage negotiations, but that it will be an equal party in follow-up negotiations over status as well.[70]

Nor is it clear whether Ghukasian could change Karabakh's opposition to the Minsk Group proposal even if he wanted to. Karabakh's political leadership has been remarkably cohesive to date, and it appears to make important decisions collectively. Ghukasian would have to convince his colleagues to accept any compromise. However, other important members of the leadership seem to be even more intransigent than Ghukasian.

Public opinion within Karabakh also appears to be strongly against the Minsk proposal. All three candidates in the recent presidential elections expressed their commitment to Karabakh's independence and security, and all three made clear their opposition to the Minsk plan. Indeed, most Armenians, including those in Karabakh, fear and distrust the Azeris, and they are convinced that were Baku to win control of Karabakh, it would either ethnically cleanse Armenians from the region or discriminate against them and force them to emigrate, just as Baku allegedly drove Armenians out of Nakhichevan in the Soviet period. Complicating the situation further is the fact that Armenian DPs from Azerbaijan, as well as some from Armenia proper in search of housing and land, have been moving into Karabakh and the occupied districts, particularly Lachin and Kelbajar, occupying homes and tilling fields that had belonged to Azeris before the war.

It is therefore very unlikely that the Karabakh Armenians will accept a repatriation program that allows Azeri DPs to return to areas of Karabakh under Stepanakert's control. Neither is it likely that Azeri DPs would be willing to return under those conditions. Presumably the Minsk proposal does not require this. It *is* possible, however, that Stepanakert could be persuaded to accept a face-saving arrangement that formally preserved Azerbaijan's territorial integrity but left Stepanakert in control of its own military, with full self-government within Karabakh, and a lifeline to Armenia through the Lachin corridor, as long as there were some kind of international guarantees against an attack by Azerbaijan and as long as Baku had no legal writ in Karabakh territory.

COMMON PATTERNS AND VARYING PRESSURES

Despite the differences in the risks of war and the opportunities for a settlement between the three cases, there are also a number of common patterns that warrant emphasis. The first is the growing appreciation by the warring parties that outside powers will not solve their problems and that they will ultimately have to come to terms with each other. Immediately after their victories on the battlefield, the separatists in all three cases were unduly optimistic about their prospects for winning diplomatic recognition and formal independence. While these hopes are still prominent in Chechnya, where fighting has ended more recently, even the Chechens are beginning to understand that the international community's default position is overwhelmingly in favor of territorial integrity, not self-determination.

While this may make the secessionists bitter, the international community's position is entirely sensible—there is simply no objective way to determine what groups qualify as "nations" with the right to "self-determination" except in cases where the relationship is clearly colonial—that is, where the citizens (or subjects) of a particular region are not full citizens of the metropole. Nor does the international community wish to create a situation whereby the legitimization of secession in certain cases induces others to launch wars of secession elsewhere. And most states are fearful of encouraging demands for self-determination and secession within their own borders. Indeed, Turkey, Iraq, or Lebanon, which might otherwise have supported the Abkhaz or the Chechens, or Iran, which might have been a significant ally for the Karabakh Armenians, confront active or potential separatist threats within their own borders and are therefore very reluctant to support secessionists elsewhere.

Nor is there a realistic chance, despite the hopes and efforts of the Chechens, of forming some kind of pan-Caucasian confederation that would allow Azerbaijan and Georgia to accept the loss of sovereignty over Karabakh or Abkhazia. Not only are confederations inherently impractical, but political differences, divergent interests, and enmity between the peoples of the region are far too great for any pan-Caucasian confederation to form, let alone last. Moreover, neither the Azeris nor the Georgians, with whom the Chechens have been hoping to form an alliance, wish to undermine their own territorial integrity or provoke Moscow unnecessarily.

As time passes, it has therefore become increasingly clear that neither the international community acting in concert nor any single power acting independently will, or indeed can, be the arbiter of their conflicts. Once they accept this, they have three choices: accept the status quo, try to resolve their differences by force, or negotiate. For the separatists, however, the use of force is not really an option because they already control their territories and are in no position to invade and occupy more territory.[71] At the same time, they appreciate that "no peace, no war" is a significant impediment to the normalization of life within their territories—not only does it mean an ongoing risk of renewed fighting, but it makes the already daunting task of economic reconstruction even more difficult. Accordingly, the only way for them to break the impasse is to negotiate a compromise, which leads inevitably to consideration of some form of autonomy.

Although hostile to separatism, the international community is generally supportive of autonomy as a means for reconciling territorial integrity and national self-determination. Essentially, the argument is that autonomy can turn a zero-sum game into a positive-sum game by making possible a wide range of compromises that de jure preserve territorial integrity while allowing self-government for minorities, indeed to the point where the national government has virtually no authority within the area whatsoever. Exactly what form autonomy should take, however, and what groups deserve it, is not specified by those international organizations, such as the Council of Europe, that promote autonomy as a means for resolving secessionist or interethnic tensions. In practice, of course, the specific arrangements that are possible and efficacious differ between cases, and ultimately the specifics of any autonomy arrangement is a political, not a normative, question.

Accordingly, the autonomy-based proposals suggested by international organizations or major powers as the basis for the settlement of a particular secessionist conflict are intended to contribute to negotiation and not serve as blueprints for a solution imposed from the outside. Of course, resting behind the proposals may be an implicit or explicit threat that should a particular party prove obdurate, it will lose the sympathy of the proposal's sponsors and risk diminished economic, military, or political support or increased support for its opponents. Still, the sponsors make clear that the terms of a final settlement must be decided upon by the contending parties themselves.

Once the parties to the conflict conclude that it is in their interest to attempt to negotiate a political settlement, it usually becomes clear that a staged approach is more practicable than a package settlement because coming to an agreement on status is so highly charged and will likely, if tackled immediately, derail the peace process. This is not only because of the many practical problems, including security guarantees, that are inherent in power-sharing arrangements. Equally important are the symbolic implications of status. Those engaged in secessionist conflicts rarely believe that they are fighting for economic benefit—rather, they are usually motivated by deeply rooted normative beliefs and the conviction that justice is overwhelmingly on their side (the Russians being a partial exception), and the basis for those beliefs are usually twofold.[72]

First, both sides assert what amounts to an ownership claim to the disputed territory, a claim that is rooted in history and law. This land, they contend, *belongs* to us, and our enemies are trying to steal it, and indeed they may even try to eliminate us as property claimants through genocide or ethnic cleansing. Both sides usually defend this claim by reference to primary appropriation ("we were here first") and specific legal instruments (international treaties, constitutional and statutory law, etc.) or their absence ("we were incorporated into the empire by force"). The more recent and concrete the legal claim, the more vigorously it is asserted. In the post-Soviet case, these claims to ownership were reinforced by the institutional peculiarities of Soviet federalism, which afforded certain (but by no means all) nationalities their own eponymous homeland with well-defined borders and affirmative action programs for the titular nationality. These institutions and the ownership claim they help foster in turn help to explain why the Armenians are fighting over Karabakh, not their traditional heartland in eastern Anatolia, and why the Azeris have taken up arms over Karabakh, not over northern Iran where some 20–25 million Azeris reside. These normative beliefs in turn make it very difficult to compromise over symbolic issues because doing so might be interpreted as undermining their ownership claim, which explains why Moscow and Grozny have found it easier to agree on the need for a "common economic space" and the reconstruction of the Baku-Grozny-Tikhoretsk pipeline than on the seemingly inconsequential issue of what passports Chechens carry when traveling abroad.

Second, combatants on both sides generally believe that their people are a "nation" and deserve to be recognized as such, and that the mark of a "real" nation, at least in the twentieth century, is full independent statehood—only statehood makes it possible to take one's place at the table beside other "real" nations of world.[73] For ardent separatists, anything less than recognition by the international community and a seat at the UN is therefore viewed as an insult and an implicit denial of their status as a genuine nation. Ardent defenders of territorial integrity, on the other hand, fight to preserve the borders of their "national state" because their state, like any other land, supposedly has the right to defend its territorial integrity by force. And again both sides fear that compromise over status will undermine their claim that their nation deserves its own state just like all the other "real" nations in the world.

As a result, if and when both sides finally accept that normalization requires a negotiated settlement, they discover that reaching agreement on status is extremely difficult and that it is usually more productive to pursue a "staged" approach that allows to negotiate over force separation, the deployment of a peacekeeping force or international monitors, the establishment of a demilitarized or weapons exclusion zone, the restoration of transportation and communication links, and so on. Staged agreements, however, have problems of their own. In particular, one or both parties may fear that a first-stage settlement will turn out to be the final settlement. The Karabakh Armenians, for example, are very suspicious that a first-stage agreement will force them to make military and territorial concessions that will leave them vulnerable should an agreement on status prove unreachable. The Azeris, on the other hand, are concerned that a first-stage agreement will make it impossible for them to use, or threaten to use, force to compel the Karabakh Armenians to compromise on status in the future. Still, the choice may be between a first-stage agreement and no agreement at all.

While staged agreements may be easier to reach than package settlements, they are not a solution to the other key obstacle to a political settlement in either Abkhazia or Karabakh: displaced persons. It is very difficult for both Tbilisi and Baku to postpone repatriation because of the immediacy of the humanitarian and economic crisis created by the DPs and because of the political influence of the DPs. The DPs also fear that their prospects for returning to their homes or reclaiming their property diminishes over time, which reinforces their unwillingness to be patient. This creates considerable pressure in Azerbaijan to reach a first-stage agreement that allows the 500,000 DPs from the occupied districts to return to their homes. For Georgia, it means that any first-stage agreement will have to provide at the least for repatriation in the Gali district, as well as for some kind of partial and/or staged repatriation program for the remainder of the republic.

Likewise, the character of the fighting during the three secessionists wars affects the relative prospects for, and character of, a peace settlement. In Chechnya, the fighting for the most part did not take the form of intercommunal "ethnic" violence between Russians and Chechen civilians living in the republic. Rather, it was between the Chechen resistance and the Russian military, and indeed the great bulk of Russian civilian casualties were caused by Russian artillery fire and aerial bombardment of urban areas, particularly Grozny. Nor did the Chechens attempt to "ethnically cleanse" the republic of Russians. In contrast, there was a great deal of intercommunal violence in Abkhazia and Karabakh, and indeed many atrocities were committed by and against civilians on both sides. This is particularly true in Abkhazia, where the settlement patterns of Abkhaz and Georgians were more mixed than in Karabakh, where Armenians and Azeris tended to live in compact settlements. There is therefore more "ethnic hatred" in Karabakh and Abkhazia than in Chechnya. In the case of Karabakh, this is compounded by the historical enmity between Armenians and Azeris, and Armenian memories of the genocide of 1915 and repression by "Turks" and the Ottoman and Turkish governments. The Russian electorate, in contrast, is both less fearful and less intent on retribution, which has made it easier for Moscow to sign a no-use-of-force agreement and postpone a settlement on status. It would also make it easier for Moscow to recognize Chechen independence if its political elite could ever reach a consensus that doing so would be in Russia's national interest.

Location and, to a lesser extent, natural endowments, have also been important factors in influencing the prospects for peace settlements in the three cases. However, the reasons for this are more subtle than is often assumed. Indeed, what is striking about all three cases is that the natural endowments of the secessionist areas were extremely limited—only Chechnya has any natural resources to speak of (in this case, oil), but even there, the republic's reserves represent only a tiny portion of Russia's fossil fuel resources. On the other hand, the Caspian's oil and gas reserves have clearly contributed to the Minsk Group's interest in promoting a settlement in Karabakh, while the possibility of moving oil through Chechnya may have contributed to Moscow's decision to agree to a military withdrawal in mid-1996. Nevertheless, Caspian oil and gas reserves and the prospect of a pipeline through Armenia have done nothing to change Stepanakert's insistence on its sovereignty, not only because there is no prospect of a major pipeline through Karabakh itself but even more because its leaders are not prepared to risk the republic's security for future (and uncertain) economic gain. Moreover, many officials in Azerbaijan, and to a lesser extent in Georgia as well, are convinced that oil and gas production and pipeline revenues will eventually allow them to restore their state's territorial integrity by force, thereby making renewed fighting more likely. In certain respects, then, the region's oil and gas reserves have increased incentives for peace settlements, but in other respects they have increased the likelihood of renewed fighting.

Location and geography have been important for other reasons as well. The fact that all three separatist regions are highly mountainous helps explain the military success of the secessionists and makes national governments more reluctant to use force to reassert their sovereignty. Karabakh's reluctance to withdraw from some of the occupied territories results in part from the fact that the republic is an enclave within Azerbaijan and needs to control Lachin to preserve its link with Armenia. At the same time, the fact that Armenia, Karabakh's principal foreign backer, is only some thirty kilometers away has been an enormous benefit to Stepanakert's military capacity and economic reconstruction. In contrast, Chechnya's relative isolation from the outside world makes it easier for Moscow to accept the current impasse because it knows that the Chechens will have a difficult time rebuilding without Moscow's cooperation. Moscow can therefore hope that the Chechens will eventually agree to some kind of compromise on status. Finally, the fact that Abkhazia borders on Russia and has a Black Sea coastline with excellent ports helps explain Sukhumi's belief that it can be a viable independent state and also makes it easier for the Abkhaz to receive military support from Russia and from the Abkhaz and Circassian community in Turkey.

Finally, the nature of the regimes of the national states has had an influence on the prospects for peace in the three conflicts. Authoritarian rule and human rights abuses in Azerbaijan, for example, have reinforced the Karabakh Armenians' conviction that the Azeris cannot be trusted and that Baku is not fit to exercise sovereignty over the region. So, too, has Azerbaijan's rejection of federalism and its reputation for denying cultural autonomy or political rights to its other ethnic minorities (regardless of the accuracy of that reputation). Georgia, in contrast, has left open the possibility of establishing itself as an asymmetrical federation. In addition, democracy appears to be consolidating in the country while civil liberties are being reasonably well respected. As a result, it should prove easier for Tbilisi to convince the Abkhaz that its intentions are benign.

CONCLUSION

Secessionist wars do not end easily. The justice claims and security concerns of the warring parties inevitably make compromise difficult, particularly where the fighting has been extremely destructive of life and property. Should secessionists win control of their territory but fail to occupy the national capital or otherwise force the central authorities to recognize their independence, the result will likely be either an ongoing war of attrition or a "no peace, no war" impasse that keeps the national government from exercising its authority in the separatist area while preventing normalization of life for the separatists. On the other hand, where the forces of the national government manage to occupy the separatist area, they will likely confront prolonged guerrilla wars or terrorism. In these circumstances, even where national governments prove relatively conciliatory, it will be decades before secessionists reconcile themselves to integration into the national state.

It will therefore be extremely difficult to arrive at stable and comprehensive settlements in Chechnya, Karabakh, and Abkhazia. The best that can reasonably be hoped for are staged agreements in which both sides agree to disagree on status while building trust through limited agreements on specific issues. And even where staged agreements are signed, they will likely be difficult to implement. Nor is there any guarantee that they will be followed by agreements on more fundamental issues.

Western governments and businesses engaged in the Caucasus need to plan accordingly. In particular, it would be a mistake to plan a pipeline system for the region on the assumption that one or more of the these conflicts will be settled in the near future. Likewise, it would be a mistake to assume that oil and gas revenues will necessarily lead to a stable peace, despite earlier talk about the benefits of a "peace pipeline." With luck and prudent policies from domestic international actors, renewed warfare can be avoided in all three cases. But the prospects for comprehensive and stable settlements in the foreseeable future are bleak, while the risks of renewed fighting, particularly in Abkhazia and Karabakh, are significant and will increase in the absence of progress at the negotiating table.

A New Cycle of Instability in Georgia

10

New Troubles and Old Problems

Ghia Nodia

INTRODUCTION

Georgia may be moving in cycles since its independence. From 1991 to 1994 Georgia experienced unparalleled instability. There were two ethnic-territorial wars between the central government and separatist regions of Abkhazia and South Ossetia, which ended with the victory of the latter, the establishment of de facto independent but unrecognized states, and a refugee crisis. Georgia survived a military coup when a democratically elected but allegedly autocratic President Zviad Gamsakhurdia was ousted, followed by episodes of a civil war between Gamsakhurdia's supporters (the "Zviadists") and a new government led by Eduard Shevardnadze, former Communist leader of Georgia and foreign minister of the USSR. The fledgling civilian governmnet has also struggled with warlords and their militias. This political turmoil has been accompanied by a nearly complete economic collapse.[1] However, this instability was followed by an almost miraculous recovery in 1995–97, when all fighting stopped, warlords were put in jail, political life stabilized, democratic freedoms were introduced, and economic reforms lead to fairly fast growth.[2]

However, throughout 1998 the country was haunted by an extremely unpleasant string of episodes, which may or may not lead to a new cycle of general instability, but which nonetheless create a fear of such a cycle. Some problems that caused trouble a few years ago have yet to be solved and threaten to exacerbate the situation: ethnic-territorial conflicts in Abkhazia and South Ossetia are suspended but not resolved; the public is still divided concerning the legal and practical ramifications of the anti-Gamsakhurdia coup, and some Zviadists are still ready to fight for the restoration of what they call the "legitimate government" (though Gamsakhurdia himself committed suicide—or, according to other views, was killed—on New Year's Eve, 1994); relations between the center and the Adjarian Autonomous Republic within Georgia are uncertain and increasingly strained; the ethnic Armenian population in the south appears unsatisfied with its standing; the status of the Russian military bases on the Georgian territory is dubious and open for controversy; and state institutions are inefficient, corrupt, and not trusted by the public.

I will first make a short overview of the events which have led to fears of a new wave of instability, and then try to analyze the problems that lie at their roots and assess how the security situation in the country may develop.

OLD AND NEW TROUBLES (RE)EMERGED

Kill the President and Pick Up the Pieces:
Zviadists, the Russian Connection, the Assassination Attempt, and Its Aftermath

The first sign of insecurity came on February 9, 1998, with an unsuccessful attempt on the life of Georgian president Eduard Shevardnadze. The attempt was carried out in the unusual manner of a military operation having some fifteen to twenty people shoot rocket-propelled grenades at the presidential car. Shevardnadze survived, thanking God, the armor of his Mercedes car, and the agility of his driver (in that order) for his survival. Two of his bodyguards were killed as well as one assailant, an ethnic Chechen Russian national from Daghestan. Initially, responsibility for the attempt was placed on neo-Communist forces in Georgia and their Russian patrons (because of the similarities to a previous failed attempt on Shevardnadze's life in August 1995, when Igor Giorgadze, then Georgian security chief with obvious Russian connections, was the alleged mastermind), but a few days later several members of a group allegedly involved in the attempt were arrested. Even though this group turned out to be Zviadists, the arrests did not completely calm fears of the "Russian hand" as major Zviadist leaders now reside in Russia.

The story had an aftermath. Later in February a group who may have been a part of the organization that carried out the assassination attempt took hostage four officers of the UN Observers' Mission in Georgia (which monitors a cease-fire in Abkhazia). Their major demand was to start negotiations between the current and "legitimate" governments, that is, between the Shevardnadze government and the current parliament and the representatives of the parliament that was ousted along with Gamsakhurdia. After President Shevardnadze held a meeting with the vice-speaker of the ousted parliament, Nemo Burchuladze, the hostages were released after six days in captivity. Negotiations with the Zviadist representatives did not continue, although the government renewed talks about the necessity of "national reconciliation"—starting by "reconciling" with certain members of the hostage-takers. The end of the story was bloody: the leader of the group, Gocha Esebua, was killed in a standoff with police. At his funeral, irreconcilable terrorists shot and killed one of the "reconciled."

The whole episode, onerous as it was, did not necessarily imply a major trouble by itself. It showed how weak the Zviadists actually were: their actions clearly betrayed want of unity (many Zviadists condemned the action) and coherent strategy, and reminded the population of Georgia of desperate attempts by die-hard fanatics. A larger concern was that it also reminded the people of the fragility of state institutions in Georgia. Most politicians expressed the view that had the assassination attempt been successful, it would have been followed by major turmoil. The security services proved utterly unprepared for the hostage crisis, and this showed that they would have had certain difficulty with stronger and better organized opponents.

The "Six-Day War" in Gali, the White Legion, and the Abkhazian Success

Much more serious trouble awaited the Georgian government in Abkhazia. Though negotiations between Georgia and Abkhazia have been under way since 1994, when the majority of the fighting during the postindependence civil war ended, no progress whatsoever had been reached by the fall of 1998. However, since 1994 some forty to fifty thousand refugees spontaneously returned to the Gali district, a region in south Abkhazia bordering with Georgia proper, where the prewar population was overwhelmingly ethnic Georgian. The returnees had no formal security guarantees, save for being in the twelve-kilometer-wide security zone, which was considered to be off-limits for the Abkhaz army, but not for the Abkhaz police. The task of providing such guarantees was claimed by a Georgian guerrilla movement, the White Legion, which is widely believed to have emerged with the covert support of the Georgian government (though both guerrillas and the government deny this). The Abkhazian government in exile (representing the pro-Georgian part of the Abkhazian population, who are refugees), supported the guerrilla movement openly and urged the Georgian authorities to do so as well. Guerrilla groups carried out terrorist actions against both Abkhaz authorities and Russian peacekeepers who they believed were siding with the Abkhaz.

The guerrilla movement strengthened over time, while the general situation in Abkhazia—isolated, impoverished, and wrought with crime—tended to deteriorate. By April–May of 1998 the guerrillas and the Abkhazian government in exile (the role of the Georgian government per se is uncertain) felt confident enough to carry out symbolic actions signifying that Georgian jurisdiction now extended to Gali, such as raising the Georgian flag in one of the Georgian villages, openly distributing humanitarian aid, and organizing a widely publicized visit of two Georgian MPs elected from the region. The secessionist authorities would not tolerate such challenges. Responding to another guerrilla terrorist action, the Abkhaz moved fifteen hundred militia to Gali and conducted operations that targeted guerrillas and the residents of those villages where they had their base. The Georgian government had a choice to get involved in a war or to watch the uneven fight. It did something in between, moving in small armed units, simultaneously announcing the aim of helping to evacuate civilians, but then withdrawing the forces very quickly. By May 26, when a new cease-fire was signed after six days of fighting, the guerrillas were defeated and almost all of the local Georgian population fled, creating a new wave of refugees estimated at thirty to forty thousand people. According to different estimations, the hostilities left some two hundred to four hundred people dead on both sides. After the cease-fire was signed, the Abkhaz continued the campaign of looting and burning houses so that refugees had less incentives to return. Occasional terrorist attacks, apparently carried out by Georgian guerrillas from the White Legion and Brothers of the Forest, continued as well. Russian peace-keepers did not intervene in any of these developments, or at least there is no evidence of their doing so.

The Gali events led to a deterioration of the situation in neighboring Megrelia and dealt a considerable blow to President Shevardnadze's position. The Georgian government was seen as recklessly provoking the Abkhaz without being able to protect the population exposed to punitive attacks. Some thirty to forty thousand very angry people who blamed the government for their new misfortunes gathered in the region of Megrelia, a traditional stronghold of the Zviadists and the ancestral land of Gamsakhurdia, where Shevardnadze was extremely unpopular anyway. The state treasury was almost emptied—all money was sent to the troublesome region in an effort to prevent a major explosion there. This prompted a fiscal crisis, from which the government had not recovered by the end of 1998.

The government, however, assessed the May events as a (Russian) provocation aimed at dragging Georgia into major fighting in Abkhazia, and claimed credit for not falling for it. Both assessments may be fair: but then Shevardnadze is shown to be in a very weak position. Sensing this weakness, the opposition and different interest groups became much more aggressive. While several less important opposition parties demanded the president's resignation, others targeted reform-minded young leaders from Shevardnadze's party, the Citizens' Union of Georgia (CUG), demanding a greater share of power. Several opposition factions started to boycott the parliament sessions, provoking a power crisis. Shevardnadze and the CUG managed to avert it, though, first shifting attention to the possibility of constitutional changes (which did not take place) and then to the government reshuffle that occurred in August.

New Battlegrounds? The Removal of the Gali Buffer Zone and the Spread of Violence to the Regions of Georgia Proper

Before May, the Gali district represented an effective buffer zone between Abkhazia and Georgia proper. It was almost exclusively inhabited by the returned Georgian refugees. The Abkhaz authorities had no actual control over the territory. Being wary of Georgian guerrillas, their representatives only dared to show up in Gali villages during the day, never at night. The guerrillas, on the other hand, hardly ventured to the north of Gali. Hence, Abkhaz forces were not in contact with the territory of Georgia proper before the May war. The main result of the May war, apart from a new wave of refugees, was that this buffer zone was now gone. Abkhazia was only divided from the rest of Georgia by a natural border—the Inguri River.

The dissolving of the buffer zone contributed to the continuous low-key hostilities on both sides of the line dividing Abkhazia and Georgia proper. Land-mine incidents continued in the Gali district, causing casualties among Russian peacekeepers. The White Legion, despite their defeat in the May war, made public statements that they would continue their activities in Abkhazia. As a result of the disappearance of the buffer zone, the Georgian territory bordering with Abkhazia, Zugdidi, and Tsalenjikha districts were put in a much more vulnerable position. Georgian civilians were kidnapped for ransom and murdered if payment was not made. Shooting exchanges continued across parts of the border not coinciding with the Inguri River. Several times small Abkhaz armed groups invaded the Zugdidi district to attack local villages, sometimes damaging homes. Militant claims abounded: an Abkhaz militiaman was shown on Russian television saying of Zugdidi, "Soon, it will be a district center in Abkhazia."

Continuous tensions threatened to develop into a new full-scale war—something both Georgian and Abkhaz authorities definitely wanted to avoid. Starting in August, several rounds of negotiations occurred at the level of prime ministers (the Georgian side was headed by the minister of state—an approximate equivalent of a prime minister). Until then, the continuous meetings of delegations were more ritualistic in their character: the parties knew they were expected to negotiate, but believed that in fact the solution depended on Russia, and each hoped to reach a separate deal with the latter. Until then, they could just enjoy visiting places like Geneva. This time the negotiators appeared to mean business—they needed to prevent a new war and to at least reduce violence in respective border zones. An agreement on coordinating efforts to curb terrorism was reached. The number of violent incidents, though they continued to occur, was gradually reduced. One of the trends in negotiations tended to be the relative reduction of the role of Russia, which had earlier dominated the negotiating process. The parties currently appear to understand they have to rely more on their own negotiating skills. A meeting between Shevardnadze and Ardzinba is being prepared, where the two leaders are expected to sign a major document on the return of refugees.

The Cagey Strongman in the Southeast: Aslan Abashidze and the Strained Relations with Adjaria

Though relations between the central government and Adjaria in Georgia—also called the Adjarian Autonomous Republic—had always been strained, during the last year open conflict developed between the center and the region. Although legally the problem of Adjaria is reminiscent of Abkhazia and South Ossetia because all three had the status of territorial autonomy within Soviet Georgia, Adjaria is different by virtue of a fact that Ajars are ethnic Georgians who follow the Muslim religion (Adjaria was the only confessionally-based autonomous unit in the former Soviet Union). There have never been any public separatist movements in Adjaria. The local political and military strongman, Aslan Abashidze, calls his party the All-Georgian Union of Revival (later renamed the Democratic Union for the Revival of Georgia, DURG), thus having stressed his commitment to Georgian unity. At the same time, however, he did not allow the central government to "meddle in his affairs," having created a territory which is de facto out of reach of the central power. The main achievement for which he usually takes credit was that he kept the 1991–94 turmoil out of Adjaria, not letting any warlords in; this gained him a certain level of popularity nationwide.

Despite the ongoing tensions, Shevardnadze's government maintained ostensibly good relations with Abashidze until the end of 1997, with the ruling CUG keeping a formal coalition with the DURG. However, the CUG refused to make a concession to Abashidze on an important issue for him—proclaiming Adjaria a free economic zone. An open split ensued, after which Abashidze intensified his criticism of the center for its allegedly anti-Adjarian stance. Relations reached a new crisis point in April 1998, when the faction of Abashidze's party in the Georgian parliament declared a boycott of the sessions. Abashidze's tactics seem to be to establish close contacts with all oppositional political forces on the left and on the right, thus making Batumi some kind of a second power center.

A June congress of the DURG looked suspiciously like a unification event for all the opposition. Radically oppositional groups like the United Communist Party, some Zviadist groups, groups of refugees from Abkhazia who are in the opposition, as well as more moderate parties like the Laborists, the Traditionalists, and the Popular Party, or some individuals who lost their power positions in the rest of Georgia—all hope to enhance their chances by establishing good relations with Abashidze. The latter, however, does not hurry to announce any alliances formally, but rather prefers keeping these diverse actors within the orbit of Batumi. All this prompts many commentators and pundits to speak of forming an alternative power center in Batumi and to mention Abashidze as the major alternative to Shevardnadze.

However, it is still very uncertain which way this second power center will develop, if at all, and whether Abashidze really has any aspiration for national leadership. The diversity of groups rallying around Abashidze hardly allows for any ideological identity. If one keeps in mind that the major target of Abashidze's criticism are pro-Western reformist forces in the current Georgian government, and that his major political links outside Georgia are the Russian military and Communist/nationalist opposition, then Batumi may be a natural stronghold for the neo-Communist opposition. But Georgian political groups have never been notable for ideological consistency, so there is no necessity for them to display it this time.

The standoff between Tbilisi and Batumi has recently acquired one more dangerous dimension. Following the departure of the Russian naval guards and expected withdrawal of the Russian land border troops from the Georgian-Turkish border (see below, "Relations with Russia"), guarding the Adjarian sector of both the naval and land borders has become an issue. Abashidze claims that the Adjaria Autonomous Republic should be in charge of guarding its border without interference from Tbilisi, while the central government insists that guarding the border is the responsibility of the central authorities, though the actual duty may be carried out by residents of Adjaria. So far, the center has tried not to exacerbate tensions on this issue, but it must eventually be resolved one way or the other.

Avoiding Javakheti: The Next Karabakh?

Javakheti is a small region in South Georgia on the border with Armenia where the population is predominantly ethnic Armenian. This region, notable for its harsh climate and weak economy, has never been conspicuous in Georgian politics. Still, it is a point of lingering concern as the Georgian public fears the development of an Armenian irredentist movement similar to that in Nagorno-Karabakh. Reports on the activities of the local Armenian-nationalist Javakh organization, whose agenda reportedly included territorial autonomy for the region (which the Georgian government fears could be the first step to secession), occasionally stirred the Georgian public. Due to the poor conditions of communications, Javakheti is largely isolated from the rest of Georgia and much more accessible to Armenia. The local population hardly speaks any Georgian and has only a very vague understanding of what is going on in the rest of the country. Needless to say, the sense of Georgian citizenship is not extremely strong.

Fears about Javakheti are exacerbated by the presence of a Russian military base, which, considering the close security relations between Russia and Armenia, could presumably be a factor in the local situation. Whatever Russian attitudes, however, the local population has a double interest in maintaining the Russian military presence. First, in lieu of other economic opportunities, the base is the major job-provider in the region. According to different estimates, some 60 to 70 percent of its personnel is local. Second, the locals see the base as a security guarantee. Javakheti also borders with Turkey, which Armenians see as their traditional enemy, and the Armenians in Javakheti are not absolutely sure that the Georgian government can or will protect them from Turkish provocations. There is definite conflict between the interests of the Georgian government, which only reluctantly accepts the Russian military presence in its territory, and the local Armenian community. If and when the government asks Russia to remove its bases, this conflict will become more open.

However, so far the problem of Javakheti exists only on the level of fears and suspicions. Cooperation between the Georgian and Armenian governments, the latter of which clearly wants to avoid any complications with Georgia while dealing with Karabakh and Azerbaijan, has contributed to this. Not only are the governments cautious: people in general as well as various political and social groupings in the south Caucasus feel the fatigue of conflict and are no longer easy to mobilize under nationalist slogans.

An episode in August 1998, however, moved Javakheti to the forefront of public attention: a Georgian military detachment was moving in the direction of Akhalkalaki (the major town in Javakheti) to reach the site of joint maneuvres with Russian troops but was stopped by a group of local residents who promised to violently resist the troops if they attempted to enter the town. The Georgian detachment turned back, and this was the end of the actual incident. But the region and the leaders of the Javakh organization found themselves in great demand for interviews by Georgian and other media. The Javakh leaders denied that their organization was political by its nature and dismissed allegations that they were ready to fight for territorial autonomy. They did, however, express discontent over the policy of the Georgian government toward the region. Most interestingly, soon after this incident the Adjarian leader Abashidze made a surprise proposition of Javakheti joining the autonomous region of Adjaria. This could hardly be considered a serious project in its own right, as it would be an Armenian-Muslim alliance. The proposition of a political alliance between two such groups and regions was met with obvious uneasiness in Tbilisi. The Georgian government responded by instigating more intensive contacts with the Armenian government (which officially denies the existence of any problem in Javakheti) as well as with the Javakh organization.

The Ghost of Gamsukhurdia and the Mutiny in Senaki

Throughout the summer and early fall, Georgian politicians predicted some new debacles, usually having in mind another terrorist act against the president or attempts to organize mass disturbances. The prediction came true, though, in a somewhat unexpected scenario. On October 19 a mutiny broke out in Senaki, a part of Megrelia in western Georgia. Some one hundred officers and soldiers, joined by about the same number of civilians, marched to take Kutaisi, the second largest city in Georgia. There they demanded the restoration of the "legitimate government." The mutiny was lead by Akaki Eliava, erstwhile Zviadist paramilitary leader, who fought against the Shevardnadze government in 1992–93 but then "reconciled" with Shevardnadze and eventually became a colonel in the Georgian army. The appeal to the Georgian people issued by the rebels was signed by Akaki Eliava and Nemo Burchuladze, the former vice-speaker of the parliament ousted with Gamsakhurdia, who had met with Shevardnadze during the hostage crisis in February. Although initially the mutiny looked like a serious challenge to the government, by the end of the day the regular army easily quelled it. The whole episode left three people dead (with two of the rebels crushed in their armored vehicle, presumably because they did not know how to steer it properly) and several wounded. Most soldiers returned to their barracks, while the leaders fled. By November some thirty-five alleged participants were arrested, though Eliava was not among them. Most Zviadist organizations distanced themselves from the mutiny. The most obvious explanation of the episode was that Eliava counted on a considerable part of the army and of the population joining it after initial, even small, military success—which proved to be a miscalculation.

Another Cold Winter and More Economic Problems

During 1996–97, Georgia had the highest growth rate in the former Soviet Union, although it started from a very small base after the Soviet economic collapse. It managed to stabilize its new currency, the *lari*, and dramatically cut its inflation rate. High growth was projected for 1998 as well.[3] However, in 1998 Georgia underwent a severe budget crisis. It started after the Gali crisis in May, but there was no subsequent normalization. The major reason, according to most assessments, was corruption and inefficiency in tax collection and customs services.[4] Target figures for growth, established by the government, were not reached. So because the budget was only 11 to 12 percent of the gross domestic product (while in other transitional economies this figure is between 18 and 30 percent[5]), it is planned to increase the budget by 15 to 20 percent. The Russian financial crisis also had a negative impact, especially damaging Georgian exports to that country and therefore its trade balance.[6] Especially alarming for Georgia was the IMF's dissatisfaction with the pace of its economic reforms and its refusal to issue the next tranche of the stabilization credit until its recommendations were implemented.[7] It is widely believed by the Georgian government that if the IMF credit does not come soon enough a general economic crisis will follow. The extent of the political damages of such a crisis are hard to predict, but it certainly will not be good for the security situation either.

THE BIG QUESTION: WHY NOW?

The natural question that arises in this context is, why did all of these problems emerge now after several fairly calm years? Is the security situation going to deteriorate further or has the cycle of instability already peaked? The Georgian ruling elite tends to see the major causes of the recent destabilization as external, namely with problems in Georgian-Russian relations. Other commentators put greater weight on internal Georgian weaknesses. Both directions deserve further exploration.

Escaping the Maw of the Bear: The Catch-22 of Relations with Russia

Russia continues to be the major player in the region, and any security issues in Georgia are usually considered in the context of its relation to Russia. These relations, however, are uncertain and controversial. Officially, there is no open conflict with Russia, but a number of issues have yet to be resolved, and most Georgian politicians see major security threats for the country coming from their northern neighbor. The major source of Georgian-Russian disagreement is usually seen as being due to a Russian desire to strategically dominate its "near abroad" while Georgia sees the guarantee of its genuine independence in direct cooperation with the West. The issue of the oil pipeline route from the Caspian, in which both countries are competing, has become largely a symbol of geopolitical contest rather than an economic issue. Many Russian politicians believe that losing the competition for the pipeline would imply losing Russian clout over the south Caucasus, while the Georgians often see a pipeline as a symbol of independence and of being linked to the West. As the decision on the big, or "main oil," pipeline was expected in the fall of 1998, with a pipeline through Georgia (leading to the Turkish port of Ceyhan) considered the most feasible scenario, Georgian political elites claimed Russia desired to destabilize Georgia in an effort to diminish its political integrity, thus weakening Georgia's chances for winning the pipeline game. Most of the above mentioned troubles (the February assassination attempt, the six-day war in Gali, greater assertiveness of the Adjarian leader, and the October mutiny[8]) were at various times openly ascribed by Georgian political leaders to just such a Russian conspiracy. However, no specific evidence was ever produced. This caused strong irritation in Russia. Whether or not these accusations of the "Russian hand" are legitimate, it is a fact that both Georgia and Russia see their relations primarily in the context of a geopolitical competition, however unequal it may be. This breeds strong mistrust between them.

Against this backdrop, the issues of the Russian military presence in Georgia in the form of military bases, peacekeepers in the conflict zones of Abkhazia and South Ossetia, and border troops on the border with Turkey have become especially sensitive. Both Russian and Georgian attitudes to this presence are controversial. Russia is interested in keeping its military presence in order to mark the area as being in its zone of influence. If Russia leaves, Russian strategists fear the void will be filled by others. However, the Russian Federation obviously lacks the resources necessary to maintain the readiness of its troops, especially after the financial crisis in the fall of 1998. At the same time, the presence of the Russian military has not succeeded in fostering its political and economic interests in Georgia. To the contrary, the Russian presence alienates Georgians politically and pushes them toward other contacts and alliances, such as GUAM, a coalition between Georgia, Ukraine, Azerbaijan, and Moldova, which appears anti-Russian to some. The Georgian political elite considers the Russian military presence as an imposed condition and as a security threat. They feel that if Russia has an intention to manipulate the situation in Georgia and especially to destabilize it when she wants (as Georgians tend to believe), then her military outposts are obvious tools for doing that. Following this logic, it is no coincidence that Russian bases are deployed in such politically sensitive areas as Adjaria, Javakheti, and Abkhazia. However, the Georgian leadership abstains from openly and clearly demanding the Russian military withdrawal because they are afraid that, if too disgruntled, Russia may use its influence to upset the fragile political balance in Georgia.

Vague attitudes in the Georgian government often make outsiders wonder whether Georgia really wants or does not want the Russian military on its land. Georgia neither welcomes the Russian troops there nor asks them to leave. Russian military bases are there on the basis of an agreement signed by the Georgian president and Russian prime minister in October 1995; but the Georgian parliament has never ratified this agreement and is not going to ratify it until Russia agrees to help Georgia to regain Abkhazia. The latter condition leaves all in a quandary, for the condition is not in the body of the agreement but was, at least from the Georgian point of view, presumed at the time it was signed.[9] This makes the presence of the Russian military bases in a way half-legal. They are neither finally endorsed nor finally rejected. Russian peacekeepers in Abkhazia have to have their mandate extended every six months. This means new bilateral bargaining at each extension negotiation. The Georgian strategy—which was never formulated, but can be deduced from the actual behavior—is to use the legal uncertainty of the Russian military presence in Georgia as a lever on the Russian government and, on the other hand, to make the Russian military feel as uncomfortable as possible so that if they leave it will be following their decision, not an open Georgian demand.

In 1998, this strategy appears to have borne fruit in one area. According to the agreement signed by the Georgian and Russian heads of border services in November, Russia will gradually transfer to Georgia its control over the Georgian-Turkish border, completing its withdrawal by mid-1999.[10] The naval guards have withdrawn already, following the agreement signed in June. As to the military bases, though, they are apparently going to stay, but personnel cuts are expected.[11] Given Russian financial problems, however, the possibility of complete withdrawal of the Russian bases is estimated by experts as more probable than before.

Although Russian military withdrawal may be desirable for Georgia in the long run, the process itself may prove hazardous. Even if Russia decides to withdraw, this decision will not be unanimous and will probably cause disagreements between political forces, which may be destabilizing for Georgia, as those who disagree may try to do something to prove that Russian presence in Georgia is still needed. But even if one completely rules out any intentional destabilizing impulses coming from Russia, any withdrawal or reduction of the Russian military forces implies some change in internal power balance in Georgia. Local actors may try to respond to this change in a way that is destabilizing. Adjarian leader Abashidze or Armenian nationalist leaders in Javakheti may get some encouragement from the outside, as Tbilisi politicians tend to think. But they would not necessarily be passive without this kind of encouragement. Both consider the Russian military presence as part of their political capital, and they have their own motives to take measures to prolong it or to find some compensation for it. So, the Georgian government has a task not just to get rid of unwanted military presence, but also to find specific means to alleviate those fears which will inevitably be, or are already, raised by the prospect of the Russian military withdrawal.

The Internal Dimension: From a Failed State to a Weak One

External factors—such as the fact that Georgia found itself in the middle of real or imagined global geopolitical competition, which intensified by 1998, and that any change in the regional military balance tends to upset fragile internal political balance in Georgia—are valid and should not be denied their explanatory value. However, they must be considered together with the formidable internal weaknesses of the Georgian state. While, as it was said above, Georgia made considerable progress as compared with the turbulent years of the early 1990s, most of the problems which have caused that turbulence have not actually been solved. Many were postponed while others were suspended or denied. Some point out the success of the Shevardnadze government in destroying (or coopting) certain powerful militias that laid claim to political legitimacy. The most powerful of these, the *Mkhedrioni*, was crushed after its leaders were accused of carrying out an attempt on President Shevardnadze's life. However, there were other claims to political power laid by uncontrolled armed groups within the internationally recognized Georgian state. The October 1998 mutiny perhaps shows that even within the Georgian army the leadership may not be entirely controlled by the government. Georgian guerrillas voting in Abkhazia are another exception. Despite reports that they may be covertly controlled by the Georgian government, the informal nature of this control would make such opposition inefficient in the long run, and the guerillas may eventually become a source of trouble not just for the separatist Abkhazian regime, but for Georgia proper.

Success in the Shevardnadze government's efforts in neutralizing militias is of considerable importance because it is one necessary condition for Georgia to meet the basic Weberian definition of statehood: excercising monopoly over legitimate use of violence. A second condition is no less important, and is also no better fulfilled by the Georgian state at this time: Georgia does not have clear territorial boundaries marking the sphere of its jurisdiction. The status of de facto independence for the provinces of Abkhazia and South Ossetia is unacceptable for the Georgian state; and despite all the rhetoric, the Georgian authorities display readiness to live with this uncertainty for a long time. Although it is quite clear that no comprehensive solution is going to be reached in the foreseeable future through negotiations, at least in the Abkhazian case, Georgia rejects both the possibility of accepting the independence of Abkhazia and of taking any military effort to regain the breakaway territory. In addition to that, there are zones of uncertain jurisdiction, such as Adjaria, where an open challenge of the local strongman to the state's right to exercise control over the border—one of the most basic authorities of the central government—is an extremely telling example of fundamental weakness. While the cases of Abkhazia and South Ossetia openly challenged state authority and were met by military action—which proved to be a mistake but at least showed the will to meet challenges to the integrity of the state—in the case of Adjaria the center is hesitant to openly recognize the problem as a serious one. The situation in Javakheti is less dramatic, but the episode with the Georgian military forces showed that the extension of Georgian jurisdiction over that territory is not without question, and the government does not hurry to provide clear answers. A decision taken by parliament in 1995 not to include the issue of territorial arrangement of state power in the national constitution was the most manifest expression of this policy of postponement. This restraint may not be without a rationale. The calculation is that once Georgia becomes economically and politically stronger, it will have a better negotiating position than all those who openly or otherwise challenge its integrity. The previously described strategy in Russian relations is another example of this general policy of postponing problems for the future and accepting ambiguity in the present.

Arguably, the government hardly has an alternative to this strategy, as any alternative would involve taking risks that Georgia is not ready to face. But the hazards are also obvious. Not every Georgian is as ready to live in a state of continued ambiguity. Refugees are the most obvious example, for the perpetuation of their "displaced" status is the necessary precondition of the Georgian strategy to regain its lost territory (i.e., their homes). Abkhazian authorities are also unhappy with the status quo of uncertainty, because for them it means permanent fear of renewed war, isolation, and lack of economic development. Finally, the militia groups, such as the White Legion, are obviously unwilling to live forever with the status quo. Overall, such a strategy creates a chronically weak image for the government and thus reduces its legitimacy.

The problem of the Zviadists deserves special mention. From the government perspective, it is not postponed but rather wished away. The Georgian political elite seems to believe that after pro-Gamsakhurdia paramilitary groups were defeated in fall 1993 and Gamsakhurdia disappeared from the scene, the movement of his followers became politically irrelevant and would die out eventually. The fact that Zviadist groups were splintered, involved in continuous bickering among each other, and produced no credible leaders appeared to reinforce this assessment. But the events of 1998—whoever may be standing behind them—proved this dismissal to be premature. The failure of the Zviadists to create a strong political movement only pushed them in the direction of terrorism. The bottom line is that the coup of 1991–92 divided the nation and created a genuine crisis of political legitimacy. There is a whole region, Megrelia, where the memory of the punitive missions and fighting in 1992–93 persists, that considers itself a loser in a civil war. The fact that it borders on Abkhazia and most Georgian refugees from there are Megrelians exacerbates the problem still further. Gamsakhurdia may be severely criticized for many things, including his reputation of extreme ethnic nationalism and autocratic tendencies, but he was a democratically elected president and his military ouster constituted an original sin of the new Georgian independence. Unfortunately, this cannot just be forgotten or dismissed. The point on which the Zviadists insist—that the events of 1991–92 require a legal and political assessment—is a valid one. Some future Georgian government will have to face it. Until then, the issue of the coup of 1991–92 will haunt Georgia as one of the "postponed problems."[12]

Success or failure of the "strategy of postponement" depends on the government's ability to use years of relative calm to build viable and efficient state institutions. The record of institution building in Georgia, however, is a mixed one at best. Most experts consider rampant corruption in state institutions among the major security threats for Georgia.[13] Parliament is usually considered a relative success. After 1995 it became a fairly efficient institution that pushes for democratic reforms in the country. This success is largely ascribed to the organizing talent of its speaker, Zurab Zhvania, and his team of young reformers. However, it is not clear how much this small team controls the Citizen's Union of Georgia—the party under whose auspices they act—and how much the Citizen's Union can be called a party at all. Given Zhvania's low ratings and the relentless attacks on the reformer's team from different directions, their political future is uncertain.

The executive branch is considered to be much less successful than parliament at building institutions and fighting corruption. The two key groups of state agencies in charge of the most basic functions of a state, law enforcement and tax collection, cause the greatest concerns. Both have become synonymous with corruption and inefficiency. This is no surprise as these two features reinforce each other. No agency that is unable to reduce corruption within its ranks to a reasonable level can be very efficient. It has already been noted that inefficiency in tax collection has already caused the budget crisis, which in its turn threatens to bring about a major economic crisis. The police are also widely considered one of the most corrupt institutions. The government's very dependency on the police, however, limits its ability to fight corruption within the force. Many reform-minded politicians privately admit that while the general security situation is fragile (due to the many challenges to sovereignty), the government is afraid to alienate the police by seriously cracking down on corruption in its ranks. Police corruption is dangerous not only because it reduces its efficiency and credibility, but it creates an important impediment for economic growth. Extortion by the police creates an informal tax burden for small businesses that prevents them from being able to pay official taxes.

Another important social-psychological factor should be taken into account. The credibility of Shevardnadze's government has been mainly based on the fact that he managed to stabilize the country after years of turmoil. Shevardnadze is far from being popular, but the fear of possible new troubles is probably still the major factor which stops Georgians from publicly expressing dissatisfaction against their government. People might be unhappy, but nobody wants to take chances. However, this factor works as long as memories of recent disorders are still fresh. As these memories fade, people will start taking relative stability for granted and their level of demands will increase. Soon it will no longer be enough that people do not shoot in the streets; the people will demand that salaries are paid regularly and electricity is supplied twenty-four hours daily. The very fact of "normalization" of the political and public life implies new challenges to the Georgian government.

Back to the Future?

How is Georgia to meet these challenges? Is it doomed to repeat the cycle of turmoil of 1991–94, or is the worst over? There are both pessimistic and optimistic arguments. As far as the security situation in Russia has an impact on Georgia, recent trends show that those political actors who are traditionally more nationalistically oriented and give greater priority to Russia's geopolitical ambitions are becoming stronger. This may lead to the issues of geopolitical competition over the region becoming more powerful as well. The fact that the economic crisis leaves less resources for Russia to commit to this competition may lead to refocusing it—or to making the Russians more bitter. Most likely there will be no internal consensus within Russia on her policy toward the Caucasus, which makes actual Russian behavior in the region less predictable—and, hence, less stabilizing.

Similarly, Georgia's economic fate is also tied to Russia. Whether or not the Georgian government will be able to prevent a big economic crisis is unclear. As it is commonly believed, one of the results of Asian and Russian economic crises is general investor mistrust to emerging economies—especially those close to Russia. As the prospects of the Georgian economic recovery depend so heavily on foreign investments and exports to Russia, this trend is also hardly favorable. Unfortunately the corruption and inefficiency of the agencies involved in collecting tax revenues serve as a weight that hinders the government's efforts and forces the target figures for budget revenues to remain low in absolute terms. While the application of draconian measures may help, at least in the short term, the recent mutiny in western Georgia, along with the situations in Abkhazia, Adjaria, and Javakheti, may be interpreted as good indicators of exactly how bad the situation in Georgia is.

PART THREE

Toward a Solution:

Stemming the Flow
of Weapons
and Controlling Trade
as a Policy Tool
in the Southern Tier

Developing Nonproliferation Export Controls in Georgia in the Context of the Emerging Eurasian Transportation Corridor

11

Mamuka Kudava and Cassady Craft

INTRODUCTION

The entire region from the Black Sea to the Caspian Sea, including all the littoral states from the Balkans to Central Asia through the Caucasus, is becoming a hub of regional and international trade and transportation networks. The economic and security interests of many countries in the West as well as in Russia, Iran, Turkey, and other states are clear. The energy resources of the South Caucasus[1] and Central Asia present enormous potential for the West; at the same time, it is also obvious that Russian control of the region's energy transit routes implies an unacceptable risk for the West and new independent states (NIS) that are involved. Finally, because the breakup of the Soviet Union left fifteen states to worry about the old Soviet weapons and manufacturing infrastructure that they inherited, it became clear that a grave threat to international security existed in the underdevelopment of the means to control these weapons, materials, and technologies in the NIS. Even though energy security provides the impetus behind almost all of the countries' activities in these regions, it also provides the backdrop against which we will analyze the development of nonproliferation export controls in the critical and representative state of Georgia.

There are three prerequisites for energy security: political stability, secure and cost-effective lines of transport, and a positive financial and investment climate entailing agreed legal rules that dovetail with dominant international norms and are not subject to arbitrary change.[2] The development of nonproliferation mechanisms, including border and export control systems, could prove instrumental in supporting energy security in the region. In this chapter, we provide a brief overview of the developing political and economic processes ongoing in the region, and then analyze the importance of nonproliferation export control development in providing the needed energy security in Georgia.

THE EURASIAN TRANSPORTATION CORRIDOR—A SILK ROAD OF THE TWENTY-FIRST CENTURY?

The New Oil Rush

The main reason the international community devotes increased attention to the South Caucasus region is, of course, the vast amount of natural resources in the Caspian Sea Basin and the necessity of building the pipelines and other infrastructure for their transit to the world market. The scope of these interests is illustrated by the fact that the proven oil and gas reserves of the Caspian Sea region, estimated to hold 100 to 200 billion barrels of oil worth $2 to $4 trillion at current market prices, are second in size only to those in the Middle East. In an immediate sense, it is unfortunate that there is no "easy" means of getting these resources to markets. The Caspian Sea itself is a landlocked lake; Central Asia is very remotely located, and the Transcaucasus region (the North Caucasus areas of Russia as well as the South Caucasus) has been fraught with political and military struggles for power. The isolation of the Caspian Basin and lack of an East-West transportation net due to the Cold War–era political and economic relationship between the Soviet Union (of which Central Asia, the Caucasus, and the Caspian Sea were a part) and NATO Europe means that a "transportation corridor" must be built. The political and economic environment of the entire region in southern Russia, the former Soviet states in the Central Asian and South Caucasus regions, and the other important states situated close by (Iran and Turkey, especially) means that the development of the resources in the Caspian Basin and a subsequent transportation infrastructure will not be easy. As this chapter should make clear, it is only when one views the cross-linkages between political and economic policies, as well as domestic, regional, and international relationships, that solutions begin to appear.

We analyze Georgia because of its interesting future role in the creation of a Eurasian transportation corridor. By modernizing its Black Sea ports, Georgia hopes to fulfill its promise as a natural transit link for energy resources flowing from the Caspian Sea to the Black Sea and from the Black Sea to the Turkish Mediterranean port of Ceyhan. However, Western expertise in pipeline construction and maintenance are needed to ensure that Georgia fully benefits from the potential conferred upon it by its geographic location. In 1996 the Azerbaijan International Oil Consortium (AIOC) decided to transport Azerbaijan's "early oil" through two pipelines, one of which (the western pipeline running from Baku to Ceyhan) passes through Georgia. Georgia's position as a key link in this route is enhanced by the fact that other countries, such as the United States,

Turkey, Azerbaijan, Kazakhstan, and Turkmenistan, advocate a broad strategic approach to the transit of the "main" Azerbaijani oil and Central Asian hydrocarbon resources through the Western-based pipeline as well. In other words, each of these players, albeit for differing reasons and to different degrees, wishes for strategic reasons to avoid two possible routes: a southern route, which would extend a pipeline from the Caspian Sea to link up with the existing Iranian pipelines and would empty into the Persian Gulf; and a northern route, which would transit the Northern Caucasus portion of Russia, including Chechnya.

The Eurasian Transportation Corridor—A Modern Silk Road?

The development of oil and gas pipelines is only the first step in building a greater Eurasian transportation corridor that will include the development of road and rail links to allow growing trade through and within the Caspian Basin and Transcaucasus. Such infrastructure development will increase in importance as the economies of the South Caucasus and Central Asian nations grow and diversify, allowing them to expand their ties to the countries beyond the NIS. Historically, the Silk Road was a network of caravan routes running from China and India through Central Asia and the Transcaucasus to Europe. The valuable oil and gas reserves of the Caucasus and Central Asia are likely to make the new Silk Road a trade and investment engine to power tremendous economic growth because of the pure cost-efficiency (in time and distance) of the Eurasian corridor.[3]

While the Georgian government is still in the process of formulating a national security policy to meet the challenges posed by the international and regional political, economic, and security environments in which the country finds itself, it is clear that the realization of the full potential of a Eurasian transportation corridor is and will be vital for the future. The profits of transporting the Caspian oil will have political ramifications in strengthening the independence and sovereignty of Georgia and the countries along the corridor. However, the crucial issue is this: if the Georgian government cannot control its borders and the activities of its businesses and citizens, and provide political stability within the country, then the powers that will finance and build the transportation corridor will be forced to avoid Georgia. Because the corridor is seen as vital for Georgia's future, it is understood that activities must be undertaken to improve the trust that international actors have in the Georgian government's ability to safeguard their interests.

The Political and Security Aspects of the Development of the Eurasian Transportation Corridor

In the context of establishing a modern Silk Road, several important factors must be seriously considered because they potentially influence the stability, security, and economic viability of the Central Asian and South Caucasus regions. First, the "Russian factor" must be better understood.

The Russian government has pursued a policy, according to one well-accepted line of thought, of "frozen instability" in the Caucasus.[4] Another view is that Russia's policy in the Caucasus—if one can even speak of such a thing—is confused, sometimes contradictory, and often destabilizing.[5] Russian activities in the Caucasus (real or imagined) have contributed to anti-Russian feelings, leading to claims that in Georgian public and political circles, the main threat to the existence of the country throughout the entire period of independence came from the north—from Russia.[6] Russia's policy, perhaps, follows from convictions that an independent region of the South Caucasus, with pipelines and other transportation infrastructure running from there to Turkey and the West, "would prevent Russia from exercising a monopoly on access to the region and would thus also deprive Russia of decisive political leverage over the policies of the new Central Asian [and South Caucasus] states."[7]

At the same time, it should be noted that there are healthy aspects of Russia's relations with the countries of the region. The resolution of conflicts there, which will certainly reqire either Russian cooperation or complicity, will be followed by the opening of closed roads and rail links that, if it includes the Abkhazian region of Georgia, would create the possibility of a profitable and practical north-south axis of the Eurasian corridor. This infrastructure development would bring many more economic and political benefits for the Transcaucasus region than the continuation of any policy akin to "frozen instability." The latter policy only promises the "Balkanization" of the Transcaucasus region, with the "clashes of civilizations" predicted by Huntington and Brzezinski.[8] Russian cooperative behavior in the region would create natural political, social, and economic relationships within the region that would benefit all states.

Gunrunning and Drug Lords:
The Other Implications of the Region's Transit Functions

Along with the existing and potential legal and economically useful transit capabilities of the South Caucasus and Georgia, the region can also be used for the transportation of high- and dual-use technology; conventional, chemical, biological, missile, and nuclear weapons and materials; and the illicit trafficking of drugs and contraband. The end of the Cold War and the breakup of the Soviet Union resulted in proliferation dangers emanating from the transit potential of the South Caucasus region. The most prominent of these fears was that the obvious proliferation chain from Russia to Iraq, Turkey, Iran, or Syria would run through the Central Asian states or the South Caucasus.[9]

In addition to the problems of the movement of weapons of mass destruction (WMD) or materials was the fear of a "brain drain" of unemployed (or unpaid), but highly trained ex-Soviet scientists and weapons-making technicians to rogue states. Some felt that it would "be impossible in newly emerging democracies to keep thousands of people in an iron cage. The virtual certainty is that some crucial expertise will travel southwards."[10] In particular, it was feared that states like Russia, Armenia, or Georgia could furnish Soviet-trained nuclear scientists and nuclear materials to those countries with nuclear weapons programs.

If the South Caucasus becomes a major aspect of the new Silk Road, the proliferation concerns mentioned above would need to be addressed (we will discuss how this is being done in Georgia in the sections below). However, there are other items—drugs, contraband, and conventional weapons among them—transiting the South Caucasus region that also pose a serious threat to the realization of the full potential of the Eurasian transportation corridor. These items, by their very nature, threaten the economic health (via the black market) and security of the state. Unfortunately, their transit also threatens the attractiveness of the South Caucasus route for the Silk Road by virtue of establishing an international reputation for the region as a place where drugs, guns, and nuclear materials are smuggled through porous borders, with corrupt official taking bribes and protecting organized criminal groups along the way.

WHY EXPORT CONTROLS?

Export controls for nuclear, chemical, biological, missile, and dual-use materials, equipment, and technology contribute—together with other instruments such as safeguards, regional diplomacy, disarmament and arms-control initiatives, and security assurances—to the strength of the nonproliferation regime.[11] Although export controls are not the only pillar of the regime, they play an important role in the relationship between countries, facilitate the development of economic cooperation, and constitute the necessary preconditions for the export and import of high technology and dual-use goods. Also, the political will and international commitments of a country to have effective export controls together with internal regulations and legislation is a basis for the development of bilateral and multilateral cooperation. In short, export controls can play a vital role in establishing the bona fides of a country that desires to play a prominent role in the creation of the Eurasian transportation corridor.

While establishing export controls, Georgia has kept in mind that an effective system would strengthen international nonproliferation efforts as well as enhance its national security and economic potential. Failure to establish proper export controls in the South Caucasus region not only jeopardizes international security but also contributes to regional arms races and domestic instability. The creation and maintenance of nonproliferation export control systems are beneficial for the following reasons:

1. The realization of the Eurasian transportation corridor promises the revitalization of foreign trade in the region. Without relevant export control

systems, Western investors cannot cooperate as fully with the countries along this route. This fact is especially relevant to advanced technology sectors where South Caucasus states need the most aid to develop effectively in the coming years.

2. Without firm guarantees of proper export controls, Georgia and similar states will lose opportunities to be used as routes for the transit of various goods and technologies that their territories provide by virtue of their location. Also, with sound export controls, Western companies will consider the transit of goods through Georgia as being reliable. All of these things would facilitate the maintenance of the infrastructure included in the Eurasian transportation corridor and give regional governments additional revenues.

3. Export control development will strengthen Georgia's security by providing the country with more leverage in international political and economic affairs and enhance the country's international and regional prestige. This will establish it as a more important and reliable partner of the international community and the West.

4. Export controls will help to create a positive financial and investment climate and give real guarantees to foreign investors, hence encouraging capital investment and high technology transfer from the West. This is necessary not only because Western countries are legally bound to condition their high technology transfers on the establishment of export controls, but also because international direct investment is strongly tied to the confidence that investors have in realizing a steady return on their initial investments.

5. Enhanced export controls in Georgia can make illicit transfers of all kinds much more difficult and therefore enhance national security. Because customs and border controls will be strengthened and equipped through foreign assistance for nonproliferation export control and law enforcement aid, Georgia would benefit enormously in terms of national security. In particular, participation in a common information net designed to maintain the timely exchange of information on illicit movement of goods, services, products, technology, drugs, and weapons would be of enormous value.

6. If Georgia is perceived as having effective export controls and expresses its clear will to satisfy related international norms and criteria, it will have access to a greater array of defense-related equipment, technology, and armaments. Georgia produces virtually no military commodities and does not have the strong technological base within its economy needed to become self-sufficient in this area. Rather, most of the few defense enterprises and defense production associations in Georgia are dependent on deliveries from Russia or the other NIS. Due to this, Georgia will be mainly dependent on the import of military equipment into the foreseeable future. Without a sound system of export controls, the import of much Western military equipment is not possible because foreign exporters need firm guarantees that high-technology weapons and dual-use goods will not go to countries of proliferation concern. Because these restrictions are of lesser concern to the Russian Federation, Georgia would still be able to acquire Russian weapons for its defense needs.[12]

However, such an arrangement would leave Georgia reliant on its biggest external security threat for the weapons needed for its national security! It would also probably require Georgia—at least at this time and in the near future—to agree to military basing, economic concessions, or other arrangements with the Russian government that would allow a continued Russian military presence within Georgian borders as well as strategic economic domination by its neighbor to the north. It is emphatic that neither of these situations is ultimately acceptable for a politically independent and economically robust Georgian state.

7. Because control of borders is one of the primary functions of a sovereign government, the issue of developing export controls (which rely on border controls to be effective) must be considered in light of their role in the most basic, and therefore important, undertaking that faces the Georgian government at this time. The challenges rendered by the difficulties in Abkhazia, South Ossetia, and Ajaria are ultimately unacceptable to the Georgian state because they affect the sovereignty of the government. For much the same reason, the fact that border guards from the Russian Federation perform border control functions in other areas of Georgia is unacceptable. Because of the importance of these final issues, they are discussed in greater detail in the following section.

CHALLENGES AND CONSTRAINTS FOR EXPORT CONTROL DEVELOPMENT IN GEORGIA

Fully capitalizing on the transit potential of Georgia, as well as other South Caucasus and Central Asian states, is impossible without an effective system of export controls, and especially border controls. Furthermore, export and border control development is not possible without first addressing the sovereignty issue. This is well understood and continues to be a high priority in the Georgian political establishment. The two main challenges for the establishment of effective border and export control systems in Georgia are the sovereignty challenges of the Russian military presence and the uncontrolled territories.

The Russian military presence, which includes Russian border forces, peacekeeping forces madated by the Commonwealth of Independent States (CIS) forces, and four military bases, creates difficulties in the fulfillment of international obligations from the Georgian side. Because Russian border guards protect the border with Turkey according to a 1994 agreement, they control one of the most economically vital portions of Georgia's borderline. Not only do Russian forces in this manner threaten economic interests and usurp the physical sovereignty of the Georgian state, even more serious is the fact that their lack of respect for the rights of Georgian citizens and at times simply unlawful actions in defiance of the Georgian authorities create a legal and political challenge for the Georgian government as well. The Russian problem includes the existence of Russian military airports on Georgian soil. Because these are almost completely uncontrolled by Georgian authorities, it is extremely difficult to monitor the transit of goods into and out of the country. It is commonly accepted that the territory of Georgia is used for illegal drug and weapons trafficking from the north to south and east to west.[13] For instance, in 1997 there was the big "Yerevangate" scandal (still being "investigated" by the Russian parliament) regarding *billions* of dollars' worth of illegal Russian arms shipments to Armenia. There is an indication that the military armaments were delivered to Armenia from Russian military units stationed in Georgia. This fact undoubtedly worries the Georgian government because, as stated by President Aliev of Azerbaijan, "in principle, all countries in the region may suffer as a result of the shipments." Although Georgia has an agreement (signed in October 1993) with Russia "on the Procedures of the Passing of Military Technology of the Russian Federation, as well as Armaments and Equipment, and on the Procedures of Transit of Other Military Cargo through the State Border of the Republic of Georgia," the Russian military, whom many suspect have a primary interest in smuggling weapons and drugs in close association with organized criminal groups from outside Georgia, often violate it by not informing the Georgian authorities about the routes and equipment transferred.

In situations where Georgian law enforcement officials stop (or attempt to stop) Russian military personnel in order to prevent illicit drug, black market, or weapons trafficking (which all have important effects on the Georgia economy), political troubles ensue. Needless to say, these do not enhance Georgian-Russian relations.[14] This is particularly disheartening because, while Russia is seen as the biggest external threat to Georgia, it is also Georgia's natural trading partner. Thus, the political problems forced upon Georgia by Russian unwillingness to either control their military forces (who are perhaps acting in a freelance manner) or to comply with the agreements negotiated between the two states have potential interregional, and for Georgia international and economic repercussions, as well.

The uncontrolled territories of Georgia that exist because of separatist regimes, particularly in the region of Abkhazia, create what are to this point insurmountable difficulties for border and export control development. Simply put, without positive control of its entire geographic space, neither Georgia nor any other state can possibly assure the international community that it controls all products, goods, and technologies that transit through it. The criminal essence of the regime that controls the Abkhaz region generates difficulties and threatens much of the progress of the Georgian government in the nonproliferation field. Two examples provide illustrations as to why this is so. Two kilograms of 40-percent-enriched uranium 235 that was kept in the Black Sea port city of Sukhumi (in Abkhazia) have reportedly disappeared. A number of reported cases of drug smuggling have occurred in a second uncontrolled territory, Tskhinvali in South Ossetia. This territory has an outlet to Russia through the Roki mountain pass, and is not under the control of Georgian authorities. As a 1997 U.S. State Department report states, "seizures of opiates elsewhere in the Transcaucasus, Central Asia, Turkey, and Western Europe suggest that there is drug trafficking through Georgia."[15] One can surmise that where drugs flow, so may other materials and weapons, especially given the proximity of the defiant, if not completely independent, Chechen region. These examples make clear that only restoration of territorial integrity and extension of the authority of the central government over all territory of the country will allow Georgia to take full responsibility in the sphere of border and export controls. This will help to prevent drug smuggling and illicit trafficking of conventional weapons and WMD materials that, due to the geographic location of the territories of Abkhazia, Chechnya, Nagorno-Karabakh, and Kurdistan can create problems not only for Georgia, but for other countries in the region including Turkey, Russia, Armenia, and Azerbaijan. It will also allow Georgia to repair the damage done to its international reputation—an important event in light of the hopes for a Silk Road through the country.

While the presence of Russian military forces and the uncontrolled territories present the greatest challenges to Georgian border and export control development, the country also faces constraints on its ability to implement such policies. In many ways these constraints represent problems that are every bit as intractable as the challenges noted above.

The difficult economic situation of Georgia leaves less governmental resources than are necessary for the full establishment of an export control system in implementation as well as in policy and institutional development. In reality, there are similar societal problems with political ramifications throughout the NIS. Because the people do not feel compelled to completely follow the laws (e.g., they may not pay taxes or serve their time in the military), a civic breakdown occurs when the government cannot obtain the requisite resources to provide necessary services. Further, because shortfalls in tax collection may be the result of increased black market activity as the citizens hide income or assets, border and export controls are doubly affected (due to less resources and more trafficking).

The lack of experience in the nonproliferation field, or lack of a "nonproliferation culture," in Georgia is also an important inhibitor of export control development. Before the dissolution of the Soviet Union, Georgia did not have its own legislation and export control structure. These issues were handled by the relevant Soviet ministries. Unlike Russia and to some degree Ukraine and Belarus, Georgia had to begin the construction of nonproliferation export controls from scratch. It lacks the resources and expertise to establish systems that comply fully with international standards. One specific component of the insufficiency of nonproliferation expertise was undoubtedly a lack of skilled specialists, which caused a delay in serious consideration of nonproliferation policy and the initiation of the establishment of an export control system. This problem also resulted in a lack of appreciation among leaders and the Georgian citizenry on the importance of designing and implementing export controls to meet international conditions for expanded access to high technologies.

Further, the delay of Western attention inevitably affected Georgian nonproliferation export control development. While Russia, Ukraine, Belarus, and Kazakhstan were given immediate attention and nonproliferation aid by the West because they possessed nuclear weapons, other countries—including the South Caucasus states—were outside the "nuclear four" and merited less attention because they had no nuclear weapons and less technologies and capabilities of proliferation concern. Although the Western concentration on and assistance to the "nuclear four" countries was understandable, it contributed to the delay in development of nonproliferation policy making in the other countries of the former Soviet Union. This delay, as we have argued above, now threatens the most vital aspects of these states' political, economic, and even social development.

AN OVERVIEW AND ASSESSMENT OF THE GEORGIAN EXPORT CONTROL SYSTEM

A Brief Outline of the Early Georgian Regulatory Process

In order to understand the importance of export controls for the security of Georgia, it is necessary first to examine how the government has attempted to establish and maintain export controls to date. In spite of the numerous problems indicated above, the first efforts to establish an export control system in Georgia were made quite soon after national independence was restored after the seventy-year domination by Soviet Russia. As in many other states developing nonproliferation export controls from scratch, the earliest basis for export controls came from commodity control decrees and regulations that covered a variety of commercial items, including weaponry. For example, the first export control lists were issued by the no-longer-existent Cabinet of Ministers, and a March 1992 decree on foreign economic relations banned the export of certain items, including weapons.

In July 1993, a decree on quotas and licensing of commercial imports and export items (including, again, weapons) was issued. It applied to international trade in Georgia with any foreign company, unless otherwise stipulated in intergovernmental agreements. On March 31, 1994, the Cabinet of Ministers passed Decree No. 265 entitled "On Quotas and Licensing of Import and Export Goods and Services," which established that the export or reexport of any weapons were prohibited. Despite several other decrees and resolutions that for the most part have liberalized the restrictions on importing and exporting commercial products to and from Georgia, the ban on weapons and munitions trafficking is still considered in force. Finally, on February 8, 1995, the Georgian parliament passed Law No. 504, prohibiting the transit and import of toxic and radioactive waste. This provided an important step in moving export control awareness closer to items of nonproliferation concern.

The Turning Point in the Development of Nonproliferation Export Controls

While the above commodity control efforts attempted to regulate mainly what in an economic sense was strategic trade (things like meat, rice, and timber were included), the true starting point for establishing the intellectual, policy, political, economic, and security rationales for creating an effective, internationally accepted nonproliferation export control system was the Washington Forum on Export Controls and Nonproliferation for Senior Government Officials, held in September 1996. This forum consisted of briefings by U.S. government officials to representatives of eight Central Asian and South Caucasus states. This event initiated the involvement of these countries in international export control arrangements. Of paramount importance was the U.S. statement that export controls in the so-called Southern Tier of the former Soviet Union were needed to prevent the export of high technologies, weapons, dual-use goods, and radioactive materials from Russia to nearby countries wishing to have or improve their WMD programs. The message of the forum was clear—the United States was ready to begin serious cooperation in the South Caucasus and Central Asian regions if certain guarantees were proffered by these states. One such guarantee was the creation and maintenance of effective export control systems. The participation of these previously neglected states of the NIS made clear that to control fully the transit of goods through these regions, training and advanced technological equipment from the United States was needed.

From that time, Georgia started intensively working to develop the legal and institutional basis of nonproliferation export controls. The National Security Council of Georgia actively considered the costs and benefits of an export control system, concluded that there should be great importance attached to its development, and initiated work on specific elements of such a system. Upon the National Security Council's recommendation, Georgian president Shevardnadze issued a decree on December 2, 1996, that created an interagency working group authorized to work out the necessary proposals for preparing a legislative and material-technical basis for the control of high technology, radioactive materials, raw materials, and "special destination" products. The interagency working group consists of representatives from various ministries and regularly gathers to discuss developments in the export control system in Georgia, identify existing problems, and so on.

The Draft on Export Control Law

The draft on Export Control Law submitted to the Georgian parliament in fall 1997 was developed by collaborative effort of the interagency working group in cooperation with experts from the U.S. Department of Commerce. The parliamentary Subcommittee on Military Industry of the

Committee on Defense and Security took the lead in drafting a law that will provide a sound legal basis for nonproliferation export controls in Georgia. It explicitly states that one of the main principles behind regulating exports in Georgia is to adhere to international obligations regarding the nonproliferation of WMD. The law gives the government of Georgia the responsibility for developing an export control system and for defining the responsibilities of executive branch agencies in that sphere. In addition, the government is responsible specifically for granting export permission for items subject to export control. Although the government has yet to complete its drawing up of control lists, the draft law states that the following categories of items will be subject to export controls:

- conventional arms and military technology, raw materials, materials, special equipment and technology, and services connected with their production;
- nuclear materials, technology, equipment, facilities, special non-nuclear materials and products, dual-use equipment and technologies, radiation sources and isotope products, *and lists of items established by international nonproliferation regimes*;
- chemical and dual-use technologies that could be used in the creation of a chemical weapon, in accordance with *lists of items established by international nonproliferation regimes*;
- disease agents, their genetically changed forms, and fragments of genetic material that could be used in the creation of bacteriological (biological) weapons; as well as *lists of items established by international nonproliferation regimes*;
- equipment, materials, and technologies that could be used in the creation of a missile weapon, *and lists of items established by international nonproliferation regimes*; and
- scientific-technical information, services, and results of intellectual activity that are connected to military products.

Of special note, as indicated by the italicized statements above, is the commitment made to the international nonproliferation regime. Not only is this a symbolic step for Georgia, but it will also require real efforts to alter the existing, rudimentary system that is based on the old Soviet *nomenklatura* lists and licensing procedures that did not conform to many of the regime lists. The law also outlines the process for obtaining an export license and explicitly states that nuclear materials can only be exported if the importing country guarantees that:

1. the items will not be used in the production of nuclear weapons or for the achievement of any military goal;
2. the items will be placed under International Atomic Energy Agency (IAEA) safeguards;
3. the items will be placed under physical protection at levels not less than those recommended by the IAEA;
4. the items will be reexported only if the third country can guarantee the

three conditions above. In the case of highly enriched uranium (HEU), plutonium enriched to over 20 percent, or heavy water, reexport will take place only with the written permission of the relevant authorities within Georgia.

In order to make Georgia more compliant with the guidelines of the international nonproliferation regime after the adoption of the umbrella Export Control Law, there are plans to issue several executive decrees and regulations that will identify agencies involved in export controls, the delegation of authorities among them, etc. These decrees will be followed by agency regulations. Work in this direction is currently underway.

The Current Georgian Export Control System

For controlled goods and services (e.g., munitions, armaments, etc.) an export contact has to be registered prior to obtaining a license. These contracts are registered by the Ministry of Foreign Economic Relations (MTFER) and have to be obtained prior to applying for an export license. Applicants are responsible for the authenticity of all information provided and must seek the registration of a contract by submitting a copy and original of the contract, a bank account statement, and an application in order to be considered. This application must be acted upon within ten working days from the date when it is submitted, and if approved the applicant is given a registration card, sealed and signed by an official of MTFER. The registration card has to be submitted to the customs service as the product is being shipped. In case of a failure to do so, customs officials will not allow the export transaction, even in the case where a license is presented.

Once a contract is obtained for exporting a controlled item, an applicant may be granted one of two types of licenses: a general license covering a period of no more than twelve months or a single-use license authorizing a solitary transaction. Export licenses are issued by the MTFER within a period of fifteen days after the submission of an application. According to Resolution No. 35 of the Cabinet of Ministers (January 23, 1995), an enterprise seeking an export license must submit an application with the following documentation: (a) an export contract; (b) a notice from the enterprise's partner bank confirming that the enterprise has submitted a copy of the contract and notified the bank about the planned transaction; (c) license fees; (d) a certificate stating the source or origin of the goods and services; and (e) for goods and services produced in Georgia, a certificate of quality. A rejection must be based on substantial grounds, and the applicant is entitled to notification in writing. Any rejected applicant is permitted to appeal to the courts.[16] Because of the nature of the Georgian production economy, the MTFER only rarely will review nonproliferation-related applications.

The customs service of Georgia is required to maintain strict control over export and import of licensed products and submit statistical data to the Ministry of Economics, MTFER, and the State Committee of Social-Economic Information on a quarterly basis. There are also, however, many reports in Georgian newspapers on the dangerous level of corruption in customs as well as in the border forces. The Sarpi checkpoint at the Georgian-Turkish border comes closest to international nonproliferation standards, while others are in various stages of development. Others are patrolled by Russians, as mentioned above. Border forces continue to receive nonproliferation training, mostly within the framework of U.S.-Georgian cooperation. There are, however, also cooperation programs between Georgian border forces and their Ukrainian, Turkish, Greek, German, and Bulgarian counterparts. Georgian border guards declared that they would take full control of Georgian territorial waters on the Georgian part of the Black Sea beginning in July 1998. This step is of utmost importance considering that the important links of the Eurasian transportation corridor and pipeline infrastructure—the Georgian Black Sea ports of Poti and Batumi—should be properly secured.

Georgian Involvement in International Nonproliferation-related Activities

Georgia has membership in only a couple of the arrangements of the nonproliferation regime, but will attempt to bring its policies into adherence with the others as its capabilities develop. Georgia acceded to the Nuclear Nonproliferation Treaty on March 7, 1994, and became a member of the IAEA in February 1996. During the IAEA General Conference in September 1997, Georgia signed the strengthened (additional) safeguards protocol. Georgia has undertaken the commitment to apply the protocol provisionally, pending its ratification by parliament. The protocol grants the IAEA complementary legal authority to implement strengthened safeguard measures through providing greater access for the IAEA to information about states' nuclear programs, both current and planned. It also provides for more access to locations, including nuclear sites and research and manufacturing facilites that could be relevant to nuclear activities. Inspectors will also make use of advanced analytical technology under this protocol.

The protocol is now being ratified by the parliament of Georgia. Once the protocol enters fully into force, Georgia will be one of the first countries to start implementing the strengthened safeguards system. Georgia's nuclear facilities that will fall under the protocol consist of a pool-type research reactor (8-megawatt thermal) that started up in 1959 and has been shut down since 1989. This reactor, near the town of Mtskheta, is currently under IAEA safeguards. The Institute of Physics and Technology, which conducted research and development activities at Sukhumi (in the Abkhaz region) is not currently under IAEA safeguards and probably will not become so until the sovereignty issue is settled.

Georgia is an observer in the export control cooperation agreement known as the Minsk Accord that was signed in Belarus in 1992. There are nine signatories to the Minsk Accord, and while Georgia is not one of them, it participates in the annual meetings as an observer. While initially promising, however, the Minsk Accord has largely failed to facilitate coordination within the CIS on export controls.

Because illicit trafficking of nuclear materials contains a significant threat to global security, many national leaders participated in meetings held in Moscow in June 1996 to address this threat. The main result of these discussions was the expansion of cooperation in all fields of proliferation detection and information exchange, as well as in the areas of investigation and prosecution of proliferants. The fundamental responsibility of each country is to ensure on a national level the consistent physical protection, control, and accounting (MPC&A) of all possessed nuclear materials. Georgia adheres to the principles of this program, and considers it one of the key components of a complete export control system.

On May 31, 1995, in Gudauri, Georgia, security chiefs from the CIS countries signed an agreement on combating organized crime that included protocols on nuclear smuggling, terrorism, drug trafficking, and illegal armed formations.[17] But this document, like the Minsk Accord mentioned above, has had little, if any, real effects. Any cooperation on these issues are overshadowed by allegations from certain CIS countries that other CIS member states shelter criminals and terrorists.

While WMD are the weapons that threaten the most damage, conventional arms are those that kill in practice. Furthermore, items of a dual-use nature pose the most difficult economic and security questions for governments.[18] The Wassenaar Arrangement, the successor to the Coordinating Committee for Multilateral Export Controls, has a stated objective of contributing to regional and international security by promoting transparency and greater responsibility with regard to transfers of conventional arms and dual-use goods and technologies. In the future, as its defense industry develops, Georgia could legitimately be interested in joining the Wassenaar Arrangement. But, first of all, it must achieve sufficiently reliable export controls over arms and dual-use technologies. Georgia's stance toward the other parts of the nonproliferation regime—the Australia Group, Zangger Committee, Nuclear Suppliers Group, and Missile Technology Control Regime—is very similar. The intention to adhere to the full range of regime control lists is made obvious by the clauses of the draft Export Control Law italicized above.

A CONFLUENCE OF INTERESTS: U.S.-GEORGIA COOPERATION IN NONPROLIFERATION ACTIVITIES

Fortunately enough, the United States and other Western countries have interests in the Eurasian transportation corridor that are similar to those that drive export control development in Georgia. First and foremost, all players in the Caspian oil sweepstakes have a priority of safe, secure, and reliable transportation of oil and other resources through the corridor. in order to ensure this, stability in Georgia and along the rest of the corridor must be enhanced. One means of doing this, as alluded to above, is to devote attention and resources toward solving the major problems that prevent Georgia from being able to uphold its end of the bargain. Foreign assistance for nonproliferation and other anticrime activities has been a useful way of doing so.

U.S.-Georgia cooperation in the nonproliferation field began, as mentioned above, in fall 1996. After the Washington Forum on Export Controls and Nonproliferation for NIS "Southern Tier" countries, an interagency export control delegation consisting of representatives from the departments of state, commerce, and defense; the FBI; the customs service; the coast guard; and the Nonproliferation Center visited Georgia in December 1996. The main aim of the visit was to gather information on the situation related to Georgia's export control system and the existing legislative and material-technical base, and to prepare recommendations for U.S. government assistance to Georgia in this field. The team had meetings in various governmental agencies as well as with relevant parliamentary committees and also visited control-exit points in Poti on the Black Sea, Sarpi on the border with Turkey, and the "Red Bridge" crossing at the Georgia-Azerbaijan border. Practical steps for future cooperation were discussed and approved as a result of this visit.

In May 1997, the U.S. government invited a Georgian delegation to participate in an export control–related legal and technical forum, "Partnership and Cooperation in Export Controls," hosted by the Bureau of Export Administration, Department of Commerce. The Georgian delegation was briefed by officials from the departments of commerce, state, energy, and treasury, as well as the Nonproliferation Center and the customs service. During these discussions, U.S. officials examined and made comments on a draft of the Georgian Export Control Law.

An important element in U.S.-Georgian nonproliferation cooperation has resulted from the opening of the Cooperative Threat Reduction (CTR) program's assistance to the non-nuclear four states of the former Soviet Union. The utility of "CTR II" spreads far beyond the technical application of resources: it has a latent diplomatic value through its facilitation of communication on key mutual security concerns; it serves as a significant bargaining chip in regional security affairs; and it enhances U.S. global nonproliferation policy.[19] More concretely, CTR II assistance provides equipment and training for the safe storage of weapons materials and for export controls. After working for several years to implement the initial four CTR umbrella agreements with Russia, Belarus, Ukraine, and Kazakhstan, in 1997 the United States signed agreements to begin CTR II programs in Moldova, Georgia, and Uzbekistan. U.S. deputy assistant secretary of defense Susan Koch asserts that the purpose of these programs is to "encourage [these states] to become full members of the international [non-proliferation] community." As the threat of nuclear leakage has gained prominence as a policy concern, the increasing importance of export controls has led to funds being programmed for this task as part of the State Department's Nonproliferation and Disarmament Fund as well.

In addition, it was considered that with the substantial influence of organized crime in the NIS, export controls are a cornerstone of regional nonproliferation efforts and complement the MPC&A activities funded by the U.S. Department of Energy and IAEA in the region. The original MPC&A cooperation between the United States and Georgia began in early January 1996 with the initial site survey of the research reactor site at the Institute of Physics outside of Mtskheta (about twenty kilometers from Tbilisi). In early 1997, Georgian officials announced the completion of a "quick-fix" effort at establishing materials security at the Institute of Physics, which contained about 4.3 kilograms of 90-percent-enriched (i.e., weapons-grade) uranium 235 and 800 grams of spent reactor fuel. A large brick obelisk was built to secure the material, and intrusion detection sensors, video cameras, and a central alarm station were installed as well. In mid-April 1998, all of the nuclear material (highly enriched uranium and spent fuel) was removed from the Institute of Physics in a tripartite operation by the Georgian, U.S., and British governments.

Further cooperative relations were built on the basis of bilateral relations between the United States and Georgia. On July 17, 1997, President Shevardnadze and U.S. secretary of defense William Cohen signed an agreement on "the Cooperation in the Area of Prevention of Proliferation of Weapons of Mass Destruction and Promotion of Defense and Military Relations." This umbrella agreement was a historic step enabling preparation for additional cooperative bilateral defense activities between the United States and Georgia. As Secretary Cohen asserted after the signing ceremony, "this program is going to ensure that Georgia remains a 'sturdy brick' in the wall holding back the spread of weapons of mass destruction." According to the document, cooperation is envisaged in the following areas:

- establishing verifiable measures against the proliferation of WMD and technology, materials, and expertise related to such weapons from Georgia;
- preventing unauthorized transfer and transportation of nuclear, biological, or chemical weapons and related materials; and
- promoting defense and military contacts and other cooperative military activities.

The endeavors above resulted in U.S. assistance in the nonproliferation field, particularly export controls, beginning in 1997. There have also been other purposes of this assistance, foremost among which have been efforts to assist the countries of the South Caucasus to secure their borders and effectively control the trafficking of illegal narcotics, to contain and inhibit transnational organized criminal activities, to provide international military education and training, and to assist these countries in developing capabilities to maintain national border and coast guards and customs controls. In addition to the State Department's export control programs, it has been proposed that Georgia participate in the following programs: Department of Defense/Customs Service Counterproliferation Program; Department of Defense/FBI Counterproliferation Program; and the Department of Defense's Military-to-Military Counterproliferation Program. All of these activities are interrelated and have several similarities:

1. they are nuclear, biological and chemical (NBC) weapons and NBC-related materials counterproliferation programs;
2. they provide for training a community of relevant officials from Eastern Europe, the Baltic States, and the NIS; and
3. they provide for the procurement of equipment for use by the above governments.

Finally, the U.S. Congress has even begun to understand the importance of the South Caucasus's resources to U.S. security, and also the interrelated nature of the political, economic, and security issues at stake. For fiscal year 1998, Congress passed legislation—popularly known as the "Silk Road Strategy Act of 1997"—making available $250 million for assistance for the Southern Caucasus. Of this, $92.5 million will be available for Georgia and $87.5 million for Armenia (because of its blockade of Armenia—an act of war—Azerbaijan is not eligible for such aid due to the sanctions placed upon it by stipulation of Section 907 of the U.S. Freedom Support Act). In addition to these sums, 28 percent of the funding is set aside for reconstruction and remedial activities related to the destruction wrought during conflicts within the region. Within that 28 percent, $15 million is devoted to developing border security telecommunications infrastructure, $5 million to train border and customs control officers, and $5 million shall be available for urban and commercial development.

All of these activities discussed in this section illustrate the importance of a multifaceted approach to the economic, political, and security challenges of the Georgian element of the Eurasian transportation corridor. One question remains: Without the corridor, would the United States and other states have such an interest in the region?

CONCLUSION: THE DEVELOPMENT OF EXPORT CONTROLS AND THE EURASIAN TRANSPORTATION CORRIDOR

The development of the new Silk Road, or Eurasian transportation corridor, which will link Central Asia with Europe through Georgia and the South Caucasus, is in the process of becoming reality. The establishment of nonproliferation export controls in Georgia and the South Caucasus is directly linked to the process. Without effective systems of export controls in the states along the Silk Road, this trading infrastructure will be less secure, less stable, and have much less value. In other words, it will not meet the needs of energy security in the region. On the contrary, sound export controls in Georgia and the other South Caucasus and Central Asian states would greatly facilitate the realization of the project by assuring businesses of increased regional stability, increased accountability, the safety of products in transit through the region, and the creation of a more positive financial and investment climate overall.

There are several challenges that directly affect both the sovereignty and the creation of an export control system in Georgia. The presence of foreign troops on the state's territory, uncontrolled regions, a difficult economic situation, and the pervasiveness of criminal, illegal, and unlawful activities within the state all present major challenges and constraints. Fortunately, U.S. assistance for Georgian export control development has taken into account the domestic, regional, and international situation in Georgia, and almost all of these programs are multifaceted in their approach to nonproliferation, i.e., they address the issues of criminality and border control as well as the traditional nonproliferation elements of MPC&A and export controls. The role of Western assistance, along with the already declared clear political will of the government of Georgia, are crucial to the establishment of effective export controls that meet international standards.

In spite of the many external and internal restraints, the establishment of an export control system in Georgia is underway. Growing attention toward this process has resulted in its serious consideration in the political circles of the country. While the first phase of the creation of the system— the establishment of a legislative basis, the initiation of coordination between relevant governmental agencies, etc.—approaches its end and some improvements have already been achieved, still much more must be done in order to meet the relevant requirements and international standards. Because of the perceived importance of the Eurasian transportation corridor, Georgia must continue, and indeed redouble, its efforts toward developing export control standards that are complementary with those in the West.

Reconciling Disparate Views on Caucasus Security

12

Nonproliferation at a Vital Crossroads[1]

Cassady Craft

INTRODUCTION

It is widely perceived in the West that the development of nonproliferation policies, institutions, and procedures is a governmental commitment
to enhance international security by slowing the spread of dangerous mass
destruction weapons technology. This relationship is so tight that the
development of these programs is, at least in the United States, often seen
as virtually an end in itself because nonproliferation has become a "core"
security concern. Of course, despite the correlation between nonproliferation and security, the one still serves the other; nonproliferation is a
means by which states, especially the United States and the West, preserve
both physical security and their "rightful place" in the international system. It is sometimes less clear that nonproliferation policies can serve to
enhance security initiatives not directly related to the spread of weapons of
mass destruction (WMD), and yet retain their basic usefulness as a means
to core security preservation.[2] In this sense, (non)proliferation policies are
more obviously a means to an end—an end not of preventing proliferation,
but of enhancing some other vital security need such as border control or
expansion of sovereignty. In short, the differences between these two rationales for antiproliferation policies require careful attention by all of those
concerned with their design, implementation, and evaluation. In a sense,
nonproliferation reached a vital crossroads in the Caucasus in the early to
mid-1990s, one where diplomats in the West, who seek nonproliferation
development, and the Caucasus states of Armenia, Azerbaijan, and Georgia, who seek (non)proliferation, were confronted with both the difficult
problem of creating a semblance of policies to prevent weapons of mass
destruction proliferation and also the enhancement of stability in local

security environments. This vital crossroads in antiproliferation efforts took place in a region that, due to its geographic position and physical characteristics, was considered one of the most fertile potential transshipment points in the world. This paper reports that while there was initial misunderstanding of the issues involved and the stakes of the game in both the West and the Caucasus states, cooperation on antiproliferation policy development in the Caucasus region has undergone considerable development in attending the disparate views of security that the policies of necessity must serve.

THE END OF THE SOVIET UNION AND THE REALIZATION OF A POTENTIAL PROLIFERATION CROSSROADS IN THE CAUCASUS

The end of the Soviet Union left the new independent states (NIS) with only pieces of the Soviet economic infrastructure, political traditions, military forces, and conventional and WMD weapons complex. Problems surrounding the consolidation and control of these issues in the young states dominated their early histories. Despite very large differences in their military-related inheritances, they all faced common challenges: harnessing the productive forces of the economy; establishing political sovereignty and the legitimacy of government; training and maintaining military forces; creating systems of materials protection, control, and accounting (MPC&A); and, controlling exports of weapons-related and dual-use goods, services, and technologies useful for military purposes. In doing so, they faced the necessity of making policy choices with severely constrained resources, i.e., their leaders had to prioritize which policy options to pursue in light of enhancing national, and perhaps international, security. In making these policy choices, leaders of the Caucasus states, it is argued here, committed themselves to policies of (non)proliferation. These policies had less to do with nonproliferation as a near goal of government action (as it is in the United States), but rather used their development as a means to attain greater security in terms of the more pressing problems of political, economic, and military disruptions.

By now it is clear that many scholars and government officials consider it a matter of vital interest to the West for the states of the NIS, including the Caucasus states, to develop nonproliferation policies. Considerable thought, effort, and resources have been committed to encourage these governments to seek, as an explicit goal of governmental action, to eliminate the potential for the legal or illegal trade in WMD technologies and materials contained and transiting their borders.[3] Some of the NIS states— Ukraine, Belarus, and Kazakhstan—gave up the nuclear weapons that they inherited and began to develop nonproliferation systems (MPC&A and export controls) almost immediately. The Russian Federation inherited the majority of the Soviet weapons, military-industrial infrastructure, and expertise and institutions for MPC&A and export controls, and also was able to rapidly coalesce and refine its nonproliferation policies in word, if not always in deed. Other states, such as those in the Caucasus, inherited no weapons but did possess sensitive industry, materials, and technology.[4] Furthermore, their vital geographical location necessitates systems of control. Yet these states lagged behind in their attempts to develop nonproliferation structures. In at least one case, the "other" national security concerns were so strong that the "non" in (non)proliferation policy was removed; for example, Armenia purchased ballistic missiles—weapons of indiscriminate, mass destruction—from Russia.

The remainder of the article is arranged as follows. First, I provide a brief overview of the political, military, economic, and proliferation-oriented problems that the Caucasus states inherited upon independence. Second, nonproliferation policy and institutional development in the Caucasus is analyzed, paying particular attention to the economic principle of opportunity costs as an important explanatory factor. Finally, a conclusion is offered that makes clear why nonproliferation policies are likely to develop further in the Caucasus.

NATIONAL AND INTERNATIONAL SECURITY PROBLEMS INHERITED BY THE CAUCASUS STATES

The security problems inherited by the Caucasus states after their independence may be separated into two categories: basic political, economic, military, and relational, i.e., national security related; and those that involved the security of other states due to proliferation potential, or international security related.

The first and, from an analytical point of view, most important of these concerns the challenges to sovereignty and legitimacy of the governments erected in the Caucasus after independence. Each of the three states struggled initially with the transition from authoritarian Communist rule to democracy. In all, the transition has been incomplete, with Georgia widely considered the most democratic of the three, being labeled a "one-man democracy" by some analysts.[5] Unfortunately for Georgia and Azerbaijan (and indirectly for Armenia, as well), the partial transition left powerful and more or less distinct political groups with separatist ambitions within the national territory of the state. In Azerbaijan, conflict over the legitimacy of the government between ethnic Armenians in Nagorno-Karabakh and the duly elected Azerbaijani government has in all reality destroyed the sovereignty of the state given the military situation in Nagorno-Karabakh and the so-called occupied territories. Because of ethnic ties, the Armenian government has little choice but to remain at least indirectly involved in the situation due to concerns over the irredentist sensitivities concerning the ethnic Armenians in Karabakh.

In Georgia, likewise, a strong revolt of Abkhazians and forces loyal to the former president, Gamsakhurdia, left the government without control of the major port city of Sukhumi, and only the most tenuous grip on the capital city, Tbilisi, in the summer of 1993. Subsequently, even after the peace brokered by the Russian Federation and with the stationing of Commonwealth of Independent States (i.e., Russian) peacekeeping forces in the region (and also in South Ossetia), the Tbilisi government has no control and its sovereignty is challenged in the Abkhaz region (and to an extent, in the region of Adjaria and South Ossetia). Exacerbating the problems are claims that the current governments are illegitimate, put in power by Russian mandate in Georgia and Azerbaijan, and maintained through fixed elections, at least in Armenia and Azerbaijan.[6]

If these basic problems of legitimacy of government and sovereignty were not pressing enough, the states all face considerable economic dislocation. None had consistent growth in their economies for the first five years of independence (see Table 12.1). Debt has increased, foreign trade is tenuous, unemployment high, currencies are weak, inflation rampant, and they are each vulnerable to economic pressures from foreign powers—especially Russia. These economic dynamics create a "crunch," where there are few resources for the governments to wield in order to perform even the most basic tasks of governance, such as collecting much-needed taxes.

Given such resource scarcity, careful priorities must be delineated when considering competing programs, even for the military aspects of national security. Military security needs in the Caucasus are largely dominated by the basic issues of state-building noted above, i.e., establishing control over national borders. However, there are external factors to be considered as well.[7] Azerbaijan and Georgia must worry over their borders with Russia, even if they are considered indefensible.[8] Azerbaijan worries over the intervention of Armenia in the Nagorno-Karabakh dispute, and must plan to

Table 12.1: Economic Performance in the Caucasus States

	1992	1993	1994	1995	1996
Armenia					
—Real GDP Growth (%)	−52.4	−14.8	5.4	6.9	5.8
—Inflation rate (% ave)	830	1,920	5,060	280	18.7
—Current Account ($m)	−50	−67	−104	−279	−493
Azerbaijan					
—Real GDP Growth (%)	−22.6	−23.1	−19.7	−12	1.3
—Inflation rate (% ave)	616	1,130	1,664	411.8	19.8
—Current Account ($m)	488	58	−120	−378	−751
Georgia					
—Real GDP Growth (%)	−44.2	−29.3	−11	2.4	11.4
—Inflation rate (% ave)	809.9	3,125.4	15,606.5	162.7	39.4
—Current Account ($m)	−319	−485	−446	−474	−530

Source: The Economist Intelligence Unit, *EIU Country Report*, Third Quarter, 1997

defend against an Armenian invasion if and when it moves to retake the occupied territories. It has also been invaded by Iranian military forces since independence, causing another area of concern.[9] Finally, if Azerbaijan is to develop economically, it must secure its national borders and take action to enhance regional cooperation and security in order to ensure safe travel for its oil and the functionality of related pipelines and other infrastructure.

Armenia has a historical distrust of Turkey, which may mass overwhelming mechanized forces only a short day's drive away from its capital city, Yerevan, because of loopholes in the Flank Agreement of the Conventional Forces in Europe treaty. There is also the enmity between Armenia and Azerbaijan, and questions regarding the stability of Christian Armenia's relations with its second-largest trading partner, Iran, an Islamic state.

Finally, Georgian officials worry especially over the internal and external security dynamics of the creation of a "transportation corridor," which may include the "main oil" pipeline carrying crude from the Caspian drilling fields to the Black Sea as well as Western goods to the Caucasus and Central Asia via a new "silk road." The creation of such a trade corridor is seen to have important implications on Georgian national security due especially to the Abkhazian, Ossetian, and Chechen turmoils, on the opposite side of the Caucasus range, which have provided illustrations of irregular forces attempting to hold hostage, damage, or destroy pipelines and other transportation infrastructures in attempts to wring political concessions from the Georgian and Russian governments.

While these basic political, economic, and military problems are difficult for the Caucasus governments to handle, they are not the only policy nuts that they have to crack. In addition, there are the international security problems that they have inherited including parts of the Soviet military inventory, nuclear infrastructure, as well as their complete lack of MPC&A and nonproliferation export control systems upon independence, and their problems which abound from their geographic location. Because the dimensions of these issues are generally less well-known than those discussed above, I will devote greater attention to them in detail.[10]

Of the multiple international security-related problems faced by the Caucasus states, the foremost probably concerns conventional weapons.[11] There are problems related to weapons which were left on their territory, transited through these states on their way to other regions, or transferred into the region from Russia and other states of the NIS. A large number of military items were left in the Caucasus immediately after independence because the region was an important area in terms of the defense of the Soviet Union from the West/NATO. In addition, Baku and other Azerbaijani ports were part of the embarkation areas for a Soviet invasion of northern Iran in the event that these plans were executed.

If these weapons were not enough, the early civil wars in the region

(Nagorno-Karabakh and Abkhazia among them) caused great influxes of additional weapons. Over $1 billion worth of weapons have been transferred to the Caucasus from Russia, Ukraine, and Uzbekistan. Included in these transfers are high-tech conventional weapons, such as T-80 main battle tanks, armored fighting vehicles, and weapons of mass destruction: thirty-two SCUD-B ballistic missiles and portable delivery systems that are allegedly chemical weapons–capable.[12] Additional "transfers" are widely believed to take place between Russian peacekeeping and border control forces and various governmental groups, as well as insurgent groups and criminal elements, in the Caucasus. Further, the illicit transit of weapons (and drugs) through the region is widely seen as an important problem because this black market feeds off of, and reinforces, the strength of organized criminal elements in the region. Finally, there are rumors of transfers of Russian weapons to entities surrounding the Caucasus, including Iran and Kurdish rebels, by various actors within the Russian Federation. These transfers are said to occur without official knowledge or approval of the Russian government.

A second set of problems for the Caucasus states concerns their inherited parts of the nuclear infrastructure of the Soviet Union. Included here are such facilities as Armenia's nuclear power reactors, nuclear research center, and spent fuel and radioactive waste; Azerbaijan's many radioactive waste sites; and the research reactor and highly enriched uranium at the Mtskheta site in Georgia (until it was removed in the spring of 1998), as well as the isotope-production reactor in Sukhumi, a part of the separatist Abkhaz region of Georgia.[13] Each of these facilities represents a proliferation threat and must be monitored by the local governments as such.

Unfortunately, upon independence, these governments inherited very little of the Soviet MPC&A infrastructure and virtually none of its export control system. Early efforts to develop nonproliferation policies and institutions were dominated by the Russian Federation. In 1992, virtually all the NIS states committed themselves to the Minsk Accord, which required the transfer of all tactical nuclear weapons to Russia, established the basis for NIS export controls, and modeled them after the Soviet/Russian system. However, according to one Georgian official, Tbilisi's real efforts to begin to develop an export control system did not start until November 1996—about four years after independence.[14] This is probably true for Armenia and Azerbaijan as well. While each of the Caucasus states almost immediately established by presidential decree that importing or exporting weapons and proliferation-sensitive materials was illegal, in terms of Western-style nonproliferation export control development, by late 1997 none of their efforts had fully matured.[15] Russian forces have since the independence of the Caucasus states provided at least partial border controls for Armenia and Georgia under the Commonwealth of Independent States' Border Forces Agreements (Azerbaijan is one of the few NIS states which never joined this agreement).[16] Unfortunately Russia provides little—if any—support for MPC&A efforts in the Caucasus states, a function that has subsequently been left to the states themselves and the aid of the International Atomic Energy Agency, the United States, and others.

A final international security-related problem confronts the Caucasus states. They are in a tenuous geographic position between East and West, Europe, the NIS, and the Middle East. They, along with the Central Asian states, are likely transit routes for the illicit movement of drugs, weapons, and WMD goods, services, and technologies to and from elsewhere in the former Soviet Union, Europe, and states such as Iran, Iraq, China, India, and Pakistan. Neither this fact, nor the knowledge that the Caucasus region lies in the "fault line" between the Christian and Islamic worlds, escapes Caucasus officials.[17] Finally, as even U.S. State Department officials admit, the Caucasus is an area where many "regional powers" deign to struggle for influence.[18] Of particular importance is the competition between Turkey, Iran, Kazakhstan, Russia, and the West over the cultural identity, political leanings, and economic development of the individual, and collection of, Caucasus states.

OPPORTUNITY COSTS, POLITICAL REALISM, AND THE DEVELOPMENT OF (NON)PROLIFERATION POLICIES IN THE CAUCASUS[19]

From the Western viewpoint, it is likely that nonproliferation system development in the Caucasus would be most effective if nonproliferation was seen by Caucasus officials as virtually an end in itself, i.e., that preventing the spread of weapons of mass destruction and their technologies was a goal worthy of great levels of political and economic (if not military) sacrifice. However, Caucasus officials have not, for most of their history, regarded nonproliferation as an end, but (non)proliferation as a means to greater, and holistic, national security. In short, nonproliferation policies themselves do not increase the absolute or relative power of the Caucasus states. However, (non)proliferation may very well be one of several means by which economic, political, military, and relational aspects of the national security may be increased.

The desire in the West to mirror image the Caucasus states and thus attribute to them the prioritization of nonproliferation as a virtual end of security policy was only one of several important misconceptions concerning antiproliferation policy developments in this vital crossroads during the early 1990s. Another important misconception in the United States along these lines was the viewpoint made explicit by the Cooperative Threat Reduction (CTR) programs that the so-called nuclear four states of Russia, Ukraine, Belarus, and Kazakhstan were the only important potential players in the proliferation arena that was the NIS. Finally, U.S. officials believed that nonproliferation policies could develop in a meaningful sense in isolation from the true "core" security problems of the Caucasus states.[20]

There were other misperceptions concerning the development of non-proliferation policies that may have included both Caucasus and Western officials and analysts. For Caucasus officials there was initially a widespread belief in the flip side of the CTR rationale; in states that have neither nuclear weapons nor "anything else" of proliferation concern, nonproliferation development was not necessary or useful. Other misunderstandings concerned the role that Russia would play in the nonproliferation policy development in the NIS (or the Russian-dominated CIS as it was, significantly, referred to then). The two most important aspects of the Russian involvement was the instigation of the Minsk Accord on nonproliferation export control development in 1992 and the evolution of the former Soviet Department of Border Forces. In terms of the Minsk Accord, it was initially believed by those in the West that these were important, and perhaps sufficient, commitments by the NIS states to nonproliferation export control development for international security purposes (i.e., nonproliferation as a near end of security policy).[21] In reality, the commitments provided by the Minsk Accord were virtually worthless. They were, in the truest sense, commitments in words instead of deeds. The same is largely true in terms of the commitment of former-Soviet and almost entirely Russian "CIS" border forces to enact some semblance of border control. As this is seen by many as the most crucial element of nonproliferation controls in developing states, and the inarguable fact was that none of the Caucasus states were initially able (and are still probably unable) to control their borders with their indigenous military forces, many saw this as a positive development. However, the Russian border troops have not adequately safeguarded the security and nonproliferation interests of their own country, much less those of Georgia and Armenia (Azerbaijan has never accepted Russian border forces). Indeed, counterclaims have been made by several scholars and analysts that these forces have served in the opposite capacity—as instruments of proliferation activity throughout the region.[22]

Because nonproliferation policies and institutions are only some of many potential means of addressing the larger security needs of the Caucasus states, the subject of "opportunity costs" becomes vital. As Steven Rhoads reminds us, any given policy contains costs which, "leave us with fewer resources available to further values in other policy areas. In other words, whenever the costs (and benefits) of one program increase, the expenditures on and benefits obtained from some other program (or from private expenditures) decrease. This is the opportunity cost insight, the understanding that spending and regulatory decisions that use scarce resources or require their use incur costs in terms of forgone alternatives (that we no longer have the capacity to undertake) elsewhere."[23] Political Realism admonishes leaders to consider the prudence of competing policy options according to their consequences. The consideration of opportunity costs, then, are not adverse to Realists, and indeed are encouraged.

The concept of opportunity costs has arisen in the literature concerning the development of nonproliferation policies. Kathleen Bailey, in developing a cost-effectiveness theory of nonproliferation export control development, argued that "[e]xport controls divert resources of governments—particularly in countries that do not have large bureaucracies and budgets—that might be more profitably devoted to other nonproliferation efforts."[24] In utilizing a holistic view of security, Bailey implies that the opportunity costs of developing systems for the end of nonproliferation are potentially realized to the detriment of other aspects of political, military, and economic security. In the Caucasus states, given the political, military, and economic problems noted above, such opportunity costs are not lightly taken. Indeed, their leaders have even struggled with these very costs when developing (non)proliferation policies as a means of addressing other security concerns. Because of the opportunity costs of policy development, Caucasus leaders early in the states' histories ignored nonproliferation problems largely alone as alluded to above. The crux of the matter was that nonproliferation policy was (and to a great extent, still is) perceived as of lesser value in promoting the national security of the Caucasus states (see Figure 12.1).

(Non)proliferation policy was, however, almost immediately seen as a sometimes effective means of increasing state power. In Armenia, for example, it is clear that the early (1992–94) development of MPC&A policies for the Metsamor nuclear power plant and spent-fuel storage facilities was driven by the need for energy, the desire to avoid sanction by the International Atomic Energy Agency, and because there were linkages made between such development and Western developmental aid. Thus, these policies were seen as a means to increase the state's power by reducing its energy reliance on Russia to more manageable levels, not as a nonproliferation policy goal. In late 1996, when an Armenian government official was asked about the development of nonproliferation export control policies in the Caucasus region, his reply was, "We do not have the leisure to ponder the best way to develop an export control system. We are fighting wars and trying to stabilize an inherently unstable region."[25] In other words, the opportunity costs of further development of a nonproliferation system were too great, and nonproliferation was not seen as a goal of foreign policy.

When more recently asked about the development of nonproliferation policies, however, government officials stated that protection of the Metsamor site is beneficial to Armenian national security, because otherwise the state would be vulnerable to Azerbaijani or Turkish terrorist activities. While this may be seen as somewhat of a shift in Armenian priorities, it is telling that Armenian officials never claimed that nonproliferation policies were useful in meeting any threat to the country due to Iranian acquisition of nuclear weapons or technology (an undeniable problem if nonprolifera-

Figure 12.1: Security Prioritizations in the Caucasus and the West: (Non)proliferation as Means to Policy Ends and Nonproliferation as a Policy Goal

	Core Interests	Secondary Interests	Peripheral Interests
Armenia	Struggle with Azerbaijan; security vis-à-vis Turkey	Economic development; regional leadership	(NON)PROLIFERATION; ↓ acceptance by West
Azerbaijan	struggle with Armenia/ Nagorno-Karabakh; relations with Turkey; relations with Russia	exploitation of Caspian Sea oil; economic development	(NON)PROLIFERATION?
Georgia	maintenance/expansion of sovereignty	improve relations with West; transportation corridor; stability in S. Ossetia; improve relations with Russia;	(NON)PROLIFERATION; ↓ Black Sea security
West	NONPROLIFERATION (prevention of new WMD powers in SW Asia)	conflict resolution ↓ economic prosperity	democracy, human rights

Key: Solid lines/arrows indicate primary relationships with italicized circumstances; broken lines/arrows indicate potential relationships with italicized circumstances.

tion is a goal of Armenian policy). Quite simply, Iran is not currently seen as a threat to Armenia in this manner. Iran is Armenia's second largest trading partner (behind Russia), and thus plays a vital role in its economy. Thus, it is inescapable that compliance with the Western nonproliferation regime mandates in terms of creation of compatible control lists and agreement on proscribed destinations (which include Iran) are seen as "too stringent" by Armenian officials.[26] (Non)proliferation system development is still seen, apparently, as a means to an end in Armenia.[27]

Furthermore, interviews with Armenian government officials indicate that Armenia sees (non)proliferation as an important means of obtaining acceptance by the West. Such acceptance is useful for Armenian security needs because it allows the state to "win the public relations battle" with Azerbaijan.[28] Thus, while Armenia has received hundreds of millions of dollars in U.S. humanitarian and developmental assistance, Azerbaijan receives virtually none because it suffers from sanctions by the United States and other international actors due to its policies concerning the Nagorno-Karabakh conflict.

Likewise, in Georgia, the stated impetus behind the recent creation of an umbrella export-control law was the "national security" implications of the development of Georgia as a "transportation corridor," and the need to strengthen the border forces of the state so that sovereignty may be maintained where it is established and expanded to the separatist Adjaria, South Ossetia, and Abkhaz regions.[29] According to government officials, the corridor poses coinlike security predicaments for Georgia. On one face, a transportation corridor may benefit the Georgian economic plight by enticing Western companies to invest in infrastructure, technology, and communication within the country. Such economic benefits are only possible, it is felt, if (non)proliferation policies are developed; without such policies, the types of technology that Western countries can transfer to Georgia is limited. On the other face of the coin are the threats posed by an increase in traffic of goods, services, and technologies through the region. Given the power of criminal and rebel elements, any item moving within Georgian borders can be potentially diverted. This poses national security problems of three sorts. First, such diversions serve to strengthen the criminal and separatist elements, undermine sovereignty, and weaken the state itself—grave threats in themselves to the Georgian government.[30] Second, the diversion of weapons, materials, or technology of proliferation concern that are transiting Georgian territory obviously pose national security concerns because of their potential use by terrorists, separatists, or criminals. Finally, diversion of goods which pose no proliferation risk nonetheless has national security implications because of the economic damage done when these products are sold on the black market where the government cannot collect vitally needed taxes or tariffs. Only the second of these indicates that nonproliferation system development in Georgia is more properly seen as a goal rather than a means to achieve goals such as political consolidation and gaining control of the economy.

In Azerbaijan, members of the Elçibey government, which was in power prior to the ascension of Heydar Aliev (currently president of Azerbaijan), clearly saw the opportunity costs involved in diverting resources from the "war effort" against Karabakh and Armenia to the fight against proliferation. Development of MPC&A and export controls was not seen as important upon independence because there was, according to these former officials, "no sensitive industry in Azerbaijan."[31] Developing border controls in order to stop the transit of proliferation-sensitive items was seen as a foolish diversion of scarce resources because those wishing to illegally send items from Russia to Iran would certainly use the Caspian Sea rather than move them across the Azerbaijani border. Diversion of significant resources from the effort against Karabakh and Armenia, with which Azerbaijan considers itself at war, was not deemed prudent by Azerbaijan's past leadership.

It is clear that nonproliferation in Azerbaijan was not considered a worthy goal for a state under considerable duress due its dispossession of over one fifth of its national territory. However, since the cease-fire was negotiated in Nagorno-Karabakh, Azerbaijan has devoted some resources to (non)proliferation. Thus, it is only fitting that the greatest concern of Azerbaijan in developing (non)proliferation policies and institutions has been: (1) the prevention of Karabakh forces from gaining power through access to potential radiological materials useful for terrorist activities and (2) to develop the capability to control the borders of Azerbaijan (including the border with Armenia) so that conventional weapons and supplies going to Karabakh can be halted. It is perceived that if Azerbaijan is not seen as proactive in efforts to develop such (non)proliferation policies (especially border control), then Russia would see an opportunity to increase its political and economic pressure on Azerbaijan to join the CIS border forces agreement (and therefore allow Russian border forces to take control of Azerbaijan's borders), accept Russian troops as peacekeepers in Nagorno-Karabakh, and to allow Russian military bases upon the territory of Azerbaijan.[32] Again, it is difficult to find evidence that Azerbaijan would control its borders so that proliferation related items transiting on their way to Iran or elsewhere would be detained because this is a worthy goal of Azerbaijani foreign policy.

CONCLUSION:
WHY NONPROLIFERATION POLICIES ARE LIKELY TO DEVELOP FURTHER IN THE CAUCASUS

It is clear from the above that there are opportunity costs involved in the development of nonproliferation policies in terms of the national securities of the individual Caucasus states. To date, most, if not all, nonproliferation policy development has occurred only when such developments could be utilized for the enhancement of (non—meaning not) proliferation-oriented aspects of political, military, economic, and relational security. Such a view toward opportunity costs are typical of the Realist notion of prudent choices made within a larger security orientation.

Nonproliferation policy and institutional development as such, rather than as a means to implement a holistic general security effort, in the Caucasus is much more important to those in the West concerned with international security (a concept arguably created by the West, for the West) than to the Caucasus states themselves. Given the asymmetric importance of the development of such policies, it is of vital importance for the West to devote increased attention to the security matters of the Caucasus states.[33] As noted by one U.S. State Department official,

> If reform in the nations of the Caucasus and Central Asia continues and ultimately succeeds, it will encourage similar progress in the other NIS. . . . It will contribute to stability in a strategically vital region that borders China,

Turkey, Iran, and Afghanistan, and that has growing economic and social ties with Pakistan and India. The consolidation of free societies, at peace with themselves and with each other . . . will open up a valuable trade and transport corridor along the old Silk Road, between Europe and Asia. The ominous converse is also true. If economic and political reform . . . does not succeed . . . the region could become a breeding ground of terrorism, a hotbed of religious and political extremism, and a battleground for outright war.[34]

There is much to be gained, much to be lost, and perhaps, little time left to make additional efforts to encourage such reforms. (Non)proliferation policy development and institution building in the Caucasus is important—and will therefore continue along these lines—because of an additional, and related, dynamic. The region abounds with a history of militarized disputes and potential for their reescalation which would break the successfully negotiated, but ultimately unacceptable, cease-fires in the region. When combined with the acquisition of weapons of mass destruction in the form of ballistic missiles by Armenia, the region is truly dangerous. The potential escalation of this nascent arms race, especially given the weakness of MPC&A and nonproliferation export control efforts in the other regions of the NIS and the Caucasus themselves, is sobering. It threatens the regional security of the Caucasus states and their neighbors, as well as the larger international security of the West because of the potential disruption of trade, loss of investment, destruction of property, and the threatening of the Caspian Sea oil exploration and extraction. Last, but certainly not least, the damage such proliferation-related escalation will do to nonproliferation norms concerning weapons of mass destruction in the international community is great. For the West, then, both non- and (non)proliferation policy are concerned with the plight of the Caucasus.

The bad news is that the Caucasus states probably will not (and perhaps cannot), on their own, devote the resources needed to create Western-style nonproliferation policies and institutions with a corresponding capability of effective implementation. Indeed, one could argue that because of the limits of the likely benefits of their (non)proliferation policies in terms of their larger security needs, they are unlikely to be cost effective in any case. The good news: each state in the Caucasus sees in its national interests the creation of better diplomatic relations, trade, and investment opportunities with and by the West, and they see (non)proliferation aid as a means to address their core national security concerns.

To insist on development of nonproliferation systems as a goal for the Caucasus and the West brings out the worst of the asymmetry of interests between the two. To devote increased resources to create linkages between (non)proliferation policies and institutions and broader national and international security issues heightens their convergence of interests. As we move away from the vital nonproliferation crossroads in the Caucasus of the early 1990s, it appears that U.S. government officials have come to understand this. To this effect, a great portion of (non)proliferation aid devoted to the Caucasus has come from the FBI, Department of Defense, and U.S. Customs Service programs which integrate all aspects of border control with nonproliferation development. Furthermore, other U.S. government agencies have directly provided much-needed support to Caucasus nonproliferation development efforts, as the U.S. Department of Commerce's provision of legal support for the Georgian government in their efforts to develop an export control law. Even more importantly, the U.S. government has taken direct military action to reduce the threat of proliferation from the Caucasus when in the spring of 1998 the U.S. military removed weapons-grade highly enriched uranium from the Tbilisi Institute of Physics in a multilateral counterproliferation operation.[35] Finally, the U.S. Congress enacted the Silk Road Strategy Act of 1997, which provided considerable sums to Armenia and Georgian nonproliferation export control development. While most aid to Azerbaijan is still circumscribed by Section 907 of the Freedom Support Act in protest of Azerbaijan's blockade of Armenia, the U.S. State Department has recently been allowed to conduct nonproliferation programs in cooperation with the government in Baku due to the perceived contribution of these programs to the national security of the United States.[36]

All of these above success stories represent important steps away from the vital proliferation crossroads in the Caucasus toward a safer haven. However, as exemplified by the recent Azerbaijani interdiction of Russian-origin missile parts transiting the Russo-Azerbaijan border for Iran, this haven has not yet been reached. It is important for U.S., Western, and international governmental and non-governmental actors to stay the course in helping integrate the Caucasus states more fully into the international nonproliferation regime. Only then will the full extent of the disparate views of security in the Caucasus be fully reconciled.

Perspectives on Security in Kazakhstan

13

Dastan Eleukenov

During the last seven years of independence, the Republic of Kazakhstan has established itself as a state with its own interests and goals. Even with all the diversity of the complex foreign policy objectives, methods, and concepts that the young state had to use in achieving sovereignty, one is able to single out a core element, a basic principle. It can be expressed in a single word: *integration*. There are quite a few advocates of integration—the tendencies of interdependence within the global community are quite obvious. In such a global context, it is difficult to find discrepancies in understanding the meaning of this term. On the regional level, however, difficulties arise. One can with some degree of certainty maintain that for the Baltic countries, for example, integration has a concrete meaning: it amounts to joining the European Union and NATO. For other independent nations of the former Soviet Union (FSU) integration means a more general goal of joining the global community as equal members. In this respect, Kazakhstan is not an exception, but has an important addition: it emerged as an independent state by using integration as a tool of foreign policy.

From the very beginning, Kazakhstan viewed integration tendencies both as the "first principle" that guides the driving forces of today's world and as a tool in everyday work. It is a well-known fact, for instance, that the Commonwealth of Independent States was founded in Almaty, on the initiative of Kazakhstan, which prevented chaos and bloodshed on the FSU territory, and slowed the process of alienation of the former brotherly nations.

Kazakhstan's active integration policy was perceived quite differently by the CIS states. And there is an explanation for this: CIS states, having chosen various paths of development, after seven years enjoy various degrees of advancement. Therefore, some countries' call for integration is not always readily accepted by others: they are simply not ready for it. To overcome this difficulty, we developed a concept of varying speed integration, which emphasizes cooperation of states that are pursuing similar reforms at differing but similar paces.

Other well-known initiatives advanced by Kazakhstan as part of the integration initiative are the Eurasian Union, Central Asian Union (and its peacekeeping batallion, Customs Union), the Conference on Coordination and Trust Measures in Asia (CCTMA), and many other Kazakh projects within these and other institutional frameworks. The result that Kazakhstan expects is stability on all regional levels—from Central Asia to Eurasia as a whole—because stability is the primary condition for the success of economic reforms. It is essential to securing long-term regional stability that the majority of these initiatives receive support, most importantly from regional neighbors: Kyrgyzstan, Uzbekistan, Russia, and others. I will consider some of these initiatives in the following sections.

STRATEGY 2030

Using the "first principle," it is easier to systematize Kazakhstan's actions in international relations, including Kazakhstan's views on security, and their reflection in its policies. However, the strategy and priority systems of Kazakhstan have never been simple to the degree of a short description. Such a concise definition is greatly assisted by the document published in 1997 by President Nursultan Nazarbayev, known as *Strategy Kazakhstan-2030*, or simply *Strategy-2030*.[1] The long-term priorities highlighted in the document are few and deserve full listing, especially because the importance of the priorities is eloquent by itself:

1. National security;
2. Internal stability and consolidation of the society;
3. Economic growth based on an open-market economy with high levels of foreign investment and internal savings;
4. Health, education, and well-being of the citizens of Kazakhstan;
5. Energy resources;
6. Infrastructure, especially transportation and communications;
7. A professional state.

National security occupies a deserved first spot in Kazakhstan's set of priorities. The strategy to ensure it consists of five components:

1. To have reliable and friendly relations with neighbors:
   - to develop and improve equal and trustful relationships with Russia, our closest and historically friendly neighbor;
   - to develop similar good-neighbor relations with China, on the mutual advantage principle;
   - to improve relations and integration processes with Central Asian states;
   - to improve relations with Middle Eastern states.

In determining this element, Kazakhstan assumes that all present and future potential threats to national security do not and will not have the nature of direct military intervention or violate of the country's territorial integrity.

2. To improve relations with the main industrial democracies. Many of these states, including the United States, already realize that the establishment of an independent and prosperous Kazakhstan meets their national interest. They view Kazakhstan as the stronghold of stability and security in Central Asia, and as their key partner in the region.

3. To use help and assistance of international institutions and fora, such as the United Nations, International Monetary Fund, World Bank, and the Asian, European, and Islamic Bank of Reconstruction and Development. This element is designed to ensure wide international support for Kazakhstan.

4. To use natural resources. They can become a solid foundation for defending the sovereignty and territorial integrity of the country.

5. To develop a sense of patriotism and country loyalty in citizens of Kazakhstan.

As we see from the above, the undisputed priority in ensuring the security of Kazakhstan is given to foreign policy efforts and the formation of a dense network of relationships with its neighbors and the world's leading powers. Pursuing this, Kazakhstan cannot afford to depend entirely on its relationship with one country. An important part of the process is the creation of a beneficial climate for long-term investments into the country. Kazakhstan is against military solutions to any conflicts. The best weapon that ensures the protection of national interests and power parity for the short and long term is the policy of integration; development of the Central Asian Union among Kazakhstan, Kyrgyzstan, and Uzbekistan; and noninterference in the affairs of other states. At the same time, much attention will be given to the development and modernization of the armed forces, improvement of their combat readiness, and equipment with the latest weapons systems. Among the important national security priorities are also strong demographic and migration policies designed to slow the dangerous tendencies in population decline. Although energy resources occupy a space in the lower half of the list, it still is the fourth most important element in the strategy of ensuring the national security of Kazakhstan. It also answers the question whether Kazakhstan will bet on oil exports as its main source of revenue: the significance of energy resources is high, but Kazakhstan will not "put all its eggs in one basket."

EURASIANISM

It appears that Kazakhstan's most organically integrated approach was implemented in the international arena in the idea of the Eurasian Community (EAC), advanced by President Nazarbayev in his speech at Moscow

State University in March 1994. The full description of the project should, of course, be entrusted to the experts, because its contents are much wider than the scope of this work. I will address a few of those points.

The fact that the idea of EAC was proposed by President Nazarbayev, not Russia, which has traditionally been very keen on the idea of Eurasianism, confirmed the reputation of the Kazakh leader as the most consistent proponent of integration. For Kazakhstan, a state that recently regained independence and which also has a unique ethnic make-up, the most important aspect of this project is the alternative that it presents to the recently advanced and very popular theory of the "clash of civilizations."

The end of the twentieth century offered some support for the "clash of civilizations" theory. For a country such as Kazakhstan, with its unique ethnic composition, the clash of civilizations in Central Asia marks the "end of history" in the nonmetaphoric sense. However, European and Oriental societies have cooperated, virtually without conflicts, in the Asia-Pacific region (APR) until recently with good results. Certainly, no one aspires to achieve full unification, which is impossible, even if all agree to it: the Soviet Union failed to produce "a unified commonality—the Soviet people." On the other hand, the current Asian crisis may be an indication of insufficient interdependence of West and East. If all existing ways of handling the economy are ignored, especially those developed by the West, the infatuation with national market models may lead to a collapse.

Until now, discussions on the problem of the relationship between the Eastern and Western civilizations have been limited to the issues of the APR. It is clear that the same issues will be salient for Central Asia in the future, especially since the percentage of European population here is higher than in the APR. So far, intercivilization issues in the Central Asian region have focused on conflict prevention, especially of interethnic conflicts, which is by itself an enormously important endeavor. It would be, however, an unforgivable mistake to locate the only source of internal instability in one's geopolitical and ethnic situations. The appearance of new independent states in Central Asia created a large intracontinental tangent region between East and West, comparable in size to the APR. Central Asian states should therefore be taking into account the APR experience, seeking prosperity on the basis of the cooperation of civilizations.

The idea of Eurasianism facilitates security in the nations of the continent because it urges both key states of the region (Kazakhstan and Russia) as well as many other nations to pursue common unifying sentiments. The EAU draft document is still under consideration, but Kazakhstan, ever since gaining independence, has put Eurasianism at the center of its policies. Here lie the roots of Kazakhstan's aspirations for integration.

A quote from an article by Alexander Bovin captures the spirit of the above arguments:

The future of Russia as a great power, as one of the poles and power centers in twenty-first-century world politics, will depend on whether it can realize its Eurasian status, whether we can join the international community as an effective and useful political, cultural, and economic bridge between Eurasia's East and West. In the framework of this conceptual plan, it is obvious that Russia will hardly use all its potential without deep relationships with the post-Soviet republics of Central Asia, particularly Kazakhstan. It is also obvious that Kazakhstan, located in the very heart of the Eurasian continent, must build its foreign policy within the Eurasian system of coordinates: only a broad Eurasian approach is capable of taking the country along the road of prosperity. And it is not surprising that President Nazarbayev consistently promotes the idea of a Eurasian Union, or Community, as an integration project of the twenty-first century.[2]

Conference on Cooperation and Trust Measures in Asia

Without doubt the work to convene the Conference on Cooperation and Trust Measures in Asia (CCTMA) is among the top priorities of the foreign policy of Kazakhstan. It was initiated by President Nazarbayev and presented to the international community in 1992 at the UN General Assembly.

The core idea is to renew the earlier unsuccessful attempts to establish a security structure on the Asian continent, where, contrary to other continents, it does not exist. Several months after the proposal, in March 1993, representatives of twelve Asian nations met in Almaty to discuss Kazakhstan's initiative. Thus, the work on CCTMA has begun. Later, the participants created a special working group to prepare the Council of the Ministers of Foreign Affairs of the states interested in convening the CCTMA.

The purpose of the conference is to improve the relationships among the member states and to ensure stable living conditions for Asian peoples. The foundation for the activities of the conference would be the provisions of the UN Charter and other principles of international law. The range of issues considered by the Special Working Group includes such important themes as a respect of sovereign rights; prohibition of violence or threats of force; territorial integrity of member-countries; peaceful settlement of disputes; noninterference in the internal affairs of members; disarmament and arms control; economic, social, and cultural cooperation; and human rights.

The initiative received tremendous support from a large part of Asia geographically, demographically, and by the size and political clout of the interested countries.[3] Among observers are such international organizations as the UN, OSCE, the Arab League, and the Interstate Council of Kazakhstan, Kyrgyzstan, Uzbekistan, and Tajikistan. The process of convening the conference acquires real political contours and is becoming a fact of international life.

Significant progress in advancing the initiative occurred in 1997, when the first official document paving the way to the ultimate goal was adopted at the conference of the CCTMA's countries' deputy foreign ministers. Considering the great amount of political, economic, cultural, and religious diversity of the member nations, as well as the presence of old conflicts, one may readily admit that reaching a consensus will not be an easy task. A consensus has also been reached, however, on the final version of the basic political document: a Declaration on the Principles of Relationships among the CCTMA members.

International Organizations and Security Agreements

Kazakhstan's armed forces are growing and becoming stronger. A substantial treaty and legal basis for cooperation with other nations, especially with our neighbors, has been established and is improving. Nevertheless, the future of comprehensive security arrangements is in multilateral diplomacy. Many experts, impressed by the globalization of international processes, pronounce their favorable judgment in this respect. Indeed, international organizations, which are particularly security-related, play an increasingly important role in current international relations and the formation of the new world order.

Unfortunately, it is utterly impossible in one article to reflect the views of Kazakhstan on the importance of international security arrangements.[4] Year by year, the activity and involvement of the young state in its work is growing. Kazakhstan attributes extreme importance to participating in such organizations as the UN and the OSCE. Kazakhstan also actively participates in the activities of the IAEA. The republic, as well as other states of Central Asia and the Transcaucasus, does not fail to use the opportunities provided by international organizations. Multilateral diplomacy is a priority of Kazakhstan's foreign policy, based on the concept of integration.

Kazakhstan's efforts in bilateral relations are also persistent and active: they resulted in establishing a reliable "security belt" around the nation's borders. Kazakhstan has no potentially threatening disputes with any country. Moreover, within the last years, relationships with neighboring states have improved, while relationships with the United States, major European and Asian powers, and Australia are steadily progressing.

The list of historic documents signed with our neighbors alone is illustrative, and will continue to grow. Among them are the Kazakhstan-Russian "Declaration of Eternal Friendship of 1998," oriented toward the twenty-first century; an agreement on the delimitation of the borders with the People's Republic of China; the 1996 Shanghai and 1997 Moscow agreements on the measures of trust in military affairs and on arms reduction in borderline districts; and the 1997 "Treaty on Eternal Friendship with Kyrgyzstan and Uzbekistan." One can conclude from this treaty that the foundations of Kazakhstan's relationships with its neighbors are so strong that no economic disagreements (which are common occurrences in international affairs) can overshadow the main goal: maintenance of stability in Central Asia.

Another equally important conclusion is that a threat to the stability in the region should be addressed jointly. Of greatest concern for the region is the situation in neighboring Afghanistan and along the Tajik-Afghan border. We cannot overestimate the importance of the Joint Declaration of the Central Asian States and Russia, which resulted in the Treaty on Collective Security, signed in the midst of a threatening development on the southern borders of the region. The fragility of truce between the government and opposition forces in Tajikistan is the subject of constant attention of the leaders of Central Asian nations. Tajikistan's joining the Treaty on Unified Economic Environment among Kazakhstan, Kyrgyzstan, and Uzbekistan is significant as much as it is a natural step toward the integration of Central Asia.

These four states jointly develop regional mechanisms of cooperation in military and foreign policy affairs: the Four Power Inter-Governmental Council and councils of foreign and defense ministers. On the initiative of President Nazarbayev, a Central Asian Peacekeeping Batallion was created, which in the future will operate under UN auspices. In 1997–98, the battalion conducted joint maneuvers with U.S., Russian, Turkish, Azeri, and Georgian troops in the spirit of the Partnership for Peace program (PFP). The experience of the alliance in peacekeeping operations is very valuable for the Central Asian region. It is important that this work results in the creation of a united and viable batallion.

This work, however, has so far not covered two important issues in the sphere of disarmament and arms control, namely WMD nonproliferation and technology export controls.[5] I would like to point out two issues: the development of nonproliferation export controls in Kazakhstan and the initiative of the Central Asian states to create a nuclear-weapons-free zone in Central Asia (CANWFZ). The consideration of the national policy regarding the export of armaments, military hardware, and dual-use technologies, which occurred on May 20, 1998, at the meeting of the Security Council of Kazakhstan under the chairmanship of President Nazarbayev, became a long-awaited event. The meeting resulted in a unified position on controlling the export of arms, military hardware, and dual-use items. The law "On Export Controls over Armaments, Military Hardware, and Dual-Use Items" affirms the priority of the political interest in enforcing export controls. Therefore, the new export contracts will take into consideration not only economic benefit, but also the need not to jeopardize Kazakhstan's good relations with its partners as well as its image as a peaceful democratic state.

An important aspect of export controls was Kazakhstan's joining the international nonproliferation regimes, such as the Nuclear Suppliers

Group, the Wassenaar Arrangement (conventional weapons, dual-use technologies), Missile Technology Control Regime, and the Australia Group (chemical and biological weapons). Minister of Foreign Affairs K. Tokayev said in his speech at the Conference on Disarmament in Geneva on May 19, 1998, that beginning in 1997, Kazakhstan has adhered to the principles of the NSG in its activities involving the export of nuclear materials and technologies. Besides, by possessing the scientific and technological potential for missile building and having a rocket launch site on its territory (Baikonur), Kazakhstan, in Tokayev's opinion, can offer a substantial contribution to the MTCR and actively develop cooperation in the peaceful use of missile technology.

The idea for creating the CANWFZ has been tossed around for some time. The work on developing such a project started practically simultaneously in Kyrgyzstan, Kazakhstan, and Uzbekistan.[6] The example of Kazakhstan is well known and can serve as a model for other countries to emulate. As the Americans, who love technical metaphors, like to say, Kazakhstan appeared on the world radar screen not long ago, but its mark is already recognized by many. Kazakhstan is known not only for being a country of immeasurable natural resources, but also for making a substantial contribution toward the noble cause of disarmament: Kazakhstan was the first to shut down the nuclear test site at Semipalatinsk, the first to dispose of its nuclear weapons inheritance (formerly aimed at the United States), supported the indefinite extension of the Nuclear Nonproliferation Treaty (NPT), and was one of the first CIS countries to adopt a comprehensive law on controlling the export of armaments, military hardware, and dual-use items. The security guarantees provided for Kazakhstan by the nuclear powers are an adequate response to Kazakhstan's unilateral decision and a means whereby to ensure a favorable position in the international arena.

It is not surprising that neighboring Kyrgyzstan and Uzbekistan recognized the importance of nonproliferation. The CANWFZ initiative, advanced by Uzbekistan, was actively supported by Kazakhstan and Kyrgyzstan, which on February 28, 1997, resulted in the "Almaty Declaration," where heads of all three states declared their intention to pursue this endeavor. Little time has passed since then, but the progress achieved is impressive. The involved and creative approach of the participants in negotiating the treaty helped the United Nations and independent experts do their job. There is every reason to believe, moreover, that the fruits of cooperation will be another confirmation of the earlier conclusions.

Contrasting with the nonproliferation efforts made by Central Asia, the nuclear explosions in India and Pakistan sounded a sharp note of dissonance. On May 13, 1998, the Ministry of Foreign Affairs of Kazakhstan issued a stern memorandum regarding the nuclear tests in India. As a nation that voluntarily abandoned its nuclear legacy and firmly adheres to the nonproliferation regime, Kazakhstan cannot but declare its deep concern over the fact that the development of nuclear weapons in India jeopardizes the intent of the international community to achieve some progress in the area of nuclear disarmament and nonproliferation. The tests conducted by India negatively affected the situation in the region. Unfortunately, as the Foreign Ministry stated, the world is facing the real threat of an escalating nuclear arms race and the continued spread of nuclear weapons. The conclusion arrived at in Astana, Turkey is troubling: the next century is not likely to be less dangerous than its predecessor. To thwart that, Minister Tokayev proposed making real steps toward nuclear disarmament. As the meeting of deputy foreign ministers in Bishkek in July 1998 with participation of the five nuclear powers and the UN showed, the Indian and Pakistani nuclear tests even increased the interest toward the process of creating the CANWFZ.

It is appropriate to mention that regardless of the events in South Asia, the nonproliferation activities in Central Asia are undergoing a renaissance of sorts after a brief interlude when Kazakhstan joined the NPT in December 1993. In particular, several NGOs working on nonproliferation issues have been established in Almaty.

The Legal Status of the Caspian Sea

The growing foreign policy and geo-economic importance of the Caspian region encouraged politicians and political scientists of many countries to become well versed in the geography of the region: names of oil fields and figures describing oil reserves in Tengiz, Chirag, Azeri, or Gunesli; estimates of oil reserves in the Kazakhstani Shelf; etc. They carefully monitor each other's share in each project, how much it will cost when fully implemented, and what the expected payoffs are for the participants. The estimated amount of all oil reserves in the region is 30 billion tons, while Kazakhstan's reserves of hydrocarbon minerals under the Caspian Sea and the continental part of the country approximates 20 billion tons in the oil equivalent.

Newspapers and magazines are filled with outlines of future oil pipelines toward the outside world: from Baku and Tengiz to Novorossiysk, Baku-Batumi, Transcaspian (from Kazakhstan to Azerbaijan, or Tengiz-Aktau-Makhachkala-Baku-Batumi-Ceyhan), or through Iran to the Persian Gulf and to the east to China, while Bulgaria, Greece, Rumania, and Ukraine do not want to be passed over. As far as the vast reserves of Turkmenian gas are concerned, the potential oil pipeline routes include Afghanistan and Pakistan. The list of all the countries and oil companies already active in the Caspian region is extensive. Further consideration reveals a number of local problems along the routes, such as regional conflicts, separatist movements, and terrorism. Another concern surrounding pipelines is the ecological impact. Finally, of particular importance is the issue of the legal status of the Caspian Sea. Besides the problem of sharing the oil fields, other issues must also be resolved.

There is no shortage of studies originating from the unforgettable recipes of Realpolitik, which are based on such positions as "where there is oil, there is war," and which seek to assign certain roles to states in the assumed struggle for influence and power. The unregulated conflicts in this region provide food for such analyses. Sadly, the conclusions drawn from such analyses call for a strong hand that should take control, rather than relinquish it, over Caspian oil and gas reserves. Standing at the doorstep of the twenty-first century, we really need to emphasize the potential of energy resources to promote economic development, stability, and prosperity anywhere in the world, rather than just conflict.

Such diverse scenarios and personalities on the Caspian scene cannot be mastered at one glance. Just the legal basis of the Caspian Sea can be an issue for an entire conference with representatives from many countries, experts in oil extracting and fishing, political scientists, diplomats, lawyers, ecologists, etc.[7] Since it is impossible to encompass all concerns, I would like to discuss only two issues closely related to Kazakhstan's security concerns: the legal status of the Caspian Sea and the oil pipeline route. The interest of major world powers in this project, including the United States, Russia, Japan, China, the United Kingdom, and others, is well known.

Kazakhstan's position on this issue can be characterized as relatively compromising. For example, Kazakhstan advocates establishing a condominium regime with regards to navigation, fishing, and ecological cooperation. Its principled position is in delineating the seabed and its resources among all Caspian nations, which would have an exclusive right for the survey and exploitation of mineral resources, laying pipelines and cables in their respective economic zones. In this case, outer zone borders lie along the median line from the shores of coastal states, while side borders are drawn from the point of the land border crossing the shoreline perpendicular to the median line.

This position was reflected in the recently signed agreement with Russia on the delimitation of the northern part of the Caspian Sea using the median line principle. The next step is to prepare a special protocol, which would establish the coordinates of national sectors on the seabed. Concluding this agreement would indicate both countries' conviction over the urgency of the Caspian status issue.

The work on establishing the legal status of the Caspian Sea will continue both on bi- and multilateral levels, since the other three Caspian countries propose other solutions. Azerbaijan, for example, considers such a method of delineation artificial. Finding a compromise, however, is an art in itself. Objections to the Kazakhstani proposal sometimes indeed look artificial, such as a suggestion, for example, that freely navigating ships would collide with oil rigs positioned on the national seabed sectors.

Apparently, delineating the Caspian according to the "pie principle" is regarded as strengthening sovereignty and political independence. But any decision made on the basis of consensus cannot infringe on anyone's rights.

A condominium on the usage of the surface and depth of the Caspian Sea meets the desires of everyone to make the Caspian a zone of peace, good neighborly relations, and cooperation. It also corresponds with the integration approach advocated by Kazakhstan. At the same time, the extension of the condominium principle on the use of the seabed and its resources, even given its simplicity, would create complex problems related to the rights of ownership, attracting investments, governability, and sharing the profits. Theoretically, a total condominium would be possible if all Caspian nations possessed equal financial, industrial, and modern technological potential for sea oil extraction. And if such potential is roughly equal, it is because it approaches zero. It would slow the economic development of the entire Caspian region. Fortunately, a pragmatic approach dictates another scenario for the status of the Caspian, which generates some optimism. At the July 1998 meeting of the foreign ministers of Kazakhstan and Iran, the head of the Kazakh agency expressed his satisfaction with the remarkable progress achieved recently by all coastal states in merging their positions on the continuing dispute over the status of the Caspian Sea.

A decision should be found soon, especially since oil companies have been surveying and extracting oil at sea for some time. The activities of the U.S. oil companies in western Kazakhstan are also well known. Therefore, the issue of exporting oil to world markets is gaining importance. It concerns the strategic interests of many states, including the United States, which introduced the post of a special counselor to the president and the secretary of state on Caspian energy policy.

The Issue of Oil Export

The lack of oil exporting facilities is already felt in Kazakhstan. It hinders the growth of oil and gas extraction and the completion of the Tengiz-Novorossiysk pipeline belonging to the Caspian Oil Pipeline Consortium (CPC), scheduled for late 1999. It is known that the pipeline will pass through Russian territory, and the Kazakh side has frequently declared its preparedness to cooperate with its Russian partners in oil export activities. The CPC project is now undergoing an expert evaluation at the Russian Ministry of Ecology, and, when on October 1, 1999, the conclusion is issued, the work will begin.

However, the CPC should not be the sole outlet of Kazakh oil to the world market. First, its capacity (67 million tons per year) will in time become insufficient. Secondly, and most importantly, Kazakhstan is an adherent to a multioptional approach in oil transportation. It is impossible to integrate into a world economic community via one pipeline. Presently, there are no more proponents of monopolistic ownership of the oil tap. It would be unwise of anyone to insist on a monopoly of the transit. Professionals prefer to make money and participate in administration, which means possessing influence through cooperation in the joint projects. What is the preferred pipeline route for Kazakhstan? This is an important question, because discussions on such a priority take time, and the hope of obtaining revenues from oil exports becomes more distant. In addition, in five years Kazakhstan will be producing so much oil that only construction of new pipelines will resolve the issue of investment return into the Kazakh oil industry. Therefore, the pipeline project that has all problems solved, contractors found, and, most importantly, financing planned, will become a reality.

Much is said about the danger of the existing and potential pipeline routes going through regions of instability. One must admit that reasons for concern do exist. But potential instability should not determine the routes for a number of reasons. First, diversification and multiplicity of routes makes terrorist acts on the pipelines pointless. Secondly, if necessary, measures can be taken to guarantee the security of the routes. In any event, if economic feasibility and political will exist, such a project could be implemented: as one oil industrialist pointed out, "We are used to the pipelines going through unstable regions. It is our business to deal with it." Finally, a taboo laid on the completed pipeline by the attitudes of the local population, which would benefit from its presence, should provide a stabilizing factor.

On the issue of the location of a second pipeline, one may with a certain degree of certainty say that it will be neither west nor south. The western direction is linked with high costs associated with the construction of the Transcaspian pipeline, but the most important for the construction is practical work and concrete proposals for financing. The impulse for the implementation of this option could possibly be provided from the recently begun work on technical and economic assessment for the construction of the Transcaspian pipeline from Turkmenistan through Turkey, which is funded by the U.S. Agency for Trade and Development, and Anron, a U.S.-based company. The U.S. government noted that Turkmenistan acted swiftly and consistently in the decision-making process. It is also possible that there is an implicit invitation to other Caspian states to act likewise. As far as Kazakhstan is concerned, its active investment attraction policies indicate that it hardly needs such invitations. It is more likely that the Americans are still probing a possibility for a larger project for transporting oil across the Caspian seabed. Even a nonexpert would realize that transporting oil across the seabed is an easier task from the ecological standpoint alone.

It is known that the southern direction through Iran and the Persian Gulf, according to expert evaluations, is optimal with regard to cost of construction and exploitation of the pipeline. However, this cost is still rather high, and large investments are required. Iran does not have such funds, while other potential investors fear U.S. sanctions. While U.S. pressure may be lifted in the near future, the pressure of potential competitors in the Gulf project is present and real.

The second pipeline may very likely go in the eastern direction—to China and the Pacific Ocean. Presently, the technical and economic assessment is underway, and due to be completed in March 1999. It is no secret that the victory of the Chinese oil company over a tender for the Uzen oil field in western Kazakhstan was an unpleasant surprise for the American competitors, who obviously underestimated the potential of the growing oil industry in China. Despite the ambitious nature of the project to lay a pipeline across the vast territory of Kazakhstan, it is this potential that brings some measure of assurance to the feasibility of the project. The project also meets the general position of Kazakhstan on the multiple options of the pipeline route direction. Its implementation will allow oil production to increase. Finally, it is the largest joint project of the two neighboring countries, which promises to become a solid foundation for bilateral relations as a whole. Considering the geostrategic position of Kazakhstan, one may surmise that transporting oil to China will increase stability in the region.

At the same time, Kazakhstan's reaction to the growing economic cooperation with China, particularly on the joint oil project and pipeline construction, is not exactly defined. There have been fears expressed that the project would create a channel for illegal migration of Chinese workers. In Kazakhstan, the idea of creating localities for compact settlement of Chinese workers is not entirely popular, especially given the current situation of high unemployment. Kazakhstan therefore is working on developing measures to license foreign workforce employment. As far as the above-mentioned project is concerned, it provides for separate agreements on the number and duration of employment of Chinese workers and engineers for each separate contract. Thus, the grounds for mutual suspicions are eliminated, which only facilitates the maintenance of good neighborly relations with the PRC.

The proposals for the construction of the pipeline in the western and southern directions, which are reportedly being considered by the government of Kazakhstan, will be viable and practical enough to make the gap between switching on pipelines three and four minimal. Then the "Great Silk Road" will revive as the "Great Oil Road." In this case, the prospect of Kazakhstan's integration, as one of the primary exporters of energy resources in the next century, into the world economy will become feasible.[8]

Incidentally, in September 1998, Kazakhoil, the national oil company, signed a packet of agreements with the world's largest oil companies, which is an important event in itself. This is yet another "contract of the century," along with CPC and China, which is worth $2 billion. The importance of this fact is enhanced by comparing it to the current flight of investors and capital from many countries. Kazakhstan considers it not only a confirmation of its success in creating a benign investment environment, but a testament to the overall stability in the country as well. Indeed, Kazakhstan's security policies bring their benefits.

Simultaneous with the signing of the above mentioned agreement Kazakhstan also announced the sale of a one-seventh share of the state holding in the Caspian pipeline consortium for $550 million. President Nazarbayev announced that all this money will go to settle the wage and pension arrears to teachers and pensioners, and for other urgent needs. As Prime Minister N. Balgimbayev said, "People cannot wait for the promised oil revenues, money is needed now, and the government found a way to obtain it."

Security of Transportation Routes

U. Kasenov, a well-known Kazakh scholar, said in his latest work with regard to regional security[9] that the existing and emerging international security mechanisms cannot ensure safe development of the Central Asian and the Caucasus region because "new geopolitical and geo-economic realities in Eurasia and new challenges to Asian security are not reflected in the mission statements and participation pool of such organizations as NATO, OSCE, CIS, or the Economic Cooperation Organization (ECO)."[10] Indeed, are international security structures ready to meet the challenge of an international conflict involving major powers, should the scenarios of the proponents of Realpolitik come into being?

Of all the above-mentioned organizations, only NATO and OSCE are designed to prevent and address international conflicts and conduct peace-keeping operations. The adaptability of OSCE to the new conditions is well known. It has radically changed since 1990: from a Conference on Security and Cooperation it became an Organization, with the number of participants increasing from thirty-three to fifty-four. A number of important policy declarations have since been issued. OSCE emphasizes preventive diplomacy with regard to international conflicts. This partly explains OSCE's inability to cope with ongoing conflicts. The ability of the OSCE to respond to conflict is also limited by decision-making rules within the institution, namely the need for consensus.

While attempts have been made to dispose of this weakness and introduce a "consensus minus one" mechanism, the proposal is blocked by countries that fear that such a clause can be used against their interests. The issue of security is a vital one, and it is unlikely that a certain organization dealing with security issues would willingly relinquish the consensus principle. Multilateral diplomacy, therefore, is not a panacea. The strength of international organizations is in the synchronized will of states and their readiness to use agreed-upon mechanisms. Other international security structures also react to global changes, and NATO is one of them. The process of the alliance's expansion is the news of the day. NATO established a Euro-Atlantic Partnership Council and signed the Founding Agreement with Russia. The question remains as to whether these organizations adequately adapt to the changes in the international environment. NATO's capability to project force beyond the limits of its geographic responsibility is not questioned by anyone. But thoughts of the alliance's armed operations within the CIS are quite unpleasant, and may only become acceptable if and when Russia becomes a member.

It appears that the optimal solution for now is strengthening the tools of preventive diplomacy in the OSCE arsenal. The decision to open OSCE missions in all Central Asian states is a positive development.

Integration is a dominant strategy of modern times, and it requires joint efforts directed through international organizations. That is why Minister of Foreign Affairs K. Tokayev said in his address at the Conference on Disarmament in Geneva that Kazakhstan is firmly committed to strengthening international security, promoting cooperation among states, and expanding the role of international organizations in resolving global problems and conflicts.

APPENDIX[11]

Long-Term Priority 5:

Energy Resources

> "Wealth is not in the possession of wealth, but in the ability to use it expediently."
>
> —*Miguel de Servantes Saavedra*

Kazakhstan possesses immense volumes of natural, particularly energy, resources. The territory of our country is rich in oil and gas reserves, which brings us to the top-ten oil-possessing countries. Kazakhstan also has significant reserves of coal, uranium, gold, and other valuable minerals. We also have large potential for using wind and sun energy. Despite all that, we have not been able to provide for our internal needs from these resources for a number of years. This is due to the Soviet system of distribution and the absence of the required infrastructure. Similarly, the lack of communications for the export of oil and gas to international markets drastically reduces our ability to obtain funds to implement development plans. The strategy for the use of energy resources will include the following elements:

1. We shall conclude long-term cooperative agreements with main international oil companies to attract best international technologies, know-how, and large capital in order to utilize our resources quickly and

effectively. We have already signed a number of large contracts; others are in the preparatory stage. We seek long-term partners, whose goals coincide with ours. In the contracts, we will strictly and reasonably maintain the interests of Kazakhstan, protect the environment, ensure the employment and preparation of our workforce, and try to solve urgent social issues. In the use of our natural resources we will adhere to transparent agreements, which meet best international standards and the interests of Kazakhstan. Herein lies the guarantee of international support, of stability of our revenues, and fairness of contracts.

2. The second part of our strategy is in building a system of oil and gas pipelines for exporting these commodities. Only a large number of independent export routes will ensure our own independence from a single neighbor and price reliance on a single consumer.

3. Our strategy for the use of fuel resources is aimed at attracting the interests of large powers to Kazakhstan and its role as a world fuel supplier. Countries that may invest in the development of our oil and gas industry are the United States, Russia, China, Japan, and those of Western Europe. Economic interests of these powers in the export of our resources in a stable manner will facilitate the development of an independent and prosperous Kazakhstan.

4. We will finance, with the use of foreign investors, the development of the internal energy infrastructure and resolve the problems of self-sufficiency and competitiveness.

5. And finally, the strategy implies economical use of future revenues from these resources. We must have strict control over our strategic resources, be thrifty, and use our resources wisely, saving some of our wealth for future generations.

14 Security Challenges for Kyrgyzstan

Orozbek Moldaliev

Today the world is keenly interested in political and economic developments in Central Asia. Many of the world's major research centers in the West and in the East have held annual conferences and seminars on the complex security problems confronting the region. The Western scholars attending these events frequently misinterpret events in Central Asia and predict a whole range of scenarios for the future of the region. The Western misconceptions of security problems are to some extent connected with the West's limited knowledge about the region. The outside world knows the ancient history of the nomadic peoples of Central Asia well, including Genghis Khan, Tamerlane, and Bābur. Unfortunately, however, our region was lost from the middle of the last century until the beginning of the 1990s. Thanks to renewed attention by the West, Central Asia has reappeared on the international stage. Just as Central Asia was once the "axis of history" and stimulated European progress and "the revolution of the great seafarers," so once again Central Asia is drawing the attention of Western governments.

HISTORICAL OVERVIEW

The Kyrgyz people are one of the ancient nomadic peoples of Central Asia. Although the history of the relations of these people to the outside world is little known, it can be instructive. By the end of the sixth century A.D. the Kyrgyz had a state system and written language; from the ninth to tenth century they played a dominant role in Central Asia from Mongolia and the Yenisey River to Kashgar and Tien Shan. This was a feudal state, which ensured its security primarily by military means, sometimes combining its military might with diplomatic efforts. The "Kyrgyz great power" epoch ended after the Mongol invasion. The Kyrgyz lost their state system, while retaining their independence and a part of their former territories. The Kyrgyz state empire was not an economic and political whole; instead it was a union of clan and tribal entities.

From the thirteenth until the nineteenth century the Kyrgyz repeatedly suffered from the encroachments of powerful neighbors. In order to survive "in the crossroads of three adjacent powers"—Kokand, China, and Russia—they had to have wisdom, foresight, and the ability to understand geopolitical priorities and threats to national security. In the middle of the nineteenth century the Kyrgyz territory became an object of the colonial policy of Russia. The hopes on the part of the Kyrgyz clan and tribal nobility to preserve elements of the Kyrgyz state system were not realized. The territory of Kyrgyzstan was divided into several *uyezds* and *volosts*,[1] which were made a part of the Turkestan region of the Russian Empire. This encroachment caused discontent among the Kyrgyz, who aimed at having self-government and consistently opposed Russia's interventionist policy. This opposition to interference led to the Kyrgyz and Kazakh uprisings in 1916, which were supported by the other peoples of Central Asia. However, this anti-Russian uprising jeopardized the existence of the entire Kyrgyz nation, part of which attempted to flee to western China by dodging the "Cossacks" and eventually dying of cold and hunger in the mountain passes. These events are viewed as some of the most tragic pages of Kyrgyz history.

The Russian period of domination in the history of Kyrgyzstan brought new elements into the notion of security: the Kyrgyzstan-China border gained a legal status and the region obtained strategic meaning due to the rivalry among Russia, Great Britain, and China. Establishment of Soviet power in Central Asia rescued the Kyrgyz from the genocide of tzarist Russia and the tragedies stemming from refugees attempting to flee for China. Nonetheless, threats to the physical existence of the people stemming from civil war, migration, and social shocks (like forced collectivization) continued until the 1930s.

The nationalities policy of Moscow and social-economic conditions created by Soviet "socialism" spawned internal ethnic instability. The most serious security threat to the Soviet state revolved around events in Osh in June 1990, when fomenting interethnic tensions were unleashed by Gorbachev and his policies of *glasnost* and democratization, leading to a bloody clash between the Kyrgyz and Uzbeks. As a result of this clash 230 people died (according to some sources of information more than 1,000 died), 91 were reported missing, state property was destroyed, and the government suffered from serious financial losses. Other security threats to the people of Kyrgyzstan stemmed from Soviet economic experiments in Kyrgyzstan, which led to social dislocation and the participation of the Soviet Union in nuclear activity, which led to major ecological concerns in Kyrgyzstan. The importance of the Soviet period in the history of Kyrgyzstan was in the opportunity for national development. By the end of the twentieth century Kyrgyzstan gained independence. If Kyrgyzstan can respond to the challenges of newfound independence and statehood, its future will be bright. If it fails in its efforts to build a prosperous state, the country is threatened with disintegration.

In the early 1990s many analysts doubted the possibility of the Kyrgyz republic emerging as a unified state. There were good reasons for such pessimistic forecasts: the country is situated far from the sea, lacks known oil and gas reserves, and depends on Moscow both militarily and economically; its industry once depended on imported raw materials and was mostly oriented toward the Russian Federation's military-industrial complex. Moreover, the severing of economic ties threatened Kyrgyzstan, which was a major exporter of raw materials to other republics. Adding to the list of problems was the fact that the country was a multiethnic state with powerful neighbors like China and Russia. This was the complex environment in which Kyrgyzstan found itself following the disintegration of the Soviet Union. Fortunately, owing to the help of the international community—primarily democratic states—Kyrygyzstan managed to stand and pass the first stage of development, which entailed gaining a national orientation, gaining recognition in the international arena, and forming national policies and international priorities.

DANGERS AND THREATS TO THE SECURITY OF KYRGYZSTAN

New states attempting simultaneously to solidify independence and to institute radical reforms while in a deep economic crisis are bound to be sensitive to numerous risks and conscious of their vulnerability. Kyrgyzstan is no exception. In particular, it must consider economic security threats and not just military threats which seem less pressing given the social, political, and economic challenges posed by independence. The following threaten to become major security problems:

- external or internal activities aimed at undermining the sovereign and territorial integrity of the state;
- a growing gap between the state's economic and technological capabilities and those of industrialized states;
- a decline in industrial output, food shortages, and a resulting dependence on foreign sources for food and resources;
- the danger of becoming a raw material supplier unable to obtain advanced technologies;
- regionalism, the problem of relations between the center and the periphery;
- ethnic tensions and conflicts within the country and in adjacent nations;
- organized crime, corruption, terrorism, and drug trafficking;
- militarized conflicts near the borders;
- transit and proliferation of weapons of mass destruction (WMD);
- further degradation of the ecological situation; and other factors.

External Threats

It is widely understood that a state may become a victim of hostile external powers, on the one hand, and internal disorder on the other hand. External threats to Kyrgyzstan's security (for example, regional instability and high conflict potential of Central Asia and its surroundings, drug trafficking, refugees, migrants, etc.) are conditioned by the geopolitical position of the republic on the "Southern tier of instability." Prolonged war in Afghanistan has threatened the entire region with a whole range of security threats, including arms and drug smuggling and a potential spillover of the conflict into neighboring states. The situation in Afghanistan has undermined the ability of Central Asia to open its doors to the South, to the warm seas. Furthermore, Afghanistan may become a serious destabilizing factor in Central Asia as our closest neighbors—Tajikistan, Uzbekistan, Russia, Iran, and Pakistan—meddle in the country's affairs. Although the negotiation process has been under way for a year in Tajikistan, it remains a threat because the arrangements of political forces are unclear and the political equilibrium is fragile. Negotiations and attempts to quell civil discord are threatened by frequent acts of violence such as the assassination of staff from the United Nations Observer Mission. Without the United Nations or others attempting to mediate conflict in Tajikistan, the country may plunge into civil war once again.

Drug production and trafficking in Afghanistan has become a means of survival for its people and the backbone of the Afghan economy. In the provinces adjacent to the Afghan border, drug dealers store dozens of tons of opium and are now building and assembling secret laboratories for processing opium into morphine and heroin. Prior to 1997 Afghanistan harvested nearly 700 tons of raw opium annually. Now it harvests about 3,000 tons capable of yielding 300 tons of heroin, which is convenient for transportation and very expensive (in Osh the heroin sells for $4,000–$8,000 per kilo; in Moscow it goes for $170,000 a kilo). This quantity of drugs may put the whole world on its knees. The most profitable activity of organized crime syndicates is drug trafficking. If drug trafficking is not arrested, organized crime will only continue to flourish in the region.

Kyrgyzstan is becoming a transit corridor and a staging post for the transportation of drugs to other countries of Central Asia, the Commonwealth of Independent States (CIS), Europe, and the United States. Drug dealers in Asia are joining forces and arming. They are increasingly buying sophisticated weaponry and technologies, including surface-to-air missiles such as Stingers. Criminal gangs are merging with corrupt officials, who are sometimes former law enforcement officers, involved in fighting drug trafficking. Drug trafficking has resulted in a dramatic rise in criminal activity and drug abuse in the Kyrgyz Republic. National authorities alone cannot address the problem of drug trafficking in Kyrgyzstan. Until peace is achieved in Afghanistan and Tajikistan the problem will linger.

The civil unrest in Afghanistan and Tajikistan is the cause of another serious problem for the Kyrgyz Republic—the problem of migration and refugees. Beginning in 1993, Kyrgyzstan officially began accepting refugees from these territories. As of today there are sixteen thousand of them registered, mainly from Afghanistan and Tajikistan. A mass influx of refugees into densely populated regions of Kyrgyzstan aggravated the socioeconomic situation in the republic, especially in the southern part of the country (refugees refuse to settle in the sparsely populated zones because of the climatic conditions and significant distances to the capital). Lately representatives of the UN humanitarian workers arrived in Kyrgyzstan to help resolve issues of employment, medical assistance, and humanitarian aid for refugees. While official refugees arrive in Kyrgyzstan in a relatively organized way, and are monitored, the increasing influx of illegal migrants has occurred in an uncontrolled fashion. According to some experts, the number of illegal immigrants is approaching fifty thousand. Most of these immigrants are from CIS regions of conflict, such as Chechnya (50 percent), Abkhazia, and Nagorno-Karabakh. Many of these immigrants do not become productive citizens, but engage in drug trafficking and other criminal activities.

Islamic extremism is also cause for concern in Kyrgyzstan, especially in the south. Strong traditions of khanafism and shafism—branches of Sunnism—were suppressed by Soviet-established secularism. The emergence of politicized Islam warrants continued attention by Kyrgyz authorities. Reports about Islamic extremism and illegal activity by fundamentalist Wahhabis are often heard in the region. Two events demonstrate the nature of this threat. First, in 1992 during their pilgrimage to Mecca, Tajiks swore on the Koran that they would create an Islamic state after they returned home. On their way home from Saudi Arabia, Iranians allegedly gave them money (dollars and tumans) in Tehran. One of the leaders of the United Tajik Opposition (UTO), Turojohn–zadeh, is a well-known Wahhabi activist. Thus the ideological groundwork and financial support for Islamic activity were prepared in Iran and Saudi Arabia. Also, until January 1997 the Spiritual Directorate of the Muslims of Kyrgyzstan (SDMK) was headed by a well-known Sunnis: mufti Kimsanbai azhi and his deputy Habibulla azhi. These two leaders worked hard to prevent Wahhabism and Shi'ism from taking root in Kyrgyzstan. They courteously sent the muftis espousing fundamentalism out of the republic, refused questionable donations from Saudis and Iranians, tried to prevent the proliferation of Wahhabi and Shi'ia literature, and accepted the support and aid of Turkish Islamic organizations. At the end of 1996, the recreated State Commission of the Republic of Kyrgyzstan on Religion came to exert secret pressure on the leaders of the SDMK and started to support opponents of the organization headed by S. Kamalov. Later, the State Commission declared that the SDMK was created illegally and withdrew the directorate's registration in order to depose the mufti and his deputy. Only due to stiff resistance from the religious community was an effort by the State Commission to elevate S. Kamalov, a Wahhabi, blocked. Nonetheless, with the help of the State Commission, he legitimately managed to register his Islamic Center and to bolster the activity of his supporters in the southern region of Kyrgyzstan. The Wahhabis are growing in number and expanding their efforts to publish and spread their literature with Saudi financing. At the same time, the state has no money to publish textbooks for schools.

In addition to the financial advantages enjoyed by Wahhabis, they are able to attract youths by offering them the opportunity to study abroad on preferential terms, mostly in Saudi Arabia, Libya, Egypt, and other Islamic countries. Wahhabism attracts people who decide to follow the "true path" because of its simplified rites and norms. The danger of political Islam is that it is impossible to eradicate and to win by force. In 1997 more than twenty Wahhabi preachers were evicted from Kyrgyzstan, but more of them arrived than were expelled. Only peaceful, cultural Islam can defeat political Islam.

In 1998 an armed group of citizens from the People's Republic of China (PRC) was arrested in Bishkek for allegedly plotting to organize an armed struggle in an attempt to create the state of Uigurstan in Sinkiang, PRC. According to preliminary reports, their activity was financed by Wahhabi organizations outside the CIS.

In addition to the threats cited above, there are other threats lurking on the horizon:

- The problem of establishing well-defined borders with neighboring states;
- Water disputes related to Kyrgyz rivers flowing into neighboring states. This issue concerns the right of Kyrgyzstan to receive compensation from countries that use its water. In particular, Kyrgyzstan seeks compensation for the construction, repair, and use of reservoirs and other facilities that have national importance.

These issues have drawn the attention of scholars in the region who are actively seeking acceptable solutions to them.

The Issue of Borders

Kyrgyzstan borders China, Kazakhstan, Uzbekistan, and Tajikistan. The border with China was previously protected by the Federal Border Guard Service of Russia. Since January 1, 1999, state protection has been transferred to Kyrgyzstan completely, presenting the government with a major financial burden.

As part of the Soviet legacy, Kyrgyzstan inherited the problem of regulating the Chinese border, which has finally been addressed with the signing of the 1996 Kyrgyz-Chinese agreements "On the Kyrgyz-Chinese

State Border" and "On Meaures to Increase Trust around the Border." In 1997 the leaders of the PRC, Kazakhstan, Kyrgyzstan, the Russian Federation, and Tajikistan also signed the Agreement on the Reduction of Armaments around the Border. These documents legally guaranteed the territorial integrity and the current border between Kyrgyzstan and China.

The Kyrgyz government has generally transparent borders with neighboring states, with customs checkpoints at the border with former Soviet republics. The issue of borders in Central Asia was officially resolved in the 1991 Almaty Declaration, which stated that "former administrative borders within the Soviet Union are inviolable and are not subject to change." This principle was further reinforced by Kazakhstan, Kyrgyzstan, and Uzbekistan with the creation of the Central Asian Union (since July 1998, Central Asian Economic Community, which includes Tajikistan as a member). All Central Asian states are members of major international organizations, such as the United Nations, International Monetary Fund, World Bank, and OSCE; they adhere to international norms and rules, including the principle of the inviolability of borders.

Despite this agreement among Central Asian states on borders, there are problems related to the imprecise way in which the Soviet Union drew internal borders. After gaining independence, questions began to arise regarding the ownership of formerly communal pastures, which grew into mutual accusations and conflicts. Therefore, the countries of the region need to finally resolve the issue and to complete the delimitation and demarcation of the borders in order to put an end to political temptations.

This work is difficult for many reasons (e.g., some remote Kyrgyz territories are populated by ethnic Tajiks, who believe that the territory should be transferred to Tajikistan), but Kyrgyzstan consistently pursues a negotiated solution to the problem. Fortunately, efforts to resolve the border and territorial issues with Tajikistan are proceeding smoothly. After border issues are resolved with Tajikistan, the delimitation of the borders with Kazakhstan and Uzbekistan will be completed.

The issues of borders and territorial claims among some countries of the region are aggravated by the high population density in some locations (such as in Fergana Valley) that can be used by third parties to destabilize the situation. Another difficulty rests with the perception among much of the population in Uzbekistan and Tajikistan that their people lost significant territories during the Soviet era, despite the fact that before the 1917 revolution no nation-states existed within their current borders.

The issue of water use and access as a security matter also needs clarification. Kyrgyzstan possesses large freshwater reserves of the highest quality. The republic accumulates fresh water from the melting mountain ice and snow, and during the irrigation season gives about 35 billion cubic meters free of charge to its neighbors. The issue raised is not about payments for the fresh water, but about equal financial and technical participation of all users of this water in building and maintaining the necessary infrastructure. The following example will better illustrate this problem. During the fall/winter season's peak demand for energy, the Kyrgyz Toktogul hydroelectric power plant (HPP) stops producing, and serves as a dam to accumulate water in its reservoir for use by Uzbekistan and Kazakhstan. In order to offset the country's shortfall in energy production, Kyrgyzstan buys natural gas, oil, and coal from Kazakhstan and Uzbekistan to load up its other power plants. In summer, the HPP is idle again. Until 1991 the republic was compensated for the unproduced energy with a billion cubic meters of natural gas, a million tons of coal, and four hundred tons of heavy oil. Between the years 1993 and 1996 alone the direct cost of operating the coal and oil power plant reached 189 million som (Kyrgyz national currency equal to approximately U.S. $1.45 million).

According to international water law, Kyrgyzstan can demand compensation for its unilateral expenses. Kyrgyzstan is also suffering flooding and swamping of fertile land, repair costs for irrigation equipment and facilities, decreased production of electric energy, and other financial burdens. Why should Kyrgyzstan alter, at a loss to itself, the schedule of its energy-production facilities to accommodate the irrigation plans of its neighbors and fill up its reservoirs, fearing potential natural disasters? Why should it damage its environment by needlessly burning oil and coal? No country in the world can question the right of Kyrgyzstan to use its hydroelectric energy complex (the Naryn Cascade) as it sees fit with regard to its needs and requirements: to produce more energy in winter, and to accumulate water for winter energy production in summer. Experts have calculated possible ramifications of such unilateral actions for neighbors. Kyrgyzstan has been raising this issue since 1995, and now thinks it should not forgo its own national interest and suffer a loss given the present budget deficit.

In October 1997 President Askar Akayev signed a decree "On the General Principle of the Foreign Policy of Kyrgyzstan in the Use of Water Resources and Rivers, Formed on the Territory of Kyrgyzstan and Flowing into the Territories of Neighboring States." According to this decree, the interested parties will address the issues of water supply exclusively on the basis of international treaties. Tariffs have been established, and the decree provides for the right of Kyrgyzstan to receive compensation for construction, repair, and exploitation of water reservoirs and irrigation facilities from countries that use its water.

The official position of the Kyrgyz side has been made known to the leaders of Kazakhstan, China, and Uzbekistan in a letter from President Akayev, whereby he suggests moving to a qualitatively new level of cooperation on the water supply issue. Now all the basic principles of this cooperation should be coordinated and an optimal solution found.

High population growth rates, increased demand for irrigation, and shortages of fertile land may lead to increased tensions in the region. The issue of border disputes and water use requires a meticulous and weighed study and a negotiated solution that is advantageous to all parties. We should not forget that any attempt to redraw borders could lead to bloodshed.

Internal Threats

The economic crisis gripping Kyrgyzstan is perhaps the most pressing threat to national security because of the domino effect produced by economic downturn: a drop in production leads to unemployment, which leads to population migration, poverty, crime, and social destratification.

The issue of economic security today is one of the most important ones for Kyrgyzstan, because its survival as an independent nation directly depends on achieving economic stability. The causes of economic crisis in CIS countries are well known and need no repetition. Almost ten years have passed since economic reforms were introduced, yet there are few signs of successes as economic growth rates are low and insignificant. What is the problem? Economists and politicians cite a number of problems, such as the lack of a realistic model for making a transition to a post-Soviet society. I believe, however, that the real problem rests with the fact that during the Soviet period, private enterprise was virtually eliminated. By comparison, post–World War II European nations had a large stratum of private entrepreneurs who, using Marshall Plan funds, helped rebuild societies and facilitated the growth of the economies of Germany and Italy (a similiar scenario occurred in Japan). This middle-class entrepreneurial group is only now emerging in our country; however, its birth is undergoing tremendous difficulties. The ranks of private entrepreneurs are growing, although they are squeezed dry by taxation, bureaucracy, and organized crime. Potential investors, therefore, are wary. This presents a major problem because if Kyrgyzstan is unable to attract significant foreign direct investment, the country may find itself in debt and poverty and relegated to the margins of the global economy.

Another major internal security problem in Kyrgyzstan rests with increasing social stratification as a small segment of the population enjoys opulent wealth while the majority toil in squalor. According to the Social Foundation of Kyrgyzstan, 60 to 70 percent of the population is considered "low income," while 20 percent are classified as poor. The majority of the latter reside in the countryside, where the unemployment level is the highest. This problem is paramount for Kyrgyzstan, because the increasing stratification may lead to mass discontent and ultimately social upheaval. Many Communists and other presidential opponents play on the frustrations of the people in an effort to discredit efforts to democratize. In addition, Islamic groups can use the people's poverty and disenchantment for its political purposes, as they did in Egypt and Algeria.

The year 1998, declared the year of fighting poverty, was accompanied by a number of government programs designed to address the problem. After several years of economic catastrophe, Kyrgyzstan managed to slow inflation and to turn the economy around. In 1996 Kyrgyzstan recorded economic growth of 7 percent. The introduction of a national currency also aided the government's efforts to invigorate the economy. This success, however, is very fragile, and the growth that has been achieved so far does not go far enough in reversing the major economic downturn following independence.

Regionalism

The problem of regionalism, center-periphery relations, and of north-south relations within the country are often written about in the Kyrgyz and foreign media. These issues do require serious attention by policy makers. The situation in the south is shaped by the following factors:

- The southern regions of Osh and Jālālābad serve as home to 1.2 million Kyrgyz (60 percent of the population), 600,000 to 700,000 Uzbeks (26 percent), 126,000 Russians (6.3 percent), and 30,000 to 40,000 Tajiks, Uigurs, and Dungans;
- Recently, the city of Osh became a transshipment point for drug traffickers from Afghanistan and Tajikistan, and became their hub;
- According to intelligence reports, the Fergana Valley is the center of activity of a secret separatist organization, FANO, (Fergana, Andijan, Namangan, Osh), which aspires to unite these four regions in an independent state;
- The influence of Uzbekistan:
  - the major transportation and communication arteries go through its territory;
  - the people of the region receive large flows of Uzbek news and propaganda lauding Uzbekistan's achievements;
  - there is a large Uzbek population in the southern part of Kyrgyzstan;
- High population density, shortage of pastures and water;
- Growing social stratification and other reasons generally pertaining to the north as well.

Most of the independent media in Kyrgyzstan dismiss the notion that there is a serious north-south divide. Nonetheless, there are frequent reports suggesting that the north (the government in Bishkek) is ignoring problems in the south. The authors of these reports contend that the central government unjustifiably delays efforts to resolve water, land, and border problems in the southern regions of the country, and allows neighboring countries to use the natural resources of Osh and Jālālābad.

In addition to these disputes, the media often draws attention to other problems:

- inadequate governmental attention to the threat of landslides in the south and failure to relocate townships from dangerous landslide-prone areas.

- the impact of the construction and exploitation of the Kampyr-Ravat water reservoir, causing flooding of fertile land, damage to structures, and increased instances of tuberculosis;
- the emergence of the Osh-Horog highway, the main route used by drug traffickers;
- the government's failure to conduct a thorough investigation into the ethnic cleansing events in the Osh region;
- the government's failure to address simmering ethnic issues;
- the issue of the hydroelectric power plant, natural gas reserves, and the use of pastures;
- the influx of various religious movements into the south, especially fundamentalist Islamic groups involved in building new mosques;
- the possibility of covert persecution of southerners among government personnel.

Aggravating the problem are also accusations that Kyrgyz living in the south are underrepresented in government. If previously the objections centered on the lack of southerners among the elite (although the prime minister is from the south), now the focus is on the fact that the recruited southerners are the wrong (i.e., not qualified) ones.

Nevertheless, the dispute over the lack of government personnel from the south exists. The conflict came about for various historical and geographical reasons. First, living far from the capital, many southerners were limited in obtaining college and professional education. Second, the south is a cotton- and tobacco-growing region, and every hand is valuable there. Despite the "humane" Soviet laws and the "reliable" protection of human rights, as the Communists declare today, child labor has often been used in agriculture in such difficult and hazardous jobs as cotton and tobacco harvesting. It was only in late winter that children were able to attend school. Poor families with many children could not afford to send them to a college or university in the north. Third, graduates of schools and colleges in the north, which have been traditionally more Russified, had a better command of the Russian language, giving them an edge over their southern peers in obtaining work. This fact generated a natural psychological protest among the southerners toward the northerners, who they believed were blocking their access to positions of power.

While tensions between the government in Bishkek and the south were largely suppressed in the Soviet era, democracy allows these tensions to surface. The southern electorate is now able to voice their discontent at the ballot box. The danger is that political groups in the south will play the regionalization card and spawn divisions and greater rivalry.

Ethnic Tensions
The maintenance of ethnic peace and social stability were important issues for Kyrgyzstan even before gaining independence. Interethnic conflicts

brought about by the process of Glasnost and democratization in the Soviet Union in the late 1980s/early 1990s did not bypass Kyrgyzstan. We experienced bloody clashes in the south between Uzbeks and Kyrgyzs, and a conflict between Kyrgyzs and Tajiks over the use of water resources was barely averted.

The first seven years of independence in Kyrgyzstan were marked by relative stability. However, the dire economic situation could eventually generate mass discontent and social tension. Certain political groups and Islamic extremists within and outside of Kyrgyzstan may in turn draw strength from these sentiments, thereby further destabilizing the social situation and sparking ethnic conflict.

One of the most frequently discussed issues in the local media is the emigration of the Russian-speaking population from the country, raising concern among elites in the government. There are frequent accusations that the Kyrgyz government's personnel policies discriminate against Russians. At the same time, sociological studies conducted by the Russian Academy of Sciences and statements of Russian officials and leaders of the Russian diaspora all attest to the fairness of the ethnic policy pursued in the country.

During the Soviet era, Russians were a privileged group. They moved across the entire Soviet Union, sought better living conditions, and used their "Big Brother" status for their own gain. Now they have become an ethnic minority in many CIS countries and often charge that their rights are being infringed upon. The Russian media helps to evoke such views. Their frequently biased publications, which lay out a variety of "conceptions" on ethnic policy, have their readers and fans in the new independent states. But these publications are read not by Russians alone, and declarations of the Russian elite on their privileged geopolitical status and special, "messianic role" in the new world only provoke the Russian-speaking population in the CIS, bring about suspicions in the CIS regarding Moscow's integration policies, and create ethnic tensions.

Of course, it is hard for Russia to accept the loss of the territorial possessions gained throughout the centuries. It is unwilling to accept that its "younger brothers" have grown up, started their own families, and, thanks to Russia itself, managed to start their own life. This is a natural process, and Russians need to make peace with it.

Corruption

Corruption is a dangerous social phenomenon and a serious destabilizing factor for the democratic reform efforts underway in Kyrgyzstan. Corruption breeds a sense of distrust among the population toward the authorities, lowers political activity, and creates mass pessimism and low morale. Last year, for example, voters in one of the districts of Bishkek boycotted the elections of the local deputies.

In 1995 President Akayev said that corruption reached the seventh floor of the Government Building (that is where the administration and the apparatus of the prime minister are located). The IMF managing director Michel Camdessus drew parallels between corruption in East Asia and Central Asia, stating "one cannot help but observe the similarities between the relationships that existed among enterprises, banks, and government in some East Asian countries under the system of "crony capitalism" and the tendencies one can observe—which still survive or start developing again—in a number of transition economies."[2] The validity of this observation is reinforced by Minister of Finance T. Koychumanov, who stated, "Credits, large credits at that, were given not to people on the street, but to those possessing great power. That is why, perhaps, it is so hard to get our money back now."

The General Prosecutor's Office of Kyrgyzstan initiated 145 criminal proceedings in recent years involving 150 elected deputies, at all levels, charged with various economic crimes. Many of them, using their legislative immunity, try to evade responsibility. The Kyrgyz population wholeheartedly approved the proposal of President Akayev to change the immunity principle provided to parliamentary deputies.

Environment

Kyrgyzstan still possesses areas untouched by human activity, including beautiful landscapes, pure water, and air. However, the economic crisis threatens Kyrgyzstan's pristine environment as the population is pushed into irrational use of natural resources—clearing of forests, overcultivation of fertile land, violation of irrigation standards, etc. There are over 130 mining waste sites covering 1,950 hectares of land. Radioactive and non-ferrous metal waste sites are of the greatest concern. Most of them are located in zones known for mud- and landslides, and along mountain rivers, thereby creating an ecological hazard involving territories of adjacent states and the entire Aral Sea basin. The need to strengthen control over the activities of industrial enterprises producing poisonous substances was proven again last year, when cyanides were dumped into Lake Issyk-Kul, causing mass poisoning of the population.

The degradation of fertile land is also a cause of great concern and may result in the country becoming dependent on other countries for food. Due to cutbacks in spending on irrigation systems, the amount of dry land is increasing. Fifty-one percent of fertile land is currently eroding, resulting in significantly smaller harvests.

Weapons Proliferation

The threat of weapons of mass destruction has garnered the attention of policy makers in Kyrgyzstan for several reasons. The economic crisis in the former Soviet Union means that individuals are frequently willing to sell anything that is marketable. Furthermore, law enforcement agencies in the former Soviet Union are ill equipped to deal with the problem of illegal export of items used for making weapons of mass destruction. For example, the border and customs checkpoints in Kazakhstan have no special detection equipment for intercepting nuclear materials. In fact there are few tools in place currently to prevent the transfer of sensitive nuclear technology through the region.

CONCLUSION

The new post–Cold War era has altered the meaning of the term "security" from a purely military concept to one embracing economics, the environment, and more. I have demonstrated that for Kyrgyzstan national security threats stem not only from the fact that the country is surrounded by major powers with questionable intentions, but also from a number of domestic problems. For a new state like Kyrgyzstan, managing both these internal and external threats represents a major task.

Kyrgyzstan is addressing the problem of defending its national security and independence at both the domestic and international levels. It participates in international and regional organizations and institutions such as the UN, OSCE, World Trade Organization, CIS collective security arrangement, NATO's Partnership for Peace , the Central Asian Customs Union, and the Central Asian Economic Community.

The United States is playing an important role in the reform effort under way in Kyrgyzstan. After the collapse of the Soviet Union, Washington initially focused on Moscow, but later switched its priorities with regard to Central Asia and began developing relationships directly with regional states. The United States eventually opened an embassy in Bishkek, and since then Kyrgyzstan has enjoyed warm relations with Washington. Presently, U.S. interests in Central Asia run along two fronts: economic and geopolitical. These interests entail preventing Russia and China from controlling oil reserves in Central Asia, preventing militarized conflicts in the region, maintaining the present balance of power among the United States, Russia, and China, and ensuring that conflicts in neighboring Afghanistan do not spill over into Central Asia.

The United States renders significant assistance to the process of reforms in Kyrgyzstan and promotes Kyrgyzstan's integration into the world community through the work of various foundations, NGOs, and the American International Development Agency. However, in order for effective assistance to be rendered, the West must develop a better understanding of the region and its traditions. This knowledge will enable the United States and other states to provide the assistance necessary for ensuring that democracy and economic reforms prove successful.

NOTES

INTRODUCTION

1. U.S. Department of State, *Turkmenistan Country Report on Human Rights Practices for 1997*, released by the Bureau of Democracy, Human Rights, and Labor, January 30, 1998.
2. Svante Cornell, "Iran and the Caucasus," *Middle East Policy* 5: 4 (January 1998): 51–67. The Azerbaijan Popular Front (APF) and the South Azerbaijan National Liberation Committee (SANLC), operating from the Azerbaijani republic, have at times pressed for reunification of Southern Azerbaijan (northern Iran) and Northern Azerbaijan (Azerbaijan proper).
3. Ronald G. Suny, *The Soviet Experiment: Russia, the USSR, and the Successor States* (Oxford: Oxford University Press, 1997): 79–122.
4. See Ted Gurr and Barbara Harff, "A Framework for Analysis of Ethnopolitical Mobilization and Conflict," in *Ethnic Conflict in World Politics* (Boulder, Colo.: Westview Press, 1994): 77–97.
5. For example, in 1989 clashes in the Uzbekistan part of the Fergana Valley (a swathe of common territory arcing through Uzbekistan, Tajikistan, and Kyrgyzstan) between Uzbeks and Meskhetian Turks (originally from the Djavakheti region of southern Georgia, they were deported by Stalin in 1944 and resettled in Uzbekistan) left scores dead and hundreds wounded. In 1990, Kyrgyz and Uzbeks in the Osh region of Kyrgyzstan clashed in brutal fighting, which left almost two hundred dead and over one thousand wounded.
6. See Roman Frydman, Kenneth Murphy, and Andrzej Rapaczynski, "Capitalism with a Comrade's Face," *Transition* 2: 2 (January 26, 1996).
7. Regional nonproliferation efforts are currently underway in both the Caucasus and Central Asia. For example, representatives of the Central Asian states and the five nuclear countries—the U.S., China, Russia, Britain, and France—as well as those of the United Nations met in Bishkek, the Kyrgyzstan capital, for a two-day conference on ways to create a nuclear-free zone in Central Asia. See Breffni O'Rourke, "Central Asia: Dangerous Encirclement Prompts Call for Nuclear Free Zone," Radio Free Europe/Radio Liberty Report (hereafter *RFE/RL*), *Newsline* (July 10, 1998).
8. See the statement of Glenn E. Schweitzer before the Permanent Subcommittee on Investigations, Committee on Government Affairs, United States Senate, March 13, 1996.
9. "Narcotics in Central Asia," International Narcotics Control Strategy Report, 1997, released by the Bureau for International Narcotics and Law

Enforcement Affairs, U.S. Department of State (Washington, D.C., March 1998): 24–27.

10. Jolyon Naegele, "Azerbaijan: The Refugee Burden Looms Large," *RFE/RL, Newsline*, Prague, May 15, 1998. The refugee problem also plagues war-torn Tajikistan and Georgia, with over 12,000 and 36,000 displaced persons respectively.

11. In Tajikistan, the head of the OSCE mission and one mission member started work in Dushanbe on February 19, 1994. The Permanent Council decision of July 6, 1995, provided for the opening of three branch offices, initially for a six-month period, in Kurgan-Tyube, Shartuz, and Dusti. These branches opened officially on October 1, 1995. The OSCE mission in Georgia—to address the conflicts in South Ossetia and Abkhazia—opened in December 1992.

12. The CAU evolved from a January 1994 agreement between Kazakhstan and Uzbekistan providing for the abolition of customs barriers to create a common economic space. Kyrgyzstan acceded to that agreement almost immediately. From its inception, the union was intended as a model for closer economic integration within the CIS. Over the past three years, it has developed supranational coordinating structures—including an executive committee of heads of state and government, and a council of foreign ministers—that are far more effective than its CIS equivalents. The leaderships of the three member states reportedly coordinate their positions on all regional issues. Moreover, the union has created a Central Asian peacekeeping battalion, which has the official recognition of the UN, and the Central Asian Bank for Cooperation and Development.

CHAPTER 1

1. Even before the collapse of the Soviet Union, during the period of reform that led to serious infighting among the central authorities in Moscow, different factions manipulated interethnic tensions to advance their goals. See Shireen T. Hunter, *The Trans-Caucasus in Transition: Nation-Building and Conflict* (Washington, D.C.: Center for Strategic and International Studies, 1994). Also see Thomas Goltz, "The Hidden Russian Hand," *Foreign Policy* 92 (Fall 1993).

2. U.S. policy toward the Transcaucasus and Central Asia was expressed as early as January 1992 by the then U.S. Secretary of State James Baker, during a trip to the region. On this trip, he made it clear that containing Iranian influence was one of the main components of U.S. strategy toward the region. See Thomas L. Friedman, "U.S. to Counter Iran in Central Asia," *New York Times* (February 6, 1992).

3. Paul Goble, for instance, characterized U.S. policy toward the post-Soviet states as "Russia plus branch offices." See Paul Goble, "Ten Issues in Search of a Policy: America's Failed Approach to the Post-Soviet States," *Current History*, 92: 576 (October 1993).

4. Indeed, Nursultan Nazarbaev, president of Kazakhstan, wondered, since Russia dominated the Soviet Union, from whom Russia wanted to become independent.

5. See Richard C. Hovannissian, "Historical Memory and Foreign Relations: The Armenian Perspective," in S. Frederick Starr (ed.), *The Legacy of History in Russia and the New States of Eurasia* (Oxford: Oxford University Press, 1994).

6. Ibid.
7. Ibid.
8. Edward Mortimer, "Azerbaijan: Turbulent Region With a History of Foreign Interventions," *Financial Times* (January 24, 1990).
9. On this revisionist thinking, see Rafael Ishkanian, "The Law of Excluding the Third Force," in Gerard J. Libaridian (ed.), *Armenia at the Crossroads: Democracy and Nationhood in the Post-Soviet Era* (Watertown, Mass: Blue Crane Books, 1991).
10. Nevertheless, some Armenian commentators have noted that the question of the Armenian Genocide has not been given much priority. See Salpi Hartounian Ghazarian, "Selective Remembrance: The Changing Politics of Genocide Recognition," *Armenian International Magazine (AIM)*, 4: 4 (April 1994): 14–16.
11. On the Turkish-Israeli alliance, see Daniel Pipes, "A New Axis: The Emerging Turkish-Israeli Entente," *National Interest* 50 (Winter 1997–98): 31–36. And on Azerbaijani-Israeli relations, see Bulent Aras, "Israel's Strategy in Azerbaijan and Central Asia," *Middle East Policy* 4: 4 (January 1998): 68–79.
12. On the tripartite agreement among Iran, Armenia, and Greece, see "Armenia, Greece, Iran to Expand Regional Cooperation," *Foreign Broadcasting Information Service (FBIS)* NES-97-356 22 (December 1997).
13. Hovamissian, op. cit.: "The underlying Armenian-Iranian bond has been demonstrated by the tolerance and even benevolence with which Iranian rulers have treated their Armenian minority for nearly four hundred years."
14. According to this plan, in exchange for Karabakh, Armenia would give Azerbaijan the Zangezur region, which would then link Nakhichevan to western Azerbaijan.
15. The details of the Minsk Group proposal were not made public, but what was leaked indicated that it was based on a step-by-step approach. See Edward W. Walker's chapter in this volume (p. 176).
16. See Ronald G. Suny, *Looking Toward Ararat: Armenia in Modern History* (Bloomington: Indiana University Press, 1993): 34–43.
17. Aliev was not Moscow's ideal choice, but rather the best that Moscow could get. See Shireen T. Hunter, "Unwilling Partners: Gaidar, Aliev, and 'the Moscow Connection,'" *AIM* 5: 7 (September 1994): 30–31.
18. This point was made to the author by a high Armenian official.
19. On the Russo-Armenian Treaty and its benefits and disadvantages for Armenia, see Hakob Chakryan, "The Armenian-Russian Treaty Creates Essential Conditions for Russian Influence in the Balkans and the Middle East," *Yerevan Azg*, reproduced in *FBIS/SOV* 97: 300 (October 27, 1997). Also see Saak Sarkisyan, "Russian Military Presence: Pros and Cons," *New York Times* (August 23, 1997): 36–37.
20. See Richard C. Hovannissian, *The Republic of Armenia: From Versailles to London 1919–1920* (Berkeley: University of California Press, 1982): 140–67.
21. Ibid.
22. See Hakop Astrian, "Bad Oil, Bad Blood," *AIM* 5: 4 (April 1994): 12–13.
23. For a more detailed analysis of these issues and historical sources, see Shireen T. Hunter, "Greater Azerbaijan: Myth or Reality," in M.R. Djalili (ed.), *Le Caucase Post Sovietique: La Transition Dons le Conflict* (Brussels: Bruylant and Paris, 1995): 115–142.

24. Some of these ultra-Turkists claim that even Sumerians were Turkic. On these and similar views, see, among others, Zia Gokalp's works, such as *The Principles of Turkism* (Leiden: R.J. Brill, 1968).

25. This theory, too, is not based on historic evidence. To begin with, the Indo-Europeans, notably the Medes and the Persians, entered the area long before the Turkic elements, which did not begin to enter the region until the ninth and tenth centuries A.D. These Turkic invasions, however, did not completely eliminate the Iranian people of the region, although large numbers of them were killed. The languages spoken in what is now Iranian Azerbaijan and the republic of Azerbaijan were dialects of Persian, known as Azeri and Arram. Thus if there were any colonization, it was done by Turks and not by the Russians. For more information, see *Ahmad Kasravi Azeri Ya Zaban-e-Bostan-e-Azerbaijan (Azeri or the Ancient Language of Azerbaijan)* (Tehran: Sharq publishing, 1956).

26. Ibid.

27. These notions form the basis of Azerbaijan's irredentist claims toward the Iranian province of Azerbaijan. The notion of a Russo-Iranian conspiracy is even more outlandish than those about the ethnic and cultural history of the region. Iran fought two long wars with Russia—1804–1813 and 1824–1828—in order to protect its Transcaucasian possessions. The Treaty of Turkmenchai in Iran is known as the "shameful" treaty. In fact, it is very difficult to imagine how a country could conspire to lose a part of its territory.

    The Communist Party of Azerbaijan SSR, in a congratulatory telegram sent to the Democratic Party of Azerbaijan in Iran, praised it for struggling to free "The Southern part of our homeland that for years has been suffering under the cursed hands of Persian chauvinists." From *Azerbaijan* 18 (September 1948).

28. Aliev argued that he was not pressured into joining the CIS. See "National Assembly Meets to Discuss Joining of CIS," *FBIS/SOV*-93-181 (September 21, 1993).

29. Despite sending a special mediator (Vladimir Kazimirov) to resolve the Karabakh problem in 1993 and proposing several peace plans, Russia was unable to settle the dispute.

30. For example, Elçibey has created the "Movement for Unification of the two Azerbaijans."

31. In particular, the West was jolted by the victory of Vladimir Zhirinovski's ultranationalist party, which captured 21 percent of the votes in the parliamentary elections.

32. For a view that indicates this emerging fear, see William E. Odom, "A New Russian Empire May Be Coming," *International Herald Tribune* (October 26, 1996).

33. See Daniel Sneider, "Turkey and Russia Back Rivals in Azerbaijan Power Struggle," *Christian Science Monitor* (June 30, 1993).

34. Ibid.

35. On Hikmat Cetin statement, see "Cetin on Azerbaijan Policy," *Turkish Times* (June 15, 1993).

36. "Azerbaijan Asks Turkey to Train More Officers," *RFE/RL Daily Report* 2 (January 1994).

37. See "Aliev, Turkey's Demirel Sign Friendship Accord," *FBIS/SOV*-94-028 (February 10, 1994).

38. See Daniel Pipes, op. cit.
39. Divisions among the Georgians are both regional, such as between the Mingrelians and the rest, and religious, such as between the Azhard, who are Muslims, and other Georgians, who are Christians.
40. See Shireen T. Hunter, op. cit., p. 120.
41. Ibid., p. 132.
42. Ibid., p. 133.
43. On the differences of opinion between Russia and Georgia on the question of Russian bases, see "Georgian Foreign Minister on Unresolved Issues With Russia," *FBIS/SOV*-98-300 (October 27, 1998). On Georgia's efforts to use Ukraine to dilute Russian presence, see "Ukraine: Ukrainian Peacekeepers Needed in Caucasus," *FBIS/SOV*-98-278 (October 5, 1998). According to this report, the Ukrainian foreign minister has expressed his country's readiness to provide peacekeeping forces in Georgia and Abkhazia.
44. The Georgian defense minister visited Turkey in October 1998. See "Turkey: Georgian Defense Minister Arrives on Official Visit," *FBIS/SOV*-98-286, October 13, 1993).
45. It seems that Shevardnadze initially was not fully aware that U.S.-Iran hostility was related to Middle East problems and thus not amenable to his mediation.
46. See "Israeli Premier Cancels Georgia Visit Over Health Problems," *FBIS/SOV*-98-252 (September 9, 1998). Several bilateral agreements were to be signed during this trip.

CHAPTER 2

1. R. G. Suny argues that regional security in the Caucasus requires strong, authoritative states. See Ronald Grigor Suny, "Living With the Other: Conflict and Cooperation Among the Transcaucasian Peoples," in *The Transcaucasus Today: Prospects for Regional Integration, June 23–25, 1997, Edited Conference Report, American University of Armenia*: 51.
2. On the Caucasian states' foreign policy see Archil M. Gegeshidze, "Georgia's Foreign Policy: Objectives, Results, and Prospects": 22–28; Edmund M. Herzig, "Azerbaijan's Foreign Policy: Implications for Regional Cooperation": 29–33. Both articles are in *The Transcaucasus Today: Prospects for Regional Integration, June 23–25, 1997, Edited Conference Report, American University of Armenia*.
3. On this point see Roy Allison, "The Network of New Security Policy Relations in Eurasia," in *Security Dilemmas in Russia and Eurasia* (London: The Royal Institute of International Affairs, 1998): 12–29.
4. On this point see Alexander Rondeli, "Security Threats in the Caucasus: Georgia's View," *Perceptions* 3: 2 (June–August 1998): 43–52.
5. Coit Blacker calls such powers "interested outsiders," willing to play a consistently constructive role in the search for a comprehensive peace in the region. See "The Challenge of Statehood: Independence and Cooperation in the Caucasus," in *The Caucasus Today: Prospects for Regional Integration, June 23–25, 1997, Edited Conference Report, American University of Armenia*: 13.
6. Bahram Amir Ahmadi calls the Caucasus a "geopolitical buffer region," See Bahram Amir Ahmadi, "Caucasus: Geopolitical Buffer Region," *Caucasica* 2: 24–35.

7. Martin Wight. *Power Politics*. Edited by Hedley Bull and Carsten Holbraad. (London: Leicester University Press, Royal Institute of International Affairs, 1995), p.160.

CHAPTER 3

1. *Turkey and the World: 2010–2020*, press release, Ministry of Foreign Affairs, Republic of Turkey, foreword.
2. See Graham E. Fuller, Ian O. Lesser, and Paul B. Henze, *Turkey's New Geopolitics* (Boulder, Colo.: Westview Press, 1993); Andrew Mango, *Turkey: The Challenge of a New Role* (London: Praeger, 1994); Graham E. Fuller, *Turkey Faces East: New Orientations Toward the Middle East and the Old Soviet Union* (Santa Monica, Calif.: RAND, 1992).
3. *Turkey and the World: 2010–2020*, press release, Ministry of Foreign Affairs, Republic of Turkey, foreword, by Ismail Cem, Foreign Minister (1998). Hugh Pope, *Independent*, June 1, 1992, cited in Philip Robins, "Between Sentiment and Self-Interest: Turkey's Policy Toward Azerbaijan and the Central Asian States," in *The Middle East Journal* 47: 4 (Autumn 1993): 595.
4. This does not mean that there are no significant difficulties standing in the way of these modest goals. Armenia, and more importantly, Russia consider the new Turkish factor in the Transcaucasus a security problem. Hence the Turks have to take into consideration the Russian and the Armenian fears and suspicions, while coping with Iran's rivalry for influence within the same region. Nevertheless, it is my contention that earlier predictions of rampant Ankara-sponsored "Pan-Turkism" failed to materialize. See Bruce Pannier, "Turkey and Iran in Former Soviet Central Asia and Azerbaijan: The Battle for Influence that Never Happened," (Parts 1 & 2) in *Perspectives on Central Asia*, 2: 14 (May 1998); published by the Center for Political and Strategic Studies.
5. See R. Nation, "The Turkic and Other Muslim Peoples of Central Asia, the Caucasus, and the Balkans," in V. Mastny and R. Nation, eds., *Turkey between East and West: New Challenges for a Rising Regional Power* (Boulder, Colo.: Westview Press, 1998), pp. 97–112, and Elmira Akhmedly, "Istanbul Has Special Relations with Baku," *Current Digest of the Post-Soviet Press* (January 1996): 22–23.
6. For a comprehensive view of Turkish objectives in the Transcaucasus, see Shireen T. Hunter, *The Transcaucasus in Transition: Nation-Building and Conflict* (Washington, D.C.: Center for Strategic and International Studies, 1994), pp. 161–70; and Suha Bolukbasi, "Ankara's Baku-Centered Transcaucasia Policy: Has It Failed?" *The Middle East Journal* 51: 1, (Winter 1997).
7. See D. Sezer, "Turkey in the New Security Environment in the Balkan and Black Sea Region," in V. Mastny and R. Nation, eds., *Turkey Between East and West: New Challenges for a Rising Regional Power* (Boulder, Colo.: Westview Press, 1996), pp. 72–73.
8. See Bolukbasi (1997).
9. See Stephen Kinzer, "A Perilous New Contest for the Next Oil Prize," *New York Times*, September 21, 1997, and Rosemarie Forsythe, *The Politics of Oil in the Caucasus and Central Asia: Prospects for Oil Exploitation and Export in the Caspian Basin* (Oxford: Oxford University Press, 1996).

10. Since mid-1993, Moscow has been expressing concern over what it describes as efforts to create a pan-Turkist alliance. A pan-Turkist movement, moreover, could materialize in Russia, whose Turkic-speaking population is 47 million. Iran (12 million) and China (9 million) have voiced similar internal security concerns. See Shireen T. Hunter, *Central Asia Since Independence* (Westport: Præger Press, 1996), p. 138, and I. Tiouline, "Russian Diplomacy: The Problem of Transition," in Medhi Mozaffari, ed., *Security Politics in the Commonwealth of Independent States: The Southern Belt* (New York: St. Martin's Press, 1997), pp. 35–53.

11. See Levon Chorbajian, *The Caucasian Knot: The History and Geopolitics of Nagorno-Karabakh* (New York: Zed Books, 1996).

12. See Emil Danielyan, "Armenia: Government to Raise Genocide Issue with Turkey," *RFE/RL*, June 4, 1998, and Richard Hovanissian, *The Republic of Armenia: Between Crescent and Sickle: Partition and Sovietization* (Berkeley: University of California Press, 1996). See also Liz Fuller, "Armenia Warns Against Turkish Base in Azerbaijan," *RFE/RL*, March 23, 1999.

13. Floriana Fossato, "Moscow Starts Delivery of S-300 Missiles to Armenia," *RFE/RL*, February 18, 1999. The S-300 is the same missile system that was to be deployed by Greeks Cypriots, and over which Turkey threatened preemptive measures until the system was transferred to Crete.

14. The relationship between Tbilisi and Ankara has been one of relative stability and little acrimony. See Jolyon Naegele "Turkey: Foreign Relations Good With Two of Eight Neighbors," *RFE/RL*, August 13, 1998. In particular, Western diplomats in Ankara say Turkey's friendship with Georgia, largely reflecting Ankara's support for Georgian leader Eduard Shevardnadze, is mutually beneficial. Trade is booming, with Turkish consumer goods heading to Georgia and tank-full loads of cheap oil and gasoline clogging roads at the Georgian-Turkish frontier. The two countries are also involved in joint civil engineering projects such as the Kars-to-Tbilisi railroad, a hydropower project on the Coruh River, the modernization of Batumi's airport, and the planned Baku-Ceyhan pipeline, which would transit Georgia.

15. See John F. Wright, "The Geopolitics of Georgia," in J. Wright, S. Goldenberg, R. Schofield, eds., *Transcaucasian Boundaries* (London: University College of London Press, 1996), pp. 138–140.

16. Ibid.

17. See Ghia Nodia, "A New Cycle of Insecurity in Georgia: New Troubles and Old Problems," Chapter 10 of this volume, p. 188.

18. See Liz Fuller, "Georgia/Turkey: Agreements Secure Bilateral Trade and Defense," *RFE/RL*, March 10, 1999. Shevardnadze has ruled out the possibility that Georgia might host Turkish military bases on its territory.

19. Author's interviews, Georgian Ministry of Foreign Affairs, Tbilisi, August 1998.

20. See Jacob M. Landau, *Pan-Turkism: From Irredentism to Cooperation* (London: Hurst, 1995).

21. See Yuri Fyodorov, *Russia, the Caucasus, and Central Asia; The 21st Century Security Environment* (New York: M.E. Sharpe, 1999), and Paul Goble, "Turkey: Analysis From Washington: Ankara Resists Russian Pressure," *RFE/RL*, May 15, 1998.

22. See R. Nation, "The Turkic and Other Muslim Peoples of Central Asia, the Caucasus, and the Balkans," in V. Mastny and R. Nation, eds., *Turkey*

between East and West: New Challenges for a Rising Regional Power (Boulder, Colo.: Westview Press, 1998), pp. 97–112; and, Thomas L. Friedman, "U.S. to Counter Iran in Central Asia," *New York Times*, February 6, 1992; John E. Yang, "U.S., Turkey Pledge Aid to New States," *Washington Post*, February 12, 1993; "U.S. Struggle Against Radical Islamic Movements Viewed," *Foreign Broadcast Information Service*, Western Europe (henceforth *FBIS-WEU*)-93-158, August 18, 1993.

23. The *1998 Turkish Ministry of Defense White Paper* notes: "Turkey is a stabilizing and balancing element in the Balkans, Caucasus, and the Middle East where risks and threats such as extreme nationalism, fundamentalism, proliferation of weapons of mass destruction, terrorism, and ethnic conflicts have emerged."

24. Late President Özal noted: "Whatever the shape of things to come, we will be the real elements and most important pieces of the status quo and new order to be established in the region from the Balkans to Central Asia. In this region, there cannot be a status quo or political order that will exclude us. "Özal Gives Opening Speech," *FBIS-WEU* 93-057, March 26, 1993, and Jolyon Naegele, "Turkey: Foreign Policy Plan Aims for Pivotal Role in Eurasia," *RFE/RL*, August 13, 1998. See also President Demirel's observation that "Because of our central geographic position, we have to be active in many regions." "Demirel on Kurds, Ties to EC," *FBIS-WEU*-93-134, July 15, 1993.

25. See quoted in Dugyu Sezer, "Turkey's Political and Security Interests in the New Geostrategic Environment of the Expanded Middle East," Henry L. Stimson Center, Occasional Paper no. 19 (July 1994), p. 25.

26. "Paper Reports Inflation, Price Hikes," *FBIS-WEU-93-092*, May 14, 1993; "Treasury Said Facing 'Very Difficult Situation,'" *FBIS-WEU-92-094*, 1992; Chris Hedges, "Turkey Off Balance as Death Ends a Long Rivalry," *New York Times*, May 20, 1993; John Murray Brown, "Economic Woes Mount for Çiller," *Financial Times*, August 6, 1993; Jonathan C. Randal, "Turks Rethinking Regional Roles," *Washington Post*, February 24, 1993.

27. Source: *Economist Intelligence Unit Report*, Turkey, 1st Quarter 1999.

28. "Turkey Pushes for Lifting of Iraqi Oil Embargo," *The Economist*, January 16, 1999.

29. Ian O. Lesser, "Bridge or Barrier? Turkey and the West After the Cold War," Graham E. Fuller and Ian O. Lesser, eds., *Turkey's New Geopolitics: From the Balkans to Western China* (Boulder, Colo.: Westview Press, 1993), pp. 119–20; Robert Block, "NATO Adds Fuel to Balkan Arms Race," *The Independent*, London, July 21, 1993, p. 10; "Defense Industry Expands to Meet Risk of Threats," *FBIS-WEU-93-055*, March 24, 1993; and Mohammed Ziarati, "Turkish Security Policy After the Cold War," *Middle East International*, February 5, 1993, p. 19.

30. See Lale Sariibrahimoglu, "Turkey: Arming for Peace," *Jane's Defence Weekly*, August 19, 1998; Sitki Egeli, "Turks Fear Ballistic Menace," *Defense News*, May 31, 1993, p. 19; and "Missile Defense System Sought: Patriot System Faulted," *Defense News*, May 21, 1993, p. 71.

31. Unlike many other members of the anti-Soviet alliance, Turkey has not emerged from the Cold War with a sense of enhanced security. Foreign Minister Hikmet Çetin, for example, stated in 1993 that "because its geopolitical and geostrategic location places Turkey in the neighborhood

of the most unstable, uncertain and unpredictable region of the world, it has turned into a frontline state faced with multiple fronts. It is at all times possible for the crises and conflicts in these regions to spread and engulf Turkey." See Malik Mufti, "Daring and Caution in Turkish Foreign Policy," *Middle East Journal* (Winter 1998): pp. 32–50.

32. See William Hale, *Turkish Politics and the Military* (New York: Routledge, 1994).

33. Yury Chubchenko, "Caspian Oil Is Divided in Istanbul," *Current Digest of the Post-Soviet Press*, April 1998, pp. 23–24; and Patrick Crow, "Caspian Realities," *The Oil and Gas Journal*, November 2, 1998, pp. 43–49.

34. For extensive coverage and analysis of the early years of the Nagorno-Karabakh issue, see *Nagorno-Karabakh: White Paper* (Yerevan: Armenian Center for International and National Studies, 1997). The author would also like to acknowledge Mkrtich Zardarian and Alexander Grigorian for their ideas on this issue (Yerevan, 1998). See also, Susan Ellingwood, "At the Crossroads: Nagorno-Karabakh," in *Breaking the Cycle: A Framework for Intervention*, Roderick Von Lipsey, ed. (New York: St. Martin's Press, 1997).

35. See Svante Cornell, "Turkey and the Conflict in Nagorno-Karabakh: A Delicate Balance," *Middle Eastern Studies* (January 1998): 51–72.

36. Ibid.

37. On October 25, 1996, Armenian deputy foreign minister Vardan Oskanyan observed that Turkish public opinion—which perceives Armenia as the "aggressor" in the Karabakh conflict—constitutes a serious obstacle to improved bilateral relations. See Jolyon Naegele, "Caucasus: Burden of History Blocks Turkish-Armenian Border," *RFE/RL*, July 28, 1998.

38. See Elizabeth Fuller, "Nagorno-Karabakh: Can Turkey Remain Neutral?" *RFE/RL Research Report*, April 3, 1992, pp. 36–38; and Dmitriy Kulik, "Türkes' Expansionist Pan-Turkic Aspirations Scored—Look Who's Come to Us: 'Grey Wolves' Dream of Expanding Turkey From China to the Balkans," *FBIS-SOV-97-15*, January 15, 1997, *Komsomolskaya Pravda*.

39. See Andrew Mango, "Testing Time in Turkey," *The Washington Quarterly*, (Winter 1997): 3.

40. With respect to diplomatic recognition, Yerevan is similarly disposed. For example, Armenian foreign minister Vartan Oskanian recently said that "Armenia will always face a serious threat from both Azerbaijan and Turkey. Turkey makes normalization of bilateral ties with Armenia conditional on a Karabakh settlement in Azerbaijan's favor and this is unacceptable." Anna Saghabalian, "Oskanian Sees 'Serious Threat' From Turkey, Azerbaijan," *RFE/RL Armenian Report*, August 29, 1998.

41. See, for example, Michael Gunter, "The Armenian Terrorist Campaign Against Turkey," *Orbis* (Summer 1993).

42. Ter-Petrossian's ouster, former Karabakh president, Robert Kocharian, cited the former's conciliatory stance on Karabakh and warming relations with Turkey as proof of his administration's vulnerability. See "Armenian President Announced His Resignation," *RFE/RL Armenia Report*, February 3, 1998.

43. President Yilmaz also pledged to supply electricity to Armenia if Yerevan agreed to shut down the Medzamor nuclear power plant. See Lowell

Bezanis, "Turkey Offer to Help Armenia," *OMRI Daily Digest*, April 1, 1996, and *Turkish Daily News*, May 29, 1996.

44. See Sulejman Alijarly, "The Republic of Azerbaijan: Notes on the State Borders in the Past and in the Present," in Wright, et al., eds., op. cit., pp. 130–32. Also, Shireen Hunter notes: "When Russia made a bid to reestablish itself in Azerbaijan, by among other things toppling the pro-Turkish government of Elçibey, and despite the embarrassment that this caused Turkey, the West essentially accepted the Russian *fait accompli*" (1994, 160).

45. On June 11, 1996, Azerbaijani president Aliyev told a visiting delegation of Russian parliament deputies in Baku that Azerbaijan "gives priority" to relations with Russia. He also said he was "pleased" that the emigration of ethnic Russians from Azerbaijan had slowed, and offered to help find a settlement to the Ossetiyan-Ingush conflict. Aliyev has evidenced his political acumen on several occasions, balancing Turkey and Russian efforts at influencing Baku. See Lowell Benzanis, "Azerbaijan between Russia, Turkey," *OMRI Daily Digest*, June 12, 1996.

46. Recently, Baku has made a decidedly Western move by joining the GUAM (Georgia, Ukraine, Azerbaijan, and Moldova) grouping of states— a grouping seen as an alternative security regime to the CIS—and by seeking Turkish and U.S. military assistance. The latter overtures are seen as countermeasures against increased Russian and Armenian military cooperation. See Stephen Kinzer, "Azerbaijan Asks the U.S. to Establish Military Base," *New York Times*, January 31, 1999.

47. See Amberin Zaman, "Azerbaijan Looks to Ankara," *Middle East* (July 1992): 8–9.

48. See Thomas Goltz, *Azerbaijan Diary: A Rogue Reporter's Adventures in an Oil-Rich, War-Torn, Post-Soviet Republic* (New York: Sharpe, Inc., 1998), and author's interview (Athens, October 1998). With respect to Azeri-Iranian relations, see Shireen Hunter, "The Evolution of the Foreign Policy of the Transcaucasian States," Chapter 1 of this volume, regarding Azerbaijan's irredentist claims toward the Iranian province of Azerbaijan (northern Iran).

49. "Nagorno-Karabakh Plan Proposed," *FBIS-WEU-92-059*, March 26, 1992; "Lachin Corridor Territorial Redistribution Plan Outlined," *FBIS-USR-92-109*, August 28, 1992; "Cetin Said to Propose 'Exchange,'" *FBIS-WEU-93-066*, April 8, 1993; Paul A. Goble, "Coping With the Nagorno-Karabakh Crisis," *Fletcher Forum of World Affairs*, Summer 1992, pp. 19–26.

50. Raymond Bonner, "War in Caucasus Shows Ethnic Hate's Front Line," *New York Times*, August 2, 1993.

51. "Security Crisis With Iran Affects Economic Ties," *FBIS-WEU-93-150*, August 6, 1995.

52. See Svante Cornell, "Turkey and the Conflict in Nagorno-Karabakh: A Delicate Balance," *Middle Eastern Studies* (January 1998): 51–72.

53. Jolyon Naegele, "Turkey: Foreign Policy Plan Aims for Pivotal Role in Eurasia," *RFE/RL*, August 13, 1998.

54. See "Georgia, Turkey Sign Accord," *Jane's Defense Weekly*, March 16, 1999; and Steven Shabad, "The Caucasus: Turkish Inroads," *World Press Review* (March 1996).

55. Increased Russian military relations with neighboring Armenia are viewed

warily in Tbilisi as well as in Ankara; see Sean Boyne, "New Russian Accord Causes Concern in Turkey," *Jane's Intelligence Review*, August 1, 1996, p. 5.

56. See Elizabeth Fuller, "Turkey: A Diplomatic Return to the Caucasus and Central Asia," *RFE/RL*, September 8, 1997.

CHAPTER 5

1. S. Frederick Starr, "Making Eurasia Stable," *Foreign Affairs* 75: 1 (January/February, 1996): 80–92.
2. Ibid., 81.
3. "U.S. Defense Secretary Praises Uzbekistan's Stability," *Agence France Presse* (Nexis), (April 6, 1995).
4. See, for example, Steve Chan, "In Search of the Democratic Peace: Problems and Promise," *Mershon International Studies Review* 1997 41: 59–91; Dean V. Babst, "Elected Governments: A Force for Peace," *The Wisconsin Sociologist* 1964 3: 9–14; Steve Chan, "Mirror, Mirror, on the Wall . . . : Are Freer Countries More Pacific?," *Journal of Conflict Resolution* 1984 28: 617–48; James L. Ray, "Wars Between Democracies: Rare or Nonexistent?," *International Interactions* 1993 18: 251–76; Bruce M. Russett, *Grasping the Democratic Peace: Principles for a Post–Cold War World*, (Princeton: Princeton University Press, 1993); Zeev Moaz and Bruce M. Russett, "Normative and Structural Causes of Democratic Peace, 1946–1986," *American Political Science Review* 1993 87: 624–38.
5. Jack S. Levy, "The Causes of War: A Review of Theories and Evidence," in Tetlock, et al. (eds.), *Behavior, Society and Nuclear War*, Vol. 1 (New York: Oxford University Press, 1989): 270.
6. Data are taken from Raymond D. Gastil, "Freedom in the World 1997" (New York: Freedom House, 1997); and Kim R. Holmes, Bryan T. Johnson, and Melanie Kirkpatrick, "1997 Index of Economic Freedom" (Washington, D.C.: Heritage Foundation, 1997).
7. An OLS regression yielded a statistically significant relationship for the democracy variable, after controlling for quantity of U.S. foreign aid supplied to states (on a per capita basis, and as a percentage of the recipient's GDP), and the economic openness of the state. The standardized coefficient for the democracy variable was also significantly higher than for the other variables (beta = 0.56).
8. Address by Strobe Talbott, "A Farewell to Flashman: American Policy in the Caucasus and Central Asia," talk delivered at the Central Asia—Caucasus Institute, July 21, 1997, *www.sais-jhu.edu/casa/10–02.htm*.
9. Ibid.
10. Karimov has sometimes dismissed domestic opposition and efforts to democratize elsewhere in the former Soviet Union as "pseudo-democracy." See "Uzbekistan: Karimov on Reform, Democracy, Opposition," *FBIS-SOV*-96-173 (World News Connection), speech by Karimov at opening of Supreme Council in Tashkent, August 29, 1996.
11. Barnett R. Rubin, "Central Asia: Problems of Wealth, a Wealth of Problems," *Freedom in the World: The Annual Survey of Political Rights & Civil Liberties, 1996–1997* (New York: Freedom House, 1997): 48.
12. Heather Clark, "Uzbekistan fights the 'phantom fundamentalists,'" *Agence France Presse* (Clarinet) (November 7, 1998).

13. "Uzbekistan," *The Economist Intelligence Unit Country Report* (2nd Quarter, 1998): 10.

14. "Uzbekistan: Karimov on Reform, Democracy, Opposition," *FBIS-Central Asia* 29 (August 1996).

15. "Uzbekistan," *The Economist Intelligence Unit Country Report* (4th Quarter, 1996): 44.

16. See *Freedom in the World: The Annual Survey of Political Rights and Civil Liberties, 1996–1997* (New York: Freedom House, 1997).

17. "Kyrgyzstan: Kyrgyz President Favors Reform of Election System," *FBIS-Central Eurasia* (World News Connection) (June 4, 1998).

18. Birgit Brauer, "Human Rights Struggling to Catch On in Central Asia, Abuses Rise as Rulers Stifle Foes," *The Record* (Nexis) (April 12, 1998): A14.

19. See Alan Cranston and Michael D. Green, "Kyrgyzstan Takes Quiet Path to Democracy," *The Christian Science Monitor* (May 4, 1994): 14.

20. "Akayev Views Role of Democracy," *FBIS-Central Eurasia* (World News Connection) (October 4, 1994).

21. Namatbaeva, op. cit., 175.

22. "Akayev Speaks on Reforms, Presents Prime Minister," *FBIS-Central Eurasia* (World News Connection) (March 31, 1995).

23. For a full account of Karimov's politics, see William Fierman, "Political Development in Uzbekistan: Democratization," in Dawisha and Parrot (eds.), *Conflict, Cleavage and Change in Central Asia and the Caucaus* (Cambridge: Cambridge University Press, 1997): 360–408.

24. See *Freedom in the World: The Annual Survey of Political Rights and Civil Liberties, 1996–1997* (New York: Freedom House, 1997).

25. Ibid., 517.

26. Colin McMahon, "The Rehabilitation of Tamerlane," *Chicago Tribune* (January 17, 1999).

27. "Uzbekistan: President Speaks on Need for Democracy," *FBIS-Central Eurasia* (December 8, 1998). In his speech Karimov appears to suggest that democracy is the goal but that the people must first be educated and the state must inculcate democratic values.

28. Ibid.

29. See "U.S. Department of State—Uzbekistan Country Report on Human Rights Practices for 1997," at *www.state.gov/www/global/human_rights/1997_hrp_report*.

30. According to the State Department report, in June of 1997 authorities convicted Rahmatjon Otaqulov of narcotics and ammunition possession. Most observers believe that the contraband was planted by the arresting officers.

31. See U.S. Department of State Report on Human Rights in Uzbekistan.

32. See State Department Report on Human Rights, 1997.

33. "Uzbekistan," *Economist Intelligence Unit* (1st quarter, 1994): 73.

34. See Roger D. Kangas, "Uzbekistan: Evolving Authoritarianism," *Current History* (April 1994): 179. The government claims that attacks on the leaders of these groups is the work of "hooligans."

35. Ibid.

36. Ibid.

37. See "Uzbekistan," *The Economic Intelligence Unit* (2nd quarter, 1998): 6.

38. Lucian Kim, "Uzbeks Try to Blunt Islam's Rise," *Christian Science Moni-*

tor (November 20, 1998). See also, "Kyrgyz Paper Condemns Uzbek Anti-Wahabbi Witch Hunt," *FBIS-Central Eurasia* (January 28, 1998).

39. Sanobar Shermatova, "Uzbekistan: Contradictions of Karimov's Policy Examined," *Moskovskiye Novosti (FBIS-Central Eurasia)* (February 10, 1998).
40. Daniel Williams, "Uzbeks Caught Between Secular, Islamic Currents," *The Washington Post* (September 27, 1998).
41. Ibid.
42. Michael Ustinger, "Uzbekistan," *Focus Central Asia, Annual Review* (December 1995).
43. Ibid.
44. Statistics on trade and investment in Uzbekistan are maintained by the U.S. Department of Commerce's web-site, *www.iep.doc.gov/bisnis*.
45. See "U.S.-Uzbekistan Joint Commission: Trade, Investment, and Energy Committee," at the Department of State web-site, *www.state.gov/www/regions/nis/*.
46. Fiona Dunne, "World Bank to Contribute to Uzbek Health, Environment," *RFE/RL* (September 23, 1998).
47. "Silk Route gets 126-million-dollar facelift," *Agence France Presse* (September 15, 1998).
48. Robin Wright, "Los Angeles Times Interview: Askar Akayev," *Los Angeles Times* (September 7, 1997).
49. Maria Carlino, "Uzbekistan Gets Closer to US as it Privatizes," *Journal of Commerce* (March 5, 1997).
50. Sander Thoenes, "Uzbek Bid to Curb Market Forces Backfires," *Financial Times* (January 15, 1997).
51. Daniel Williams, "Uzbeks Caught Between Secular, Islamic Currents," *Washington Post* (September 27, 1998).
52. Interview with Uzbek assistant to President Karimov, July 1996.
53. See "Uzbekistan," *The Economist Intelligence Unit* (4th quarter, 1998).
54. See Breffini O'Rourke, "Kyrgyzstan: Reforms Promise to Reap Rewards," Radio Free Europe/Radio Liberty, *www.rferl.org/nca/features/1998*, (August 21, 1998).

CHAPTER 6

Note: An earlier version of this paper originally appeared in *Caspian Energy Resources: Implications for the Arab Gulf*, published by the Emirates Center for Strategic Studies and Research, Abu Dhabi, United Arab Emirates.

1. Vote by the Azerbaijan Supreme Soviet. However, this was not formally ratified until October 17.
2. The Belovezhsky Agreement, concluded on December 8, 1991, between the leaders of the three Slav republics, marked the end of the Soviet Union.
3. In the all-Union referendum on the future of the Soviet Union, held on March 17, 1991, Turkmenistan returned a vote of over 94 percent in favor of remaining within the Union.
4. The spelling "Karabakh" is preferred by some authors, while others use "Karabagh."
5. Most of the commentaries on the war in Karabakh, while purporting to be objective, tends to favor either the Armenians or the Azerbaijanis. For

instance, compare the report by Human Rights Watch/Helsinki, *Azerbaijan: Seven Years of Conflict in Nagorno-Karabakh* (New York: Human Rights Watch, 1994), with the work by Levon Chorbajian, et al., *The Caucasian Knot: The History and Geo-Politics of Nagorno-Karabagh* (London: Zed Books, 1994).

6. The economic problems of Kazakhstan are well documented in Yelena Kalyuzhnova, *The Kazakstani Economy: Independence and Transition* (London: Macmillan, 1998). For an overview of economic trends in all three countries see European Bank for Reconstruction and Development, *Transition Report 1998* (London: EBRD, 1998).

7. The hydrocarbon resources of the Caspian Sea have already spawned a considerable literature. Some of the most useful works are Rosemarie Forsythe, *The Politics of Oil in the Caucasus and Central Asia: Prospects for Oil Exploitation and Export in the Caspian Basin:* Adelphi Paper 300, International Institute for Strategic Studies (Oxford: Oxford University Press, 1996); John Roberts, *Caspian Pipelines* (London: Royal Institute of International Affairs, 1996); Ottar Skagen, *Caspian Gas* (London: Royal Institute of International Affairs, 1997); IDE Spot Survey, *The Caspian Basin Oil and Its Impact on Eurasian Power Games,* Manabu Shimizu (ed.) (Tokyo: Institute of Developing Economies, June 1998).

8. Andropov also had KGB connections, and indeed headed the organization for a period, but for most of his career he was a Party functionary. Aliev's sponsor for elevation to the Politburo was more probably Brezhnev, though he died just before the appointment had been implemented.

9. Aliev gained 98.8 percent of the vote. He ran against two virtually unknown candidates. Elizabeth Fuller, "Azerbaijan at the Crossroads," in Roy Allison (ed.), *Challenges for the Former Soviet South* (London: Royal Institute of International Affairs, 1996): 129, pointed out that "Some observers attributed Aliev's political comeback to interference by Moscow...." A concise chronicle of Aliev's return to power is given by Audrey Altstadt, "Azerbaijan's Struggle Towards Democracy," in Karen Dawisha and Bruce Parrott (eds.), *Conflict, Cleavage and Change in Central Asia and the Caucasus* (Cambridge: Cambridge University Press, 1997): 124–29.

10. According to Ermukhamet Ertysbayev, "Nekotoryye aspekty prezidentskoy izbiratel'noy kampanii v Kazakhstane," *Tsentral'naya Aziya i Kavkaz* 1: 3 (1999): 44–55, "almost 99 percent of Kazakhstanis" voted for Nursultan Nazarbaev in December 1991.

11. Turkmenistan was the first member of the CIS to take the decision to prolong the term of office of the incumbent president by referendum. Uzbekistan followed suit the following year.

12. See El'bar Ismailov, "Vlast' i oppozitsiya nakanune i v period prezidentskoy izbiratel'noy kampanii v Azerbaydzhane," *Tsentral'naya Aziya i Kavkaz* 1: 2 (1999): 37, with reference to Azerbaijan. The situation is similar in the other two states.

13. The most breathtakingly ostentatious monument is the seventy-five-meter arch that was unveiled in January 1999 to commemorate the third anniversary of Turkmenistan's Declaration of Neutrality. It is surmounted by a gold-plated twelve-meter statue of President Niyazov, who stands aloft with arms raised toward the sun; the statue rotates, so that it is always facing the sun. Situated in the center of Ashkhabad, the capital, the arch

is intended to symbolize a traditional Turkmen hearth; it has a café on its upper tier.

14. "Insulting the honor and dignity of the President" is a charge that is not infrequently invoked in Azerbaijan; see, for example, cases cited in Ulvi Hakimov, *Azerbaijan Bulletin* 57 (December 23, 1998), Azerbaijan National Democracy Foundation, Baku. In Kazakhstan, too, law protects the honor of the president, and this is sometimes used to clamp down on potential dissidents.

15. See reports by Amnesty International, for instance, *Turkmenistan: Measures of Persuasion* (March 1996); *Kazakstan: Ill-treatment and the Death Penalty* (July 1996); *Azerbaijan: Time to Abolish the Death Penalty* (March 1997). See also Human Rights Watch, *World Report 1999*, Human Rights Developments.

16. Azerbaijan's flag has, top to bottom, three parallel horizontal bands of blue, red, and green, with an eight-pointed white star and crescent moon, horns pointing to the right, in the center of the red central band, reminiscent of the Turkish flag. The flag of Kazakhstan has a bright blue background, representing the sky, with a golden sun in the center, wreathed with the outspread wings of a steppe eagle, and down the lefthand (hoist) side a broad vertical band of decorative folk motifs, also in gold. The Turkmen flag is dark green, with a white crescent moon, horns facing to the left, signifying a bright future, and five stars to represent the five provinces. There is a vertical purple band of traditional carpet designs from the five provinces down the lefthand (hoist) side, with two crossed olive branches at the bottom.

17. To give just a few examples, in Azerbaijan, the city of Kirovabad, named after a Bolshevik hero, was given back its historical name *Gandja*; in Baku, Lenin Square was renamed *Azadlig* (Freedom). In Turkmenistan, the port of Krasnovodsk was renamed *Turkmenbashi*; the provinces of Ashkhabad and Chardzhou were renamed *Ahal* and *Lebap* respectively. In Kazakhstan, the port of Shevchenko, named after a Ukrainian poet, was renamed *Aktau*, while the port of Guriyev became *Atyrau*.

18. The *manat* in Azerbaijan in August 1992; the *manat* in Turkmenistan and the *tenge* in Kazakhstan in November 1993.

19. For a fuller discussion of Islam during the Soviet period see Shirin Akiner, "Islam, the State and Ethnicity in Central Asia in Historical Perspective," *Religion State and Society* 24: 2–3 (1996): 91–132.

20. The most striking example of Turkmenistan's new rituals is the oath of allegiance, which is repeated every day in the media, in schools, and at all public ceremonies. It runs, in part, "Turkmenistan, beloved fatherland . . . for the slightest calumny about you, may my tongue become powerless; at the moment of treason . . . may my breath be cut off." For the full text, see Michael Ochs, "Turkmenistan: The Quest for Stability," in Dawisha and Parrott, op. cit., 328.

21. Murad Esenov, "Konstitutsiya Turkmenistana," *Tsentral'naya Aziya* 2 (1996): 21–25, highlights the ambiguities in the role of the People's Council. In effect, it represents a fourth branch of power, although this is not provided for in the constitution.

22. See Martha Brill Olcott, "The Growth of Political Participation in Kazakhstan," in Dawisha and Parrott, op. cit., for a fuller account of this period. President Nazarbaev gives his own explanation of events in his

autobiography *My Life, My Times and the Future* . . . , translated and edited by Peter Conradi (Northamptonshire: Pilkington Press, 1998): 87–95.

23. Altstadt, op. cit., 129–31.

24. The distinction between "formal" parties and "informal" movements dates back to the Soviet period. Today, there is no difference between the various types of groupings other than the fact that regulations for registering a party are much tougher than for registering any other form of organization.

25. There were many other parties that did not succeed in securing registration. A good account of the positions of different parties is given by Ismailov, op. cit., 36–41.

26. It was registered in spring 1994 and by 1995 claimed to have 64,000 members (Altstadt, op. cit., 148).

27. According to information provided by the first secretary of the Communist Party, Serikbolsyn Abdildin, in January 1999, it numbered 48,000 members; of these, 18,000 were under fifty years of age.

28. The deputy chairman of the Movement for Democratic Reform, Khalmurat Soyunov, outlines the problems facing the opposition in Turkmenistan in "Budushcheye Turkmenistana nerazryvna s demokratiyey," *Tsentral'naya Aziya* 1 (November 1995): 20–25; a similar position is taken by Ashir Ioliyev, "Demokratiya po-Turkmenbashi—svoboda slova uprazdnyayetsya," *Tsentral'naya Aziya* 6: 33–37.

29. Turkmen political refugees played a large part in launching the journal *Tsentral'naya Aziya*, later renamed *Tsentral'naya Aziya i Kavkaz*, published in Sweden since 1995.

30. The Feminist League in Kazakhstan, for example, canvassed presidential candidates before the elections in January 1999 and succeeded in focusing some attention on gender issues.

31. Fuller, op. cit., 144–47.

32. See Adam Dixon, "Kazakhstan: Political Reform and Economic Development," in Allison, op. cit., 96–97.

33. In 1997–98, in Azerbaijan, total active armed forces numbered 66,700, with basic terms of service being seventeen months; in Kazakhstan, 35,100, with basic terms of service being thirty-one months; in Turkmenistan, approximately 18,000, with terms of service being twenty-four months. (Source: International Institute of Strategic Studies, *The Military Balance 1997/98*, Oxford, Oxford University Press, under relevant country entries.)

34. See Shirin Akiner, "Soviet Military Legacy in Kazakhstan," *Jane's Intelligence Review* (December 1994): 552–54.

35. *Jane's Sentinel: Russia and the CIS, Security Assessment*, 1996 Edition, under entry for Azerbaijan.

36. For an outline of the legal and regulatory framework for the media in these two countries, see Yasha Lange, *Media in the CIS: A Study of the Political, Legislative and Socio-economic Framework* (Dusseldorf: European Institute for Media, 1997): 54–61, 105–09 respectively. Military censorship was introduced in Azerbaijan in 1993, but abolished three years later. Political censorship was introduced in late 1994, but lifted in August 1998.

37. See Lange, op. cit., 213–17.

38. In 1998 it was estimated that a hundred newspapers were published in Azerbaijan, including fifteen dailies and thirty weeklies. There were two

state television channels and three privately owned Baku-based companies. (Source: *Monitoring the Media Coverage of the October 1998 Presidential Elections in Azerbaijan: Final Report*, European Institute for the Media,
Dusseldorf, 1999). As of 1997, there were 234 registered television and
radio stations in Kazakhstan, and 725 newspapers (Lange, op. cit., 110).
However, most networks reach only a small geographic area. By law, television networks are required to provide 50 percent of their material in
Kazakh. In Turkmenistan, as of 1997, there were two television channels,
one broadcasting in Russian and Turkmen, the other predominantly in
Turkmen; there were also thirty-two periodicals, although only seventeen
appeared regularly (Lange, op. cit., 218–20).

39. Several such cases are listed in the *Presidential Elections in Azerbaijan: Final
Report* (op. cit.), and *Monitoring the Media Coverage of the Kazakhstan Pres-
idential Elections: Final Report* (Dusseldorf: European Institute for the
Media, 1999).

40. For example, in Kazakhstan in January 1999 several people told the
author that they knew "for a fact" that President Nazarbaev had been
named by a Western publication as the eighth richest man in the world.
Whether or not this is true—and it is probably not true—nevertheless, it
reflects a general belief that the president is very wealthy; the further
implication is that he amassed his fortune at the expense of the people.

41. Elections to the Supreme Soviets of the USSR and of the Soviet Republics
were held every five years, to local government every two-and-a-half
years.

42. As Ochs (op. cit., 329) points out, it is not clear why Niyazov decided to
hold the referendum, rather than participating in another presidential
election in 1997, which he assuredly would have won.

43. *Central Asia Newsfile* 7: 1 (January 1999): 74.

44. According to the Central Electoral Committee of Kazakhstan, over 90
percent of the electorate took part in the referendum and over 95 percent
of those who voted were in favor of the extension *Central Asia Newsfile* 3:
5 (May 1995): 31.

45. Other reasons included concerns over the effect that the Russian elections,
also scheduled for 2000, might have had on the electorate in Kazakhstan.
In particular, it was feared that the Russian Communists might be gaining in popularity and that this would boost the chances of the Communist Party in Kazakhstan. The explanation favored by officials was that the
president needed a clear mandate in order to implement long-term
reforms. (Sources: conversations held by the author, during a visit to
Kazakhstan in January 1999, with government officials, opposition
activists, and political analysts, as well as with a cross section of the public.)

46. Ertysbayev, op. cit., 44–55.

47. The German presidency, on behalf of the European Union, commenting
on the Kazakh presidential elections, expressed regret at "the setback that
the conduct of the election has inflicted on the process of democratization and the rule of law in Kazakhstan." *Bulletin Quotidien Europe* 7388
(January 22, 1999).

48. Richard Giragosian, *TransCaucasus: A Chronology*, vol. 8, January 1999,
Washington, D.C.: Armenian National Committee of America, e-mail
version.

49. For a good survey of Turkey's hopes, disappointments, and achievements in the region see Gareth Winrow, *Turkey in Post-Soviet Central Asia* (London: Royal Institute of International Affairs, 1995).

50. Azeri separatists in Iran, who seek unification with Azerbaijan, are intermittently active. See *RFE/RL Iran Report* 2: 2 (January 11, 1999), quoted in *Caghdas Azerbaycan Volu*, distributed through the Research Centre for Turkestan, Azerbaijan, Crimea, Caucasus and Siberia, S.O.T.A. Haarlem, The Netherlands. It should be noted that population estimates for Azeris in Iran range from under five million to over twenty million.

51. Kazakhstan shares a long border with Siberia; much of northeast Kazakhstan is culturally, ethnically, and economically more closely linked to Russia than to other parts of Kazakhstan. Azerbaijan borders the Republic of Daghestan, a constituent republic of the Russian Federation. The Lezghi people, one of the main ethnic groups of the Caucasus, are divided between Azerbaijan and Daghestan. From time to time, the Daghestani Lezghis have laid territorial claim to parts of Azerbaijan.

52. This is particularly the case with Kazakhstan and, consequently, good relations with Russia are more of a priority for Kazakhstan than for the other countries. In May 1992 Kazakhstan signed a bilateral treaty of friendship with Russia; in March 1996, Kazakhstan, along with Russia, Belarus, and Kyrgyzstan, signed the "Agreement of Four," forming an inner core of integration within the CIS. The aims of the agreement were to create a united economic area and customs union, to harmonize legal systems, coordinate foreign policy, and to provide mutual support in the fight against terrorism.

53. Some progress was made on this issue in 1998. In April 1998 Kazakhstan and Russia reached agreement on the division of the Caspian seabed (though not the surface of the sea) into national sectors. In July the Russian and Azerbaijani governments issued a joint statement expressing their readiness to conclude a similar agreement on the demarcation of the seabed. In August it was agreed that a Turkmen-Iranian working group should be created to draw up "a plan of action" on the legal status of the Caspian Sea. However, many problems still remain, not least the tension between Azerbaijan and Turkmenistan over conflicting claims to offshore oilfields.

54. See Forsythe, op. cit., and Roberts, op. cit., for a good exposition of possible export routes.

55. By the beginning of 1995 Aliev's main political opponents—Ayaz Mutalibov, a former president; Rahim Gaziyev, a former defense minister; and Suret Huseinov, a former prime minister and instigator of a coup against Aliev in October 1994—were all based in Moscow. Kazakh opposition leaders also have close links with Moscow, including Akezhan Kazhegeldin, a former prime minister of Kazakhstan and currently the only serious rival to Nazarbaev. There are likewise several Turkmen political dissidents in Moscow. In 1993 a group of them established the Turkmenistan Foundation under the leadership of the former foreign minister Abdy Kuliyev. The aims of the foundation included the annulment of the referendum of January 1994 extending Niyazov's term of office. The Russian authorities generally tolerate such activities; however, they have also on occasion cooperated with the Turkmen government in taking action against the dissidents as, for instance, when they arrested Murad

Esenov and Khalmurat Soyunov, leading members of the opposition (Ochs, op. cit., 346–47).

56. Azerbaijan joined the CIS in 1991, but under President Elçibey withdrew from the organization. When President Aliev came to power he took Azerbaijan back into the CIS.

57. Altstadt, op. cit. 130–31; *Presidential Elections in Azerbaijan: Final Report*, op.cit.

58. OSCE/ODHR, *Election Assessment Mission, Republic of Kazakhstan, January 11, 1999, Preliminary Statement.*

59. A version of this section appeared in Shirin Akiner, *Central Asia: Conflict or Stability and Development?* (London: Minority Rights Group, 1997): 11–14.

60. In 1997 estimated at 19.3 percent of the labor force in Azerbaijan; 4.1 percent in Kazakhstan (i.e., unemployed registered with the Public Employment Service); recent data not available for Turkmenistan (EBRD, *Transition Report, 1998*, 206–33, under country entries). Unofficial estimates are far higher, however.

61. Recent estimates from officials and research institutes in Kazakhstan put the proportion of those living below the poverty line at 60–75 percent of the population.

62. See Michael Kaser and Santosh Mehrotra, "The Central Asian Economies after Independence," in Allison, op. cit., 287–93.

63. The "mafia" in the former Soviet Union have no connection with the Mafia in Italy. The term is used loosely to refer to organized criminal groups.

64. Turkmenistan lies on one of the main drug-trafficking routes leading from Afghanistan to the Middle East. Key transhipment points are Takhta-Bazar and Kushka on the Turkmen-Afghan border and Serakhs on the Turkmen-Iranian border. According to the Turkmen National Security Committee, drug seizures in 1998 amounted to 24 tons. Of the seven-hundred-odd death penalties handed down in 1998 in Turkmenistan, 90 percent were for drug-related crimes. (Reuters, January 7, 1999; *Central Asia Newsfile* 7: 1, January 1999.)

65. For example, the Kazakhstan International Bureau for Human Rights and Rule of Law.

66. The major assassination attempt on President Karimov of Uzbekistan on February 16, 1999, showed that even with heavy security arrangements, it is difficult to ensure the complete safety of these leaders.

67. On January 17, 1999, President Aliev was unexpectedly flown to a military hospital in Ankara for treatment. Official reports stated that he was suffering from bronchitis; unofficial reports hinted at serious heart problems. He returned home on January 30, 1999.

68. On September 1, 1997, President Niyazov underwent heart surgery in Germany. He is said to have made a good recovery, but it is difficult to know for certain what the long-term prognosis is.

69. Saparmurad Niyazov proclaimed a program for a "Decade of Prosperity" in 1992, and in September 1998 Nursultan Nazarbaev put forward his program "2030 Vision." However, in both cases these were general statements of intent rather than concrete plans for reform.

70. Ilham Aliev is currently vice president of SOCAR, the Azeri State Oil Company; there are rumors that he will be made speaker of the Mejlis in

the near future, as a prelude, perhaps, to assuming greater responsibility in state affairs. The daughter of Nazarbaev, Dariga, has made a successful career in media management and is currently general director of Khabar, the semiprivatized former state television company. The son of the Turkmen president is best known for his profligacy in foreign casinos.

71. In January 1999 Azeri officials were suggesting that NATO should establish bases in Azerbaijan in order to balance the Russian presence in Armenia (Reuters, January 25, 1999; *TransCaucasus: A Chronology*, February 1999).

72. A complete census enumeration, the first since the end of the Soviet period, was carried out in February–March 1999; full results were not available at the time of going to press, hence population figures for Kazakhstan are approximate. Recent demographic data are also not available for Turkmenistan and Azerbaijan.

73. *Kazakhstan: 1998 Country Profile* (London: EBRD). It should be noted that estimates of GDP per capita vary considerably from one source to another, owing to the unreliable nature of official data.

74. *Turkmenistan: 1998 Country Profile* (London: EBRD). See comment in note 73 above.

75. *Azerbaijan: 1998 Country Profile* (London: EBRD). See comment in note 73 above.

76. For more information on the history of Kazakhstan see Martha Brill Olcott, *The Kazakhs* (Stanford: Hoover Institution Press, 1987); Shirin Akiner, *The Formation of Kazakh Identity: From Tribe to Nation State* (London: Royal Institute of International Affairs, 1995).

77. For more information on the history of Azerbaijan, see Tadeusz Swietochowski, *Russian Azerbaijan, 1905–1920: The Shaping of National Identity in a Muslim Community* (Cambridge: Cambridge University Press, 1985); Audrey Altstadt, *The Azerbaijani Turks: Power and Identity Under Russian Rule* (Stanford: Hoover Institution Press, 1992).

78. The Kazakh (originally called "Kirghiz") Autonomous Soviet Socialist Republic was created within the Russian Soviet Federal Socialist Republic in August 1920. In December 1936 it was elevated to the status of Union Republic, thus becoming the Kazakh Soviet Socialist Republic.

79. A number of good works have been written on the organization and functions of the Soviet system. A useful starting point is Gordon B. Smith, *Soviet Politics: Continuity and Contradictions* (London: Macmillan, 1998).

CHAPTER 7

1. International Institute for Strategic Studies, "Caspian Oil: Not the Great Game Revisited," *Strategic Survey 1997/98* (London: International Institute for Strategic Studies, 1988).

2. E. W. Anderson, *An Atlas of World Political Flashpoints* (London: Pinter, 1993).

3. L. S. Kaplan, "Historical Aspects," in J. Simon (ed.), *NATO Enlargement: Opinions and Options* (Washington, D.C.: National Defense University, 1995).

4. A. Boyd, *An Atlas of World Affairs* (London: Routledge, 1998).

5. Kaplan, op. cit.

6. Stephen M. Walt, *Revolution and War* (Ithaca, NY: Cornell University Press, 1997).

7. K. Naumann, "The Reshaping of NATO from a Military Perspective," *RUSI Journal* (June 1997): 7–11.

8. C. L. Barry, "Creating a European Security and Defense Identity." *Joint Force Quarterly* 15 (Spring 1997): 62–69.

9. E. B. Atkeson, "The Changing Face of NATO and the Need for Change in Responsibilities," in S. J. Blank, *NATO after Enlargement: New Challenges, New Missions, New Forces* (Carlisle, Penn.: Strategic Studies Institute, U.S. Army War College, 1998).

10. H. Plater-Zyberk, *NATO Enlargement—Benefits, Costs and Consequences* (Camberley: Conflict Studies Research Centre, Royal Military Academy, Sandhurst, 1996).

11. C. Blandy. *The Caspian: A Sea of Troubles* (Camberley: Conflict Studies Research Centre, Royal Military Academy, Sandhurst, 1996).

12. M. A. Smith, "Oil and Gas Interests in the Russian Political Equation," *Occasional Brief* 59 (Camberley: Conflict Studies Research Centre, Royal Military Academy, Sandhurst, 1998).

13. P. Ross, "Routes and Finance: The Key Azeri Developments," *Petroleum Review* (October 1998): 40–41.

14. E. W. Anderson, *An Atlas of World Political Flashpoints* (London: Pinter, 1993).

15. S. A. Mikoyan, "Russia, the U.S. and Regional Conflicts in Eurasia," *Survival* 40: 3 (Autumn 1998): 112–126.

16. M. A. Smith, *Iran—New Focus of Russian Foreign Policy* (Camberley: Conflict Studies Research Centre, Royal Military Academy, Sandhurst, 1995).

17. S. J. Blank, "Beyond the Founding Act: The Next Stage of Russian-NATO Relations," in S. J. Blank, op. cit.

18. K. H. Kamp, "NATO Entrapped: Debating the Next Enlargement Round," *Survival* 10: 3 (Autumn 1998, 170–86).

19. Z. Brzezinski, "The Next Big Euro-Atlantic Task is to Engage Russia," *International Herald Tribune* (May 4, 1998); and S. Talbott, in J. Hoagland, "NATO is in Transition—So Why Not Talk About It?," *International Herald Tribune* (March 19, 1998).

20. S. M. Walt, "Why Alliances Endure or Collapse, " *Survival* 39: 1 (Spring 1997, 156–79).

21. International Institute for Strategic Studies, "Making a Bigger NATO," *Strategic Survey 1997/98* (London: International Institute of Strategic Studies, 1998).

22. A. J. Pierre and D. Trenin, "Developing NATO-Russian Relations," *Survival* 39: 1 (Spring 1997, 5–18).

CHAPTER 8

1. Elkhan Nuriyev, "Geopolitics and Regional Conflicts in the Caucasus," *Eurasia, Turkey* (October 1997): 15.

2. Fiona Hill, "Pipeline Dreams in the Caucasus," SDIP (Harvard University, John F. Kennedy School of Government, 1996 Seminar Series): 5.

3. Elkhan Nuriyev, "Regional Conflicts and the New Geopolitics of NATO Expansion: The Cases of the Caucasus," *Turkistan-Newsletter* 98:2–004 (January 8, 1998).

4. Ibid.

5. Fiona Hill, preface in Edward Walker, *No Peace, No War in the Caucasus:*

Secessionist Conflicts in Chechnya, Abkhazia, and Nagorno-Karabakh (SDIP, Harvard University, John F. Kennedy School of Government, February 1998).

6. Ibid.
7. ORT News Review, Moscow TV (November 1995).
8. See *Turkistan-Newsletter* 98:2–004 (January 8, 1998).
9. Fiona Hill, op. cit.
10. Edward Walker, *No Peace, No War in the Caucasus: Secessionist Conflicts in Chechnya, Abkhazia, and Nagorno-Karabakh* (SDIP, Harvard University, John F. Kennedy School of Government, February 1998): 16.
11. Fiona Hill, op. cit.
12. Zerkalo-Ayna newspaper (April 11, 1998).
13. *Turkistan-Newsletter*, 98:2–004 (January 8, 1998).
14. Voice of America, Daily Report (April 1997).
15. Raja Mohan, "The Hindu-Editorial: Caucasian Fire Circle," *The Hindu* (March 20, 1997).
16. *Turkistan-Newsletter* 98:2–004 (January 8, 1998).
17. Ibid.
18. See *Zerkalo-Ayna* (newspaper) (April 15, 1997); and Robert Hunter, "Enlarging NATO: Reckless or Requisite?" *U.S. Foreign Policy Agenda: An Electronic Journal of the United States Information Agency* 2: 4 (October 1997): 15–18.
19. Radio Liberty–Radio Free Europe, *Newsline* 15, Part 1 (April 21, 1997).
20. Elkhan Nuriyev, "Geopolitics and Regional Conflicts in the Caucasus," *Eurasia, Turkey* (October 1997): 16.
21. Ibid.

CHAPTER 9

* The author is grateful for the Hoover Institution on War, Revolution and Peace for providing him with the opportunity to conduct research for this paper as a national fellow in 1997–98. He would also like to thank the Ford Foundation for funding the Berkeley Program on the Caucasus and Caspian Littoral, which made possible research trips to the region in 1996 and 1997.
1. Even Armenia, which has been supporting the Karabakh secessionists both politically and materially, has been careful not to incur the wrath of the international community by formally recognizing Karabakh independence.
2. "Rossiisko-Chechenskii Dogovor o prekrashenii voennykh deistvii," reproduced in *The Search for Peace in Chechnya: A Sourcebook 1994–1996*, produced by Diane Curran, Fiona Hill, and Elena Kostritsyna, Strengthening Democratic Institutions Project, John F. Kennedy School of Government, Harvard University, March 1997.
3. The results of the election are analyzed by Alaoudin Chilaev in "Chechnya: Towards Independence," *War Report* (January/February 1997): 12–13.
4. The text of the treaty can be found in Otto Latsis, "Dogovor s Chechnei: Kto Pobedil, Kto Proigral?," *Izvestia* (May 14, 1997).
5. Few if any governments will accept those passports as valid without permission from Moscow, however, because doing so would suggest recog-

nition of Chechen independence. For this same reason, Moscow will refuse to grant such permission. Various compromises have been suggested that would allow Chechen officials and even citizens to travel abroad without having to use the new passports now being issued by the Russian Federation. One option is to allow Chechens to continue to use their Soviet-era international passports, although this is impossible for the many Chechen officials who did not obtain Soviet-era passports because they never traveled abroad during the Soviet period. Another possibility is for Moscow to allow Chechens to use their Soviet-era internal passports. The passport issue is particularly significant because it forces other governments to become directly involved, at least implicitly, in the status question. To date it has been resolved on an ad hoc basis, which has allowed Chechen officials to travel abroad.

6. *RFE/RL Newsline* (January 7, 1997).

7. I have analyzed the constitutional aspects of Chechen independence in greater detail in "Constitutional Obstacles to Peace in Chechnya," *East European Constitutional Review*, 6: 1 (Winter 1997): 55–60.

8. The speaker of the Russian Duma, Genadii Seleznev, has threatened to initiate impeachment proceedings against Yeltsin if he attempts to recognize Chechen independence. See *RFE/RL Newsline* (September 2, 1997).

9. See Robert Sharlet, "The Politics of Constitutional Amendment in Russia," *Post-Soviet Affairs*, 13: 3 (1997): 197–227.

10. My own view is that this fear is exaggerated and that Russian acceptance of Chechen independence would not lead other republics to press for secession. Intergovernmental relations within Russia have stabilized considerably since 1992–93, and the leaders of its other republics, including those in the North Caucasus, as well as most of the peoples residing in those republics, wish to avoid a "Chechen scenario." For an elaboration of these arguments, see Edward W. Walker, "The Dog that Didn't Bark: Tatarstan and Asymmetrical Federalism in Russia," *The Harriman Review*, 9: 4 (Winter 1996): 1–35. It *is* true, however, that instability in Chechnya could spill over into other neighboring republics, particularly Daghestan, but this instability is unlikely to manifest itself in demands for independence—most Daghestanis fear that the brittle ethnic balance in their republic would unravel should the republic press for independence. And while they opposed the Russian intervention in Chechnya and were sympathetic to the plight of the Chechens during the war (despite pre-war resentment over Chechen lawlessness and the frequent robberies of passengers on the railroad through Chechnya to Makhachkala), they also resent Chechen irredentist claims on areas of eastern Daghestan that were traditionally settled by Chechens. See Anna Matveeva, "Daghestan," *Former Soviet South Briefing Paper*, The Royal Institute of International Affairs, no. 13, May 1997.

11. The Russian constitution provides for two kinds of treaties—international treaties, which are signed by heads of state (for Russia, the president) and have to be ratified by a majority vote in the upper house of the Russian parliament (the Council of the Federation); and "treaties" on the mutual delegation of powers between the subjects of the federation (republics and regions) and the federal government, which are signed by the Russian president and the "heads of state" of the regions and republics ("gover-

nors" in the case of the regions and "presidents" in the case of republics). Some thirty-seven of these treaties have been signed to date. The accord's self-designation as a "treaty" is therefore without legal foundation.

12. Aleksandr Lebed, Yurii Luzhkov, and Gregorii Yavlinskii (all possible presidential contenders in 2000) have each argued that the war was a tragic mistake and suggested that Chechnya should be granted its independence. Whether they would in fact prove willing to take on the legal and political obstacles to Chechen independence should one of them become Russia's president (and Yavlinskii is a real long shot) can be doubted.

13. For background on the war, see Georgi M. Derlugian, "The Tale of Two Resorts: Abkhazia and Ajaria Before and Since the Soviet Collapse," Working Paper #6.2, Center for German and European Studies and the Institute of International Studies, UC Berkeley, March 1995; Elizabeth Fuller, "Abkhazia on the Brink of Civil War?," *RFE/RL Research Report*, 1: 3 (September 4, 1992); Catherine Dale, "Turmoil in Abkhazia," *RFE/RL Research Report*, 2: 3 (August 27, 1993); and Ghia Nodia, "Causes and Visions of Conflict in Abkhazia," Working Paper, Berkeley Program in Soviet and Post-Soviet Studies, UC Berkeley, winter 1998.

14. The UN distinguishes between "refugees" who are forced to flee fighting or political persecution across international borders, and "internally displaced persons" (IDPs) who are forced to flee fighting or political persecution but who do not cross international borders. I use the term "DP" to refer to both. The exact title of the agreement was, "Agreement on the Voluntary Return of Displaced Persons," which allowed the parties to finesse the question of whether ethnic Georgians who had fled into Georgia were refugees, thereby implying that Abkhazia was an independent state, or DPs, implying that it was not. With regard to the number of DPs from the conflict, the figures are, as elsewhere, disputed. See, for example, "Georgia/Abkhazia: Violations of the Laws of War and Russia's Role in the Conflict," *Human Rights Watch Arms Project*, 7: 7 (March 1995).

15. Shevardnadze was already pressing vigorously for an international PKF operating under a UN or even an CSCE (OSCE) mandate, but the Western powers, and particularly the United States, were reluctant to take on another peacekeeping operation or become involved in a conflict bordering directly on Russia.

16. UN observers had been dispatched to Abkhazia for the first time in the summer of 1993 to monitor a Russian-brokered cease-fire of July 27, 1993, that subsequently broke down.

17. See S. Neil MacFarlane, Larry Minear, and Stephen D. Shenfield, "Armed Conflict in Georgia: A Case-Study of Humanitarian Assistance," Occasional Paper #21, Thomas J. Watson Jr. Institute for International Studies, 1996.

18. Initially Armenia and (curiously) Georgia also contributed a limited number of units to the PKF, although all PKF officers were Russian.

19. By early 1997 the Abkhaz were reportedly processing only some two hundred DP applications per month.

20. For an excellent survey of internal displacement patterns and living conditions for DPs in Georgia and Abkhazia, see Catherine Dale, "Georgia/Abkhazia: Forced Migration, Internal Displacement—and a Return to Peace?," *Refugee Survey Quarterly* (Autumn 1997).

21. Information on internal conditions in Abkhazia was obtained through interviews with Ekber Menemencioglu, chief of mission, UNHCR, Georgia, Tbilisi, June 12, 1997; Martin Schümar, United Nations volunteers coordinator in Georgia, Tbilisi, June 11, 1997; and Henry T. Wooster, U.S. member, OSCE Mission to Georgia, June 13, 1997. See also Catherine Dale, op. cit.

22. The Abkhaz government-in-exile in Tbilisi (see below) reportedly has an additional three thousand irregular troops under its command, most of whom are former policemen who fled Abkhazia in 1992–93.

23. At the same time, Shevardnadze and Georgia's defense minister, Vardiko Nadabaidze, have asserted on numerous occasions that the Georgian military is ready and able to restore Georgian sovereignty in Abkhazia by force, while Shevardnadze has stated that, in the absence of progress at the negotiating table, Tbilisi will eventually be forced to resort to "other means" to restore its territorial integrity. Nevertheless, sources in Georgia indicate that the Georgian military is well aware of its limitations and that most senior officers believe that Georgia is not yet ready to launch an offensive into Abkhazia.

24. Casuality figures are unreliable and vary considerably, as would be expected in this kind of "disorderly" war. The figure cited above was provided by Paata Zakareishvili, chief of staff of the Georgian Parliamentary Committee on Human Rights, Tbilisi, May 28, 1996. A similar estimate derived from interviews of both Abkhaz and Georgian sources is given in the Human Rights Watch Report cited above ("Georgia/Abkhazia: Violations of Law," op. cit., 5).

25. Nevertheless, like most blockades it was only partially effective. Significant smuggling across the border continued, particularly exchange of Russian consumer goods for Abkhaz fruits, nuts, and vegetables, and as a result most consumer goods could be found in Abkhaz markets, albeit at very high prices given Abkhaz income levels.

26. The latter figure may be even lower—the Abkhaz are wary of population estimates because they fear that evidence of continuing out-migration will demoralize the Abkhaz and encourage Georgia to invade. Nevertheless, employees of human rights organizations active in the region report that many ethnic Abkhaz appear to have left the republic, and that the number of those remaining may be 65,000 or less. The number of ethnic Armenians in Abkhazia, however, has reportedly decreased less than others, and reports of Armenians moving into Georgian villages have contributed to tensions between Georgians and Armenians.

27. On May 25, 1997, ITAR-TASS reported that Ardzinba had declared an 11 P.M. to 6 A.M. curfew to prevent factional fighting between Abkhaz criminal organizations.

28. Georgia has been very careful in its dealings with the Chechens, both because it does not want to support separatists given the conflict in Abkhazia and because it does not want to add another source of tension with Moscow. As a result, Shevardnadze has repeatedly affirmed Georgia's support for Russia's territorial integrity, while in practical terms Tbilisi has made clear that it will not provide Chechnya with an air corridor over its territory without permission from Moscow. It has also given a lukewarm reception to Chechen proposals that a road be built between Chechnya and Georgia over the Caucasus range (an extremely expensive proposition,

and one that Georgians would be very wary of regardless because of their fear of a significant inflow of Chechen refugees). Nevertheless, many Georgians also point out that there is poetic justice in recent Chechen suggestions that Chechnya and Georgia form a federation given that the Abkhaz have occasionally expressed a desire to become a member of the Russian Federation.

29. An envoy of the Confederation of the Peoples of the Caucasus, which had supported the Abkhaz during the war and arranged for numerous volunteers from Russia's North Caucasus region to cross the border into Abkhazia to fight the Georgians, recently arrived in Tbilisi and offered the Georgians membership in the organization, indicating that the organization now supported Georgia's territorial integrity. (See *Resonance* 8: 13 (January 1998): 2, abstracted in the CIPDD Press Digest, January 13, 1998).

30. The fighting effectiveness of the Chechens during the war was confirmed by Georgian Deputy minister of state security Avtandil Iosiliani, personal interview, Tbilisi, June 11, 1997.

31. Ochamchire is located immediately to the north of Gali. Prior to the war, the population of the district was 46.2 percent Georgian and 36.7 percent Abkhaz.

32. Personal interview, Revaz Adamia, member of parliament and chair of the parliamentary Committee for Defense and Security Issues, Georgia, Tbilisi, June 11, 1997.

33. Personal interview, Martin Schümar, United Nations Volunteers Coordinator in Georgia, Tbilisi, June 11, 1997.

34. A small contingent of Abkhaz troops is also dug in along the Inguri, serving as a trip wire against a Georgian invasion. A larger contingent has taken up defensive positions to the north of the demilitarized zone.

35. Elizabeth Fuller, "Solution to Abkhaz Conflict Continues to Prove Elusive," *RFE/RL Newsline* Endnote 1: 70 (July 10, 1997).

36. Liz Fuller, "Shevardnadze's Abkhaz Brinkmanship," *RFE/RL Newsline*, Endnote, 1: 87 (August 4, 1997).

37. *RFE/RL Newsline* (November 18, 1997).

38. Personal interview with Tamaz Nadareishvili, Chairman of the Supreme Council of the Autonomous Republic of Abkhazia and Member of the National Security Council of Georgia, Tbilisi (June 12, 1997).

39. The Abkhaz, it is worth noting here, are not inherently pro-Russian and anti-Western. If anything they tend to be pro-Turkish. In fact, the "genocide" that almost destroyed the Abkhaz as a distinct people at the end of the last century was perpetrated by the Russian imperial government. Abkhazia's informal alliance with Moscow (which to a certain extent still exists, although relations are now more strained) was based mostly on the former's need for allies and the latter's desire to pressure Georgia.

40. The occupied districts are Agdam, Fizuli, Jebrail, Kelbajar, Kubatly, Lachin, and Zangelan. However, over half of Fizuli district and less than half of Agdam district are not occupied by the Karabakh army. There were five districts within the Nagorno-Karabakh Autonomous Oblast in the Soviet period: Askeran, Gadrut, Mardakert, Martuni, and Shusha (Shushi). Karabakh forces currently do not control a small amount of territory (approximately 150 square kilometers) in Mardakert and Martuni districts. A small Armenian enclave within the Azerbaijan SSR, Artsvashen, which was located along the Armenian-Azerbaijani border to the north of

Karabakh, was occupied by Azerbaijan (as a result of which the Armenians who had lived in the village fled to Armenia), while several Azeri enclave villages, the largest of which were Askipara and Kiarki, to the north of Nakhichevan, were occupied by Armenian forces (which led to the flight of its Azeri inhabitants). It should be noted that Azerbaijani officials and the international media often claim that Karabakh and Armenian forces occupy some 20 percent or more of Azerbaijan's territory, which is incorrect. Of 14.5 percent of the territory of Azerbaijan of the former Azerbaijani SSR currently occupied by Armenian and Karabakh forces, approximately 10 percent lies outside the borders of the former Nagorno-Karabakh Autonomous Oblast. See Arif Yunusov, "Statistics of the Karabakh War," unpublished paper in the author's possession, and Emil Sanamyan, "Conflict, Mythology and Azerbaijan," analysis distributed on the GROONG On-line Armenian News Network (September 17, 1997).

41. Shusha became the capital of an independent "Azeri" Khanate in 1752 (Azeri in the sense of Muslims who spoke a version of the Turkic language we call Azeri today). In 1988, the population was approximately 90 percent Azeri. However, at the turn of the century the population had been predominately Armenian. Moreover, Shusha, along with Tbilisi (Tiflis), was at one time one of the two main Armenian cities of the Transcaucasus and the center of a self-governing Armenian principality in the 1720s. It therefore contains both Azeri and Armenian cultural monuments, while the surrounding area includes a number of ancient Armenian villages. In addition, Shusha's strategic location makes the Karabakh Armenians reluctant to relinquish control of it even to an international peacekeeping force.

42. Yunosov, op. cit., estimates total casualties at 17,000 dead (11,000 Azeris and 6,000 Armenians) and 50,000 wounded (30,000 Azeris and 20,000 Armenians).

43. Azerbaijan imposed a blockade on Karabakh beginning in 1988. It also blockaded Armenia intermittently that year, and permanently from 1989 on. Turkey allowed some humanitarian aid to pass through its territory to Armenia during the winter of 1992–93 but then imposed a full blockade beginning in April 1993. Armenia's ties to the outside world, and particularly to Russia, were also affected by the interruption of railway service to Russia through Abkhazia and by the general turmoil in Georgia in 1992–94.

44. Among these were Armenians living in two districts in Azerbaijan proper, Shaumian and Getashen, most of whom fled to Karabakh. The Karabakh Armenians argue that the number of DPs from these two districts roughly balances the number of Azeri DPs from Karabakh, and that both sides should accept that repatriation of both populations is impractical.

45. The UNHCR estimates the DP population in Azerbaijan at around 670,000.

46. In 1992, the CSCE (OSCE) agreed that "elected representatives" of Karabakh Armenian authorities as well as "other representatives" (by implication, the Karabakh Azeris) would participate in the negotiating process.

47. For an overview of the negotiations, see John J. Maresca, "Resolving the Conflict over Nagorno-Karabakh: Lost Opportunities for International Conflict Resolution," in Chester A. Crocker and Fen Osler Hampson, with

Pamela Aall (eds.), *Managing Global Chaos: Sources of and Responses to International Conflict* (Washington, D.C.: U.S. Institute of Peace, 1996): 255–73.

48. See Maresca, op. cit., p. 264.

49. Azerbaijani foreign minister Hasan Hasanov claimed in September 1997 that the SCUDs were capable of carrying nuclear weapons, a charge subsequently denied by Moscow. Hasanov also asserted that Armenia might use nuclear material from its Medzamor nuclear power station to build a nuclear weapon and that Medzamor should accordingly be closed down. A Trilateral Commission made up of Russian, Azerbaijani, and Armenian representatives was supposed to investigate the charges of illegal arms transfers, but it has been ineffective because Armenia has insisted that it investigate weapons transfers to all three Transcaucasian countries, not just Armenia. Predictably, neither Azerbaijan nor Moscow has been willing to accept that demand.

50. *Moskovskii Komsomolets* (February 14, 1997).

51. Also on September 1, Russia and Armenia agreed to form a joint stock company to build a natural gas pipeline allowing Russia to deliver gas to Armenia and possibly Turkey. Armenia hopes to use Russian natural gas to deliver some three billion kilowatts of energy to Turkey per annum. Moscow is also considering a new $42.7 million loan to Armenia to help finance Armenia's troubled Medzamor nuclear power plant, in exchange for which Moscow will receive additional shares in the power plant and possible shares of other Armenia enterprises as well.

52. On September 17, Primakov issued the following statement: "I am authorized by Russian President Boris Yeltsin to state that the Treaty of the Russian Federation with Armenia is in no way targeted against Azerbaijan and will never be used in favor of those who are speaking against its territorial integrity." *ITAR-TASS* (September 17, 1997).

53. Gulazade's formal title was State Adviser for Foreign Policy, while Libaridian's was Senior Adviser. The informal talks had begun in late 1995 and were held approximately monthly.

54. As Aliev put it in September 1996, "If our lands are not freed, we will have to free them ourselves." "Presidential Vote Held in Karabakh," *UPI* (November 24, 1996).

55. Clinton named Strobe Talbott as the U.S. representative and co-chair of the Minsk Conference in early 1996, thereby reaffirming the U.S. interest in mediating a settlement over Karabakh. The U.S. cochair of the Minsk Group at the time, Joe Pressel, was replaced by Lynne Pascoe in late 1997.

56. The PKF was reportedly to have consisted of Russian, U.S., and French troops, although it is doubtful that the U.S. Congress would have agreed to send U.S. troops to Karabakh given congressional concerns about an extension of U.S. participation in the NATO peacekeeping force in Bosnia.

57. The proposal is summarized in "Po Proektu Sopredsedatelei Minskoi Gruppy Karabakhu Otvoditsia Rol' Mnogoetnicheskoi Avtonomii s Natsional'noi Gvardiei" ("According to the Proposal of the Minsk Group Cochairs Karabakh will be a Multiethnic Autonomous Area with a National Guard"), *Noyan Tapan* (June 16, 1997).

58. Personal interview, Vafa Gulazade, state adviser for foreign policy, Baku (June 6, 1997).

59. Personal interview, Gerard Libaridian, former senior adviser to President Levon Ter-Petrossian, Cambridge, Mass. (December 4, 1997).
60. Exactly what the two presidents agreed to at Strasbourg has not been made public, although reports in the Armenian press claim that Ter-Petrossian in effect agreed to the Lisbon principles in violation of a July 8, 1992, resolution of the Armenian parliament prohibiting the Armenian government from signing any document that refers to Karabakh as a part of Azerbaijan. See "Sersbka Krajina, Nagorno Karabakh: Similarities and Differences," Daniel Petrosyan, *Noyan Tapan Weekly Highlights* 44 and 45 (1997).
61. Emil Danielyan and Liz Fuller, "Is Yeltsin's Proposed Karabakh Summit A Non-Starter?," *RFE/RL Report*, Endnote 1: 140 (October 16, 1997). As it turned out, however, there was no follow-up to the proposed meeting, i.e., no formal invitations were issued.
62. Undersecretary of State Stuart Eizenstat was particularly frank about U.S. expectations of a settlement in his testimony before Congress on October 23. *Reuters* (October 24, 1997).
63. *Aravot* (Yerevan) carried by *Noyan-Tapan* (October 27, 1997).
64. Quoted in *Monitor* 3: 201 (October 28, 1997).
65. See the interview with Andrei Illarionov, "Blockade has Some Positive Effects," *Noyan Tapan* (August 28, 1997).
66. While intergovernmental relations between Armenia and Georgia are good, there are considerable tensions between Armenians and Georgians. This, plus poor roads, the interruption of railroad service, and the poor state of both economies, has contributed to the relatively low level of trade between the two countries, although trade has been growing.
67. After Yeltsin reiterated Russia's commitment to the existing borders of the successor states at the CIS summit of October 22–23, Ter-Petrossian admitted that "we have no illusions in that regard, because Russia could not act differently . . . it has its own twenty Karabakhs."
68. Deputy Secretary of State Strobe Talbott expressed the U.S. position in this regard in a major speech on July 22, 1997, at the Central Asian Institute at the School for Advanced International Studies in Washington, as follows: "Conflict resolution must be job one for U.S. policy in the region." See Sonia Winter, "Central Asia: U.S. Says Resolving Conflicts a Top Priority," *RFE/RL* (July 22, 1997); distributed on the GROONG On-line Armenian News Network (July 22, 1997).
69. As in Abkhazia, however, Stepanakert could probably mobilize a considerably larger number of reserves in an emergency.
70. Talk by Vartan Oskanian, "Oil: Stabilizing or Destabilizing Factor in the Caucasus," University of California at Berkeley (November 13, 1997).
71. The only partial exception is Karabakh, which might be in position to take more Azeri territory, including Gyandzha, as noted above. However, it would not be in Karabakh's interest to occupy additional territory because doing so would only increase its military burden while further outraging the international community, particularly if pipelines were threatened.
72. I am not arguing that normative beliefs alone motivate parties to a secessionist conflict—minority fears of assimilation and the destruction of their culture, the fear on the part of the national state that the secession of one region will lead to the secession of others, security concerns, and economic considerations can also be important.
73. This argument is elaborated in Ghia Nodia, op. cit.

CHAPTER 10

1. See also G. Nodia, "Political Turmoil in Georgia and the Ethnic Policies of Zviad Gamsakhurdia," in Bruno Coppieters (ed.), *Contested Borders in the Caucasus* (Brussels: VUBPRESS, 1996): 73–89.
2. See also G. Nodia, "Dynamics of State-Building in Georgia," *Demokratiatsiya* 6: 1 (Winter 1998): 6–13.
3. The World Bank estimated growth rates as 10.5 percent in 1996 and 11 percent in 1997, while its inflation rate fell from 64 percent in the first three quarters of 1994 to 0.5 percent during 1997. See Country Brief on Georgia on the World Bank's Internet site (*www.worldbank.org*). As late as September, the IMF projected the Georgian growth rate in 1998 at 10 percent. See "Business: The Economy Crisis for Some, Not for Others, Says IMF," BBC Online Network (September 30, 1998), *www.news.bbc. co.uk/hi/english/business/the_economy*.
4. This was the conclusion of the Georgian Audit Chamber. BS-Press News Agency (November 3, 1998).
5. As stated by Temur Basilia, the president's adviser in economic reforms. BS-Press News Agency (October 17, 1998).
6. BS-Press News Agency (November 10, 1998).
7. BS-Press News Agency (October 15, 1998).
8. On this, see, for instance, "Politics of Oil Fuels Georgia Revolt," BBC Online Network (October 19, 1998), *www.news.bbc.co.uk/hi/english/ world/europe*.
9. See the analysis of this issue in Dov Lynch, "The Conflict in Abkhazia: Dilemmas in Russian 'Peacekeeping' Policy," Discussion Paper 77 (London: The Royal Institute of International Affairs, 1998): 27–31.
10. BS-Press News Agency (November 3, 1998).
11. As Igor Sergeyev, the Russian defense minister, stated after meeting his Georgian counterpart David Tevzadze, the Georgian side did not ask for the Russian bases to leave. BS-Press News Agency (October 24, 1998).
12. Recently David Salaridze, the Georgian human rights ombudsman, appealed to parliament to make a legal and political assessment of 1991–92 events. Salaridze's links to President Shevardnadze makes one think that this initiative was probably sanctioned by the latter, giving it greater political weight. See "Juridical Assessment of the 1991–92 Events: The Outset of the National Reconciliation," Annotated Daily Headlines of the Georgian Press, compiled by the Caucasian Institute for Peace, Democracy and Development (November 10, 1998).
13. See D. Darchiashvili's chapter in this volume, p. 266.

CHAPTER 11

1. There are several names commonly used to describe the region comprising Armenia, Azerbaijan, and Georgia. Because the term "South Caucasus" is both descriptive and geographically accurate, it will be used here. The term "Transcaucasus" is at times used to indicate the South Caucasus region *and* the areas of the Russian Federation that are immediately adjacent to the Caucasus mountains.

2. Robert M. Cutler, "Towards Cooperative Energy Security in the South Caucasus," *Caucasian Regional Studies* 1 (1996).
3. Ariel Cohen, "U.S. Policy in the Caucasus and Central Asia: Building a New 'Silk Road' to Economic Prosperity," *Backgrounder* 1132 (July 24, 1997).
4. Svante Cornell, "The Unruly Caucasus," *Current History* (October 1997).
5. David Darchiashvili, "Georgia—The Search for State Security," Working Paper, Center for International Security and Arms Control, Stanford University, December 1997.
6. Zbigniew Brzezinski, *The Grand Chessboard: American Primacy and its Geostrategic Imperatives* (New York: Basic Books, 1997).
7. Ariel Cohen, "The New 'Great Game': Oil Politics in the Caucasus and Central Asia," *Backgrounder No. 1065*, The Heritage Foundation, 1996.
8. Zbigniew Brzezinski, op. cit.
9. Harald Mueller, "Non-Proliferation: A New Role for NATO?" in David Fischer, Eric Chauvistre, and Harald Mueller, *Extending the Non-Proliferation Regime—More Scope for the IAEA?* (1994).
10. Ibid.
11. Georgia's alternative military suppliers would probably be the other NIS in the form of surplus weapons.
12. Harald Mueller, ed., *Nuclear Export Controls in Europe* (Brussels: European Interuniversity Press, 1995): 12.
13. See Glenn Curtis, ed., *Armenia, Azerbaijan, and Georgia: Country Studies* (Washington, D.C.: U.S. Government Printing Office, 1995); and any of the 1993–97 versions of the Central Intelligence Agency's *World Factbook* (chapters on Armenia, Azerbaijan, and Georgia).
14. The most recent examples of these incidents on the borders, while not proliferation related, resulted in political crises. These particular issues, called the "Georgian-Russian spirits and tangerine wars," illustrate the kinds of political and economic effects that such incidents may have. In the first case, Russian border guards refused the entry into Russia of spirits transited through Georgia, causing a delay in delivery and discrediting Georgia's reliability and transit capabilities. In the second case, the tangerine harvest from the breakaway region of Abkhazia was exported to Russia without the permission of Georgian authorities.
15. *FBIS-SOV-97-099* 9 (April 1997).
16. U.S. Department of State, "Background Notes: Georgia" (July 1997).
17. "CIS Accord on Fighting Organized Crime," *OMRI Daily Digest* (June 2, 1995).
18. Harald Mueller, ed., op. cit.
19. Jason Ellis, "Nunn-Lugar's Mid-Life Crisis," *Survival* (Spring 1997).

CHAPTER 12

1. The author would like to thank the International Affairs Laboratory for Research and Education, the Center for International Trade and Security, the National Council for Soviet and East European Research, and the University of Georgia for providing funding for this research. Special thanks also to Dmitriy Nikonov for valuable assistance during my travel and research, and colleagues Richard Cupitt, Scott Jones, and Mamuka Kudava for comments on earlier drafts.

2. Throughout this article, the terms "nonproliferation system" and "nonproliferation policies and institutions" are used interchangeably. These, and the term nonproliferation itself, indicate the importance attached to preventing the spread of nuclear, chemical, biological, radiological, and dual-use goods, services, and technologies as virtually an *end* of state action. The term (non)proliferation is used when states use the development of antiproliferation- *or* proliferation-related policies as a *means* to further their broader national security—i.e., political, military, economic, and relational—interests.

3. For recent assessments of problems and solutions to the proliferation threat in the former Soviet Union, see Gary Bertsch and Suzette Grillot, eds., *Arms on the Market: Reducing the Risk of Proliferation in the Former Soviet Union* (London: Routledge, 1998); National Research Council, *Proliferation Concerns: Assessing U.S. Efforts to Help Contain Nuclear and Other Dangerous Materials and Technologies in the Former Soviet Union* (Washington, D.C.: National Academy Press, 1997); and Graham Allison, Owen Coté, Jr., Richard Falkenrath, and Steven Miller, *Avoiding Nuclear Anarchy: Containing the Threat of Loose Russian Nuclear Weapons and Fissile Material* (Cambridge, Mass.: MIT Press, 1996).

4. For information concerning the amount and types of nuclear-related industry and facilities that exist in the Caucasus, see the Monterey Institute for International Studies database, "Illicit Transactions Involving Nuclear Materials from the Former Soviet Union," and the report by William Potter, "Less Well-Known Cases of Nuclear Terrorism and Nuclear Diversion in the Former Soviet Union," *CNS Occasional Paper* (Monterey: Monterey Institute for International Studies, 1996).

5. See, for example, David Zurabishvili, "Shevardnadze's One-Man Democracy," *War Report* (September 1996).

6. Concerning the controversies over Caucasus governments' handling of elections and other legitimacy issues, see Jonathan Aves, "Politics, Parties and Presidents in Transcaucasia," *Caucasian Regional Studies* 1 (1996); Suzanne Goldenberg, *Pride of Small Nations: The Caucasus and Post-Soviet Disorder* (London: Zed, 1994); and Goldenberg, "Background Note: Reflections on Cockney," in John Wright, Suzanne Goldenberg, and Richard Schofield, eds., *Transcaucasian Boundaries* (London: UCL, 1996). For specifics on the last few elections in Armenia, see "European Parliament Condemns Presidential Elections in Armenia," *OMRI Daily Digest* (November 21, 1996).

7. Excellent reviews of the historical and contemporary interests of Russia, Turkey, and Iran in the Caucasus are provided by Bruno Coppieters, "Conclusions: The Caucasus as a Security Complex," in Bruno Coppieters, ed., *Contested Borders in the Caucasus* (Brussels: VUB Press, 1996); Margot Light, "Russia and Transcaucasia," in Wright, et al., *Transcaucasian Boundaries*, op. cit., pp. 34–53; Goldenberg, *Pride of Small Nations*, op. cit., pp. 46–69; Shireen Hunter, *The Caucasus in Transition: Nation-Building and Conflict* (Washington, D.C.: The Center for Strategic and International Studies, 1994), pp. 142–78; William Hale, "Turkey, the Black Sea and Transcaucasia," in Wright, et al., *Transcaucasian Boundaries*, op. cit., pp. 54–70; Pavel Baev, *Russia's Policies in the Caucasus* (London: The Royal Institute of International Affairs, 1997); and Fred Halliday, "Condemned

to React, Unable to Influence: Iran and Transcaucasia," in Wright, et al., *Transcaucasian Boundaries*, op. cit., pp. 71–88.

8. The influence of Russia in the region is pervasive, both because of the problems noted later concerning the existence of Russian military forces on the territories of the Caucasus states, and also because of the threat of further Russian political, military or economic interference in their affairs. For analysis of some of these issues, see Paul Goble, "Outflanked on the CFE," *RFE/RL Newsline* (May 2, 1997); and Alexander Rondeli, "Georgia in Post-Soviet Space," *Caucasian Regional Studies* 1 (1996).

9. For a general overview of post–Second World War conflicts in the Caucasus, see Guy Arnold, *Wars in the Third World Since 1945*, 2nd edition (London: Cassell, 1995), especially pp. 131–35 and 263–66. Azerbaijan must also remain sensitive to the potential claims of allegiance of ethnic Azerbaijanis living in Iran, a situation that is sensitive in relations between the two countries.

10. For additional aspects of proliferation- and nonproliferation-related issues in the Caucasus, see Craft, "Security Dimensions," in Bertsch and Grillot, eds., *Arms on the Market*, op. cit.

11. For discussion of conventional weapons transfers within and through the Caucasus, see Aves, "Politics, Parties and President," op. cit.; Light, "Russia and Transcaucasia," op. cit.; Richard Speier, "Statement before the Subcommittee on International Security, Proliferation, and Federal Services of the Committee on Governmental Affairs," U.S. Senate, June 5, 1997 (reprinted in *The Monitor: Nonproliferation, Demilitarization and Arms Control* 3, Summer 1997); Paul Goble, "Russia: Analysis from Washington—Using Minsk in the Caucasus," *RFE/RL Features* (April 8, 1997); "Baku Alarmed by Moscow Arms Supplies to Armenia," *Reuter* (April 4, 1997); and *Jane's Defence Weekly* (April 1997).

12. For details of these transfers, see Speier's testimony before the U.S. Senate noted above. Also useful is the Stockholm International Peace Research Institute's *SIPRI Arms Transfer Database* which reflects the sale or transfer of these weapons, as well as others.

13. See the Center for Nonproliferation Studies, *NIS Databases, Nuclear Profiles*, Monterey Institute for International Studies, May 1997 update.

14. Personal correspondence with Georgian Ministry of Foreign Affairs official, September 1997.

15. For example, in Armenia, "Government Enactment 537, On the Establishment of a Commission for Export Controls on Primary Products, Materials, Equipment, Technologies and Services Used in the Creation of Weapons of Mass Destruction," November 3, 1992, and "Government Enactment 121, On Matters of Export Controls on Primary Products, Materials, Equipment, Technologies and Services Used in the Creation of Weapons of Mass Destruction and Missile Delivery Systems," March 19, 1993, served as rudimentary export control "laws."

16. Richard Woff, "The Border Troops of the Russian Federation," *Jane's Intelligence Review* 7 (February 1995).

17. Samuel Huntington's *The Clash of Civilizations and the Remaking of World Order* (New York : Simon & Schuster, 1996) is apparently quite well read among officials, intellectuals, and researchers in the Caucasus states. Huntington argues that the most important future wars will be fought along the "fault lines" where differing religious cultures meet. He explic-

itly details the importance of the "fault lines" in the Transcaucasian region of Russia and the NIS (see particularly pp. 246–98). Both Azerbaijanis and Armenians referred to this work, and Georgian officials attributed their "identification" with the West to the common ties of Christianity.

18. Statement of U.S. deputy secretary of state Strobe Talbot, "A Farewell to Flashman: American Policy in the Caucasus and Central Asia," at the Johns Hopkins School of Advanced International Studies (July 21, 1997). Talbot's plea for an end to geopolitical competition between the great powers in the region is commendable, but probably in vain due to Russian, Armenian, Georgian, Azerbaijani, Turkish, and Iranian views on the subject.

19. Much of the information in this section on foreign policy decision by Caucasus officials comes from personal interviews and correspondence with government and former government officials from various ministries in Armenia, Azerbaijan, and Georgia during 1997 and 1998.

20. It could be argued as well that the Washington Conference also represented another misconception on the part of many U.S. government officials involved in nonproliferation issues. The fact that the materials presented were based on the full development of nonproliferation export controls along the lines of the overly sophisticated U.S. system, which would be impossible for a Third World state such as those in the Caucasus and Central Asia to develop due to its technical detail and redundancy, was a serious error. A simplified system of export controls would have been far more effective and useful, according to Caucasus officials interviewed by the author.

21. Author interviews with U.S. government officials, 1994–96.

22. See especially Craft, "Security Dimensions," in Bertsch and Grillot, eds., *Arms on the Market*, op. cit.; and also the sources in footnote 11 above.

23. Steven Rhoads, *The Economist's View of the World: Government, Markets, and Public Policy* (Cambridge: Cambridge University Press, 1985): 11.

24. Kathleen Bailey, "Nonproliferation Export Controls: Problems and Alternatives," in Kathleen Bailey and Robert Rudney, eds., *Proliferation and Export Controls* (New York: University Press of America, 1993): 52.

25. Interview notes of Scott Jones, with an official from the Armenian Ministry of Foreign Affairs, September 1996.

26. These effects are heightened by Armenian suspicions that the amenity with Iran, an Islamic state with a large ethnic Azerbaijani population, is unnatural or unstable. Any adverse policy passed in Armenia could potentially, it is felt, "push" this important political and economic partner into the waiting (it is assumed) arms of Azerbaijan.

27. Although in summer and fall 1998 Armenia began exerting its influence in the United States to prevent the sale of U.S.-designed nuclear-power reactors to Turkey due to concerns over a potential nuclear weapon program in that country. The fact that these efforts may have contributed to the eventual award of the reactor contract to Canadian-built light water (CANDU) reactors may represent the short-sightedness of such efforts for nonproliferation purposes given the much greater proliferation potential of the latter.

28. And, as alluded to in the footnote above, with Turkey over nuclear reactors.

29. The Russian interests in these regions are directly opposed to those of

Georgia, according to one Russian Duma official, and Russia has no intention of giving up "its" borders (especially between Adjaria and Turkey) in these regions. Personal interview with Russian Duma official, November 1997.

30. Georgian Ministry of Foreign Affairs officials were in July 1997 particularly worried about the dangers to democratic development posed by criminality. They felt that the most insidious danger from corruption was that it undermined Georgian *society*, which they feel has strong democratic yearnings, as well as the state that has tried to implement this form of government as best it could given the difficulties of postindependence events.

31. Interviews with former Elçibey-government officials, Musavat party headquarters, Baku, Azerbaijan, July 1997.

32. Note the discrepancy between Azerbaijan's policy and those of Armenia and Georgia. Both of the latter have acceded to Russia's demands regarding the CIS border controls agreement, stationing of Russian forces, and accepted Russian bases. Azerbaijani officials note the plight of the Georgians, who have for the past year or so tried to obtain the withdrawal of these Russian contingents and failed. A Russian Duma official asserted that the most effective potential nonproliferation policy available in the Caucasus region was Russian occupation of Azerbaijan and performance of border controls throughout the entire region (personal interviews, November 1997).

33. Some efforts have recently been undertaken, and provide valuable first steps. For example, there have been meetings between Turkish, U.S., and Caucasus officials at international conferences devoted to the subject of nonproliferation export control development held in Istanbul, Turkey, in summer 1995 and in Washington, D.C., in fall 1996. There have been training programs for border officials conducted by the U.S. customs service. Finally, there have been diplomatic initiatives regarding the cooperation of Caucasus governments with the United States, such as the Georgia-U.S. agreement on nonproliferation policy development (see *RIA-Novosti Hotline*, "The U.S.A and Georgia Sign Cooperation Agreement in the Military Sphere and Preventing Proliferation of Mass Destruction Weapons," July 18, 1997).

34. Statement of Strobe Talbot, "A Farewell to Flashman," op. cit.

35. See Cassady Craft, "Only Shevardnadze . . . and Not the HEU, and Let's Keep It That Way." *The Monitor: Nonproliferation, Demilitarization and Arms Control* (Spring–Summer 1998).

36. Author interview with U.S. Department of State official, fall 1997.

CHAPTER 13

1. N. Nazarbayev, "Kazakhstan-2030: An Address of the President to the Nation," Almaty, 1998.

2. Alexander Bovin, "Kazakhstanski Azimut," *Izvestiya* (July 8, 1998).

3. The list of countries includes: Russia, China, Uzbekistan, Kyrgyzstan, Tajikistan, Kazakhstan, Mongolia, Azerbaijan, Turkey, Iran, India, Pakistan, Afghanistan, Israel, Egypt, and the Palestinian Territory. Japan, South Korea, Indonesia, Malaysia, Lebanon, the United States, Ukraine, and Australia participate as observers.

4. I recommend the book by K. Tokayev, *Hoisting the Independence Banner: Essays on Kazakhstan's Foreign Policy* (Almaty: Bilim, 1997).
5. See, for example, D. Eleukenov and Keith Wolfe, "Export Controls in Kazakhstan," in Gary K. Bertsch and William C. Potter, eds., *Dangerous Weapons, Desperate States: Russia, Ukraine, Belarus, and Kazakhstan* (New York: Routledge, 1999).
6. In Kazakhstan, for example, it was conducted in 1993–94, at the Institute for Strategic Studies under the president of Kazakhstan.
7. The first such conference took place in May 1995 at the Kazakhstani Institute for Strategic Studies under the president of Kazakhstan.
8. The energy resource strategy, outlined by President Nazarbayev in *Strategy-2030*, is included in the Appendix.
9. U. Kasenov, "The Formula of Asian Security," *Business Weekly* (Almaty) (February 20, 1998).
10. The OEC (Organization for Economic Cooperation) includes all five Central Asian states: Azerbaijan, Turkey, Pakistan, Iran, and Afghanistan. Its main interest is in transportation projects.
11. The Appendix is extracted from *Strategy-2030*.

CHAPTER 14

1. *Uyezds* and *volosts* were the administrative units in prerevolutionary Russia.
2. Address by Michel Camdessus, managing director of the International Monetary Fund, at a conference on "Challenges to Economies in Transition," Bishkek, Kyrgyz Republic (May 27, 1998).

ABOUT THE CONTRIBUTORS

Shirin Akiner is an Associate Fellow at the Royal Institute for International Affairs in London. She has authored several books and articles on Central Asia.

Ewan W. Anderson is University Professor of Geopolitics at the Centre for Middle Eastern and Islamic Studies at the University of Durham. He is also a Distinguished Research Fellow of the Center for International Trade and Security at the University of Georgia.

Liam Anderson is a Senior Research Associate at the Center for International Trade and Security at the University of Georgia and an instructor in the Department of Political Science at the University of Georgia.

Gary K. Bertsch is Director and University Professor of Political Science at the Center for International Trade and Security at the University of Georgia.

Michael Beck is Assistant Director of the Center for International Trade and Security at the University of Georgia.

Cassady Craft is cofounder of IntaLAB, Inc., International Affairs Laboratory for Research and Education, a nonprofit organization in Oklahoma City that promotes global activisim.

David Darchiashvili is a researcher at the Caucasian Institute for Peace, Democracy, and Development located in Tbilisi, Georgia.

Dastan Eleukenov is an adviser to the Ministry of Foreign Affairs of Kazakhstan on national security matters.

Shireen T. Hunter is the Director of Islamic Studies at the Center for Strategic and International Studies in Washington, D.C. She previously served as director of the Mediterranean Studies program with the Centre for European Policy Studies in Brussels.

Scott A. Jones is a Senior Research Associate at the Center for International Trade and Security at the University of Georgia.

Mamuka Kudava is Head of the Military-Political Department, Ministry of Foreign Affairs of Georgia.

Orozbek Moldaliev is the Director of the Bureau for International Trade and Security, a nongovernment research institute in Bishkek, Kyrgyzstan.

Ghia Nodia is Chairman of the Caucasian Institute for Peace, Democracy, and Development in Tbilisi, Republic of Georgia.

Elkhan E. Nuriyev is Director of the Center for International Studies at the University of the Caucasus in Baku, Azerbaijan.

Alexander Rondeli is Director of the Foreign Policy Analysis and Research Center at the Ministry of Foreign Affairs of the Republic of Georgia.

Edward Walker is Executive Director of the University of California Berkeley Program in Soviet and Post-Soviet Studies.

INDEX